HORSES AND TACK

HORSES
AND TACK

REVISED EDITION

M. E. ENSMINGER

*Illustrated with Drawings
and Photographs*

HOUGHTON MIFFLIN COMPANY

BOSTON 1991

Library of Congress Cataloging-in-Publication Data
Ensminger, M. Eugene
Horses and Tack / M. E. Ensminger. — Rev. ed.
p.   cm.
Includes bibliographical references and index.
ISBN 0-395-54413-0
1. Horses.   I. Title.
SF285.E55   1990   90-37676
636.1 — dc20   CIP

Printed in the United States of America

Book design by Patricia Dunbar

HAL 1 2 3 4 5 6 7 8 9 10

"Horse Power," made for the author by his brother,
Harry Edward Ensminger.

To the memory of my beloved brother,
Harry,
who lives again in the hearts of people and in the
classic craftsmanship he left behind.

CONTENTS

PREFACE

The unique thing about the horse business, not found in any other industry, is the human values that are so much a part of it; it's a people's business, and a way of life for many. In the United States, there are more than 10½ million horses. About 25 million people go to horse shows each year; 75 million people go to horse races annually. The annual wages paid in the horse industry exceed $1 billion. There are more 4-H Club horse projects than beef cattle projects. There are 500,000 horses on the western ranges, and a mechanical device for roping a steer has not been devised.

A shorter workweek, increased automation, more suburban and rural living, and the continued recreation and sports surge, with its emphasis on physical fitness and the out-of-doors, assure a bright future for the horse industry.

The author gratefully acknowledges the contributions of all who worked on the manuscript of this book. Special appreciation is expressed to my wife, Audrey, for her assistance; to Sandra Williams and Joan Wright, who typed the manuscript; to Georgia Cheer, who did the newer art work; to Jean Nelson and Deanna Ross, who proofread the material; to Ruth K. Hapgood, senior editor, Houghton Mifflin, and Barbara R. Starton, for sharing liberally of their equine expertise, editorial talents, and pictures; and to all those who provided pictures and information.

Throughout history, the footprints of horses have been alongside the footprints of people; horses and people are inseparable, they have advanced each other. If *Horses & Tack* enhances the horse-people relationship in the decades to come, it will make for a better world, and I shall feel amply rewarded.

M. E. Ensminger

October 1990
Clovis, California

HORSES AND TACK

HISTORY AND
DEVELOPMENT OF HORSES

Figure 1.1 The history and development of horses and people are inseparable; they are part of each other. Even today, horses are a business and a way of life for many people. (Courtesy, The American Morgan Horse Association, Inc., Shelburne, Vermont)

EVOLUTION

Fossil remains prove that members of the horse family roamed the plains of America (especially what is now the Great Plains area of the U.S.) during most of Tertiary time, beginning about 58 million years ago. Yet, no horses were present on this continent when Columbus discovered America in 1492. Why they perished, only a few thousand years before, is still one of the unexplained mysteries of evolution.

Through fossils, it is possible to reconstruct the evolution of the horse, beginning with the ancient four-toed ancestor, *Eohippus* (meaning "dawn horse"). This was a small animal, scarcely more than a foot high, with four toes on the front feet and three toes on the hind feet, and with slender legs, a short neck, and even teeth. It was well adapted to traveling in and feeding on the herbage of swamplands. Gradually, the descendants of *Eohippus* grew in size and changed in form, evolving into a three-toed animal known as *Mesohippus*, which was about 24

Figure 1.2 Evolution of the horse, spanning 58 million years, as portrayed by gradual changes in the hind legs and feet. Beginning with *Eohippus* (left), the descendants grew taller, the cannon bone lengthened, and the middle toe (third toe) grew longer and stronger, forming a hoof (right). (Courtesy, The American Museum of Natural History, New York, New York)

inches in height or about the size of a Collie dog. Further changes continued, transforming the animal from a denizen of the swamp to a creature of the prairie. In conformation, the animal grew taller, the teeth grew longer, the cannon bones lengthened, and the middle toe (third toe) grew longer and stronger, forming a hoof. The horse is an excellent example, therefore, of the slow adaptation of animal life to changing conditions in environment, climate, food, and soil.

ZOOLOGICAL CLASSIFICATION

In the zoological scheme, the horse is classed as *Equus caballus*. He is distinguished from asses and zebras — the other members of the genus *Equus* — by the longer hair of the mane and tail, the presence of the "chestnut" on the inside of the hind leg, and by other less constant characteristics such as larger size, larger hoofs, more arched neck, smaller head, and shorter ears.

DOMESTICATION

The horse was probably the last of the present-day farm animals to be domesticated by man. According to early records, after subduing the ox, the sheep, and the goat, man domesticated the ass and then the camel; and, finally, the horse became his servant. Horses appear to have been domesticated first in Central Asia or Persia more than 5,000 years ago.

Figure 1.3 Przewalski's horse. This is the only surviving species of original wild horses (horses that are not feral or escaped from domestication) known to exist at the present time. Note that the animals are small, with an erect mane and no forelock. (After a painting by Charles Knight; courtesy, The American Museum of Natural History, New York, New York)

Of course, it seems incredible that all the various breeds, colors, and types of draft, light, and pony horses should have descended from a common wild ancestor. Rather, there were probably many different wild stocks giving descent to domestic horses.

MAN'S USE OF THE HORSE

The name "horse" is derived from the Anglo-Saxon word *hors,* meaning swiftness; and the word horseman comes from a Hebrew root that means "to prick or spur." Within themselves, these early characterizations tell somewhat of a story.

The horse was first used as a source of food. Records dating back some 25,000 years ago reveal that, prior to their domestication, these animals were hunted by Paleolithic (Old Stone Age) man. Following domestication, mares were milked for human food — a practice still followed in certain parts of the world. Next, man learned to use the horse to wage war. About 1500 B.C., Pharaoh pursued the Israelites to the Red Sea, using chariots and horses; and the Great Horse of medieval times was the knight's steed. As early as 1450 B.C., the sports-loving Greeks used the horse in the Olympic Games, in both chariot and horse races. The use of horses in pulling loads and tilling the soil was a comparatively recent development. The improved roads that the Ro-

Figure 1.4   Uses of the horse, past and present.

mans constructed during Caesar's campaigns beginning about 55 B.C., were largely instrumental in encouraging the breeding of horses for use in transportation — for drawing heavy loads. However, there is no evidence to indicate that the horse was used in Europe to draw the plow prior to the 10th century, and few of them replaced oxen as the main source of agricultural power until the end of the 18th century.

INTRODUCTION INTO THE U.S.

Horses were first brought directly into what is now the United States by de Soto in the year 1539. Upon his several vessels, he had 237 horses. Beginning in the year 1600, the Spaniards established a chain of Christian missions among the Indians in the New World, extending from the eastern coast of Mexico up the Rio Grande, thence across the mountains to the Pacific Coast. Each mission brought horses from the mother country.

HISTORICAL USES

The golden age of the horse extended to the advent of the automobile, truck, and tractor. During this period, everybody loved the horse. The town livery stable, watering trough, and hitching post were trademarks of every town and village. People wept when the horse fell on an icy street, and they jailed men who beat or mistreated him. The oat bag,

Figure 1.5 American Indian mounted on a horse of Spanish extraction. The coming of horses among the Indians led to greater infringement on the hunting grounds of the tribes, which was ever a cause for war. (Courtesy, Jeff Edwards, Brislawn-Edwards, Porterville, California)

carriage, wagon, buggy whip, axle grease, horseshoe, and horseshoe nail industries were thriving and essential parts of the national economy. Every schoolboy knew and respected the village blacksmith.

During this era, much romance and adventure surrounded the horse. Again and again, he proved his worth through such dramatic performances as the Pony Express. Also, the horse served as a status symbol, the ultimate expression of which was a fantastic dinner staged on horseback in the plushest restaurant of the day by the New York Riding Club.

HIPPIES ON HORSEBACK

A horseback dinner was staged in Louis Sherry's restaurant, at the corner of Fifth Avenue and 44th Street, New York City, on March 28, 1903, with Cornelius K. G. Billings — Chicago utilities heir, racing enthusiast, and self-styled "American Horse King" — as host. To publicize his newly opened $200,000 stable at 196th Street and Fort Washington Road (now Fort Tryon Park), Mr. Billings converted the grand ballroom of Sherry's into a woodland paradise by means of $10,000 worth of full-scale scenic props, artificial foliage, potted palms, and a tanbark floor covering, borrowed, at Mr. Sherry's insistence, from the Barnum and Bailey circus. Thirty-six mystified horses were conveyed up to the ballroom by freight elevators, and the uncomfortable guests — members of the New York Riding Club — attired in white ties and tails, gingerly astride their favorite mounts, drank and ate to the merriment of music, while their steeds munched oats out of troughs decorated with gold foil, and costumed lackeys cleaned up behind them.

Miniature tables were attached to the saddle pommels (drive-in style), and apprehensive waiters dressed in riding attire served drink after drink, and course after course, topped off by Jack Horner pies — huge, ornamental concoctions which, when cut open, revealed a covey of nymphs in their birthday suits. Only one guest fell off his horse.

PONY EXPRESS

This mail service operated as a private venture under contract, and carried U.S. mail on horseback from St. Joseph, Missouri, to Placerville, California, before railways or telegraph. It was started in 1861, and it had a brief existence of but 18 months before it was supplanted by a telegraph line. The riders' steeds were fleet horses, not ponies. The horses were stationed at points 10 to 15 miles apart, and each rider rode three to seven animals successively, covering about 75 miles before passing the pouch to his successor. There were 80 riders, some 420 horses, and 190 relay stations. Riders were paid $25 per week.

The fastest trip ever made was in 7 days and 17 hours, when Lincoln's first inaugural address was carried to the West Coast. But the normal schedule was 8 days, which was about 24 days faster than the schedule of Butterfield's Overland Stage Line on the southern route. The maintenance of the schedule through the wilderness, often in blinding snows and howling storms and in the face of Indian dangers, won for the service a fame that has not been diminished with the passing of time.

The Pony Express lost money. The average charge for sending a letter during the period was $3, but it cost about $16 per letter to operate the service; thus, the private venture lost $13 per letter, and it is estimated that the Pony Express cost its backers $390,000.

Despite its short life, the Pony Express was credited with many important contributions, not the least of which was its help in keeping East and West joined together during the crucial early days of the Civil War.

GROWTH AND DECLINE OF HORSES IN THE U.S.

Ironic as it may seem, the development of manufacturing and commerce was responsible for both the rise and fall of the horse and mule industry in the U.S. The early growth of American industry created a large need

Figure 1.6 The statue of a Pony Express horse and rider which stands in the St. Joseph, Missouri, Civic Center. It was erected in 1941, when the Postal Department honored the Pony Express riders with a commemorative postage stamp. (Courtesy, St. Joseph Museum, St. Joseph, Missouri)

for horses to transport the raw and manufactured goods and to produce needed agricultural products for those people who lived in the cities and villages. However, the relentless wheels of progress steadily lifted from the horse his role in both agriculture and war.

A century ago, muscles provided 94 percent of the world's energy needs; coal, oil, and waterpower provided the other 6 percent. Today, the situation is reversed in the developed nations. They now obtain 94 percent of their energy needs from coal, oil, natural gas, and waterpower, and only 6 percent from the muscle power of men and animals.

At their height, in 1915, there were 21,431,000 horses in the U.S., most of which were draft animals. Mules reached a peak in 1925, at

Figure 1.7 Horsepower.

Table 1.1 Size and Density of Horse Population of Ten Leading Horse-Producing Countries of the World in 1986, by Rank

Country	Horses[1] (thousands)	Human Population[2] (thousands)
China, People's Republic of	11,000	1,069,628
United States	10,840	247,498
Mexico	6,135	88,087
U.S.S.R.	5,800	287,015
Brazil	5,500	153,992
Argentina	3,000	32,617
Mongolia	1,971	2,093
Colombia	1,950	31,821
Ethiopia	1,590	47,709
Poland	1,272	38,389
World Total	65,064	5,052,000

[1] *Production Yearbook 1986,* Vol. 40, FAO of the United Nations, Rome, pp. 195–197.

[2] *The World Almanac and Book of Facts 1989,* pub. by Newspaper Enterprise Assn., Inc.

5,918,000 head. With the advent of the machine age — the automobile, truck, and tractor — the draft horse and mule declined.

Today, the horse is rising to a more happy position in contributing to the fields of recreation and sport; and further expansion in light horses

Figure 1.8 The way it used to be done.

Size of Country		Horses per	Horses per	
(sq. mi.)	(sq. km.)	Capita[3]	(sq. mi.)	(sq. km.)
3,705,390	9,596,960	0.01	3.0	1.1
3,539,289	9,166,759	0.04	3.1	1.2
761,604	1,972,554	0.07	8.1	3.1
8,649,496	22,402,195	0.02	0.7	0.3
3,286,470	8,511,957	0.04	1.7	0.6
1,065,189	2,758,840	0.09	2.8	1.1
604,247	1,565,000	0.94	3.3	1.2
439,735	1,138,914	0.06	4.4	1.7
471,776	1,221,900	0.03	3.4	1.3
120,727	312,683	0.03	10.5	4.1
57,800,000	149,702,000	0.01	1.1	0.4

[3] Horses per capita computed from most recent census figures available.

appears inevitable. In 1986, there were 10,840,000 horses in the U.S. The ten leading states, in order by horse numbers, were: Texas, California, Oklahoma, Colorado, New York, Ohio, Michigan, Pennsylvania, Washington, and Kentucky.

WORLD HORSE NUMBERS

Table 1.1 shows the size and density of the horse population in the ten leading countries in 1986. As shown, the numbers totaled 65 million head. This was far below the 1934–1938 prewar figure of 96.4 million head. This decline in numbers since 1938 can be attributed chiefly to mechanization of agriculture in certain areas.

The leading countries, in order by horse numbers, were: China, U.S., Mexico, U.S.S.R., Brazil, Argentina, Mongolia, Colombia, Ethiopia, and Poland.

CLASSIFICATION OF HORSES

Horses may be classified as light horses, draft horses, or ponies, according to size, build, and use.

- *Light horses* stand over 14-2 hands high,[1] weigh 900 to 1,400 lb., and are used primarily for riding, driving, racing, or utility purposes on the farm. Light horses generally are more rangy and are capable of more action and greater speed than draft horses.
- *Draft horses* stand 14-2 to 17-2 hands high, weigh 1,400 lb. or more, and are used primarily for drawing loads and other heavy work.
- *Ponies* stand 14-2 hands high and under and weigh up to 900 lb. The breeding, feeding, care, and management are essentially the same for ponies as for larger light horses; the only differences result from their diminutive size.

[1] A hand is 4 inches; thus, 14-2 hands is 58 inches.

TYPES, USES, AND BREEDS
OF HORSES

Figure 2.1   There are many types and breeds of horses, used
for diverse activities. Broadly speaking, though, horses are used
for either riding or driving, and riding horses are classified as
either English or Western, depending on the type of saddle
used. *Upper photo:* English pleasure horse. (Courtesy, North
American Morab Horse Association, Hilbert, Wisconsin) *Lower
photo:* Western pleasure horse. (Courtesy, The American
Morgan Horse Association, Shelburne, Vermont)

The improvement of horses dates back to the time when man first domesticated them and sought to improve them more nearly to fulfill his needs. Through selection, different types and breeds evolved, better adapted to different uses and better meeting different human desires.

TYPES AND USES OF HORSES

In no class of animals have so many diverse and distinct types been developed as in the horse. The descendants of the Oriental light-legged horse have, for generations, been bred and used for riding and driving purposes — first as the chariot and riding horses of Egypt, Greece, and Arabia; later, as the running horse of England; and, finally, for purposes of recreation and sport in the U.S. and throughout the world. In due time, further refinements in breeding light horses were made, and these animals were adapted for more specific purposes. In this manner, light horses specifically adapted to the purposes enumerated in Table 2.1 have evolved.

In attempting to produce animals to meet these specific purposes, new breeds of light horses have been developed. In certain cases, however, the particular use or performance is so exacting that only one breed appears to be sufficiently specialized; for example, in running races the Thoroughbred is used almost exclusively, and harness races are now synonymous with the Standardbred breed.

BREEDS OF HORSES

A breed of horses may be defined as a group of horses having a common origin and possessing certain well-fixed, distinctive, uniformly transmitted characteristics that are not common to other horses. There are about 300 breeds of horses in the world.

There is scarcely a breed of horses that does not possess one or more distinctive breed characteristics in which it excels all others. Moreover, any one of several breeds is often well adapted to the same use. Certainly, if any strong preference exists, it should be an important factor in determining the choice of a breed, although it is recognized that some breeds are better adapted to specific purposes than others.

A discussion of the common U.S. breeds of light horses and ponies and their characteristics follows.[1] It is noteworthy that most U.S. breeds

[1] No person or department has authority to approve a breed. The only legal basis for recognizing a breed is contained in the Tariff Act of 1930, which provides for the duty-free admission of purebred breeding horses provided they are registered in the country of origin. But this applies to imported animals only. In this book, therefore, no official

Table 2.1 LIGHT HORSE SUMMARY

Type	Primary Use	Breeds	
Riding Horses and Ponies	Three-gaited saddle horses	American Saddlebred Andalusian Appaloosa Arabian Cleveland Bay Hanoverian Hungarian Horse Lipizzan Morab Morgan	National Show Horse Paint Horse Palomino Pinto Quarter Horse Spanish-Barb Spotted Saddle Horse Thoroughbred Trakehner
	Gaited horses	American Saddlebred Missouri Fox Trotting Horse National Show Horse	Paso Fino Peruvian Paso Tennessee Walking Horse
	Stock horses	Grades, crossbreds, or following purebreds: American Mustang Appaloosa Buckskin Chickasaw Galiceno Hungarian Horse	Morgan Paint Horse Pinto Horse Quarter Horse Spanish-Barb Spanish Mustang Thoroughbred
	Equine sports horses	Purebreds, crossbreds, and graders of the following breeds: Akhal-Teke American Creme/ American White	Lipizzan Thorcheron Thoroughbred Trakehner
	Ponies for riding	American Walking Pony Connemara Pony Gotland Pony National Appaloosa Pony	Pony of the Americas Quarter Pony Shetland Pony Welara Pony Welsh Pony and Cob
Racehorses[1]	Running racehorses	Thoroughbred	
	Quarter racehorses	Quarter Horse	

Table 2.1 LIGHT HORSE SUMMARY (*cont.*)

Type	Primary Use	Breeds	
	Harness racehorses (trotters and pacers)	Standardbred Trottingbred	
Driving Horses and Ponies	Driving horses: Heavy harness horses Fine harness horses Roadsters	Hackney American Saddlebred (predominantly, although other breeds are also used) Standardbred	
	Driving ponies: Harness show ponies Heavy harness ponies	Hackney Shetland Pony Welsh Pony and Cob	
All-purpose Horses and Ponies	Family horses/ponies	American Bashkir Curly American Gotland Horse	Haflinger Norwegian Fjord Horse
Miniature Horses and Donkeys	Driving Pets	Miniature Horse Miniature Donkey	

[1] In a few states, Appaloosa and Arabian horses are also being raced under saddle.

of light horses are American creations. There are two primary reasons for this: (1) the diverse needs and uses for which light horses have been produced; and (2) the fact that many men of wealth have bred light horses. For detailed information about any of the breeds, write to the appropriate breed registry, the names and addresses of which are given in this chapter in the section entitled, ''Breed Registry Associations.''

AKHAL-TEKE

The Akhal-Teke breed originated in the U.S.S.R., in Southern Turkmenia, by the ''Teke'' tribe, on the ''Akhal'' oasis. As the chief mount of the Turkoman warriors for centuries, the Akhal-Teke developed great stamina; and from the harsh desert environment, it developed the abil-

recognition of any breed is intended or implied. Rather, every effort has been made to present the factual story of the breeds. In particular, information about the new or less widely distributed breeds is needed and often difficult to obtain.

Figure 2.2 Akhal-Teke stallion, Gold Bay. (Courtesy, The Akhal-Teke Association of America, Staunton, Virginia)

ity to withstand great extremes in temperature, along with periods of privation of feed and water.

The first American purchases of Akhal-Tekes, a stallion and a mare, were made in Moscow, U.S.S.R., in 1978. Other imports followed. The Akhal-Teke Registry Association of America was formed in 1982.

The Akhal-Teke is a desert-bred horse, with a light, elegant build, and a gliding elastic action. Mature animals stand 15 to 15-2 hands high and weigh 900 to 1,000 lb.

The Akhal-Teke is used in all competitive equine sports, including endurance trials, dressage, and jumping.

The Russians now consider the Akhal-Teke as breeding stock of exceptional value.

AMERICAN BASHKIR CURLY

Horses with curly hair are known to have been raised centuries earlier by the people of Bashkiria on the eastern slopes of the Ural Mountains; hence, the name Bashkir. In this rugged climate, the Bashkiri people depended upon their curly horses for transportation, clothing, meat, and milk. In their native land, mares give three to six gallons of milk per day, which is highly prized. In addition to being consumed as fresh milk, cream, and butter, it makes a delicious cheese. Also, the milk is fermented to make a drink called "Kumiss," which the natives drink both as an intoxicating liquor and for medicinal purposes. History also records that the nomadic Mongols rode curly horses.

Figure 2.3 American Bashkir Curly stallion, Pat's Diamond Chip, owned by Pat McKendry, Morgan Hill, California. (Courtesy, American Bashkir Curly Registry, Ely, Nevada)

The modern history of curly horses in America began in 1898, when Peter Damele of Ely, Nevada, cut three curly animals from a herd of wild horses in the Peter Hanson Mountain Range. Most of today's curly horses trace to Damele ranch breeding. The American Bashkir Curly Registry was formed August 14, 1971.

The curly coat, with corkscrew mane and wavy tail, is the outstanding characteristic of the breed. The mane hair, and often the tail hair, falls out completely each summer and grows back during the winter. In build, Curlies are medium size and chunky, somewhat resembling the early-day Morgan in conformation. The breed is noted for small nostrils, a gentle disposition, and heavy milking. Many of the animals have a natural fox-trot gait. All colors are accepted. Horses weighing in excess of 1,350 lb. or having faulty conformation are disqualified for registry.

The American Bashkir Curly is used as a pleasure horse and for utility purposes, including light draft work. Because of their ruggedness, endurance, and gentle dispositions, they make ideal family trail horses and children's mounts.

AMERICAN CREME HORSE

Pale cream horses have been around for a very long time, primarily in Oregon and Washington. However, they were not given breed status until 1970, at which time the American Albino Association, Inc., established a separate American Creme Horse Division for their registration.

Figure 2.4 American Creme pair. (Courtesy, International American Albino Association, Naper, Nebraska)

The following color classifications of American Creme Horses are registered:

A — Body ivory white, mane white (lighter than body), eyes blue, skin pink.

B — Body cream, mane darker than body, cinnamon buff to ridgeway, eyes dark.

C — Body and mane of the same color, pale cream; eyes blue, skin pink.

D — Body and mane of same color, sooty cream; eyes blue, skin pink.

Combinations of the above classifications are also acceptable.

American Creme Horses are used as pleasure and stock horses, for exhibition purposes, and as parade and flag-bearer horses.

Both the American Creme Horse and the American White Horse are registered by the International American Albino Association, Inc., Naper, Nebraska, with separate divisions provided for each.

AMERICAN GOTLAND HORSE

American Gotland Horses originated on the Baltic island of Gotland, a part of Sweden. Coat colors are bay, brown, black, dun, chestnut, roan, or palomino, and some leopard and blanket markings. They average about 51 inches high, with a range of 11 to 14 hands.

Figure 2.5 American Gotland stallion. (Courtesy, American Gotland Horse Association, Elkland, Missouri)

American Gotland Horses are used for harness racing (trotting), as pleasure horses and jumpers, and as riding horses for children and medium-sized adults.

Pintos and animals with large markings are disqualified for registration.

AMERICAN MUSTANG

American Mustang horses originated along the Barbary Coast of North Africa, from which they were taken to Spain by the conquering Moors, propagated in Andalusia, and brought to America by the Conquistadores. The American Mustang Association was formed in 1962.

They may be any color, but they must be between 13-2 and 15 hands high.

American Mustangs are used for pleasure riding, show, trail riding, endurance trails, stock horses, and jumping.

AMERICAN SADDLEBRED

American Saddlebred horses originated in the U.S., in Fayette County, Kentucky. Coat colors are bay, brown, gray, roan, chestnut, black, or golden. Gaudy white markings are undesirable. Animals have a long, graceful neck and proud action. They furnish an easy ride with great style and animation.

American Saddlebreds are used as three- and five-gaited saddle horses, and as harness, pleasure, and stock horses.

Figure 2.6 American Mustang mare. (Courtesy, American Mustang Association, Yucaipa, California)

Figure 2.7 American Saddlebred mare, Plainview's Julia. (Courtesy, American Saddle Horse Breeders Association, Louisville, Kentucky)

Figure 2.8 American Walking Pony. (Courtesy, The American Walking Pony Association, Macon, Georgia)

AMERICAN WALKING PONY

American Walking Ponies originated near Macon, Georgia, in 1968. Coat colors are not restricted. Since the breed is a cross between Welsh Pony and Tennessee Walking Horse, the colors of both parent breeds occur. They range in height from 13 to 14-2 hands.

American Walking Ponies must perform a gait called the running walk. They are used for pleasure riding, and as mounts for children or small adults.

AMERICAN WHITE HORSE

The American White Horse originated on White Horse Ranch, Naper, Nebraska. They have hair as white as clean snow, with pink skin. The eyes are light blue, dark blue (near black), brown, or hazel, but never pink.

American White Horses are used as pleasure horses. Their snow-white color makes them attractive as trained horses for exhibition purposes and as parade and flag-bearer horses.

Both the American White Horse and the American Creme Horse are registered by the International American Albino Association, Naper, Nebraska, with separate divisions provided for each.

Figure 2.9 American White stallions pulling a fire engine in the Cotton Bowl parade. (Courtesy, International American Albino Association, Naper, Nebraska)

ANDALUSIAN

Andalusian horses originated in Spain. Whites, grays, and bays are most common, but there are a few blacks, roans, and chestnuts.

Andalusian horses are used for bullfighting, parade, dressage, jumping, and pleasure riding.

Animals not tracing to the Spanish Registry, which is supervised by the army in Spain, are not eligible for registry.

Figure 2.10 Andalusian stallion, Ganadero III, at Córdoba in the south of Spain. (Courtesy, Mrs. J. A. Rodenas, Long Island Dressage and Combined Training Association)

Figure 2.11 Appaloosa stallion, Dreamfinder, a National Grand Champion, owned by Rex Kennard, Oklahoma City, Oklahoma. (Courtesy, *Appaloosa Journal*, Moscow, Idaho)

APPALOOSA

Appaloosa horses originated in the U.S. — by the Nez Percé tribe of American Indians in Oregon, Washington, and Idaho — from animals that first came from Fergana, Central Asia. They have variable coat coloring but usually there is white over the loin and hips, with round or egg-shaped dark spots on the white areas.

The eyes show more white encirclement than most breeds, the skin is mottled, and the hoofs are striped vertically black and white. Appaloosas are used as stock, parade, race, and pleasure horses.

Animals are disqualified for registration if they have other than Appaloosa characteristics; if they have draft horse, pony, albino, paint, or pinto breeding, or overo or tobiano patterns; if they are gray or non-Appaloosa roan, or the progeny of a gray or non-Appaloosa roan; if they are cryptorchids; or if they are under 14 hands high at maturity, at five years of age or more.

ARABIAN

Arabian horses originated on the Arabian Peninsula. Coat colors usually are bay, gray, or chestnut, and occasionally white or black. White marks on the head and legs are common. The skin is always dark.

Figure 2.12 Arabian mare, Exquisite Lady, a Canadian champion. (Photo by Scott Trees; courtesy, International Arabian Horse Association, Denver, Colorado)

These animals have a beautiful head, short coupling, docility, great endurance, and an animated way of going. They are used as saddle, stock, show, race, and pleasure horses.

The Arabian Horse Registry of America, Inc., was established in 1908, although the name has undergone several slight changes. The International Arabian Horse Association, which is composed of state and local Arabian associations, was incorporated in 1950, to promote Arabian horses and to establish registries for Half-Arabians and Anglo-Arabians.

BUCKSKIN

Buckskin horses originated in the U.S. Coat colors are buckskin, red dun, or grulla (mouse-dun).

Buckskins are used as stock horses, pleasure horses, and show horses.

Disqualifications for registration are:

1. American Buckskin Registry Association: Palominos, chestnuts, sorrels, or bays with dorsal stripe; draft type; blue or glass eyes; white spots on body (indicating Pinto or Appaloosa blood) or white markings above knees or hocks.
2. International Buckskin Horse Association: Excessive white; showing Paint, Pinto, or Appaloosa characteristics. Also, the International

Figure 2.13 Buckskin mare, Leona Eclipse, IBHA Supreme Champion, owned by Doug La Sota, Phoenix, Arizona. (Courtesy, International Buckskin Horse Association, St. John, Indiana)

Buckskin Horse Association does not accept draft-type horses or ponies.

CHICKASAW

Chickasaw horses were developed by the Chickasaw Indians of Tennessee, North Carolina, and Oklahoma, from horses of Spanish extraction. Coat colors are bay, black, chestnut, gray, roan, sorrel, and palomino.

The breed is characterized by a short head and ears; a short back; a short neck; square, stocky hips; a low-set tail; a wide chest; and great width between the eyes. The preferred height: 53 to 59 inches (13-1 to 14-3 hands).

Chickasaw horses are used as cow ponies.

CONNEMARA PONY

Connemara Ponies originated on the west coast of Ireland. Coat colors usually are gray, black, bay, dun, brown, or cream, and occasionally roan or chestnut.

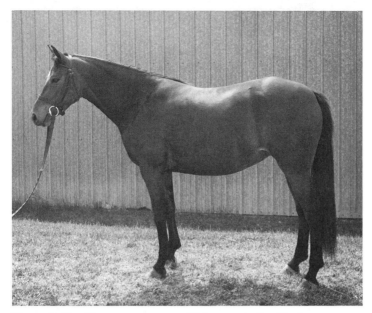

Figure 2.14 Connemara mare, Hideaway's Certified. (Courtesy, American Connemara Pony Society, Goshen, Connecticut)

These ponies are heavy boned, hardy, and docile. They range rather widely in height; hence, the American Connemara Society registers in two sections: *Section 1*, "pony," 13 to 14-2 hands; *Section 2*, "small horse," over 14-2 hands. Connemara Ponies are used as jumpers, as show ponies under saddle or in harness, and as riding ponies for medium-sized adults and children.

Animals are disqualified for registration if they are piebald, skewbald, or cream with blue eyes.

GALICENO

Galiceno horses originated in Galicia, a province in northwestern Spain. Horses of this lineage were first brought to America by the Conquistadores, but these horses were not introduced to the U.S. as a breed until 1958. The most common coat colors are bay, black, chestnut (sorrel), dun (buckskin), gray, brown, or palomino. Solid colors prevail.

At maturity, Galicenos are 12 to 13 hands high and weigh 625 to 700 lb. They are used as riding horses.

Animals are disqualified for registration if they have albino, pinto, or paint coloring, or if they are cryptorchids or monorchids.

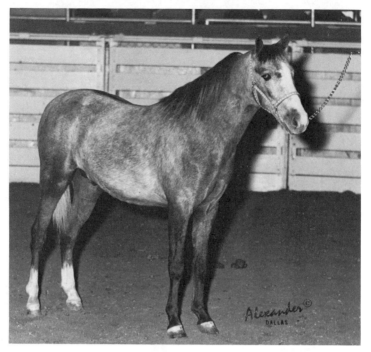

Figure 2.15   Galiceno stallion, Gray Badger. (Courtesy, Galiceno Horse Breeders Association, Tyler, Texas)

HACKNEY

Hackney horses originated on the east coast of England, in Norfolk and adjoining counties. The most common colors are chestnut, bay, or brown, and occasionally roan or black. White marks are common and desirable.

In the show ring, custom decrees that Hackney horses and ponies be docked and have their manes pulled. They have a high natural action.

Hackneys are used as heavy harness or carriage horses and ponies, and for crossbreeding purposes to produce hunters and jumpers.

HAFLINGER

The Haflinger is a very old breed, named after the village of Hafling, which was part of Austria at the end of World War I, now a part of Italy. The first importation of the breed from Austria to the U.S. was in 1958.

The Haflinger is a relatively small, stocky horse, standing from 13 to 14-3 hands high. The color is chestnut, ranging from honey blond to dark chocolate, with white or flaxen mane and tail.

Figure 2.16   Hackney pair. (Courtesy, Mrs. Dean J. Briggs, Garden Plains, Kansas)

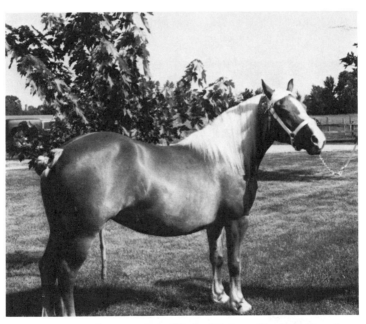

Figure 2.17   Haflinger mare, Cibyl of Dolson Creek, a Grand Champion, owned by Robert Wallace, Hemlock, Michigan. (Courtesy, Haflinger Association of America, Hemlock, Michigan)

Haflingers are noted for their versatility; they are used for all the purposes for which light horses and draft horses are used. They are family horses.

HANOVERIAN

The Hanoverian breed originated in the Hanover section of Germany, beginning in 1732. An Englishman went to Hanover and became its prince. Later, he returned to England and became King George II. During his stay in Germany he assembled outstanding individuals of certain breeds for the purpose of developing a superior horse for military use, with emphasis on size, intelligence, and temperament. Out of this effort evolved the Hanoverian breed of horses.

In Germany, the breeding, selection, and registration of Hanoverian horses are under government supervision. The State Stud, at Celle, was founded in 1735. Today, approximately 210 stallions are maintained at Celle. Each spring, these stallions are sent out to 60 stallion stations, where they breed about 16,000 registered Hanoverian mares. Without doubt, the breeding and selection program followed with Hanoverian horses in Germany is the finest equine production testing program in the world. It involves a rigid inspection of all stallions at two and one-half years of age, with only 60 selected, and the 15 top ones of these sent to the State Stud at Celle. Next, the stallions are put in intensive

Figure 2.18 Hanoverian stallion, Denar, imported foundation sire. (Courtesy, The American Hanoverian Society, Capitola, California)

Figure 2.19   Hungarian mares and foals on pasture at Bitterroot Stock Farm, Hamilton, Montana. (Photo by Ernst Peterson, Hamilton, Montana)

training and performance tested for one year in pulling, jumping, and dressage. During this time, temperament is also noted. If an animal does not measure up in any category, he is gelded.

Today, 70 percent of the horses of Germany are Hanoverians, and it is the most numerous light horse breed in Europe. In Europe, they are used for riding, driving (carriage horses), hunting, jumping, dressage, and utility purposes. In the U.S., the breed is used for all light-horse purposes, especially for jumping and dressage.

Hanoverian horses are big and powerful. Many of them stand 16.2 hands or better and weigh 1,200 lb. or more. They combine nobility, size, and strength in a unique way.

In 1978, the American Hanoverian Society was incorporated, with headquarters in Capitola, California.

HUNGARIAN HORSE

This very old breed originated in Hungary. The coat may be any color, either broken or solid.

These horses possess a unique combination of style and beauty, with ruggedness. They are used as stock, cutting, and pleasure horses, as hunters and jumpers, and for trail riding.

Animals are disqualified for registration if they are cryptorchids or have glass eyes.

LIPIZZAN

Lipizzan horses originated in Lipizza, Yugoslavia, the town from which the breed takes its name. Most mature animals of the breed are white. But Lipizzan foals are born dark (brown or gray), then turn white at

Figure 2.20   Lipizzan mare, Perlona. (Photo, J. F. Malony Photography, Seattle, Washington)

four to six years of age. About 1 horse in 600 remains black or brown throughout its life. When the latter happens, it is considered good luck.

Lipizzan horses have an elastic walk, with considerable knee action. They are used for dressage (for which purpose they are without a peer), harness horses, pleasure horses, hunters, jumpers, and parade horses.

MINIATURE HORSE

The Miniature Horse is a small model of a full-sized horse; it is not a dwarf or a freak. The breed has enjoyed great popularity and rapid growth in numbers.

The Miniature Horse is a new breed, with an old history. Miniature horses were used in England and Northern Europe to pull ore carts in the coal mines, as early as 1765. They were also bred as pets for some of the royal families of Europe. Some of these small horses were brought to the U.S. in the late 19th century and used in the mines of West Virginia and Ohio.

The American Miniature Horse Association, Inc. was organized in July 1978.

Mature animals cannot exceed 34 inches (8-2 hands) at the withers. Miniatures are of two types: (1) the more refined Arabian type, and (2) the heavier Quarter Horse type. All colors are accepted.

Figure 2.21 Miniature mare, Bond Little Lucy B, National Champion Mare, only 28¼ inches in height, owned by Charles and Barbara Ashby, Burleson, Texas. (Courtesy, The American Miniature Horse Association, Burleson, Texas)

Some people keep Miniature Horses as pets. Others exhibit them as driving horses, in single pleasure and roadster driving classes. Still others exhibit them in multiple hitches, pulling miniature wagons, stage coaches, carriages, and other vehicles.

MISSOURI FOX TROTTING HORSE

Missouri Fox Trotting Horses originated in the U.S., in the Ozark Hills of Missouri and Arkansas. They usually are sorrel, but any color is accepted.

These horses are distinguished by the fox-trot gait. They are used as pleasure and stock horses and for trail riding.

Animals are disqualified for registration if they cannot fox trot.

MORAB

Although Morgan × Arabian crosses were made in the early 1800s, the name *Morab* was not coined until the 1920s, when William Randolph Hearst became involved in a breeding program for his horses. He crossed Arabian stallions on Morgan mares to produce horses for use on his San Simeon ranch in California.

The modern Morab is predominantly Morgan and Arabian, although it may be part Thoroughbred. The breed possesses the muscular

Figure 2.22   Missouri Fox Trotting stallion, winner in the Show and Celebration. (Courtesy, Missouri Fox Trotting Horse Breed Association, Ava, Missouri)

Figure 2.23   Morab stallion, Blackwood Ben Hur, owned by Andrea Rowland, Blackwood Morabs, Walnut Creek, California. (Courtesy, North American Morab Horse Association, Hilbert, Wisconsin)

strength and ruggedness of the Morgan and the refinement and beauty of the Arabian. Mature animals average about 15 hands in height.

Morabs are used for show, pleasure riding, endurance rides, and ranch work.

Animals are disqualified if they have breed characteristics other than Morgan, Arabian, and Thoroughbred; if they have albino, appaloosa, paint, or pinto color; or if they are under 14 hands at maturity.

MORGAN

Morgan horses originated in the U.S., in the New England states. Coat colors are bay, brown, black, or chestnut; extensive white markings are uncommon.

Morgan horses are noted for their easy keeping qualities, endurance, and docility. They are used as saddle and stock horses.

Animals are disqualified for registration if they are walleyed or have white markings above the knee or hock, except that white markings on the face are acceptable.

NATIONAL APPALOOSA PONY

National Appaloosa Ponies originated in the U.S., near Rochester, Indiana. They are varicolored, but leopard, blanket-type, snowflake, or roan are the most popular colors. The skin, nose, and area around the eyes are mottled. White sclera encircles the eyes.

Figure 2.24   Morgan stallion, Shiloh Bold Command. (Photo by Karen Boulter; courtesy, The American Morgan Horse Association, Shelburne, Vermont)

National Appaloosa Ponies are used as working ponies, show ponies, and for trail riding, jumping, and racing.

Albino, pinto, or paint-colored animals are not eligible for registration.

NATIONAL SHOW HORSE

The National Show Horse was created from an Arabian × Saddlebred cross to meet a need for a beautiful show horse with athletic ability, and for new excitement and incentives in the show ring. The registry was incorporated in 1981.

Today, the National Show Horse Registry has specific rules regarding the types of horses that can be used to produce National Show Horses.

The National Show Horse combines the beauty, refinement, and stamina of the Arabian and the size and high-stepping action of the Saddlebred.

The goal of the breed founders was to produce the ideal show horse.

The National Show Horse appears to be firmly established and filling a need.

Figure 2.25   National Show Horse, Dream On. (Courtesy, National Horse Registry, Louisville, Kentucky)

Figure 2.26 Norwegian Fjord mare, Esika, a blue-ribbon mare owned by Rebecca Mayer, Fjordhest Farm, East Ryegate, Vermont. (Courtesy, Jan Exon-Equine Photography, Laramie, Wyoming)

NORWEGIAN FJORD HORSE

The Norwegian Fjord Horse is a small but powerful, all-purpose family horse — versatile and gentle. It is thought to be the oldest breed of domestic horses. In color and build, these horses resemble Przewalski's Horse, the wild horse of Asia, from which it is believed to be descended. The first records of the Fjord-like horses are found in Viking sagas and on ancient horse artifacts, dating as early as A.D. 700. In Norway, they have been selectively bred for more than 2,000 years.

Warren Delano, whose nephew was President Franklin Delano Roosevelt, was the first to import Fjord Horses into the U.S.; he brought a stallion and six mares from Bergen, Norway, in 1900. Other importations followed.

Fjordings (as their fond owners call them) are dun colored (ranging from light to dark), with a dorsal stripe, dark bars on the legs, and dark hoofs, eyes, and ear tips. They range in height from 13 to 14-2 hands. The body is compact and muscular.

In the U.S., Fjord Horses are used for draft, carriage, pleasure riding, jumping, dressage, and trail riding.

The Norwegian Fjord Horse Registry of North America was formed in 1980, for the purpose of preserving the genetic purity of the breed and promoting its use.

Figure 2.27   Paint stallion, Hot Scotch Man, World Champion at halter. (Courtesy, American Paint Horse Association, Fort Worth, Texas)

PAINT HORSE

Paint Horses[2] originated in the U.S. Coat colors are white plus any other color, but the coloring must be recognizable as paint. No discrimination is made against glass, blue, or light-colored eyes.

Paint Horses are used as stock horses, pleasure horses, and for showing and racing.

Animals are disqualified for registration unless they have natural white markings above the knees or hocks, except on the face; if they have Appaloosa coloring or breeding; if they are adult horses under 14 hands high; or if they are five-gaited horses.

PALOMINO

Palomino horses originated in the U.S., from animals of Spanish extraction. These horses are golden colored. They have a light-colored mane and tail of white, silver, or ivory; the mane and tail may not have more

[2] Two different associations have evolved for the registration of these varicolored horses. In the Pinto Horse Association of America, Inc., which is the older of the two registries, the breed is known as Pinto Horse, whereas in the American Paint Horse Association, the breed is known as the Paint Horse. Both groups of horses are similar in color. However, the Pinto and Paint differ as follows: The Pinto Association registers horses of all types and breeds, whereas the Paint Association is devoted strictly to the stock-type horse and restricts registration to registered Paints, Quarter Horses, and Thoroughbreds.

Figure 2.28 Palomino horse. (Photo by Paul E. Yard, Horse Photography, Tulsa, Oklahoma)

than 15 percent dark or chestnut hair. White markings on the face or below the knees are acceptable.

Palominos are used as stock, parade, pleasure, saddle, and fine harness horses.

The Palomino Horse Breeders of America disqualify horses with the following markings: a dorsal stripe of brown or black along the spine; zebra stripes around the legs or across the withers; or patches of white hair with underlying pink or light skin, unless caused by injury.

The Palomino Horse Association, Inc., lists the following disqualifications: buckskin, chocolate, or sorrel color; eyes blue or chalk eyed; a dorsal stripe along the spine; white or dark spots, indicating Pinto, Appaloosa, or Paint background; horses with known Albino breeding; or horses with the characteristics of draft horses.

PASO FINO

Paso Fino horses originated in the Caribbean area, where they have existed for over 400 years. They have been registered in stud books in Peru, Puerto Rico, Cuba, and Colombia.

Figure 2.29 Paso Fino stallion, El Bonito de Colombia, owned by Arthur and Lee Glatfelter, Dallastown, Pennsylvania. (Courtesy, Paso Fino Horse Association, Bowling Green, Florida)

The Paso Fino Horse Association was founded in 1972 under the name Paso Fino Owners and Breeders Association.

The coat of the Paso Fino may be any color, although solid colors are preferred. Bay, chestnut, or black with white markings are most common. Occasionally, palominos and pintos appear.

Paso Finos are used as pleasure, cutting, and parade horses and for endurance riding and drill team work.

Paso fino is Spanish, meaning "fine step." The Paso Fino gait may be described as a broken pace. The legs on the same side move together, but the hind foot strikes the ground a fraction of a second before the front foot, producing a four-beat gait.

Animals that do not possess the Paso Fino gait or do not trace directly to the purebred Paso Fino ancestry are not eligible for registration.

PERUVIAN PASO

The Peruvian Paso is original only to Peru. In this respect it should not be confused with the Paso Fino breeds whose ancestors were scattered throughout the Caribbean area.

One of the trademarks of the breed is the *piso,* or gait, a natural (inborn), smooth, four-beat, lateral gait — in essence, a broken pace.

Figure 2.30   Peruvian Paso. (Courtesy, American Association of Owners and Breeders of Peruvian Paso Horses, Burbank, California)

Another trademark of the Peruvian Paso is that it is the only breed in the world that does the *"terimo,"* a graceful, flowing movement in which the forelegs are rolled to the outside as the horse strides forward, much like the arm motions of a swimmer.

Peruvian Pasos come in all the basic solid colors, as well as grays, roans, and palominos, with some rather striking variations of these colors.

Peruvian Paso Horse Registry of North America disqualifies for registry cryptorchids, monorchids, and albino animals.

American Association of Owners and Breeders of Peruvian Paso Horses disqualifies horses with more than 25 percent of the body white, including the legs and head.

PINTO HORSE

Pinto Horses[3] originated in the U.S., from horses brought in by the Spanish Conquistadores. The coat should be half color (or colors) and half white, with many spots well placed.

The two distinct pattern markings are overo and tobiano. Overo is a colored horse with white areas extending upward from the belly and lower regions, and there may be other white markings; in tobiano the white areas on the back extend downward, and there may be other

[3] Refer to footnote 2 under Paint Horse.

Figure 2.31 Pinto Horse, Indian Sunrise, owned by Mildred Hopkins, Unionville, Ontario, Canada. (Courtesy, Mildred Hopkins)

white markings as well. Glass eyes are acceptable. The registry association has a separate registry for ponies and horses under 14 hands high.

Pintos are used for any light-horse purpose, but especially as show, parade, novice, pleasure, and stock horses.

PONY OF THE AMERICAS

Pony of the Americas originated in the U.S., in Mason City, Iowa. Their coloring is like that of the Appaloosa. They have white over the loin and hips and round or egg-shaped dark spots on the white areas.

These ponies have the characteristics of Arabian and Quarter Horses in miniature. They range in height from 46 to 54 inches and are used as mounts for juniors.

Animals are disqualified for registration if they possess any of the following characteristics: pinto or paint color; white markings with underlying light skin (1) above each leg at the top of the knees and top of the hocks, (2) behind a line running from the center of each ear to the running from one corner of the mouth to the other corner.

QUARTER HORSE

Quarter Horses originated in the U.S. The most common colors are chestnut, sorrel, bay, or dun, and sometimes black, palomino, roan, brown, or copper color.

Figure 2.32 Pony of the Americas stallion, Doc's Tough Tiger, owned by T. C. Roas, Arcadia, Florida. (Courtesy, Pony of the Americas Club, Indianapolis, Indiana)

These horses are well muscled and powerfully built, but modern animals no longer have the once-sought "bulldog" build. They are used as stock, race, pleasure, show, and equine sport horses.

Animals are disqualified for registration if they have pinto, appaloosa, or albino coloring or white markings on the underline.

Figure 2.33 Quarter Horse stallion, Chocolate Macho, Grand Champion Quarterama. (Courtesy, *The Quarter Horse Journal,* Amarillo, Texas)

QUARTER PONY

Quarter Ponies are Quarter Horses in miniature. All animals must measure 46 to 58 inches in height.

The National Quarter Pony Association was organized in 1975 to record and preserve the pedigrees of Quarter Ponies, which originated in the U.S. and were descended from Quarter Horses.

Quarter Ponies are adapted as mounts for children and juniors, and they are used for all the purposes for which their larger counterparts — Quarter Horses — are used. Some are used as cow ponies; others compete in horse shows and contests.

SHETLAND PONY

Shetland Ponies originated in the Shetland Islands. The coat may be any color, either broken or solid.

These ponies are small. Two types are recognized by the breed registry: (1) The classic type, which is somewhat short and chunky; and (2) the modern type, which is rather fine boned and long necked, with high going (a lot of knee and hock action).

Animals are disqualified for registration if they are over 46 inches high.

Figure 2.34 Shetland Pony, Michigan's Next Generation, National All-Star Champion Model Mare, owned by Taylor Pony Farm, Hudson, Michigan. (Courtesy, American Shetland Pony Club, Peoria, Illinois)

Figure 2.35 Spanish-Barb stallion, Gitano Inquieto, owned by Riverdale Farm, Platteville, Colorado. (Courtesy, Spanish-Barb Breeders Association, Berthoud, Colorado)

SPANISH-BARB

The Barb horse was taken from Africa to Spain with the conquest of Spain by the Moors in A.D. 711. From Spain, they were taken to Cuba in 1511, to Mexico in 1519, to the southwestern U.S. in 1540, and to Florida in 1565. The Spanish-Barb Breeders Association was organized in 1972.

Spanish-Barbs are small horses (the standard height is 13-3 to 14-1 hands), with short coupling (usually 5 lumbar vertebrae; at times 17 thoracic vertebrae), deep bodies, good action, and without extreme muscling. All colors are represented in the breed, but dun, grulla, sorrel, and roan are most common. Most animals are solid colored. A dorsal stripe and zebra markings occur in all duns and grullas and in some sorrels. Spanish-Barbs are used for Western and English riding, and as packhorses.

SPANISH MUSTANG

The Spanish Mustang originated in the U.S. Mustangs trace their ancestry to the feral and the semi-feral (Indian-owned) horses of Barb and Andalusian descent that were brought to America by the Spanish Conquistadores in the early 1500s and 1600s. Beginning about 1925, Robert E. Brislawn, Sr., and his brother, Ferdinand L. Brislawn, began gathering pure Spanish Mustangs. To retain the purity of the strain, the Spanish Mustang Registry, Inc., was founded in 1957, at Sundance,

Figure 2.36   Spanish Mustang stallion, Chief of Choltaws.
Raised on Medicine Springs Ranch, Finley, Oklahoma.
(Courtesy, Southwest Spanish Mustang Association, Finley,
Oklahoma)

Wyoming. Spanish Mustangs run the whole gamut of equine colors, including all the solid colors and all the broken colors. They stand 13 to 14-2 hands high. Spanish Mustangs are used for Western and English riding, and as packhorses.

The breed is characterized by having only 5 lumbar vertebrae (most breeds have 6), short ears, a low-set tail, and round leg bones.

Spanish Mustangs are used primarily as cow ponies and for trail riding.

SPOTTED SADDLE HORSE

As the name indicates, animals of this breed are spotted and saddle horses. With their loud colors and easy gaits, Spotted Saddle Horses are popular in trail rides, parades, and horse shows.

Colorful spotted horses were first brought to the U.S. by the early Spaniards. Also, spotted saddle horses were not uncommon in the foundation animals of the American Saddlebred and the Tennessee Walking Horse breeds.

On October 24, 1979, a group of breeders met in Murfreesboro, Tennessee, and formed the National Spotted Saddle Horse Association, to collect, record, and preserve the pedigrees of the Spotted Saddle Horse.

In addition to being used as pleasure mounts and jumpers, the breed has been promoted as a bird-dog mount, and for use by coon hunters in rugged mountain terrain.

During the first ten years after the registry was formed, 3,996 horses were registered. Thus, the breed appears to be off to a good start. Four pictures must accompany each application for registration.

STANDARDBRED

Standardbred horses originated in the U.S. The most common colors are bay, brown, chestnut, or black, and occasionally gray, roan, or dun.

Standardbreds are smaller, less leggy, and more rugged than Thoroughbreds. They are used for harness racing, either trotting or pacing, and as harness horses in horse shows.

DAN PATCH — Famous Standardbred

This great Standardbred horse made history soon after the turn of the century, from 1902 to 1910. In 1906, he paced the world's fastest mile, 1:55, at the Minnesota State Fair. That record stood until 1938, but it was not recognized, because a windshield was pulled in front of the sulky to break the wind. However, to the 93,000 rabid fans who witnessed the feat, and to his worshippers everywhere, the record stood.

The great horse's owner, Will Savage, was a fabulous and colorful character. Will and Dan Patch belonged to each other, when winning — yes, even in death. Mr. Savage made headlines of a sort when he

Figure 2.37 Standardbred racing champion and sire, Meadow Skipper. (Courtesy, U.S. Trotting Association, Columbus, Ohio)

Figure 2.38   Dan Patch. (Courtesy, U.S. Trotting Association,
Columbus, Ohio)

paid $60,000 for the six-year-old Standardbred pacer in 1902. Even his
friends referred to the deal as "Savage's folly." But subsequent events
proved how wrong they were.

Dan Patch brought fame and fortune to his master and to himself. A
railroad line — The Dan Patch Line — was named after him. There
were also Dan Patch sleds, coaster wagons, cigars, washing machines
(a two-minute performer like Dan), and shoes for kiddies. And Mr.
Savage built the great horse an empire, surroundings befitting his station in life. The stable was equipped with modern living quarters for 60
caretakers. Two racetracks were constructed: the best mile strip ever
built, and a covered half-miler with 8,400 panes of glass. Even during a
Minnesota blizzard, Dan and his stable mates could train in comfort —
and style.

Dan Patch was the idol of his day — the Babe Ruth, the Bing Crosby,
and the Beatles. People came to see him, as they do any other notable.
Lillie Langtry, the famous actress, arranged to have her train stopped
near Dan's so that she could go to his private car for a visit. Men vied
for his shoes, women fought to pluck hair from his mane and tail, small
boys played Dan Patch in the backyard, and people wept when he became ill.

The town of Hamilton changed its name to Savage, in honor of the
man who had put it on the map.

But there was more than a platonic relationship between horse and
owner — there was something almost supernatural between Dan and

Will. On July 4, 1916, Dan Patch and Will Savage both took ill on the same day. Those keeping vigil over the horse saw him snuff out his last race — the race with life itself — on July 11. He died at age 20. Thirty-two hours later, Dan's master, Will Savage, was dead at age 57. Both were buried at the same hour; Mr. Savage in Lakewood cemetery, and Mr. Patch under the shade of an oak tree on the bank of the Minnesota River.

TENNESSEE WALKING HORSE

Tennessee Walking Horses originated in the U.S., in the Central Basin of Tennessee. Coat colors are sorrel, chestnut, black, roan, white, bay, brown, gray, or golden. White markings on the face and legs are common.

These horses are characterized by their running walk. They are used as plantation walking horses and as pleasure and show horses.

Figure 2.39 Tennessee Walking Horse stallion, Pride's Jubilee Star, 1986 World Grand Champion Tennessee Walking Horse, owned by the Bob Parks family, Murfreesboro, Tennessee. (Courtesy, Tennessee Walking Horse Breeders & Exhibitors Association, Lewisburg, Tennessee)

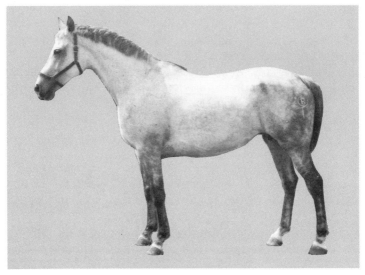

Figure 2.40　Thorcheron mare, Miss Kingsley. (Courtesy, H. Bonita Fitch, owner/breeder, and founder of the Thorcheron breed)

THOROUGHRON

The Thorcheron breed is a strong, gentle hunter/jumper type horse, developed from a Thoroughbred × Percheron cross (hence, the name Thorcheron). The initial crosses were made in 1970.

Thorcherons resemble the big hunters in Ireland, which the Irish ride to hounds. Thorcherons are short-coupled and good movers, with the refinement of Thoroughbreds and the muscle and good nature of Percherons.

THOROUGHBRED

Thoroughbred horses originated in England. The most common coat colors are bay, brown, black, or chestnut, and, less frequently, roan or gray. White markings on the face and legs are common.

These horses are noted for their fineness of conformation and their long, straight, well-muscled legs. They are used as race, saddle, stock, and polo horses, and as hunters and dressage and event horses.

Man O' War — Famous Thoroughbred

Ask the person on the street — one who may never have gone to a race — to name the greatest horse of all time and chances are that he'll say Man O' War. If there is any absolute against which greatness in a horse may be measured, it is the legendary Man O' War. "Big Red," as

Figure 2.41 The Darley Arabian, imported in 1706 by King Charles II of England. This stallion is the immortal foundation sire of the Thoroughbreds from which the Eclipse line sprang. (Courtesy, The Mercaldo Archive, Ozone Park, New York, New York)

Figure 2.42 Thoroughbred mare and foal at Spendthrift Farm, Lexington, Kentucky. (Courtesy, Kentucky Department of Public Information, Frankfort)

he was known, seemed to have limitless speed. Only once in his 21 starts did his machine-like power fail to propel him first across the finish line; that was when he was beaten by the aptly named, "Upset," at Saratoga on August 13, 1919, after an unfortunate start. As if to redress that wrong, Man O' War trounced Upset with authority the next three times they met. In 8 of his 11 starts as a three-year-old, he broke either a track or world's record.

Man O' War was born in 1917. Samuel D. Riddle bought him as a yearling at the Saratoga sale, on August 17, 1918, for $5,000.

During his career, talented writers and eloquent speakers extolled him with such superlatives as "look of eagles" and "living flame." But it fell to his groom, Will Harbut, who had quite a way with words as well as with horses, to devise the most fitting description of all. "Man O' War," as Will never tired of telling the thousands who came to see him, "was de mostest hoss dat ever was." During his lifetime, more visitors went to see Man O' War than Mammoth Cave.

Physically, Man O' War was a glowing chestnut, almost red, standing 16 hands 1⅝ in. He measured 71¾ inches at the girth and weighed 1,100 pounds in training. As a stallion, his weight reached 1,370 pounds. He was unusually long bodied and powerfully muscled in the gaskins. Estimates of his stride varied anywhere from 25 to 28 feet, although, oddly enough, it was never officially measured.

Figure 2.43 Man O' War and his groom, Will Harbut. (Courtesy, J. C. Skeets Meadors and Keeneland Library, Lexington, Kentucky)

When he was in training, Big Red's morning came early. He was given his first meal at 3:30 A.M. At 7:30 A.M., he was brushed and massaged; the bandages that he wore at all times except when in action were removed, and his legs were washed; his face, eyes, and nostrils were sponged; and he was given a rubdown with a soft cloth. After work on warm days, he was washed; then he was rubbed thoroughly, his feet were cleaned and dressed, and he was left to rest in his stall. He was fond of his caretaker; he liked to snatch his hat and carry it around as he showed off for visitors.

Most Thoroughbred horses share a universal birthday — January 1. But Big Red was different! At Faraway Farm, near Lexington, where he spent most of his life, his actual foaling date, March 29, was duly observed as a special occasion. He received telegrams, carrots, and other tokens of recognition from all over the country.

The great horse, who was the first to command a $5,000 service fee, was maintained largely for private use. He sired over 300 offspring, who won over 1,200 races and earned more than $3.5 million.

Big Red died in 1947, at the age of 30. Ira Drymon, as the Thoroughbred Club's representative, delivered the eulogy before the 2,000 people assembled and over a nationwide radio hookup. As taps were sounded and the mammoth coffin of polished oak containing the body of Man O' War was lowered to his final resting place, men, women, and children wept unashamedly. Today, above the grave stands a lifesize-and-a-half statue of the great champion.

The Man O' War legend continues on, for he lived and died and won a lasting name and fame — a rare achievement by any beast, or man.

TRAKEHNER

The breed originated in Trakehnen, East Prussia, in 1732. It evolved from the blending of the indigenous Prussian horses, Thoroughbreds, and Arabians. Although the breeding goals have changed through the years to meet the needs of the times, generally speaking the emphasis has been on the development of a horse with the size of the Thoroughbred, but more rugged, and possessing the elegance of the Arabian.

The American Trakehner Association, Inc., was formed in September 1974.

Trakehners are popular as equine sports horses, especially as dressage horses and show hunters or jumpers.

TROTTINGBRED

Trottingbreds are small harness racehorses, distinctly separate from Standardbreds (however, most of them are one-half to three-quarters Standardbred).

Figure 2.44 Trakehner stallion, Siegbert, bred and owned by Trakehner Stud, Schleswig-Holstein, Germany. (Courtesy, American Trakehner Association, Norman, Oklahoma)

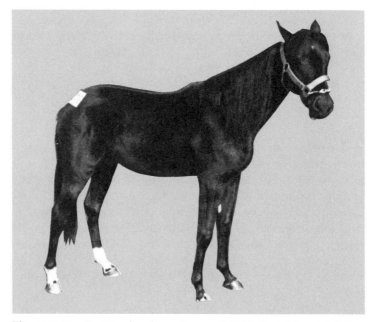

Figure 2.45 Trottingbred yearling colt, Irish Knight, sold at the 1987 auction of the International Trotting and Racing Association, Hanover, Pennsylvania, for $3,700; consigned by Shamrock Stables, Middlebury, Indiana, and purchased by Jacques Tremblay, Quebec, Canada.

The Trottingbred is a cross between Welsh, Shetland, or Hackney ponies and Standardbreds. The breed was developed in the 1960s.

Trottingbreds are miniature Standardbreds with a dash of pony; the pony breeding is necessary in order to retain the small size. To qualify for racing, Trottingbreds must not measure more than 13-1 hands.

Purebred (full-blood) Standardbreds are not allowed to compete against Trottingbreds, but they may be registered in the Trottingbred Association and used for breeding purposes.

Trottingbreds are adapted to and used for harness racing. The breed and sport are extolled as for the "little guys." Trottingbred harness racing is do-it-yourself and family oriented. Usually the Trottingbred horse is stabled and trained at the owner's home.

WELARA PONY

The Welara Pony evolved from a Welsh × Arabian cross. It resembles a miniature coach horse. Although many equestrians have long admired Welsh × Arabian crossbreds, there was no breed registry to promote the stylish ponies resulting from this breeding until 1981.

Welara Ponies range from 46 to 58 inches in height. They are most commonly used for fine harness, English pleasure, halter, hunter, and native costume classes. Also, the Welara has been hugely successful in competitive trail rides.

Figure 2.46 Welara Pony mare, Lady-B. (Courtesy, American Welara Pony Society, Yucca Valley, California)

Figure 2.47 Welsh Pony stallion, Findeln Blue Danube, owned by James W. Cloe, Okmulgee, Oklahoma. (Photo by Coleman Cowan; courtesy, Welsh Pony Society of America, Winchester, Virginia)

WELSH PONY AND COB

The Welsh originated in Wales. The coat may be any color except piebald or skewbald, but gaudy white markings are not popular. These ponies are intermediate in size between Shetland Ponies and other light horse breeds. The Welsh Pony and Cob Society of America maintains the following height divisions: *Section A,* Welsh not exceeding 12-2 hands; and *Section B,* Welsh exceeding 12-2 hands, but under 14-2 hands.

The Welsh Pony (Cob Type) and the Welsh Cob also have two sections: *Section C* is for Welsh not exceeding 13-2 hands, without lower limit; and *Section D* is for Welsh exceeding 13-2 hands, with no upper limit on height.

Welsh Ponies are used for racing, trail riding, parading, stock cutting, showing, and hunting, and as driving ponies and mounts for children and small adults.

Piebald or skewbald animals are not eligible for registration.

DONKEYS AND MULES

Small asses of the species *Equus asinas* are known as donkeys. The males are known as jacks, and the females as jennets. Compared with

Figure 2.48 Miniature Donkeys used primarily as children's pets. These small animals, standing under 38 inches high at the withers, originated in Sardinia and Sicily. They vary from mouse color to almost black, and a dorsal stripe forms a cross with a stripe over the withers and down the shoulders. (Courtesy, Daniel Langfeld, Jr., Danby Farm, Millard, Nebraska)

the horse, the ass is smaller; has shorter hairs on the mane and tail; does not possess the "chestnuts" on the inside of the hind legs; has much longer ears; has smaller, deeper hoofs; possesses a louder and more harsh voice, called a bray; is less subject to founder or injury; is more hardy; and has a longer gestation period — jennets carry their young about 12 months.

The mule is a hybrid, produced by crossing a jack (male donkey) on a mare (female horse). Donkeys and mules should be fed and cared for in the same manner as horses.

BREED NUMBERS

Table 2.2 shows (1) the annual (1987 or 1988), and (2) the total registrations to date of the breeds of light horses, ponies, donkeys, and mules. The recent annual figures reflect the current popularity of the different breeds, although it is recognized that only one year's data fails to show trends. It is noteworthy that about 275,000 horses are being registered annually in the United States at the present time.

RACING

According to some historians, the Greeks introduced horse racing in the Olympic Games in 1450 B.C. Also, it is reported that a planned horse race of consequence was run in 1377 between animals owned by Rich-

Table 2.2 Annual (1987 or 1988) and Total Registrations by Breed of Light Horses in U.S.

Breed	Annual (1987 or 1988) Registrations	Total Registrations (since breed registry started)
Quarter Horse	128,352	2,777,860
Thoroughbred	50,375	1,158,803
Arabian		
Purebred	24,570	422,829
Half-Arabian	6,500	274,200
Anglo-Arabian	188	7,353
Standardbred	17,393	632,000
Ridden Standardbred[1]	300	5,000
Paint Horse	15,518	144,076
Appaloosa	12,317	492,511
Tennessee Walking Horse	8,000	245,000
American Saddlebred	3,811	207,381
Half-Saddlebred[2]	182	1,440
Morgan	3,526	88,000
Palomino[3]	3,493	78,080
Trottingbred	3,441	10,578
Paso Fino	2,060	13,500
Peruvian Paso[4]	1,813	12,072
Missouri Fox Trotting Horse	1,800	32,800
Buckskin	852	12,540
Pony of the Americas	709	36,000
Trakehner	625	5,987
Welsh Pony and Cob	577	32,298
Shetland Pony	568	137,360
Spotted Saddle Horse	436	3,996
Andalusian[5]	355	1,903
Haflinger	298	2,000
American Bashkir Curly	163	875
National Appaloosa Pony	150	5,729
American Part-blooded Horse	147	14,450
Lipizzan	124	928
Welara Pony	93	423

Breed	Annual (1987 or 1988) Registrations	Total Registrations (since breed registry started)
Spanish Mustang	70	1,510
American White and American Creme[6]	34	3,698
Norwegian Fjord Horse	21	424
Spanish-Barb	21	381
American Walking Pony	15	300
Miniature Horse	—	30,000
Hanoverian	—	1,811
American Mustang	—	1,000
Hungarian	—	545
Morab	—	320
American Warmblood	—	71
Thorcheron	—	57
Donkeys and Mules		
Donkeys	287	3,627
Miniature Donkeys	273	7,537
Mules	107	1,003

[1] Registered in the Ridden Standardbred Association, 1578 Fleet Rd., Troy, OH 49373.

[2] The Half Saddlebred Registry was founded in May 1971 for the registration of horses of which one parent is an American Saddlebred.

[3] Palomino Horse Breeders of America: 1987 registrations, 1,746; total registrations, 53,000. The Palomino Horse Association, Inc.: 1988 registrations, 1,747; total registrations, 25,080.

[4] American Association of Owners & Breeders of Peruvian Paso Horses: 1987 registrations, 675; total registrations, 6,500. Peruvian Paso Horse Registry of North America: 1987 registrations, 1,138; total registrations, 5,672.

[5] There are two Andalusian registries. From inception to 1988, the American Andalusian Association reported a total of 703 registrations. From inception to 1988, the International Andalusian Association reported a total of 1,200 registrations.

[6] The American White and the American Creme are registered in separate divisions by the International American Albino Association, Naper, Nebraska. In 1987, a total of 34 American Creme and American White horses were registered. The number of animals registered by the association from its formation through 1987 totaled 3,698.

ard II and the Earl of Arundel. The sporting instinct of man being what it is, it is reasonable to surmise, however, that a bit of a contest was staged the first time that two proud mounted horsemen chanced to meet.

The development of horse racing in Britain dates from the 17th century, although it is known to have taken place much earlier. Records exist of racing during the Roman occupation, and during the reign of

Figure 2.49   Mandan Indian horse race. (From an oil painting
by George Catlin; courtesy, Smithsonian Institution)

Henry II races took place at Smithfield, which was the great London
horse market at the time. But it was in the reign of James I that racing
first began to be an organized sport. He took a great liking to Newmarket, where he had a royal palace and a racecourse built. Also, he established public races in various parts of the country.

The famous Rowley Mile Course at Newmarket, the home of English
flat racing, is named after Charles II. "Old Riley" was his nickname,
after his favorite hack by that name. Charles II loved racing; he rode in
matches, founded races called the Royal Plates, and sometimes adjudi-
cated in disputes.

The Jockey Club came into existence at Newmarket in 1752, with
many rich and influential men among its members. It gradually became
the governing body of English racing.

RACEHORSES

The term "racehorse" refers to a horse that is bred and trained for
racing. Today, two types of horse races are run: (1) running races (including steeplechase races) and (2) harness races.

Running Racehorses

Racehorses used for running (an extended gallop) under the saddle are
now confined almost exclusively to two breeds: Thoroughbreds and
Quarter Horses. Also, the Thoroughbred breed (including both purebreds and crossbreds) has been used widely for other purposes — especially as polo mounts, hunters, and cavalry horses. Quarter Horses

Figure 2.50 Running racehorses, Thoroughbreds, in action at the extended gallop. (Courtesy, *The Backstretch*, Detroit, Michigan)

are the cow ponies of the West and are also widely used as show and pleasure horses in the East.

Although trials of speed had taken place between horses from the earliest recorded history, the true and unmistakable foundation of the Thoroughbred breed, as such, traces back only to the reign of Charles II, known as the "father of the British turf."

Although the length of race, weight carried, and type of track have undergone considerable variation in recent years, the running horse always has been selected for speed and more speed at the run. The distinguishing characteristics of the running horse, as represented by the Thoroughbred, are the extreme refinement, oblique shoulders, well-made withers, heavily muscled rear quarters, straight hind legs, and close travel to the ground.

Quarter Horse running races are increasing in importance. Also, Appaloosa and Arabian running races have been approved in a few states.

Harness Racehorses (Trotters and Pacers)

Prior to the advent of improved roads and the automobile, but following the invention of the buggy, there was need for a fast, light-harness type of horse. This horse was used to draw vehicles varying in type from the light roadster of the young gallant to the dignified family carriage. In the process of meeting this need, two truly American breeds of horses evolved — the Morgan and the Standardbred. The first breed traces to the foundation sire, Justin Morgan, and the latter to Hambletonian 10, an animal which was linebred to Messenger, an imported racing sire.

As horse and buggy travel passed into permanent oblivion except for recreation and sport, Standardbred breeders wisely placed greater emphasis upon the sport of racing, whereas Morgan enthusiasts directed their breeding programs toward transforming their animals into a saddle breed.

The early descendants of Messenger were sent over the track, trotting (not galloping) under the saddle, but eventually the jockey races in this country came to be restricted to a running type of race in which the Thoroughbred was used. With this shift, beginning in 1879, qualifying standards — a mile in 2:30 at the trot and 2:25 at the pace when hitched to the sulky — were set up for light harness races, and those animals so qualifying were registered. On January 1, 1933, registration on performance alone was no longer granted, and registration of both sire and dam was required.

The pneumatic-tire racing vehicles, known as sulkies, were first introduced in 1892. With their use that year, the time was reduced nearly four seconds below the record of the previous year. Thus were developed harness racing and the Standardbred breed of horses, which today is the exclusive breed used for this purpose.

Figure 2.51   A field of harness horses trotting in the final quarter. (Courtesy, U.S. Trotting Association, Columbus, Ohio)

Trotters and pacers are of similar breeding and type, the particular gaits being largely a matter of training. In fact, many individuals show speed at both the trot and the pace. It is generally recognized, however, that pacers are handicapped in the mud, in the sand, or over a rough surface.

In the beginning, horses of this type found their principal use in harness races at county and state fairs. However, in recent years pari-mutuel harness racing has been established at a number of tracks. Today, harness racehorses are almost exclusively of the Standardbred breed.

RACING COLORS

The Jockey Club assigns colors to racing stables. They may be assigned for one year, or they may be assigned for a lifetime. Sometimes colors are reassigned when no longer in use, but this is not the case with the colors of very famous stables. Jockeys must wear the colors assigned to the stable.

RACING ATTENDANCE

Horse racing ranks third as a U.S. spectator sport. In 1988, 74,158,269 people went to horse races (Thoroughbred and harness racing). Baseball (major and minor leagues) ranked first, with an attendance of 89.6 million; auto racing ranked second, with 86 million fans; football (pro and college) ranked fourth, with 51 million fans; and basketball (pro and college) stood fifth, with an attendance of 46.6 million.[4]

RACING RECORDS

In running races (Thoroughbreds), Dr. Fager holds the world's record for a mile at 1:32⅕ (equal to a speed of 45.4 miles per hour), set at Arlington Park, Chicago, in 1968; and Man O' War set the world's record for 1⅜ mile at 2:14⅕, in 1920.

In harness racing (Standardbreds), Mack Lobell holds the world's trotting record for a mile at 1:52⅕ minutes, which was established in 1987; and Matts Scooter set the world's pacing record for a mile at 1:48⅖ minutes in 1988.

EQUINE SPORTS HORSES

Horses are used for many equine sports in addition to racing, including dressage, eventing, endurance rides, show hunters and jumpers, polo, and parades. Purebreds, crossbreds, and grades of the following breeds are especially well adapted to some of the equine sports described in

[4] Statistics courtesy of Triangle Publications, Inc., Hightstown, NJ.

the sections that follow: Akhal-Teke, American Creme and American White, Lipizzan, Thorcheron, Thoroughbred, and Trakehner. Representatives of many other breeds are also outstanding performers as *equine sports horses.*

- **Dressage** — *Dressage is the guiding of a horse through natural maneuvers without emphasis on the use of reins, hands, and feet.*

  The term *dressage* comes from the French verb meaning "to train." After the horse has learned to respond to the simple directions for moving forward or backward, turning, changing gait, and halting, equestrians who wish to develop the horse's strength, willingness, and agility as much as possible continue training by working on special exercises to develop these traits. This training is called dressage.

  All of the movements described as dressage or training movements are based on natural movements of the horse while at liberty. Thus, by watching horses (especially young horses) in a corral, they will be seen to execute with ease changes from one gait to another, sudden halts, changes of the leading leg at the canter when changing direction, and such intricacies of the *Haute École* ("High School") as the pirouette, the piaffe, the passage, and various airs above the ground. Why, then, must a horse be trained to do these things if it already knows how? There are two reasons: (1) the horse must learn to balance itself under the weight of the rider, and (2) the horse must learn to do these movements when so requested by the rider.

  Any horse can benefit from dressage training, which makes the horse's stride easier to adjust and the horse more supple, better balanced, and more responsive in general to the rider's aids. Dressage competition tests the progress of horse and rider toward these goals. Especially at the highest levels — as in any advanced form of competition — the harmony between horse and rider is a pleasure to watch.

- **Combined training** — also called "eventing" — is a sport that tests the horses' and riders' ability in three different areas: dressage, cross-country jumping, and stadium jumping. The same horse and rider must complete all three phases. Horses of all shapes and sizes may compete, but there are performance prerequisites for the more advanced levels.

  The jumps on a cross-country course are solid obstacles, often made more difficult by their placement on hillsides or at the edge of a woods, where a horse must jump confidently from light into dark. Types of jumps usually include ditches and up-and-down banks as well as stone walls, hedges, tree trunks, water jumps, and other vertical or spread fences that are designed to blend in with the terrain. Although the horse and rider are not judged on form — get-

Figure 2.52 Event horses and riders must be able to jump solid cross-country fences as well as show-ring fences. The jumping phases of a combined training event are preceded by a dressage test. (Courtesy, the U.S. Combined Training Association, South Hamilton, Massachusetts)

ting around the course is what counts — penalties are awarded for jumping refusals, falls, and for exceeding the time allowed. The rider has an opportunity to walk the course beforehand and plan the best approach, but the horse has not seen the jumps before he sets out on course. Stadium jumps are similar to fences encountered in show-jumping classes, with rails that come down if they are hit. Penalties are awarded for knockdowns and refusals and for exceeding the time limit.

- **Endurance rides** — *Competitive rides designed to test the stamina of horses are known as endurance trials.* The riders must take their horses over a prescribed course, which is usually of rugged terrain, and which may require anywhere from one to three days to cover. The time for the different courses varies according to the topography, elevation, and footing. Veterinarians check the horses' vital signs (temperature, pulse, respiration, etc.) and watch for signs of lameness at mandatory checkpoints, to make sure each horse is fit to continue.

One of the best-known endurance rides is the Tevis Cup Ride, held at Auburn, California, each August. The course is 100 miles long, and covers extremely rough terrain. The time limit is 24 hours, and there are three mandatory rest stops of one hour each. During the rest stops, the veterinarians check the pulse, respiration, and temperature of each horse, both at the beginning and the end of the hour, so as to determine whether its rate of recovery is satisfactory. There are two kinds of competition in the Tevis Cup Ride: (1) a race over the 100-mile course, and (2) a fitness contest, with an award for the best-conditioned horse that completes the ride within the 24-hour period.

Generally, more than 200 competitors start the Tevis Cup Ride and about 160 (or 80 percent) finish. The winning horse makes the ride in approximately 11 hours.

• **Hunters and jumpers** — *The field hunter is that type of horse used in following the hounds in foxhunting.* The sport is traditional in England, and each year its glamour is shared by more people in the U.S.

The field hunter is not necessarily of any particular breeding, but Thoroughbred blood predominates. The infusion of some cold blood (draft-horse breeding) is often relied upon in order to secure greater size and a more tractable disposition.

In addition to being of ample size and height, field hunters must possess the necessary stamina and conformation to keep up with the pack. They must be able to hurdle with safety such common cross-country obstacles as fences and ditches. The good field hunter, therefore, is rugged, short coupled, and heavily muscled throughout. Field hunters occasionally compete in hunter trials and hunter paces, but are used primarily outside the show ring. Show hunters are a more refined type, and are judged on their form over fences.

All hunters are jumpers to some degree, but high jumpers are not necessarily good hunters. To qualify as hunters, horses must do more. They must execute many and varied jumps over a long period of time.

Jumpers are a mixed group, consisting of all breeds and types; the only requirement is that they can jump. In the show ring, an unsoundness does not penalize a jumper unless it is sufficiently severe to be considered an act of cruelty. Form is not important, except to the extent that it affects the horse's ability to clear the jumps, especially when tight turns are involved. The horse is judged on his ability to "go clear" — to get around the course of jumps without refusing or knocking any down, usually within a specified amount of time.

• **Polo** — *As the name would indicate, polo mounts are horses that are particularly adapted for use in playing the game of polo.* This game, which was first introduced into this country in 1876, is played by four mounted players on each team. The object is to drive a wooden ball between goalposts at either end of a playing field 300 yards long and 120 to 150 yards wide. Long-handled regulation mallets are used to drive the ball.

At the time the game was first introduced into the U.S., there was a decided preference for ponies less than 13-2 hands in height. Later, ponies up to 14-2 hands high were accepted, and more recently, horses up to 15-2 and over have been used.

Although very similar to the hunter in type, polo mounts are generally smaller in size. They must be quick and clever in turning, and they must be able to dodge, swerve, or wheel while on a dead run. They must like the game of polo and be able to follow the ball.

The polo mount is trained to respond to the pressure of the reins on the neck, so that the rider is free to guide the horse with only one hand. Up to five or six years is required to complete the schooling of a polo horse, and as many as four to six mounts may be used by each player in a single game — all of which contributes to the expensiveness of the sport.

Polo ponies are usually of mixed breeding, but most of them are predominantly Thoroughbred. Type and training, together with native ability and intelligence, are the primary requisites.

- **Parade horses** — *Parade horses are horses of any breed, cross, or color used under elaborate Western, Mexican, or Spanish equipment in parades.* Attractive colors and good manners are important. Parade horses are shown at an animated walk and a parade gait. The latter is a prancing, cadenced trot at about five miles per hour.

BREED REGISTRY ASSOCIATIONS

A breed registry association consists of a group of breeders banded together for the purposes of (1) recording the lineage of their animals, (2) protecting the purity of the breed, (3) encouraging further improvement of the breed, and (4) promoting interest in the breed. A list of the breed registry associations is given in Table 2.3.

Table 2.3 HORSE BREED REGISTRY ASSOCIATIONS

Class of Animal	Breed	Association and Address
Light Horses:	Akhal-Teke	The Akhal-Teke Association of America, Inc. Shenandoah Farm Route 5, Box 110 Staunton, VA 24401
	American Bashkir Curly	American Bashkir Curly Registry P.O. Box 453 Ely, NV 89301

Table 2.3 HORSE BREED REGISTRY ASSOCIATIONS (*cont.*)

Class of Animal	Breed	Association and Address
	American Creme	International American Albino Association Box 194 Naper, NE 68755
	American Mustang	American Mustang Association, Inc. P.O. Box 338 Yucaipa, CA 92399
	American Saddlebred	American Saddlebred Horse Association, Inc. 4093 Iron Works Pike Lexington, KY 40511
	American White	International American Albino Association Box 194 Naper, NE 68755
	Andalusian	American Andalusian Horse Association P.O. Box 68 Tamacacori, AZ 85640
		International Andalusian Horse Association 256 S. Robertson, No. 9378 Beverly Hills, CA 90211
	Appaloosa	Appaloosa Horse Club, Inc. P.O. Box 8403 Moscow, ID 83843
	Arabian	Arabian Horse Registry of America, Inc. 12000 Zuni Street Westminster, CO 80234
		International Arabian Horse Registry of North America P.O. Box 325 Delphi Falls, NY 13051
	Buckskin	International Buckskin Horse Association, Inc. P.O. Box 357 St. John, IN 46373
	Chickasaw	Chickasaw Horse Association, Inc., The P.O. Box 8 Love Valley, NC 28677

Class of Animal	Breed	Association and Address
		National Chickasaw Horse Association Route 2 Clarinda, IA 51232
	Galiceno	Galiceno Horse Breeders Association, Inc. 111 E. Elm Street Tyler, TX 75701
	Hackney	American Hackney Horse Society P.O. Box 174 Pittsfield, IL 62363
	Haflinger	Haflinger Association of America 14570 Gratiot Road Hemlock, MI 48626
		Haflinger Registry of North America 14640 State Route 83 Coshocton, OH 32812
	Half-Saddlebred	Half-Saddlebred Registry of America, The 319 S. 6th Street Coshocton, OH 43812
	Hanoverian	American Hanoverian Society, The Office 2-E, 831 Bay Ave. Capitola, CA 95010
	Hungarian Horse	Hungarian Horse Association P.O. Box 98 Anselmo, NE 68813
	Lipizzan	United States Lipizzan Registry 12479 Duncan Plains Road, N.W. Johnstown, OH 43031
	Missouri Fox Trotting Horse	Missouri Fox Trotting Horse Breed Association, Inc. P.O. Box 1027 Ava, MO 65608
	Morab	North American Morab Horse Association, Inc. W3174 Faro Springs Road Hilbert, WI 54129

Table 2.3 HORSE BREED REGISTRY ASSOCIATIONS (*cont.*)

Class of Animal	Breed	Association and Address
	Morgan	American Morgan Horse Association, Inc., The P.O. Box 960 3 Bostwick Road Shelburne, VT 05482
	National Show Horse	National Show Horse Registry Plainview Triad North, Suite 237 10401 Linn Station Road Louisville, KY 40223
	Norwegian Fjord Horse	Norwegian Fjord Association of North America 24570 W. Chardon Road Grayslake, IL 60030
	Paint Horse	American Paint Horse Association P.O. Box 18519 Ft. Worth, TX 76118
	Palomino	Palomino Horse Association, Inc., The P.O. Box 324 Jefferson City, MO 65101
		Palomino Horse Breeders of America, Inc. 15253 E. Skelly Dr. Tulsa, OK 74116-2620
	Paso Fino	Paso Fino Horse Association, Inc. P.O. Box 600 Bowling Green, FL 33834
	Peruvian Paso	American Association of Owners & Breeders of Peruvian Paso Horses 221 N. Alameda Ave. Burbank, CA 91502
		Peruvian Paso Horse Registry of North America 1038 4th Street, Suite 4 Santa Rosa, CA 95404
	Quarter Horse	American Quarter Horse Association P.O. Box 200 Amarillo, TX 79168

Class of Animal	Breed	Association and Address
	Spanish-Barb	Spanish-Barb Breeders Association 2888 Bluff St., Box 465 Boulder, CO 80301
	Spanish Mustang	Spanish Mustang Registry, Inc., The 8328 Stevenson Ave. Sacramento, CA 95828
	Spotted Saddle Horse	National Spotted Saddle Horse Association, Inc. P.O. Box 898 Murfreesboro, TN 37130
	Standardbred	United States Trotting Association 750 Michigan Avenue Columbus, OH 43215
	Standardbred (Ridden)[1]	Ridden Standardbred Association[1] 1578 Fleet Road Troy, OH 49373
	Tennessee Walking Horse	Tennessee Walking Horse Breeders' and Exhibitors' Association P.O. Box 286 Lewisburg, TN 37091
	Thorcheron	Thorcheron Hunter Association 3749 S. 4th St. Kalamazoo, MI 49009
	Thoroughbred	Jockey Club, The 380 Madison Avenue New York, NY 10017
	Trakehner	American Trakehner Association, Inc. 1520 West Church St. Newark, OH 43055
	Trottingbred	International Trotting & Pacing Association, Inc. 575 Broadway Hanover, PA 17331

[1] The Ridden Standardbred Association accepts for registry purebred, half-bred, and partial-bred standardbreds.

Table 2.3 HORSE BREED REGISTRY ASSOCIATIONS (*cont.*)

Class of Animal	Breed	Association and Address
	Welsh Cob	Welsh Cob Society of America Grazing Field Farm Head of the Bay Road Buzzards Bay, MA 02532
Ponies:	American Gotland Horse	American Gotland Horse Association R.R. 2, Box 181 Elkland, MO 65644
	American Walking Pony	American Walking Pony Association Rt. 27, Box 605 Upper River Road Macon, GA 31211
	Connemara Pony	American Connemara Pony Society R.D. 1 Hoshiekon Farm Goshen, CT 06756
	National Appaloosa Pony	National Appaloosa Pony, Inc. Box 206 Gaston, IN 47342
	Pony of the Americas	Pony of the Americas Club, Inc. 5240 Elmwood Ave. Indianapolis, IN 46203
	Quarter Pony	National Quarter Pony Association 5131 Country Road, #25, Rt. 1 Marengo, OH 43334
	Shetland Pony	American Shetland Pony Club P.O. Box 3415 Peoria, IL 61614
	Welara Pony	American Welara Pony Society P.O. Box 401 Yucca Valley, CA 92284
	Welsh Pony and Cob	Welsh Pony and Cob Society of America P.O. Box 2977 Winchester, VA 22601
Miniature Horse:	Miniature Horse	American Miniature Horse Association, Inc. P.O. Box 129 Burleson, TX 76028

Class of Animal	Breed	Association and Address
		A.S.P.C./A.M.H.R. P.O. Box 3415 Peoria, IL 61614
Draft Horses:	American Cream	American Cream Horse Association Route 1, Box 88 Hubbard, IA 50122
	Belgian	Belgian Draft Horse Corporation of America P.O. Box 335 Wabash, IN 46992
	Clydesdale	Clydesdale Breeders Association of the United States Route 3 Waverly, IA 50677
	Percheron	Percheron Horse Association of America P.O. Box 141 Fredericktown, OH 43819
	Shire	American Shire Horse Association Route 1, Box 10 Adel, IA 50003-9702
	Suffolk	American Suffolk Horse Association, Inc. Route 1, Box 212 Ledbetter, TX 78946
Jacks, Donkeys, and Mules:	Jack and Jennet	Standard Jack and Jennet Registry of America P.O. Box 1155 Pulaski, TN 38478-1155
	Miniature Donkey	Miniature Donkey Registry of the United States, Inc. 2901 N. Elm Denton, TX 76201
	Donkey and Mule	American Donkey and Mule Society, Inc. 2901 N. Elm Denton, TX 76201
	Mules	American Mule Registry 2901 N. Elm Denton, TX 76201

Table 2.3 HORSE BREED REGISTRY ASSOCIATIONS (*cont.*)

Class of Animal	Breed	Association and Address
All Horses and Half-Breeds	Any and all colors and types of horses (including animals not eligible for registry, eligible but not registered, or registered in existing associations) including both light and draft horses.	International American Albino Association Box 194 Naper, NE 68755
	American Warmblood	American Warmblood Society Route 5, Box 1219A Phoenix, AZ 85043

The American Warmblood can be any breed or combina-tion of breeds, except that they cannot be 100 percent hot-blooded (i.e. Arabian or Thoroughbred) or 100 percent cold-blooded (most draft breeds). Pedigree history is de-sirable, but not required for registration; the only requisite is that the horse must be a warmblood.

The American Warmblood Society, which was formed in the early 1980s, is strictly a performance registry for the following events: dressage, show jumping, combined training, and combined driving. The goal is to breed and train horses to compete internationally in the equestrian events sponsored by the United States Equestrian Team, Inc.

	Half-bred Thoroughbreds	American Remount Association, Inc. (Half-Thoroughbred Registry)[2] P.O. Box 1066 Perris, CA 92370

These animals must have one Thoroughbred parent. Hunters, jumpers, and polo ponies may be performance certified.

	Half-bred Arabian	International Arabian Horse Association P.O. Box 33696 Denver, CO 80233

1. Anglo-Arabs must carry not more than ¾ and not less than ¼ Arabian blood. May be either:

[2] Formerly the Half-bred Stud Book operated by the American Remount Association, but now a privately owned registry. It records only foals sired by registered Thoroughbred stallions and out of mares not registered in the American (Jockey Club) Stud Book, or in the Arabian Stud Book.

Class of Animal	Breed	Association and Address

(a) by Thoroughbred stallions and out of registered mares;

(b) by registered Arabian stallions and out of registered Thoroughbred mares;

(c) by registered Thoroughbred or Arabian stallions and out of registered Anglo-Arab mares; or

(d) by Anglo-Arab stallions and out of either Anglo-Arab mares, registered Thoroughbred mares, or registered Arabian mares.

2. Half-Arabians are by registered Arabian stallions and out of mares that are not registered Thoroughbreds or Arabians.

Half-bred, grade, and crossbred horses, involving American Saddlebred, Appaloosa, Hackney, Morgan, Quarter Horse, Standardbred, Tennessee Walking Horse, Welsh Pony, and certain other breeds. Grade horses must not be registered in another breed association.		American Part-blooded Horse Registry 4120 S.E. River Drive Portland, OR 97222 National Grade Horse Registry P.O. Box 338 10221 Slater Ave., #103 Fountain Valley, CA 92708

SELECTING AND JUDGING HORSES

Figure 3.1 The right mounts for the right riders and uses.
Upper photo: American Walking Pony used for English pleasure
riding. (Courtesy, The American Walking Pony Association,
Macon, Georgia) *Lower photo:* Morab horse used for Western
pleasure riding. (Courtesy, Martha Doyle Fuller, Clovis,
California)

Relatively few horses are inspected and evaluated by experienced judges. Most of them are bought by persons who lack experience in judging but who have a practical need for the animal and take pride in selecting and owning a good horse. Before buying a horse, an amateur should enlist the help of a competent horseman.

HOW TO SELECT A HORSE

When selecting a horse, the buyer must first decide what kind of horse he needs. This means that he must consider the following points:

1. The mount should be purchased within a price range that the buyer can afford.
2. The amateur or child should have a quiet, gentle, well-broken horse that is neither headstrong nor unmanageable. The horse should never be too spirited for the rider's skill.
3. The size of the horse should be in keeping with the size and weight of the rider. A small child should have a small horse or pony, but a heavy man should have a horse of the weight-carrying type. Also, a tall man or woman looks out of place if not mounted on a horse of considerable height.
4. Usually the novice will do best to start with a three-gaited horse and first master the three natural gaits before attempting to ride a horse executing the more complicated gaits.
5. Other conditions being equal, the breed and color of horse may be decided on the basis of preference.
6. The mount should be suited to the type of work to be performed. After deciding on the kind of horse needed and getting an ideal in mind, the buyer is ready to select the individual horse. Selection on the basis of body conformation and performance is the best single method of obtaining a good horse. Of course, when animals are selected for breeding purposes, two additional criteria should be considered. These are (1) the record of the horse's progeny if the animal is old enough and has reproduced, and (2) the animal's pedigree. Also, show-ring winnings may be helpful.

   Proficiency in judging horses necessitates a knowledge of: (1) the parts of a horse; (2) correct conformation and stance; (3) the proper value assigned to each part (a scorecard may be used for this purpose); (4) how to determine age; (5) how to measure a horse; (6) blemishes and unsoundnesses; (7) vices; (8) the gaits; (9) defects in action; and (10) colors and markings.

PARTS OF A HORSE

In selecting and judging horses, horsemen usually refer to parts rather than the individual as a whole. Nothing so quickly sets a real horseman apart from a novice as a thorough knowledge of the parts and the language commonly used in describing them. Figure 3.2 shows the parts of a horse.

It is noteworthy that the knee joint in the horse is the counterpart of the wrist joint in man; the stifle joint in the horse is the counterpart of the knee joint in man; and the hock joint in the horse is the counterpart of the ankle joint in man.

CONFORMATION

A good horse must conform to a specific type that fits him for the function that he is expected to perform. Secondly, he should be true to the characteristics of the breed he represents.

Anyone selecting a horse should have clearly in mind the ideal for which he is looking, recognizing full well that few animals meet this high standard and that he may have to settle for less. Table 3.1 is a judging guide.

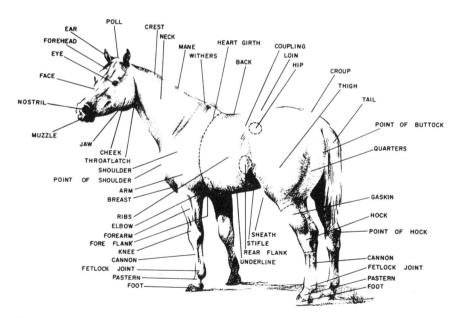

Figure 3.2 Parts of a horse.

Table 3.1 JUDGING GUIDE FOR LIGHT HORSES

Procedure for Examining, and What to Look for	*Ideal Type*	*Common Faults*
Front View:		
1. Head.	1. Head well proportioned to rest of body, refined, cleancut, with chiseled appearance; broad, full forehead with great width between the eyes; jaw broad and strongly muscled; ears medium sized, well carried, and attractive.	1. Plain headed.
2. Sex character.	2. Refinement and feminity in the broodmare; boldness and masculinity in the stallion.	2. Mares lacking feminity; stallions lacking masculinity.
3. Chest capacity.	3. A deep, wide chest.	3. A narrow chest.
4. Set to the front legs.	4. Straight, true, and squarely set.	4. Crooked front legs.
Rear View: 		
1. Width of croup and through rear quarters.	1. Wide and muscular over the croup and through the rear quarters.	1. Lacking width over the croup and muscling through the rear quarters.
2. Set to the hind legs.	2. Straight, true, and squarely set.	2. Crooked hind legs.

Table 3.1 JUDGING GUIDE FOR LIGHT HORSES (*cont.*)

Procedure for Examining, and What to Look for	*Ideal Type*	*Common Faults*

Side View:

1. Style and beauty.	1. High carriage of head, active ears, alert disposition, and beauty of conformation.	1. Lacking style and beauty.
2. Balance and symmetry.	2. All parts well developed and nicely blended together.	2. Lacking in balance and symmetry.
3. Neck.	3. Fairly long neck, carried high; clean-cut about the throatlatch, with head well set on.	3. A short, thick neck; ewe-necked.
4. Shoulders.	4. Sloping shoulders (about a 45-degree angle).	4. Straight in the shoulders.
5. Topline.	5. A short, strong back and loin, with a long, nicely turned, and heavily muscled croup, and a high, well-set tail; withers clearly defined and of the same height as the high point of the croup.	5. Sway-backed; steep croup.
6. Coupling.	6. A short coupling as denoted by the last rib being close to the hip.	6. Long in the coupling.
7. Middle.	7. Ample middle due to long, well-sprung ribs.	7. Lacking middle.
8. Rear flank.	8. Well let down in the rear flank.	8. High cut rear flank or "wasp-waisted."

Procedure for Examining, and What to Look for	Ideal Type	Common Faults
9. Arm, forearm, and gaskin.	9. Well-muscled arm, forearm, and gaskin.	9. Light-muscled arm, forearm, and gaskin.
10. Legs, feet, and pasterns.	10. Straight, true, and squarely set legs; pasterns sloping at about 45 degrees; hoofs large, dense, and wide at the heels.	10. Crooked legs; straight pasterns, hoofs small, contracted at the heels, and shelly.
11. Quality.	11. Plenty of quality, as denoted by clean, flat bone, well-defined joints and tendons, refined head and ears, and fine skin and hair.	11. Lacking quality.
12. Breed type (size, color, shape of body and head, and action true to the breed represented).	12. Showing plenty of breed type.	12. Lacking breed type.

Soundness:

1. Soundness, and freedom from defects in conformation that may predispose unsoundness.	1. Sound, and free from blemishes.	1. Unsound; blemished (wire cuts, capped hocks, etc.).

Action:[1]

1. At the walk. 	1. Easy, prompt, balanced; a long step, with each foot carried forward in a straight line; feet lifted clear of the ground.	1. A short step, with feet not lifted clear of the ground.
2. At the trot. 	2. Rapid, straight, elastic trot, with the joints well flexed.	2. Winging, forging, and interfering.

Table 3.1 JUDGING GUIDE FOR LIGHT HORSES (*cont.*)

Procedure for Examining, and What to Look for	Ideal Type	Common Faults
3. At the canter. 	3. Slow, collected canter, which is readily executed on either lead.	3. Fast and extended canter.

[1] The three most common gaits are given here. Five-gaited horses must perform two additional gaits. In selecting for gait, (1) observe horse at each intended gait, and (2) examine trained horses while performing at use for which they are intended.

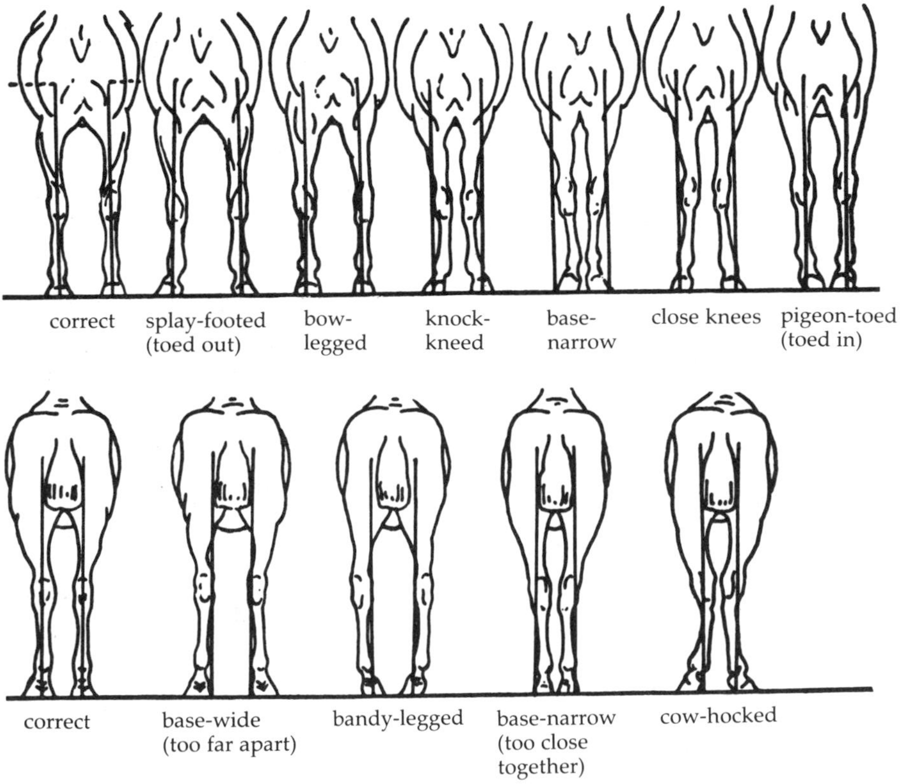

| correct | splay-footed (toed out) | bow-legged | knock-kneed | base-narrow | close knees | pigeon-toed (toed in) |

| correct | base-wide (too far apart) | bandy-legged | base-narrow (too close together) | cow-hocked |

Figure 3.3 Proper and faulty conformation of the forelegs (top row) and hind legs (bottom row). The direction of the leg and the form of the foot are very important in the horse. Horses that do not stand or travel straight may be predisposed to injuries from interfering or brushing, uneven hoof wear, and lameness. (Courtesy, U.S. Department of Agriculture)

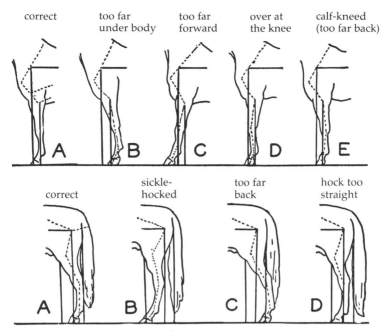

Figure 3.4 Proper and faulty conformation of the forelegs (top row) and hind legs (bottom row) when viewed from the side. Poor conformation can put extra strain on the joints, predisposing the horse to lameness problems. (Courtesy, U.S. Department of Agriculture)

STANCE

Proper stance, or underpinning, is requisite to correct movement. The legs should be straight, true, and squarely set, and the bone should be clearly defined. The pasterns should be sloping; and the feet should be large and wide at the heels. The hock should be large, clean, wide from front to back, deep, clean-cut, and correctly set. The knee should be deep from front to rear, wide when viewed from the front, straight, and tapered gradually into the leg. Since the hock and knee joints of the horse are subject to great wear and are the seat of many unsoundnesses, they should receive special attention.

HORSE SCORECARD

A horse must conform to the specific type that is needed for the function he is to perform. Secondly, he should conform to the characteristics of the breed that he represents. The use of a scorecard is a good way to make sure that no part is overlooked and a proper value is assigned to each part.

ALL-BREED HORSE SCORECARD	Points or percent:	Name or number of horse:	Name or number of horse:	Name or number of horse:	Name or number of horse:
Characteristics					
Breed type .... Animals should possess the distinctive characteristics of breed represented, including Color: Height at maturity: Weight at maturity:	15				
Form .... Style and beauty: attractive, good carriage, alert, refined. Balance and symmetry: all parts well developed and nicely blended together. Body: nicely turned; long, well-sprung ribs; heavily muscled. Back and loin: short and strong, wide, well muscled, and short coupled. Croup: long, level, wide, muscular, with a high-set tail. Rear quarters: deep and muscular. Gaskin: heavily muscled. Withers: prominent, and of the same height as the high point of the croup. Shoulders: deep, well laid in, and sloping about a 45-degree angle. Chest: fairly wide, deep, and full. Arm and forearm: well muscled.	35				
Feet and legs .... Legs: correct position and set when viewed from front, side, and rear. Pasterns: long, and sloping at about a 45-degree angle. Feet: in proportion to size of horse, good shape, wide and deep at heels, dense texture of hoof. Hocks: deep, clean-cut, and well supported. Knees: broad, tapered gradually into cannon. Cannons: clean, flat, with tendons well defined.	15				
Head and neck .... Alertly carried, showing style and character. Head: well proportioned to rest of body, refined, clean-cut, with chiseled appearance; broad, full forehead with great width between the eyes; ears medium sized, well carried, and attractive; eyes large and prominent. Neck: long, nicely arched, clean-cut about the throatlatch, with head well set on, gracefully carried.	10				
Quality .... Clean, flat bone; well-defined and clean joints and tendons; and fine skin and hair.	10				
Action.. Walk: easy, springy, prompt, balanced, a long step, with each foot carried forward in a straight line; feet lifted clear of the ground. Trot: prompt, straight, elastic, balanced, with hocks carried closely, and high flexion of knees and hocks. Discrimination: Any abnormality that affects the serviceability of the horse. Disqualification: In keeping with breed registry or show regulations.	15				
Total points or percent	100				

A scorecard is a listing of the different parts of an animal, with a numerical value assigned to each part according to its relative importance. Also, breed characteristics may be considered in a scorecard. An all-breed horse scorecard is presented on p. 84.

HOW TO DETERMINE AGE

The lifespan of horses averages about 25 years, slightly less than one-third that of man. Horses generally are at their best between 3 and 12 years of age. This may vary because of individual differences in animals or because of differences in the kind of work they do. The age of horses is, therefore, important to breeder, seller, and buyer.

The approximate age of a horse can be determined by noting time of appearance, shape, and degree of wear of temporary and permanent teeth. Temporary, or milk, teeth are easily distinguishable from permanent ones because they are smaller and whiter.

The best way to learn to determine age in horses is by examining the teeth of individual horses of known ages.

A mature male horse has 40 teeth and a mature female has 36, as shown in Table 3.2.[1] A foal of either sex has 24. The mare does not have tushes as a rule.

Even experienced horsemen cannot determine the age of an animal accurately after it is 12 years old. After this age, the teeth change from oval to triangular and they project or slant forward more and more as the horse becomes older.

Side views of the mouths of 5-, 7-, and 20-year-old horses are shown in Figure 3.7.

An animal's environment can affect wear on the teeth. Teeth of horses raised in dry sandy areas, for example, will show more than

Figure 3.5 How to look a horse in the mouth. If you hold the tongue in one hand and grasp the lower jaw with the other hand, you can look at the teeth for as long as you like.

---

[1] Quite commonly, a small, pointed tooth, known as a "wolf tooth," may appear in front of each molar in the upper jaw, thus increasing the total number of teeth to 42 in the male and 38 in the female. Less frequently, 2 more wolf teeth in the lower jaw increase the total number of teeth in the male and female to 44 and 40, respectively.

Figure 3.6

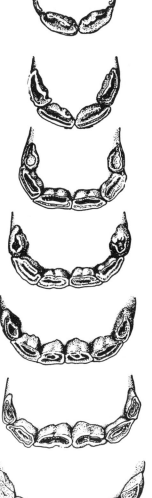

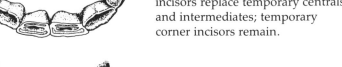

Temporary incisors to 10 days of age: first or central upper and lower temporary incisors appear.

Temporary incisors at 4 to 6 weeks of age: second or intermediate upper and lower temporary incisors appear.

Temporary incisors at 6 to 10 months: third or corner upper and lower temporary incisors appear.

Temporary incisors at 1 year: crowns of central temporary incisors show wear.

Temporary incisors at 1½ years: intermediate temporary incisors show wear.

Temporary incisors at 2 years: all show wear.

Incisors at 4 years: permanent incisors replace temporary centrals and intermediates; temporary corner incisors remain.

Incisors at 5 years: all permanent; cups in all incisors.

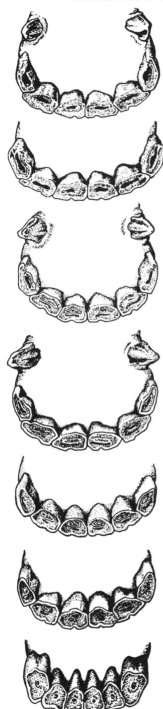

Incisors at 6 years: cups worn out of lower central incisors.

Incisors at 7 years: cups worn out of lower intermediate incisors.

Incisors at 8 years: cups worn out of all lower incisors, and dental star (dark line in front of cup) appears on lower central and intermediate pairs.

Incisors at 9 years: cups worn out of upper central incisors; dental star on upper central and intermediate pairs.

Incisors at 10 years: cups worn out of upper intermediate incisors, and dental star is present in all incisors.

Incisors at 11 or 12 years: cups worn in all incisors (smooth mouthed), and dental star approaches center of cups.

Characteristic shape of lower incisors at 18 years.

Table 3.2 Types and Number of Teeth in Horses

Types of Teeth	Number of Teeth		
	Mature Male	Mature Female	Young Animal, Either Sex
Molars or grinders.	24	24	12
Incisors or front teeth. The two central incisors are known as centrals or nippers; the next two, one on each side of the nippers, are called intermediates or middles; and the last, or outer pair, are the corners.	12	12	12
Tushes or pointed teeth. These are located between the incisors and molars in males. Females do not have tushes as a rule.	4	0	0
Total teeth.	40	36	24

normal wear; a 5-year-old western horse may have teeth that would be normal in a 6- to 8-year-old horse raised elsewhere. The teeth of cribbers also show more than normal wear. The age of such animals is hard to determine, and the age of horses with a parrot mouth also is difficult to estimate.

JANUARY 1 BIRTH DATE

Regardless of when a foal is born, its birth date is always considered as January 1. Thus, a foal born on May 1, 1990, will be ten years old on January 1, 2000. This is done from the standpoint of racing and show-ing. As a result, horsemen who race or show make every effort to have foals arrive as near January 1 as possible, thereby getting the advantage of more growth than animals born later in the year. This is especially important in the younger age groups; for example, when racing or showing a two-year-old.

A shift of the date of birth (the January 1 birthday, for purposes of racing and showing) to somewhere between March 1 and May 1 would improve conception rate and foaling percentage, simply because mares would be bred under more natural and ideal spring conditions. Thus, it would have considerable virtue from the standpoint of the horse pro-ducer. On the other side of the ledger, however, it would create prob-lems in racing and in registrations, both here and abroad. Also, such a deep-rooted tradition would be difficult to change; in fact, much consid-

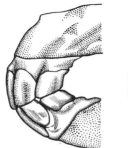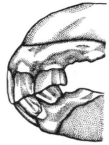

Figure 3.7 Side view of five-, seven-, and twenty-year-old mouth. Note that as the horse advances in age, the teeth change from nearly perpendicular to slanting sharply toward the front.

eration has been given to this matter. In the final analysis, therefore, stepping up breeding research is the primary avenue through which the deplorably low percentage foal crop may be improved.

OLDEST HORSE

Authentic records of very old horses are difficult to obtain. Old Bill, a horse owned throughout his lifetime by a Mr. Petrie of Edinburgh, Scotland, is reputed to have lived to age 62, according to B. S. Dystra, hippologist, of Holland.[2]

An ex-Italian army horse, Topolino, was foaled on February 24, 1909, and died in February 1960 at the age of 51.

Old Nellie, a black mare of draft breeding, raised by a Missouri farmer, was 53 years and 8 months old when she died in 1969.

Since the average life span of a horse is slightly less than one-third the life expectancy of a person in the United States, in terms of human life a 50-year-old horse would be equivalent to a man more than 150 years old.

HOW TO MEASURE A HORSE

The measurements considered important to a horse are his height, weight, girth, and bone.

1. *Height* of a horse refers to the distance from the highest point of the withers to the ground. It is expressed in hands, each hand being 4 inches (derived from the average width of the human hand). The experienced horseman estimates the height of a horse in relation to his own stature, by standing opposite the front limbs and sighting across to the top of the withers. Height may also be determined by actual measurements.

[2] *American Shetland Pony Journal,* November 1969, p. 25.

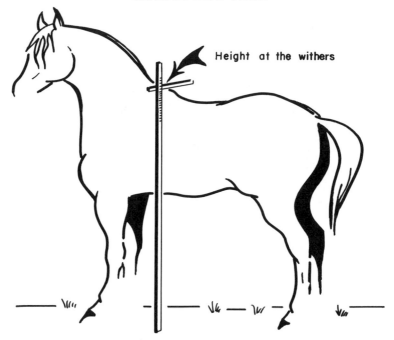

Height at the withers

Figure 3.8   The height of a horse is measured from the highest
point of the withers to the ground. The experienced horseman
deftly estimates the height of a horse in relation to his own
stature, and does not use any measuring device.

2. *Weight* is best determined by using a scale.
3. *Girth* refers to the circumference of the chest, in inches, as measured
   with a tape from behind the withers and in front of the back.
4. *Bone* is the circumference, in inches as recorded on a tape measure,
   around the cannon bone halfway between the knee and fetlock
   joints.

BLEMISHES AND UNSOUNDNESSES

An integral part of selecting a horse lies in the ability to recognize
common blemishes and unsoundnesses and the ability to rate the importance of each. A thorough knowledge of normal, sound structure
makes it easy to recognize imperfections.

Any deviation from normal in the structure or function of a horse
constitutes an unsoundness. From a practical standpoint, however, a
differentiation is made between abnormalities that do, and those that
do not, affect serviceability.

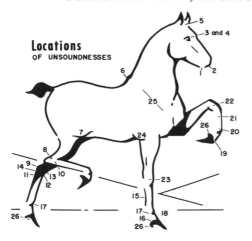

Locations
OF UNSOUNDNESSES

9. Capped hock
10. Stringhalt
11. Curb
12. Bone spavin or jack
13. Bog spavin
14. Blood spavin
15. Bowed tendon
16. Sidebone
17. Cocked ankle
18. Quittor
19. Ringbone
20. Windpuffs
21. Splint
22. Knee-sprung
23. Calf-kneed
24. Capped elbow
25. Sweeney
26. Contracted feet (heels), corns, founder, thrush, quarter or sand crack, scratches or grease heel.

General: heaves, hernia, roaring, thick wind.

1. Undershot jaw
2. Parrot mouth
3. Blindness
4. Moon blindness
5. Poll evil
6. Fistulous withers
7. Stifled
8. Thoroughpin

Figure 3.9 Location of points of common unsoundnesses.

Blemishes include abnormalities that do not affect serviceability, such as wire cuts, rope burns, nail scratches, or capped hocks.

Unsoundnesses include more serious abnormalities that affect serviceability. Unsoundnesses may be caused by any one or various combinations of the following: (1) an inherent or predisposing weakness; (2) subjecting the horse to strain and stress far beyond the capability of even the best structure and tissue; (3) accident or injury; and (4) nutritional deficiencies, particularly minerals. Unsoundnesses that can be definitely traced to the latter three causes should not be considered as hereditary. Unless one is very positive, however, serious unsoundnesses should always be regarded with suspicion in the breeding animal. Probably no unsoundness is actually inherited, but the fact that individuals may inherit a predisposition to an unsoundness through faulty conformation cannot be questioned.

A buyer should consider the use to which he intends to put the animal before he buys a blemished or unsound horse.

The locations of common blemishes and unsoundnesses are shown in Figure 3.9.

Definitions and descriptions of some common blemishes and unsoundnesses follow.

1. *Undershot jaw* — Lower jaw is longer than the upper jaw, causing malocclusion of the teeth.

2. *Parrot mouth* (overshot jaw) — Lower jaw is shorter than upper jaw.

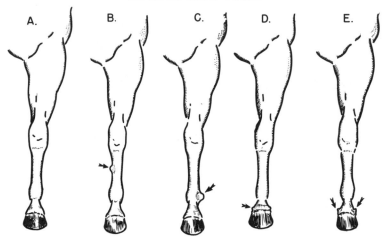

Figure 3.10 Front legs of the horse as viewed from the front:
(A) sound leg, (B) splint, (C) wind puffs, (D) ringbone, and
(E) sidebone.

3. *Blindness* — Partial or complete loss of vision. Blindness may be revealed by very erect ears, a hesitant gait, and discoloration of the eye; sometimes it can be detected by moving the hand gently as it is held close to the eye.

4. *Moon blindness* — A cloudy or inflamed condition of the eye that recurs at periodic intervals (periodic opthalmia).

5. *Poll evil* — An inflamed or infected condition in the region of the poll, usually caused by bruising.

6. *Fistulous withers* — An inflamed or infected condition in the region of the withers caused by a bruise or ill-fitting harness.

7. *Stifled* — The patella (cap) of the stifle joint has been displaced.

8. *Thoroughpin* — A puffy condition in the web (tissue) of the hock.

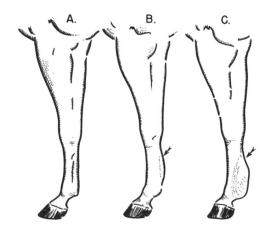

Figure 3.11 Front legs of the horse, as viewed from the side: (A) sound leg, (B) bowed tendon, and (C) filled tendon.

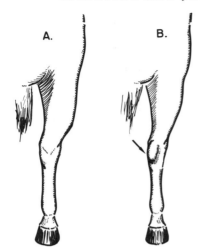

Figure 3.12 Hind legs of the horse, in three-quarter view: (A) sound leg, and (B) bog spavin.

9. *Capped hock* — An enlargement at the point of the hock.

10. *Stringhalt* — An excessive flexing upward of the hind legs when moving forward or backward.

11. *Curb* — Swelling at the rear of the leg and just below the point of the hock.

12. *Bone or jack spavin* — A bony enlargement on the inside of the hock at a point where the hock tapers into the cannon bone.

13. *Bog spavin* — A filling of the natural depression on the inside and front of the hock.

14. *Blood spavin* — A varicose vein that appears on the inside of the hock just above the location of a bog spavin.

15. *Bowed tendons* — Swollen tendons behind the cannon bones; may occur in both the front and hind legs. Descriptive terms of "high" or "low" bow are used by horsemen to denote the location of the

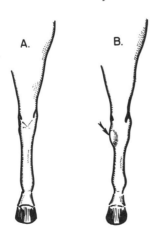

Figure 3.13 Hind legs of the horse as viewed from the front: (A) sound leg, and (B) bone spavin.

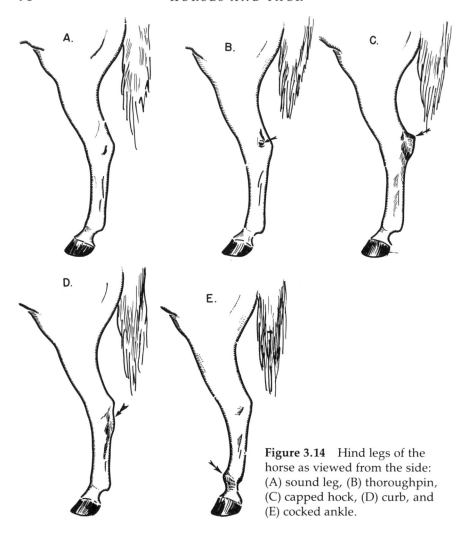

Figure 3.14 Hind legs of the horse as viewed from the side: (A) sound leg, (B) thoroughpin, (C) capped hock, (D) curb, and (E) cocked ankle.

injury; the high bow appears just under the knee and the low bow just above the fetlock.

16. *Sidebones* — Hardened lateral cartilage immediately above and toward the rear quarter of the coronet.

17. *Cocked ankles* — Fetlocks bent forward in a cocked position, usually the hind ones.

18. *Quittor* — A deep-seated running sore at the coronet.

19. *Ringbone* — A bony growth on the pastern bone, generally on the front foot.

20. *Windpuff* — An enlargement of the fluid sac, or bursa, just above the pastern on the fore and rear legs.

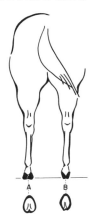

Figure 3.15 (A) sound hoof, (B) contracted heels.

21. *Splints* — Bony growths on the cannon bone, usually on the inside of the front legs.

22. *Knee-sprung* — The knees are bent forward; also called buck-kneed.

23. *Calf-kneed* — Knees tend to bend backward; opposite of buck-kneed. This condition causes more trouble than knee-sprung or buck-kneed.

24. *Capped elbow or shoe boil* — Swelling at the point of the elbow.

25. *Sweeney* — A depression in the shoulder because of an atrophied muscle.

26. *Foot ailments:*

a. *Contracted heel* — A drawing in or contracting of the heel.

b. *Corn* — A bruise in the soft tissue underlying the horny sole of the foot.

c. *Founder* — A serious inflammation of the fleshy laminae under the horny wall of the hoof, characterized by ridges running around the hoof.

d. *Thrush* — A disease of the frog (bottom middle) of the hoof.

e. *Splayfoot* — Front toes turned out, heels turned in.

f. *Pigeon-toed* — Front toes turned in, heels turned out.

Figure 3.16 Most common causes, ranked in order, for retiring horses from the track: (1) bowed tendons, (2) knee injury, (3) osselets, (4) bucked shin, (5) splint, (6) fractured sesamoid, (7) fractured fibula, (8) sand crack, and (9) suspensory ligament damage.

g. *Quarter or sand crack* — A vertical split in the horny wall of the hoof.

h. *Scratches or grease heel* — A scabby inflammation of the posterior surface of the fetlocks.

Some general ailments that affect horses are defined as follows:

1. *Heaves* — Difficulty in forcing air out of the lungs.

2. *Hernia* — The protrusion of an internal organ through the wall that contains it.

3. *Roaring* — Whistling or wheezing when breathing is speeded up.

4. *Thick wind* — Difficulty in breathing.

VICES

Stable vices are bad habits which are observed in confinement. Many of them start with poor handling and lack of exercise; once acquired they are difficult to cope with or to correct. The common ones are:

1. *Bolting* — Eating too fast; usually rectified by placing some base-ball-sized stones in the feed box, or by adding chopped hay to the animal's grain ration.

2. *Cribbing* — Biting or setting the teething against the manger (or other object) and sucking in air; remedied by buckling a strap around the neck and compressing the larynx without discomfort.

3. *Halter pulling* — Pulling on the halter when tied. It is usually a man-made vice, caused by tying the horse too low, too short, or so long that he gets a foot over the tie rope. Also, it may result when a horse has been tied to a pole or tree at the proper height but so loosely that the rope slides down on the pole or tree. At other times, the horse may be tied with a halter or rope that is too light or flimsy, or tied too closely to something terrifying, with the result that he pulls back in fright and breaks the rope.

   The number of times required to make a horse into a confirmed halter puller will vary according to the first traumatic experience and the temperament of the horse. One bad experience may make a confirmed halter puller that is hard to break.

   There are many methods of breaking a halter puller. Either a rope under the tail, or a rope around the belly, so arranged that it will tighten up when the horse flies back and breaks his halter, appears to be very successful; and there is no danger of serious injury from the use of either method.

4. *Kicking* — Striking with the hind feet without provocation. Unusual excitement or injury may cause a gentle horse to kick.

5. *Tail rubbing* — Rubbing the tail against the side of the stall or other

objects; rectified by installing a tail board. A tail board is a board projecting from the wall of the stall high enough to strike just below the point of the buttock, instead of the tail of the rubbing horse.

6. *Weaving* — Rhythmical swaying back and forth while standing in the stall.

7. *Other vices* — Balking, rearing, shying, striking with the front feet, running away, and objecting to harnessing, saddling, and grooming.

GAITS

A gait is a particular way of going, either natural or acquired, that is characterized by a distinctive rhythmic movement of the feet and legs (see Figure 3.17).

In proper show-ring procedure, horses are brought back to the walk each time before they are called upon to execute a different gait. An exception is made in five-gaited classes where the rack may be executed from the slow gait.

The walk is a natural, slow, flatfooted, four-beat gait. A four-beat gait is one in which each foot leaves and strikes the ground at separate intervals. The walk should be springy, regular, and true.

The trot is a natural, rapid, two-beat diagonal gait in which a front foot and the opposite hind foot take off and strike the ground simultaneously. There is a brief moment when all four feet are off the ground and the horse seems to float through the air.

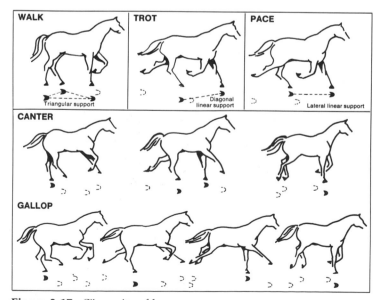

Figure 3.17 The gaits of horses.

This gait varies considerably with different breeds. The trot of the Standardbred is characterized by length and rapidity of individual strides; the trot of the Hackney shows extreme flexion of the knees and hocks that produces a high-stepping show gait.

The canter is a slow, restrained, three-beat gait. Two diagonal legs are paired and produce a single beat that falls between the successive beats of the two unpaired legs. The canter imposes a special wear on the leading forefoot and its diagonal hindfoot. It is important, therefore, to change the lead frequently.

In the show ring, the lead should be toward the inside of the ring; a right foot lead when going clockwise (see Figure 3.18), and a left foot lead when moving counterclockwise. The lead is changed by reversing direction of travel (when the ringmaster calls for "reverse and canter"). The canter should be executed in such a slow collected manner that the animal may perform in a relatively small circle.

The lope is the western adaption of a very slow canter. It is a smooth, slow gait in which the head is carried low.

The run or *gallop* is a fast, four-beat gait in which the feet strike the ground separately — first one hind foot, then the other hind foot, then the front foot on the same side as the first hind foot, and then the other front foot, which decides the lead. There is a brief interval when all four feet are off the ground. The gallop is the fast natural gait of both wild horses and Thoroughbred racehorses.

The pace is a fast, two-beat gait in which the front and hind feet on the same side start and stop simultaneously. The feet rise just above the ground level. There is a split second when all four feet are off the ground and the horse seems to float through the air.

Figure 3.18   The right lead at the lope. At the lope or canter, the lead should be toward the inside of the ring or circle.

The pace is faster than the trot but slower than the run or gallop. It allows for a "quick getaway," but it produces an objectionable side or rolling type of motion. This gait is not suited to travel in mud or snow; a smooth, hard footing and easy draft are necessary for its best execution.

The pace was once popular in England, but it lost favor soon after the development of the Thoroughbred in the 18th century.

The stepping pace (or slow pace) is the preferred slow gait for five-gaited show horses. It is a modified pace in which the objectionable side or rolling motion of the true pace is eliminated because the two feet on each side do not move exactly together. Instead, it is a four-beat gait with each of the four feet striking the ground separately. In the takeoff, the hind and front feet start almost together, but the hind foot touches the ground slightly ahead of the front foot on the same side, and each foot strikes the ground separately.

The fox trot is a slow, short, broken type of trot in which the head usually nods. In executing the fox trot, the horse brings each hind foot to the ground an instant before the diagonal forefoot. This gait is accepted as a slow gait, but it is not as popular as the stepping pace.

The running walk is a slow, four-beat gait, intermediate in speed between the walk and rack. The hind foot oversteps the front foot from a few to as many as 18 inches, giving the motion a smooth gliding effect. It is characterized by a bobbing or nodding of the head, a flopping of the ears, and a snapping of the teeth (none of which should be excessive) in rhythm with the movements of the legs. This is a necessary gait in Tennessee Walking Horses.

The running walk is easy on both horse and rider; it is the all-day working gait of the South, executed at a speed of 6 to 8 miles per hour.

The rack (formerly, but now incorrectly called single-foot) is a fast, flashy, unnatural, four-beat gait in which each foot meets the ground separately at equal intervals; hence, it was originally known as the "single-foot," a designation now largely discarded. The rack is easy on the rider, but hard on the horse. It is the most popular and flashy gait in the American show ring. On the tanbark, greater speed at the rack is requested with the command "rack on."

The traverse or *side step* is simply a lateral movement of the animal to the right or left as desired, without moving forward or backward. This trick will often assist in (1) lining up horses in the show ring, (2) opening and closing gates, and (3) taking position in a mounted drill or a posse.

DEFECTS IN ACTION

The feet of an animal should move straight ahead and parallel to a center line drawn in the direction of travel. Any deviations from this way of going constitute defects. Some defects in action are:

1. *Cross-firing*, which is generally confined to pacers, consisting of a scuffing on the inside of the diagonal fore and hind feet.

2. *Dwelling*, most noticeable in trick-trained horses, consisting of a noticeable pause in the flight of the foot, as though the stride were completed before the foot reaches the ground.

3. *Forging*, the striking of the forefoot by the toe of the hind foot.

4. *Interfering,* the striking of the fetlock or cannon by the opposite foot that is in motion. This condition is predisposed in horses with base-narrow, toe-wide, or splayfooted standing positions.

5. *Lameness*, which can be detected when the affected foot is favored when standing. In action, the load on the ailing foot is eased, and there is characteristic bobbing of the head of the horse as the affected foot strikes the ground.

6. *Paddling*, the throwing of the front feet outward as they are picked up. This condition is predisposed in horses with toe-narrow or pigeon-toed standing positions.

7. *Pointing*, a perceptible extension of the stride with little flexion. This condition is likely to occur in the Thoroughbred and Standardbred breeds — animals bred and trained for great speed with a long stride.

8. *Pounding*, a condition in which there is heavy contact with the ground in contrast to the desired light, springy movement.

9. *Rolling*, excessive lateral shoulder motion, characteristic of horses with protruding shoulders.

10. *Scalping*, that condition in which the hairline at the top of the hind foot hits the toe of the forefoot as it breaks over.

11. *Speedy cutting*, a condition of a horse at speed in which a hind leg above the scalping mark hits against the shoe of a breaking-over forefoot. In trotters, legs on the same side are involved; in pacers, diagonal legs are involved.

12. *Stringhalt*, characterized by excessive flexing of the hind legs. It is most easily detected when backing a horse.

13. *Trappy*, a short, quick, choppy stride. This condition is predisposed in horses with short, straight pasterns and straight shoulders.

14. *Winding* or *rope-walking*, a twisting of the striding leg around in front of the supporting leg so as to make contact in the manner of a "rope-walking" artist. This condition most often occurs in horses with very wide fronts.

15. *Winging*, an exaggerated paddling, particularly noticeable in high-going horses.

COLORS AND MARKINGS

Within certain breeds, some colors are preferred or required, and others are undesirable or constitute disqualifications for registration. A good horseman needs a working knowledge of horse colors and patterns because they are the most conspicuous features by which a horse can be described or identified.

BODY COLORS

The five basic body colors of horses are

1. *Bay* — Bay is a mixture of red and yellow. It includes many shades, from a light yellowish tan (light bay) to a dark, rich shade that is almost brown (dark bay). A bay horse usually has a black mane and tail and black points.

2. *Black* — A black horse is completely black, including the muzzle and flanks. If in doubt whether the horse is dark brown or black, note the color of the fine hairs on the muzzle and the hair on the flanks; tan or brown hairs at these points indicate the horse is not a true black, but a seal brown.

3. *Brown* — A brown horse is almost black but can be distinguished by the fine tan or brown hairs on the muzzle or flanks.

4. *Chestnut (sorrel)* — A chestnut horse is basically red. The shades vary from light washy yellow (light chestnut) to a dark liver color (dark chestnut). Between these come the brilliant red-gold and copper shades. Normally, the mane and tail of a chestnut horse are the same shade as the body, although they may be lighter. When they are lighter, the coloring is called flaxen mane and tail. Chestnut color is never accompanied by a black mane and tail.

5. *White* — A true white horse is born white and remains white throughout life. White horses have snow-white hair, pink skin, and brown eyes (rarely blue).

Besides the five basic colors, horses have five major variations to these coat colors. The variations are:

1. *Dun (buckskin)* — Dun is a yellowish color of variable shading from pale yellow to a dirty canvas color. A dun horse has a stripe down the back.

2. *Gray* — This is a mixture of white and black hairs. Sometimes a gray horse is difficult to distinguish from a black horse at birth, but gray horses get lighter with age.

3. *Palomino* — This is a golden color. Palomino horses have a light-colored mane and tail of white, silver, or ivory.

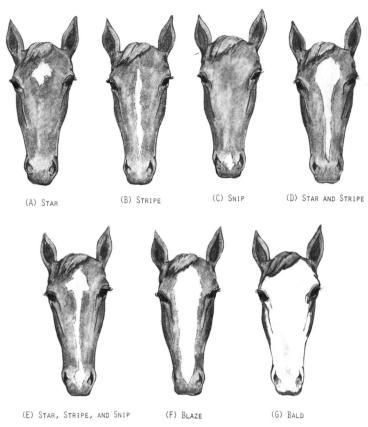

(A) Star   (B) Stripe   (C) Snip   (D) Star and Stripe

(E) Star, Stripe, and Snip   (F) Blaze   (G) Bald

Figure 3.19   The head markings of horses: (A) a **star** is any white mark on the forehead located above a line running from eye to eye: (B) a **stripe** is a narrow white marking that extends from about the line of the eyes to the nostrils; (C) a **snip** is a white mark between the nostrils or on the lips; (D) a **star and stripe** includes both a star and stripe; (E) a **star, stripe, and snip** includes all three of these marks — star, stripe, and snip; (F) a **blaze** is a broad, white marking covering almost all the forehead but not including the eyes or nostrils; (G) **bald** is a bald, or white face including the eyes and nostrils, or a partially white face.

4. *Pinto (calico or paint)* — Pinto is a Spanish word that means painted. The pinto color is characterized by irregular colored and white areas in either piebald or skewbald patterns. Piebald horses are black and white, and skewbald horses are white and any other color except black.

5. *Roan* — Roan is a mixture of white hairs with one or more base colors. White with bay is red roan; white with chestnut is strawberry roan; and white with black is blue roan.

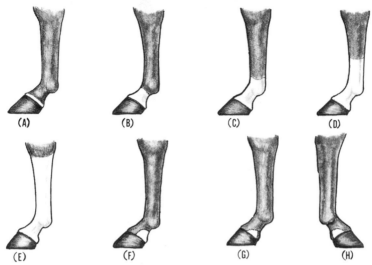

Figure 3.20 Leg markings of horses: (A) **coronet,** a white stripe covering the coronet band; (B) **pastern,** white extending from the coronet to and including the pastern; (C) **ankle,** white extending from the coronet to and including the fetlock; (D) **half stocking,** white extending from the coronet to the middle of the cannon; (e) **stocking,** white extending from the coronet to the knee, and sometimes including the knee, which is a **full stocking;** (F) **white heels,** both heels white; (G) **white outside heel,** outside heel only is white; (H) **white inside heel,** inside heel only is white.

HEAD MARKINGS

When identifying an individual horse, it is generally necessary to include more identification than just body color. For example, it may be necessary to identify the dark sorrel as the one with the blaze face. Some common head markings are shown in Figure 3.19.

LEG MARKINGS

Leg markings are often used, along with head markings, to describe a horse. The most common leg marks are shown in Figure 3.20.

OTHER CONSIDERATIONS WHEN BUYING A HORSE

In addition to the desirable qualities in conformation and action already enumerated, there should be style and beauty, balance and symmetry, an abundance of quality, an energetic yet manageable disposition, freedom from vices, good wind, suitable age, freedom from disease, and proper condition. The buyer should also be on the alert for possible misrepresentations.

F O U R

TRAINING THE HORSE

Figure 4.1 Horses may be trained for many uses. *Upper photo:* Saddlebred fine harness horse. (Courtesy, American Saddle Horse Breeders Association, Louisville, Kentucky). *Lower photo:* Spanish Mustang three-day eventer. Event horses come in all shapes, sizes, and breeds. (Courtesy, Spanish Mustang Registry, Sacramento, California)

There are as many successful ways to train horses as there are to train children. The author has observed several top professional trainers. Each used a different technique, yet all ended up with the same result — a champion. Most of them follow the basic principles given herein.

The good horseman who has followed a program of training and educating the foal from the time it was a few days old has already eliminated the word "breaking." To him, the saddling and/or harnessing of the young horse is merely another step in the training program, which is done with apparent ease and satisfaction.

BEHAVIOR OF HORSES

Each animal species has characteristic ways of performing certain functions and rarely departs therefrom. The horse is no exception. A good understanding of horse behavior enhances horse training. Some noteworthy horse behavior patterns follow.

- *Communication* — The signals consist of patterns of sound, produced by motions of the respiratory and upper alimentary tract. A *snort* is a danger signal to the whole herd; a *neigh* is a distress call; a *nicker* is a sign of relief; and a *whinny* is a call of pleasure and expectancy.

  Without doubt, this trait — being able to communicate — accounts for the foundation stock of the American Indians and the hardy bands of Mustangs — the feral horses of the Great Plains. In some mysterious manner, the abandoned and stray horses of the expeditions of de Soto and Coronado found and communicated with each other; otherwise, they could not have reproduced.

- *Courtship* — The sight of a mare elicits characteristic courtship by the stallion, including smelling the external genitalia and groin of the mare, extending his neck with an upcurled upper lip, and pinching the mare with his teeth by grasping the folds of her skin in the loin-croup area.

  Heat (estrus) in mares is marked by the mare allowing the stallion to smell and bite her, frequent urination in small quantities, mucous discharge from the vulva, spreading the hind legs, and lifting the tail sideways.

- *Dominance* — Any group of horses develops a hierarchical structure, or "peck order," in which each animal assumes a position of relative dominance. This order is maintained by sounds and gestures; challenging is kept to a minimum.

- *Fighting* — Under wild conditions, natural enemies are avoided by flight or fight, according to the situation. The teeth and hind feet are used for fighting.

- *Hearing* — Horses hear over a great range in frequencies, and they can pick up sounds too slight for man to hear.

Figure 4.2   Spanish Mustangs at play. (Photo by Mrs. Buddy Banner, Willow Springs Ranch, Oracle, Arizona)

- *Leadership* — In wild bands, there is always a stallion leader.
- *Lookout* — During the day, it is rare to see all members of a herd lying down together. One horse is almost always on the lookout.
- *Pawing* — The modern domestic horse paws the ground when excited in much the same way as did Przewalski's Horse.
- *Vision* — In its natural habitat, the adult horse keeps a sharp lookout for its natural enemies, even while grazing. Also, it is noteworthy that the eye of the horse is adapted in several ways for darkness, as in nocturnal animals. Also, its eyes are set on the sides of the head so that each eye receives a very wide and largely different scene. The lens of the horse's eye is nonelastic, but the retina is arranged on a slope, the bottom part being nearer the lens than the top part. Thus, in order to focus on objects at different distances, the horse has to raise or lower his head so that the image is brought onto that part of the retina at the correct distance to achieve a sharp image. This arrangement is advantageous to wild horses because while the head is down grazing, both near objects on the ground and distant ones on the horizon are in focus simultaneously.

  Color vision in horses has not been established.

MEMORY OF HORSES

To a very considerable degree the horse's aptitude for training is due to his memory. Many examples substantiating the excellent memory of horses could be cited, but only one will be related. Legend has it that the Arabs selected their mounts for memory and discipline by shutting them in a corral without water until they were extremely thirsty. Then they would turn them out so that they could go drink from a nearby stream. But before they reached the water, they would call them by blowing a bugle. The ones who remembered — who responded to the bugle and returned to the corral, rather than quench their thirst — were retained; the ones who forgot — who ignored the call and went for water — were culled.

CONTROLLING THE HORSE

The horse has whims and ideas of his own. But the horseman should be the boss, with the animal promptly carrying out his wishes. With the experienced horseman, this relationship is clear-cut, for he is able to relay his feelings to the horse instantly and unmistakably. For complete control and a finished performance, the horse should have a proud and exalted opinion of himself; but, at the same time, he should subjugate those undesirable traits that make a beast of his size and strength so difficult to handle by a comparatively frail and small person.

Complete control, therefore, is based on mental faculties rather than muscular force. The faculties of the horse which must be understood and played upon to obtain skillful training and control at all times are

1. *Memory* — The horse remembers or recognizes the indications given him, the manner in which he responded, and the rewards or punishments that followed his actions.

2. *Confidence and fear* — In a well-mannered horse, it is necessary that confidence in the horseman replace the fear which accompanied his existence in the wild state.

3. *Association of ideas* — Horses are creatures of habit, hence the schooling of a horse should be handled by the same competent horseman, who allows the animal an opportunity to associate the various commands with the desired response.

4. *Willingness* — A willing worker or performer is obtained through the judicious employment of rewards and punishments.

5. *Rewards* — The most common rewards are a praising voice, a gentle stroking of the hand, and treats such as sugar and carrots. Sometimes, stopping work at the right moment (when a horse just begins to master something) may be used effectively as a reward.

6. *Punishment* — The two most common types of equine punishment are the spur and the whip.

TRAINING THE FOAL

The foal should be given daily lessons of 15 to 30 minutes each, for 7 to 10 days. If trained early in life, it will be a better disciplined, more serviceable horse. Give it one lesson at a time, and in sequence; that is, be sure the pupil masters each learning experience before it is given the next one.

Put a well-fitted halter on the foal when it is 10 to 14 days old. When it has become accustomed to the halter, in a day or so, tie it securely in the stall beside the mare. Try to keep the foal from freeing itself from the rope or from becoming tangled up in it.

Leave the foal tied 15 to 30 minutes each day for 2 to 3 days. Groom the animal carefully while it is tied. Rub each leg and handle each foot so that the foal becomes accustomed to having its feet picked up. After it has been groomed, lead it around with the mare for a few days and then lead it by itself. Lead it at both the walk and the trot. Many breeders teach a foal to lead simply by leading it with the mare from the stall to the paddock and back again.

At this stage of the training, be sure the foal executes your commands to stop and go as soon as you give them. When halted, make the foal stand in show position—squarely on all four legs with its head up.

Use all your patience, gentleness, and firmness in training the foal. Never let your temper get the best of you.

Figure 4.3   Teaching the foal to lead. After the foal has been gentled to a halter, a non-skid loop, sometimes called a "come-along," is slipped over the hindquarters to teach him to move forward promptly.

Figure 4.4 Front feet of a yearling hobbled with a large, soft cotton rope. This training lesson is designed to teach the young horse to stand still (as if tied) and not get excited if he gets caught in a fence.

TRAINING THE YEARLING

The yearling should be given daily lessons of 30 minutes each, repeated until each learning experience is mastered. The horse learns by repetition. Thus, teach only one thing at a time, and repeat it in the same manner daily until mastered; then proceed to the next learning experience. Teach the yearling the following, in order:

1. *The meaning of "whoa" and his name* — The yearling should be taught "whoa" means stop. Always give the command, then call his name, as "Whoa, Duke."

2. *To stand when hobbled* — Next, the young horse should be hobbled; first the two front feet, then "sideline" (tie a front foot and a hind foot on the same side together). Hobbling is for the purpose of teaching the horse to stand still (as if tied) and not get excited if he gets caught in a fence. Many a valuable horse has mutilated himself for lack of this kind of training.

3. *To become accustomed to the saddle blanket (put the saddle blanket on; repeat for 2 days)* — Gently place the saddle blanket on the young horse's back, and move it from head to tail, until he is not afraid of having an object on his back.

4. *To get used to the saddle (saddle him; repeat for 5 or 6 days)* — Next, put the saddle on and off several times; then tighten the girth moderately and lead him around.

   Thus, the gentling of the yearling is for the purposes of teaching him the meaning of the word "whoa"; to stand patiently when hobbled or caught in a wire fence; and to get used to the saddle blanket and the saddle. After a few days of gentling like this, the yearling may be turned to pasture for a time.

TRAINING AT 18 MONTHS OF AGE

At 18 months of age, the young horse should receive additional training. At this stage, each lesson should be for 30 minutes daily, with each step mastered before moving on to the next. The trainer should always be gentle, but firm, and should not make a pet out of the horse. Let him know who is boss. When he must be punished for wrongdoing, use the whip — one time only; and do so immediately after the horse commits the act. Never discipline a horse by gouging him with spurs. When he does well, reward him by stroking his neck or shoulder and calling his name: "That's a good boy, Duke." At 18 months of age, teach the following:

1. *To drive, turn, stop, and back up; by using plowlines or long lines* — Tie the stirrups together under the horse, then run plowlines through them. Stand behind the horse and use the plowlines to drive, turn, stop, and back up.

2. *To flex his neck and set his head* — This may be accomplished either by (a) tying the reins to the stirrups, or (b) using rubber reins made from strips of old inner tube. Then turn the young horse loose in the corral or training ring for 30 minutes (he can't hurt himself).

   Also, a dumb jockey bitting rig — a contrivance fastened on a young horse — may be used to train him to place his head in the desired position. The rigging consists of surcingle, back strap, crupper, side reins, overcheck or sidecheck, standing martingale, and some sort of projection above the top of the surcingle to which reins may be attached.

   It is noteworthy that fashions in head sets change, and that not all horses should have their heads set. For example, hunters, jumpers, and cutting horses must use their heads for balance. Dressage

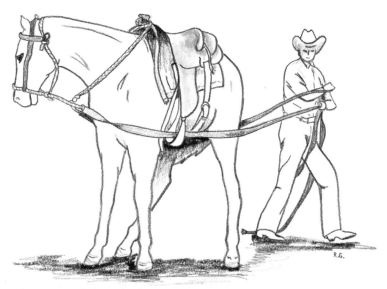

Figure 4.5 When the horse is approximately 18 months of age, use plowlines or long lines to teach him to drive, turn, stop, and back up.

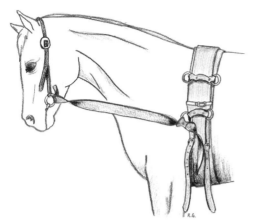

Figure 4.6 At about 18 months of age, teach the young horse to flex his neck and set his head. This illustration shows rubber reins, made from strips of an old inner tube. Leather side reins with a rubber or elastic insert can also be used to train a young horse to carry his entire body in proper balance.

horses learn to work "on the bit" through exercises that develop their balance and strengthen their hindquarters, not by having their heads set.

3. *To respond to the bosal or hackamore, ride him; introduce leg pressure —* During the first few months of riding, use a bosal or hackamore; it will alleviate the hazard of hurting his mouth with bits. If the horse is ready, do some light riding; introduce leg pressure.

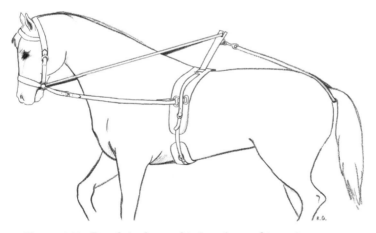

Figure 4.7 Dumb jockey, a bitting rig used to train a young horse to carry his head in the desired position.

TRAINING THE TWO-YEAR-OLD

At this stage, each lesson should be of 30 minutes duration daily, repeated until mastered. The two-year-old is ready for the following more advanced training:

1. *To respond to the aids* — Mount the horse and put him in motion by use of the aids — the legs, hands, and reins, and voice. After riding him for 5 or 6 days at the walk and trot, move him into the lope or canter; always on the proper lead — a right foot lead when going clockwise, a left foot lead when moving counterclockwise.

2. *To back* — From the ground, teach the horse to back. Hold the reins near the bosal or bit; push back (push and release) and command "Back, Duke." If necessary, push on his shoulder and/or switch him on the forelegs. Next, mount the horse and, from his back, teach him to stop and back up. If he won't back when you're mounted, have a friend stand in front of him and switch him back while you pull (pull and release) on the reins and command "Back, Duke." Backing teaches the horse to get his feet under him, which is essential for pivots and sharp turns.

3. *To pivot* (Western horse) — Each time the horse is stopped and backed up, pause for a few seconds, then collect him (with the reins, and apply a little leg pressure) and pivot. Always teach the young horse to turn on his hind feet; pull him back until his hind feet are under him, then pull diagonally on the reins.

4. *To make a sliding stop* (Western horse) — Teach the horse to make a proper sliding stop — to "stick his tail in the ground." When properly done, the rider's reining hand is low, the horse's head is low and his front feet are near the ground. Most judges prefer a stop with three or four feet on the ground, rather than the more spectacular two hind-leg stop. If the stop is on three feet, one forefoot is up slightly, ready to turn or roll back either way. Most expert western horsemen don't like a sliding stop with both front feet up in the air because the horse is not balanced and can fall over backward.

Figure 4.8 A good sliding stop. Note that the reining hand is low, the horse's head is low, and three of the feet are on the ground.

Figure 4.9   A well-trained and well-ridden barrel racing horse. This is the only women's event in rodeo. It is an excellent test of training and speed, for it is a race against time, coupled with ease of maneuverability. Each contestant must ride a cloverleaf pattern around three barrels. (Courtesy, McLaughlin Photography, Morrison, Colorado)

It takes months of training to get a horse to do the sliding stop right. First he should be stopped at the walk, then the trot, next the short lope, and finally when wide open.

In executing the sliding stop, the western rider uses his aids as follows: (a) squeezes with his legs; (b) says "Ho"; (c) sits back deep in the saddle; and (d) pulls up on the reins. The leg pressure is to alert the horse. Throwing the rider's weight back, when properly timed, drives the horse's hind feet up under him. The reins are pulled no harder than necessary, then the pressure is released so that the horse can use his head to maintain his balance.

Proper timing is important. The rider squeezes when the lead foot is off the ground and the hind feet are getting ready to come off. As the horse's hind feet come up, he shifts his weight back and starts making contact with the horse's mouth. He does not jerk, for jerking hurts the horse's mouth and makes his head fly up and his mouth gape open. Another important thing relative to timing is this: If the rider "applies the brakes" when the horse is stretched out and his front feet are in the air, he forces the horse to throw all his weight on his front feet and he'll bounce.

The really good sliding stop is performed with rhythm and balance, and is easy and smooth.

Some good horsemen train horses on the longe line — a light strap of webbing or leather 30 feet long. When the author visited the Spanish Riding School of Vienna, where the famed Lipizzan stallions perform, he learned that all basic training — including gaits, leads, stops, transitions, etc. — is given on the longe. Starting at age four, these horses are worked from the ground for one year before they are ever mounted.

The only exception to use of the longe line in training is a roping horse, because, when on the end of a rope, a roping horse is taught to run straight back from the trainer, rather than around him.

Figure 4.10   Skillful training, bitting, and shoeing made for the high natural action exhibited by this Hackney stallion. (Photo by Carl Klein, New York, New York; courtesy, Mrs. J. Macy Willets, Cassilis Farm, New Marlboro, Massachusetts)

BLOOD TESTING FOR FITNESS

Blood testing (hematology) is a means of evaluating physical fitness. All body cells require oxygen. With strenuous exercise, as in racing, the oxygen requirement increases. Oxygen is transported by hemoglobin, the protein-iron coloring matter in blood. It follows that any reduction in the hemoglobin content, or in total blood volume, will lower the oxygen-carrying capacity of the blood. When this condition is marked, anoxia (or anemia) develops, fatigue sets in, and there is lowered stamina and endurance.

Anoxia may be caused by many conditions. Usually it is due either to (1) nutritional deficiency, or (2) blood worms — both of which may be aggravated by the stress and strain of racing, endurance trials, and showing.

Most trainers accept one or more of the following as indicative of the lack of "fitness": loss of appetite; loss of weight; excessive "blowing" following work; a dry, harsh cough; rough coat; dull eye; watery instead of beady sweating; and "blowing up" over the loins. In an effort to be more exacting, some veterinarians who attend racing stables, endurance trials, and show strings now use blood examinations as a means of evaluating physical fitness.

It appears that, although there are breed differences, most horses which show consistent, good racing form have hemoglobin levels between 14 and 16 grams per milliliter, red cell counts between 9 and 11 million per cubic millimeter, and packed cell volumes between 40 percent and 45 percent. Also, other blood determinations are sometimes made. The blood testing approach is interesting and appealing. However, much more information on the subject is needed. Proof of this assertion becomes evident when it is realized that all horses whose blood pictures fall within the above range are not necessarily good performers; neither are horses with blood pictures outside this range incapable of winning. Some horses do respond to treatment, but, generally, the results have been inconsistent and disappointing. One needs to know if horses which have lower blood values, but which do not respond to treatment, carry all of the red cells and hemoglobin that they are capable of developing — and whether they have less potential for racing. Even more perplexing is the fact that this blood count can be too high, producing polycythemia. A horse with polycythemia frequently loses appetite, fails to thrive in the stable, performs unsatisfactorily, and may show cyanosis (dark bluish or purple coloration of the skin and mucous membrane due to lack of oxygen). It is also noteworthy that absolute polycythemia occurs at high altitudes or when there is heart disease or fibrosis of the lungs.

Racehorses with anemia are sometimes treated by either (1) injecting iron and/or vitamin B-12, or (2) giving orally (in the feed or water) one of several iron preparations. Sometimes vitamin C (ascorbic acid), folic acid, and the other B-complex vitamins are added.

At this time, there is insufficient knowledge of equine anemia, or of ways of stimulating the making of blood (hematopoiesis), to make a winner. The true role of therapy, if any, remains unknown.

The most that can be said at this time is that prevailing treatments usually satisfy the owner or trainer who insists that his charges "get the works." Most scientists agree, however, that "quickie" miracle shots or concoctions will never replace sound nutrition and parasite control on a continuous basis.

BREEDING HORSES

Figure 5.1   Introducing the new baby! (Courtesy, Wild Horse Research Farm, Porterville, California)

Horse owners who plan to breed one or more mares should have a working knowledge of heredity and know how to care for breeding animals and foals. The number of mares bred that actually conceive varies from about 40 to 85 percent, with the average running about 50 percent. Some mares that do conceive fail to produce living foals. This means that, on the average, two mares are kept a whole year to produce one foal, and even then, some foals are disappointments from the standpoint of quality.

HEREDITY IN HORSES

Until very recent times, the general principle that "like begets like" was the only recognized concept of heredity. That the application of this principle over a long period of time has been effective in modifying animal types in the direction of selection is evident from a comparison of present-day types of animals within each class of livestock. Thus, the speed of representatives of the modern Thoroughbred — coupled with their general lithe, angular build and nervous temperament — is in sharp contrast to the slow, easy gaits and docility of the Tennessee Walking Horse. Yet there is good and substantial evidence to indicate that both breeds descended from a common ancestry. Because of the diversity of genes carried by the original parent stock, it has been possible, through selection, to develop two distinct breeds — one highly adapted to fast running at extended distances and the other to a slow, ambling gait. Also, through selection accompanied by planned matings, this same parent stock has been altered into horses especially adept as hunters, jumpers, stock horses, polo mounts, three- and five-gaited park hacks, harness racehorses, etc.

THE GENE AS THE UNIT OF HEREDITY

The gene is the unit that determines heredity. In the body cells of horses there are many chromosomes. In turn, the chromosomes carry pairs of minute particles, called genes, which are the basic hereditary material (see below). The nucleus of each body cell of horses contains 32 pairs of chromosomes, or a total of 64, whereas there are thousands of pairs of genes.

When a sex cell (a sperm or an egg) is formed, only one chromosome and one gene of each pair goes into it. Then, when mating and fertilization occur, the 32 single chromosomes from the germ cell of each parent unite to form new pairs, and the chromosomes with their genes are again present in duplicate in the body cells of the embryo. Thus, with all possible combinations of 32 pairs of chromosomes and the genes that they bear, it is not strange that full sisters (except identical twins from a single egg split after fertilization) are so different. Actually we can marvel that they bear as much resemblance to each other as they do.

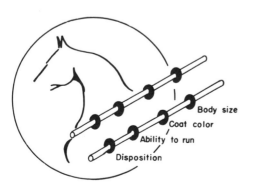

Figure 5.2 A pair of bundles, called chromosomes, carrying minute particles, called genes. The genes determine all the hereditary characteristics of horses, from length of leg to body size.

Because of this situation, the mating of a mare with a fine track record to a stallion that transmits good performance characteristics will not always produce a foal of a merit equal to its parents. The foal could be markedly poorer than the parents, or, in some cases, it could be better than either parent.

SIMPLE AND MULTIPLE GENE INHERITANCE

Simple and multiple gene inheritance occurs in horses, as in all animals. In simple gene inheritance, only one pair of genes is involved; thus, a pair of genes may be responsible for some one specific trait in horses. However, most characteristics, such as speed, are due to many genes; hence, they are called multiple-gene characteristics.

For most characteristics, many pairs of genes are involved. For example, growth rate is affected by (1) appetite and feed consumption, (2) the proportion of the feed eaten that is absorbed, and (3) the use to which the nutrients are put, whether they are used for growth or fattening — and each in turn is probably affected by different genes. Because multiple characteristics show all manner of gradation from high to low performance, they are sometimes referred to as quantitative traits. Thus, quantitative inheritance refers to the degree to which a characteristic is inherited. For example, all racehorses can run and all inherit some ability to run, but it is the degree to which they inherit the ability that is important.

DOMINANT AND RECESSIVE FACTORS

Dominant and recessive factors exist in horses. Some genes have the ability to prevent or mask the expression of others, with the result that the genetic makeup of such animals cannot be recognized with accuracy. This is called dominance. The gene that is masked is recessive. Because black is dominant to chestnut, all of the offspring will be black when a pure black stallion is crossed with a chestnut mare.

The resulting black offspring are not genotypically pure; they are Bb, where B stands for the dominant black and b for the recessive chestnut. These black, or F_1 (first cross, or first generation), animals will produce germ cells carrying black and chestnut genes in equal proportion (see Figure 5.3). Then if an F_1 stallion is crossed with F_1 mares, the F_2 (second cross, or second generation) population will on the average consist of three blacks to one chestnut.

The chestnut in the F_2 population, being a recessive, will be pure for color. That is, the mating of any two chestnut horses will always produce chestnut offspring; this is the situation in the Suffolk breed of draft horses where all animals of the breed are chestnuts. Of the three blacks in the F_2, however, only one is pure for black with the genetic constitu-

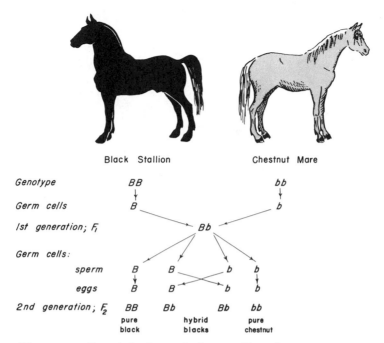

Figure 5.3 Gene inheritance in horses. Note that:

1. Each horse has at least a pair of genes for color, conveniently represented by symbols.
2. Each reproductive cell (egg or sperm) contains but one of each pair.
3. The Bb genotypes, in the first (F_1) generation, can vary in the degree of blackness, thus tending to resemble the one black parent.
4. The second (F_2) generation has the ratio of three blacks to one chestnut (phenotypically). The Bb may be black or shading into brown.
5. The pure blacks and certain hybrid blacks may not be distinguished on the basis of appearance, because the dominant B gene obscures the recessive b gene in varying degrees.
6. The chestnut (bb) is quite likely the only pure color, in this example, that can be detected on sight.

tion BB. The other two will be Bb in genetic constitution and will produce germ cells carrying B and b in equal proportion.

Dominance often makes it difficult to identify and discard all animals carrying an undesirable recessive factor. In some cases, dominance is neither complete nor absent, but incomplete, or partial, and expressed in a variety of ways. The best known case of partial dominance in horses is the palomino coloring.

Figure 5.4   Heredity has already made its contribution at the time of fertilization, but environment works ceaselessly away until death. Abundant fresh air, sunshine, exercise, a clean pasture, and plenty of milk constitute a good environment for foals. (Courtesy, *The Thoroughbred of California,* Arcadia, California)

HEREDITY AND ENVIRONMENT

Heredity and environment in quantitative traits function in horses just as they do in all animals. Generally, horse trainers believe that heredity is most important, whereas horse owners believe that environment, particularly training, is most important — especially if they lose a race. Actually, maximum development of characteristics of economic importance such as growth, body form, or speed cannot be achieved unless horses receive proper training, nutrition, and management.

The problem of the horse breeder is to select the best animals available genetically to be parents of the next generation. Because only 15 to 30 percent of the observed variation among animals may be due to heredity, and because environmental differences can produce misleading variations, mistakes in the selection of breeding animals are inevitable.

SEX IS DETERMINED BY CHROMOSOMES

The sex of an animal is determined by chromosomes. The mare has a pair of similar chromosomes called X chromosomes, and the stallion has a pair of unlike sex chromosomes called X and Y chromosomes.

The sex chromosomes in each pair separate from each other when the germ cells are formed. Thus, each of the ova or eggs produced by the mare contains the X chromosome; but the sperm of the stallion are of two types, one-half containing the X chromosome and the other half

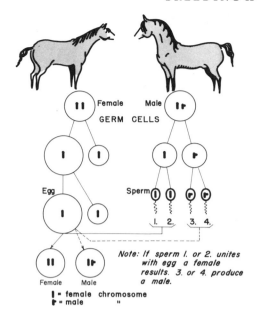

Figure 5.5 This diagram illustrates how sex is determined in horses, depending upon the chromosomal make-up of the individual horse.

the Y chromosome (see Figure 5.5). Since, on the average, the eggs and sperm unite at random, it can be understood that half of the progeny will contain the chromosomal makeup XX (female) and the other half XY (male).

OTHER FUNDAMENTALS OF HEREDITY

Other hereditary fundamentals of importance are the following:

- Both the stallion and the mare are equally important to any one off-spring. But a stallion generally can have many more offspring than a mare and, from a hereditary standpoint, is more important to the herd or breed.

- Prepotency is the ability of an animal to stamp its characteristics on its offspring so the offspring resemble that parent or each other more than usual.

- Nicking results when the right combination of genes for good characteristics is contributed by each parent. Thus, animals nick well when their respective combinations of good genes complement each other.

- Family names of horses have genetic significance only if (1) they are based on a linebreeding program that keeps the family closely related to the admired stallion or mare carrying the particular name, and (2) members of the family have been rigidly culled. Family names, therefore, lend themselves to speculation, and often have no more significance than human family names.

SYSTEMS OF BREEDING

Systems of breeding, whether planned or by chance, have made it possible to produce horses specially adapted to riding, racing, or driving. There is no one best system of breeding or secret of success for all conditions. Each breeding program is an individual case, requiring careful study. The choice of the system of breeding should be determined primarily by the size and quality of the herd, by the finances and skill of the operator, and by the ultimate goal ahead.

The systems of breeding from which the horseman may select are:

1. Purebreeding, in which the lineage, regardless of the number of generations removed, traces back to the foundation animals accepted by the breed or to animals that have been subsequently approved for infusion. Purebreeding may be conducted as either inbreeding or outcrossing, or part of each.

2. Inbreeding is the mating of animals more closely related than the average of the population from which they came. It may be done either by closebreeding or linebreeding.
    a. Closebreeding is breeding closely related animals such as sire to daughter, son to dam, or brother to sister.
    b. Linebreeding is breeding related animals so as to keep the offspring closely related to some highly admired ancestor such as half brother to half sister, female descendant to grandsire, or cousin to cousin.

3. Outcrossing is the mating of animals that are members of the same breed but that show no relationship in the pedigree for at least four to six generations.

4. Grading up is breeding a purebred sire of a given breed to a native, or grade, female.

5. Crossbreeding is mating animals of different breeds.

PERFORMANCE TESTING

The breeders of racehorses have always followed a program of mating animals of proved performance on the track. For example, it is interesting to note that the first breed register which appeared in 1791 — known as "An Introduction to The General Stud Book" — recorded the pedigrees of all the Thoroughbred horses winning important races. In a similar way, the Standardbred horse — which is an American creation — takes its name from the fact that, in its early history, animals were required to trot a mile in 2 minutes and 30 seconds, or to pace a mile in 2 minutes and 25 seconds, before they could be considered as eligible for registry. The chief aim, therefore, of early-day breeders of racehorses was to record the pedigree of outstanding performers rather than all members of the breed.

Performance testing for sport horses has been introduced in the U.S. Stallions undergo a 100-day training and observation period before they are judged over fences (including cross-country obstacles) and on the flat.

The simplest type of progeny testing in horses consists of the average record or merit of an individual stallion's or mare's offspring. Thus, the offspring of Thoroughbred or Standardbred animals bred for racing may be tested by timing on the track. Less satisfactory tests for saddle horses and fine harness horses have been devised. However, it is conceivable that actual exhibiting on the tanbark in the great horse shows of the country may be an acceptable criterion for saddle-bred animals.

THE STALLION

A stallion may become the parent of a great number of progeny. Therefore, he should be a purebred animal, a good representative of the breed selected, and a superior individual in type and soundness. If he is an older horse with progeny, the progeny should be of uniformly high quality and of approved type and soundness.

Each stallion should be studied as an individual, and his feeding, care, exercise, and handling should be varied accordingly.

We haven't improved on nature in percent foal crop. In the wild state, each band of 30 to 40 mares was headed by a stallion leader who sired all the foals in that band. With plenty of outdoor exercise on natural footing, superior nutrition derived from plants grown on unleached soils, regular production beginning at an early age, little possibility of disease or infection, and frequent services during the heat period, 90 percent or higher foaling rates were commonplace. The low fertility usually encountered under domestication must be caused to a large extent by the relatively artificial conditions that have been created.

REPRODUCTIVE ORGANS OF THE STALLION

The stallion's functions in reproduction are (1) to produce the male reproductive cells, the sperm or spermatozoa, and (2) to introduce sperm into the female reproductive tract at the proper time. A schematic drawing of the reproductive organs of the stallion follows.

The two testicles are the primary sex organs of the stallion. They produce the sperm and a hormone called testosterone, which regulates and maintains the male reproductive tract in its functional state and is responsible for the masculine appearance and behavior of the stallion.

Sperm are produced in the inner walls or surface of the seminiferous tubules, which are a mass of minute, coiled tubules. These tubules

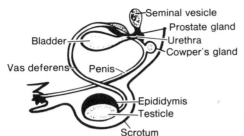

Figure 5.6 Reproductive organs of the stallion.

merge into a series of larger ducts that carry the sperm to a coiled tube called epididymis. The epididymis is the place where the sperm are stored and where they mature, or ripen.

The testicles and epididymides are enclosed in the scrotum, the chief function of which is thermoregulatory. The scrotum maintains the testicles at temperatures several degrees cooler than the rest of the body.

From the epididymis, the sperm move through a tube, the vas deferens, into the urethra. The urethra has a dual role. It carries urine from the bladder through the penis and sperm from the junction with the vas deferens to the end of the penis.

Along the urethra are the accessory glands. These are the prostate, the seminal vesicles, and the Cowper's gland. Their fluids nourish and preserve the sperm and provide a medium that transports the sperm. The fluids and sperm combined are called semen.

CARE AND MANAGEMENT OF THE STALLION

The following points are pertinent to the care and management of the stallion.

1. *Quarters* — The most convenient arrangement is a roomy box stall that opens directly into a two- or three-acre pasture.
2. *Feeding* — The feed requirements are covered in Chapter 6.
3. *Exercise* — Allow the stallion the run of a sizable pasture, but also provide additional, unhurried exercise either under saddle or hitched to a cart; by longeing; or by leading.
4. *Grooming* — Groom the stallion daily to make him more attractive and to assist in maintaining his good health and condition.
5. *Age and service* — Limit the mature stallion to not more than 2 services per day, one early in the morning and the other late in the afternoon; allow one day of rest each week.

The number of hand matings per year for stallions of different ages should be limited as follows: two years old, 10 to 15; three years old, 20 to 40; four years old, 30 to 60; mature horses, 50 to 70; and over 18 years old, 20 to 40. Limit the two-year-olds to 2 to 3 services per week; the

Figure 5.7 Stallion barn and adjacent paddock. (Courtesy, California Thoroughbred Breeders Association, Arcadia, California)

three-year-olds to 1 service per day; and the four-year-olds or over to 2 services per day. A stallion may remain a vigorous and reliable breeder up to twenty to twenty-five years of age.

There are breed differences. Thus, when first entering stud duty, the average three-year-old Thoroughbred should be limited to 20 to 25 mares per season, but a Standardbred of the same age may breed 25 to 30 mares. A four- to five-year-old Thoroughbred should be limited to 30 to 40 mares per season, but a Standardbred of the same age may breed 40 to 50 mares.

STALLION BREEDING CONTRACT

Stallion breeding contracts should always be in writing; and the higher the stud fee, the more important it is that good business methods prevail. Neither "gentlemen's agreements" nor barn door records will suffice.

From a legal standpoint, a stallion breeding contract is binding to the parties whose signatures are affixed thereto. Thus, it is important that the contract be carefully read and fully understood before signing.

A sample stallion breeding contract is shown in Figure 5.8. The contract should be executed in duplicate for each mare, one copy to be retained by each party.

BREEDING CONTRACT

This contract for the breeding season of _____ made and entered into by and between
                                                      (year)
_____, _____, herein after designated stallion owner, and
(owner of stallion)   (address)
_____, _____, hereinafter designated mare owner.
(owner of mare)   (address)

This contract covers —

The stallion, _____, whose service fee is $_____; $_____ of which is paid
                    (name of stallion)
with this contract and the balance will be paid before the mare leaves _____.
                                                                        (name of farm or ranch)

and

The mare, _____, reg. no. _____, by _____ out of
              (name of mare)   (sire)
_____, age _____, color _____.
      (dam)

The mare owner agrees that —

Upon arrival, the mare will (a) be halter broken, (b) have the hind shoes removed, and (c) be accompanied by a health certificate signed by a veterinarian, certifying that she is healthy and in sound breeding condition.

Stallion owner will not be responsible for accident, disease, or death to the mare, or to her foal (if she has a foal).

Stallion owner may, at his discretion, have his veterinarian (a) check and treat the mare for breeding condition or diseases, and (b) treat her for parasites if needed, with the expenses of such services charged to the mare owner's account and paid when the mare leaves the farm or ranch.

He will pay the following board on his mare at the time the mare leaves the farm or ranch: Feed and facilities $_____ per day (dry), or $_____ per day if mare arrives with nursing foal (wet). Payment shall be made for feed/facilities/other charges at the time the mare leaves the farm or ranch.

Should the mare prove barren, or should the foal die at birth, he will send notice of same, signed by a licensed veterinarian, within 5 days of such barren determination or death.

Should he fail to deliver the above mare to the stallion owner's premises on or before _____,
                                                                                        (date)
stallion owner shall be under no further obligation with respect to any matter herein set forth.

This contract shall not be assigned or transferred. In the event the mare is sold, any remaining unpaid fee shall immediately become due and payable and no refund shall be due anyone under any circumstances.

The stallion owner agrees that —

He will provide suitable facilities for the mare and feed and care for her in a good and husband-like manner.

Mare owner will not be responsible for any disease, accident, or injury to stallion owner's horses.

A live foal is guaranteed — meaning a foal that can stand up alone and nurse.

The stallion owner and mare owner mutually agree that —

This contract is not valid unless completed in full.

Should the above stallion die or become unfit for service, or should the above named mare die or become unfit to breed, this contract shall become null and void and money paid as part of this contract shall be refunded to mare owner.

Should the mare prove barren, or should the foal die at birth, with certification of same provided to stallion owner within the time specified, the stallion owner has the option either to (a) rebreed the mare the following year, or (b) refund the $_____ portion of the breeding fee, thereby cancelling this entire contract.

The mare will not receive more than _____ covers during the breeding season, and she will
                                        (number)
not be bred before _____, 19___, or after _____, 19___.

_____   _____   _____
      (date)   (signature, mare owner or rep.)   (address)

_____   _____   _____
      (date)   (signature, stallion owner or rep.)   (address)

Figure 5.8 Stallion breeding contract.

Incentive Breeding Contract

In addition to the provisions made in the sample stallion breeding contract, the author suggests that consideration be given to incorporating an incentive basis. Here are some guidelines for the latter:

Generally, stallion owners guarantee a live foal, which means that the foal must stand and nurse; otherwise, the stud fee is either refunded or not collected, according to the stipulations. Of course, it is in the best interest of both parties that a strong, healthy foal be born. One well-known horse establishment reports that their records reveal that of all mares settled during a particular three-year period, 19 percent of them subsequently either resorbed or aborted fetuses, or the foal or mare died. Further, their investigation of these situations showed that the vast majority of these losses could have been averted by better care and management. They found many things wrong — ranging from racing mares in foal to turning them to pastures where there was insufficient feed. To alleviate many, if not most, of these losses — losses that accrue after the mare has been examined and pronounced safe in foal, then taken away from the stallion owner's premises — the author suggests that an incentive basis be incorporated in the stallion breeding contract. For example, the stallion owner might agree to reduce the stud fee (1) by 10, 15, or 20 percent (state which) provided a live foal is born, or (2) by 25 to 33⅓ percent provided the mare owner's veterinarian certifies that the mare is safe in foal 30 days after being removed from the place where bred, with payment made at that time and based on conception rather than the birth of a live foal.

Figure 5.9 Mares and foals on pasture. The objective: a 100-percent foal crop. (Photo by J. Noye, Versailles, Kentucky; courtesy, Dr. W. C. Kaufman, Paris, Kentucky)

THE MARE

Characteristics found in the broodmare are likely to be reflected in the offspring. It is fundamental that "like tends to produce like." The broodmare should possess an abundance of feminity in addition to being sound and of good type. She should be of good ancestry, whether purebred or grade. Also, when selecting a broodmare for breeding, it is best to select one that is three or four years old. Where an older mare is selected, make certain that her breeding habits have been regular and normal.

REPRODUCTIVE ORGANS OF THE MARE

The mare's functions in reproduction are to (1) produce the female reproductive cells, the eggs or ova; (2) develop the new individual, the embryo, in the uterus; (3) expel the fully developed young at the time of birth, or parturition; and (4) produce milk for the nourishment of the young.

The part played by the mare in the generative process is much more complicated than that of the stallion. It is imperative, therefore, that the modern horseman have a full understanding of the anatomy of the reproductive organs of the mare and the functions of each part. The schematic drawing below shows the reproductive organs of the mare.

The two ovaries are the primary sex organs of the mare. They are bean-shaped organs 2 to 3 inches long. The ovaries produce eggs. Each egg is contained in a bubble-like sac on the ovary, called a follicle. There are hundreds of follicles on each ovary. Generally, the follicles remain unchanged until puberty when one of them begins to grow because of an increase in the follicular liquid in it; the others remain small. The egg is suspended in the follicular fluid.

When the growing follicle is about an inch in diameter, a hormone causes it to rupture and discharge the egg. This is known as ovulation

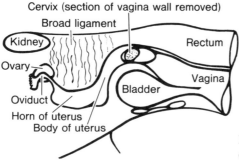

Figure 5.10　Reproductive organs of the mare.

and is the time when mating should take place. The egg is trapped in a funnel-shaped membrane, called the infundibulum, that surrounds the ovary. The infundibulum narrows into a tube called the oviduct. The oviduct then carries the egg to the uterus, or womb, the largest of the female reproductive organs, where the unborn young, or fetus, will develop.

The lining of the uterus is soft and spongy. It contains a vast network of blood vessels that provide a "bed" for the fertilized egg to settle into and develop. At birth, the heavy layers of muscles of the uterus wall contract with great pressure to force the new animal out through the cervix and vagina.

BREEDING HABITS AND CARE OF THE MARE

A knowledge of the mare's normal breeding habits will help to improve the fertility rate. However, not all mares that conceive give birth to live foals. So, improved care and management of the pregnant mare are important, also. The age of puberty (sexual maturity) for mares is 12 to 15 months. During the breeding season, the mare exhibits sexual receptivity to the stallion every 15 to 19 days; the duration of heat is usually three to seven days. The interval between heat periods is commonly 15 to 19 days. The optimum time to breed is 20 to 24 hours before ovulation. The highest rate of conception is obtained by serving the mare daily or every other day during the heat period, beginning with the third day. The gestation period ranges from 310 to 370 days, and averages 336. A handy rule-of-thumb method that may be used to figure the approximate date of foaling is: subtract one month and add two days to the date the mare was bred. Hence, the mare bred May 20 should foal April 22 the following year.

The following points are pertinent to the care and management of the mare.

1. *Age to breed.* Well-grown fillies may be bred as two-year-olds, but most fillies are not bred until they are three years old.

2. *Normal breeding season and time of foaling.* Mares are seasonal breeders. From about mid-April to mid-September, the mare cycles and exhibits sexual receptivity to the stallion every 15 to 19 days (see the following graph). At this time of year, the mare is most fertile, the heat cycles are more regular and evident, and the mare is more likely to conceive. Also, a foal conceived in the spring may be dropped on pasture the following spring with a minimum danger of becoming infected with parasites or diseases. Abundant fresh air, sunshine, and exercise contribute to the proper development of the youngster. Persons who race or show horses want foals to be born as soon as possible after January 1.

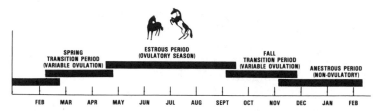

Figure 5.11 Mare seasonality. From about mid-April to mid-September, the mare cycles and exhibits sexual receptivity to the stallion every 15 to 19 days.

3. *Conditioning for breeding.* Mares are conditioned by proper feeding and adequate exercise. To achieve high conception rates, mares should not be too thin or too fat. Try to check the natural tendency of barren or maiden mares to become overweight.

   Mares may be exercised by riding them under saddle or driving them in harness. When this is not practical, they usually will get enough exercise if allowed to run in a large pasture.

4. *Signs of heat.* In season, mares generally exhibit (a) relaxation of the external genitals, (b) more frequent urination, (c) teasing of the other mares, (d) apparent desire for company, and (e) upon sight or sound of a stallion, mares in good standing heat will assume a squatting posture with raised tail, urinate frequently, and have spasmodic "winking" of the vulva.

   Mares in foal may have false heat. Breeding such mares may result in abortion. An experienced horseman who is familiar with the peculiarities of the individual animal can detect false heat when the mare is teased and can prevent such an accident.

BREEDING THE MARE

A young, shy mare should be presented to the teaser stallion fairly often as the breeding season approaches. This will acquaint her with the breeding procedure.

Since actual ovulation takes place toward the end of the heat period, the mare should be mated every day or every other day beginning with the third day after she first comes into heat.

No phase of horse production has become more unnatural or more complicated with domestication than the actual breeding operation. This is so because breeders try to get mares bred in about 4 months instead of 12 and have arbitrarily limited the breeding season to late winter and early spring. The following facts and pointers are pertinent to the breeding operation.

1. Hand mating, in which the animals are coupled under supervision, is the most common. It guards against injury to both the stallion

Figure 5.12 Examining a mare prior to breeding. (Courtesy, Gem State Stables, Boise, Idaho)

and the mare. However, corral or pasture breeding may be preferable under certain conditions. For example, corral breeding may be resorted to when only one person is handling the breeding operation, and pasture breeding is sometimes followed on the ranges of the West. In corral breeding, the stallion and the mare are turned together in a corral; in pasture breeding, the stallion is turned to pasture with a band of mares.

2. Breed only healthy mares to a healthy stallion. Require that all mares from the outside be accompanied by a health certificate signed by a veterinarian.

3. Teasing is the best way in which to make certain that a mare is in season.

4. Serve the mare daily or every other day during the heat period, beginning with the third day.

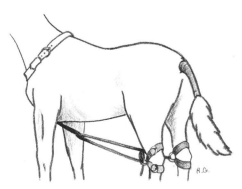

Figure 5.13 A hobbled mare, with tail properly bandaged, ready for service. Hobbles are used only to protect the stallion as he approaches and dismounts, and not in any way to force the mare into submission to service when she is not ready.

5. After making certain that the mare is in season, wash the reproductive organs of the stallion and the external parts of the mare that are likely to come in contact with the reproductive organs of the stallion; bandage the upper 6 to 8 inches of the mare's tail. Place a twitch and hobbles on the mare and allow the sexual act to be completed. Return the mare for retrial approximately 21 days later.

SIGNS AND TESTS OF PREGNANCY

Pregnancy may be determined by (1) cessation of the heat period, (2) rectal palpation, (3) blood tests, and (4) ultrasonography. All tests but the first one must be made by experienced technicians.

CARE OF THE PREGNANT MARE

The pregnant mare is inclined to be inactive. She should be separated from barren mares, which are likely to be playful and frisky.

Pregnant, idle mares should be turned to pasture in which there are shade and water. A simple shelter is all that is needed; an open shed is satisfactory in temperate climates, even in winter. Pregnant mares that are used under saddle or in harness may be given quarters like those of other horses used similarly.

The nutritive requirements of the mare are discussed in Chapter 6 of this book; hence, the reader is referred thereto.

Mares that have the run of a large pasture will usually get sufficient exercise. Stabled mares should be exercised moderately for an hour daily under saddle or hitched to a cart. Continue this routine to within a day or two of foaling. During the last couple of days, mares may be led.

CARE OF THE MARE AT FOALING TIME

Keep a written record of the date the mare is due to foal. (Remember that the gestation period can range from 310 to 370 days, with an average of 336 days.) This record enables the caretaker to make plans for foaling.

Giving birth is a critical time in the life of a mare. All the advantages gained by selecting genetically desirable and healthy parent stock and by providing the best environmental and nutritional conditions during the gestation period can be dissipated quickly through carelessness or ignorance at this time.

Signs of Approaching Parturition

These signs are a distended udder, which may be observed 2 to 6 weeks before foaling; a shrinkage or falling away of the buttocks muscles near the tailhead and a falling of the abdomen 7 to 10 days before foaling; filling out of the teats 4 to 6 days before foaling; and the appearance of wax on the ends of the nipples 4 to 6 days before foaling. As foaling time draws nearer, the vulva becomes full and loose; milk drops from the teats; and the mare becomes restless, may break into a sweat, urinates frequently, and lies down and gets up. But there are times when all signs fail, so be prepared 30 days in advance of the expected time.

Foaling Place

Provide a foaling place 7 to 10 days before the event is expected, so that the mare becomes accustomed to the new surroundings. When the weather is warm and it can be arranged, allow the mare to foal in a clean pasture away from other livestock. Avoid foaling in an unsanitary paddock or in a lot filled with droppings, because infections, such as "navel ill," often follow.

During bad weather, use a foaling stall. It should be at least 12 feet square; it should have a smooth, well-packed clay floor; and it should be free of obstructions (such as low mangers or racks) on which the mare and foal might hurt themselves. If possible, it should be located away from other occupied stalls. Before occupancy, the foaling stall should be cleaned and disinfected with 13 ounces of lye in 10 gallons of water; use one-half strength solution in scrubbing mangers and grain boxes. Sprinkle the floor and walls lightly with quick lime or burnt lime. Provide plenty of bedding for the occasion.

Foaling Time

The following information and procedures may be helpful during foaling:

1. The feed should be decreased and wheat bran should be added. Feed a wet bran mash if the mare is constipated.
2. An attendant should be near but not in sight.

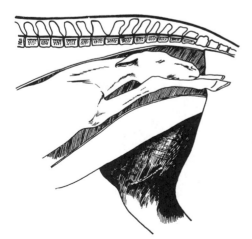

Figure 5.14 Normal presentation. The back of the fetus is directly toward that of the mother, the forelegs are extended toward the vulva with the heels down, and the nose rests between the forelegs.

3. Foaling begins with the rupture of the outer fetal membrane, which is followed by the escape of a large amount of fluid. The inner membrane surrounding the foal appears next and labor becomes more marked.

The mare foals rapidly in the normal presentation of her young. The entire birth procedure generally does not take more than 15 to 30 minutes. The mare usually will be down at the height of labor. The foal generally is born while the mare is lying on her side with her legs stretched out.

In normal presentation of the foal, the front feet with heels down appear first (see Figure 5.14), followed by the nose and head, then shoulders, middle (with back up), hips, and finally hind legs and feet.

Summon a veterinarian at once when the presentation is not normal. There is great danger that the foal will smother if birth is delayed. If the feet are presented with the bottoms up, it is a good indication that they are the hind ones and there is likely to be difficulty.

If the mare does not appear to be making any progress in parturition after reasonable time and effort, make an examination and give her help before she has exhausted her strength in futile efforts at expulsion. Often, the fetus dies when parturition is retarded because of twists or knots in the umbilical cord or is unduly delayed for other reasons.

Figure 5.15 Newborn foal. (Courtesy, California Thoroughbred Breeders Association, Arcadia, California)

4. Make certain that the newborn foal is breathing and that the membrane has been removed from its mouth and nostrils. If the foal fails to breathe, give it artificial respiration immediately. This may be done by blowing into its mouth, by working the ribs, by rubbing the body vigorously, and by lifting it up and dropping it gently. Then rub and dry the foal with towels, treat the navel cord with tincture of iodine, and let the mare and foal rest for a time.

Remove the expelled afterbirth from the stall and burn or bury it; it is usually expelled within 1 to 6 hours after foaling. If it is retained longer than 6 hours, or if the mare seems lame, blanket her and call a veterinarian. Clean and rebed the stall after the mare and foal are up. Give the mare small quantities of lukewarm water at intervals and feed considerable wheat bran for the first few days after foaling; take 7 to 10 days to get the mare on full feed. Be observant; if the mare has much temperature, call a veterinarian. The normal temperature is 100.5° F. Also, regard with suspicion any discharge from the vulva.

BREEDING AFTER FOALING

Mares usually come back in heat 7 to 10 days after foaling (foal heat), but the time can range from 3 to 13 days. Some horsemen rebreed mares during the first heat after foaling, usually on the eighth or ninth day, providing the birth was normal and the mare suffered no injury or infection. Other horsemen prefer to rebreed mares during the heat period that follows the foal heat (25 to 30 days from foaling), provided there is no discharge or evidence of infection.

Mares with infected genital tracts seldom are settled in service. If they are bred, the infection may spread to the stallion — thence to other mares. If they conceive, there is danger that the foals will be undersized and poorly developed.

DRYING UP THE MARE

Permanently separate the mare and foal at weaning time. Decrease the mare's ration before and during weaning. Rub an oil preparation (such as camphorated oil or a mixture of lard and spirits of camphor) on the udder, but do not milk out the udder until 5 to 7 days later when it is soft and flabby. At that time, the little secretion that remains, perhaps not more than half a cup, may be milked out.

MANAGEMENT FOR HIGH FERTILITY

In order to improve the conception rate of mares above the general average, good management of both mares and stallions must go hand in hand with superior nutrition; and, in addition, the microbiological, surgical, and endocrinological facets of veterinary medicine should be encompassed as necessary. Good management calls for

1. Keeping broodmares in strong, healthy breeding condition, but avoiding overfeeding and overweight.
2. Controlling parasites.
3. Providing exercise.
4. Flushing mares, beginning 4 to 8 weeks ahead of the breeding season. Flushing refers to having the mares gain in weight. This is best accomplished by more liberal feeding at this time. When properly flushed, mares should start to shed their hair coats at the time breeding begins. Of course, if they are overweight, proper flushing is impossible. When mares are too fat, slim them down well ahead of the breeding season, by (a) cutting down on the quantity of the feed and by using low-energy feeds (like cereal straws), and (b) stepping up the exercise.

A combination of proper condition (not overweight), nutritious feed, flushing beginning 4 to 8 weeks ahead of the breeding season, parasite control, and adequate exercise of both the mare and the stallion will result in a higher conception rate, and the mares will breed both earlier and more nearly at the same time.

On a horse-breeding establishment, a barren mare or an infertile stallion make for added costs — and there is no financial return. Moreover, most horses are quite valuable; hence, any mating that fails could have been a valuable horse.

THE FOAL

After the newborn foal starts breathing and has been rubbed dry, put it in one corner of the stall on clean, fresh straw. The mare usually will be less restless if this corner is in the direction of her head.

Protect the eyes of a newborn foal from bright light.

TREATMENT OF THE NAVEL CORD

If left alone, the navel cord of the newborn foal usually breaks within 2 to 4 inches of the belly. If it does not break, cut it about 2 inches from the belly with clean dull shears or scrape it in two with a knife. A torn or broken blood vessel will bleed very little, but one cut directly across may bleed excessively. Treat the severed cord immediately with tincture of iodine, or other reliable antiseptic; then leave the mare and foal alone so they can rest and gain strength.

Figure 5.16 Treating the navel cord of a newborn foal with iodine.

VALUE OF COLOSTRUM

Colostrum is milk secreted by the dam for the first few days after parturition. It differs from ordinary milk in that it is more concentrated; is higher in protein content, especially in globulin; is richer in vitamin A; contains antibodies that protect the foal temporarily against certain infection; and is a natural purgative that removes fecal matter accumulated in the digestive tract.

To be effective in protection against disease, however, colostrum must be ingested within a few hours after birth, preferably within 15 to 30 minutes, because "gut closure" occurs about 24 to 30 hours after birth. After this point, the foal digests the large molecular weight proteins in the colostrum, breaking down the components with special immunizing properties so they are no longer available.

THE FIRST NURSING

A strong, healthy foal will be on its feet and ready to nurse within one-half to two hours after birth. Before allowing the foal to nurse for the first time, wash the mare's udder with a mild disinfectant and rinse thoroughly with clean, warm water.

A big, awkward foal occasionally needs assistance and guidance when it nurses the first time. If the foal is stubborn, forced feeding will be useless. Back the mare onto additional bedding in one corner of the stall and coax the foal to the teats with a bottle and nipple. An attendant may hold the bottle while standing on the opposite side of the mare from the foal.

A very weak foal should be given the mare's first milk even if it is necessary to draw this milk into a bottle and feed the foal one or two times by nipple. An attendant sometimes must steady a foal before it will nurse.

BOWEL MOVEMENT

Regulation of the bowel movement of the foal is very important. Constipation and diarrhea (scours) are common ailments.

Excrement impacted in the bowels during prenatal development — material called meconium — may kill the foal if it is not eliminated promptly. A good feed of colostrum usually will cause natural elimination. This is not always the case, however, especially when foals are from stall-fed mares.

Observe the foal's bowel movement 4 to 12 hours after birth. If there has been no fecal discharge by this time, and the foal seems sluggish and fails to nurse, give it an enema. Use 1 to 2 quarts of water at body heat (101° F) mixed with a little glycerin, or use 1 to 2 quarts of warm, soapy water. Inject the solution with a baby syringe that has about a 3-inch nipple, or use a tube and can. Repeat the treatment until normal yellow feces appear.

If the foal is scouring, reduce the mare's feed and take away part of her milk from the foal at intervals by milking her out.

Diarrhea or scours in foals may result from infectious diseases or dirty surroundings. It is caused by an irritant in the digestive tract that should be removed. Give an astringent only in exceptional cases and on the advice of a veterinarian.

Conditions that may cause diarrhea are contaminated udder or teats, nonremoval of fecal matter from the digestive tract, fretfulness or temperature above normal in the mare, too much feed affecting the quality of the mare's milk, a cold damp bed, or continued exposure to cold rains.

CARE OF THE SUCKLING FOAL

Weather conditions permitting, there is no better place for a mare and foal than on pasture. When the foal is from 10 days to 3 weeks old, it will begin to nibble on a little grain and hay. To promote thrift and early development, and to avoid any setback at weaning time, encourage the foal to eat supplementary feed as early as possible. The foal should be provided with a low-built grain box especially for this purpose or if on pasture, it may be creep fed.

Foals normally reach one-half of their mature weight during the first year. Most breeders of Thoroughbreds and Standardbreds plan to have their two-year-old animals at full height. Such results require liberal feeding from the beginning. A foal stunted in the first year by insufficient feeding cannot be developed properly later in life. It is well recognized that forced development must be done expertly if the animals are to remain durable and sound.

Figure 5.17 Born alive, and off to a good start in life. (Courtesy, *Thoroughbred Record,* Lexington, Kentucky)

RAISING THE ORPHAN FOAL

Occasionally, a mare dies during or immediately after parturition, leaving an orphan foal to be raised. At other times, a mare may fail to give sufficient milk, or she may have twins. In such cases, the foal may be (1) shifted to another mare, known as a foster mother or nurse mare, or (2) placed on mare's milk replacer, or synthetic milk, that is mixed and fed according to the manufacturer's directions.

It is important, however, that the orphan foal receive colostrum, preferably for about the first four days of life. For this purpose, colostrum from a mare that produces excess milk or one that has lost her foal should be collected and frozen from time to time; then, as needed, it may be thawed and warmed to 100° to 105° F and fed.

For the first few days, the orphan foal should be fed with a bottle and rubber nipple. Within about two weeks, it may be taught to drink from a pail. All receptacles must be kept sanitary (clean and scald them each time they are used) and feeding must be at regular intervals. Dry feeding should be started at the earliest possible time with the orphan foal.

The following formula may be used for feeding the orphan foal if a substitute milk must be used:

1 pint of lowfat cow's milk (about 3% fat)
4 ounces of lime water
1 teaspoon of sugar

Two teaspoons of lactose or corn syrup may be used to replace the sugar, and one large can of evaporated cow's milk may be used with one can of water to replace the fresh milk. The foal should be fed about one-half pint every hour. Give large foals slightly more than a pint. After 4 or 5 days increase the interval to 2 hours. After a week, feed every 4 hours and increase the quantity accordingly.

CARE OF THE FOAL'S FEET

Foals may damage their limbs when the weight is not equally distributed because of unshapely hoofs. On the other hand, faulty limbs may be helped or even corrected if the hoofs are trimmed regularly. Also, trimming helps educate the foal and makes shoeing easier at maturity. If the foal is run on pasture, trimming the feet may be necessary long before weaning time. A good practice is to check the feet every month or six weeks and, if necessary, trim a small amount each time rather than a large amount at one time. Tendons should not become strained because of incorrectly trimmed feet. Usually, only the bottom rim of the hoof should be trimmed, although sometimes the heel, frog, or toe of the hoof may need trimming. The hoofs are trimmed with a rasp, farrier's knife, and nippers. A rasp is used more than the other tools.

Before the feet are trimmed, the foal should first be inspected while standing squarely on a hard surface and then inspected at the walk and the trot.

WEANING

Foals usually are weaned at four to six months of age. Thorough preparation facilitates weaning.

It may be advisable to wean the foal at a comparatively early age if either the foal or mare is not doing well, if the mare is being given heavy work, or if the mare was rebred on the ninth day after foaling.

If by using a creep or a separate grain box the foal has become accustomed to eating a considerable amount of hay and about ¾ lb. of grain daily per 100 lb. of body weight, weaning will cause only a slight disturbance or setback. If the ration of the dam is cut in half a few days before the separation, her udder usually will dry up without difficulty.

Move the mare to new quarters from the stall she shares with the foal. Remove anything on which the foal might hurt itself during the first unhappy days that it lives alone. Make the separation of the foal from the mare complete and final. If the foal sees, hears, or smells its dam again, the separation process must be started all over again.

Turn the foal out on pasture after a day or two. If there are several weanlings together, some of them might get hurt while running and frolicking in the pasture. Guard against this by first turning out two or three less valuable individuals and letting them tire themselves; then turn out the rest.

At this stage, if numerous weanlings are involved, separate them by sexes. Put the more timid ones by themselves. Do not run weanlings with older horses.

CASTRATING

Geldings, or castrated males, are safer and easier to handle than stallions. Therefore, a colt should be castrated unless he is to be saved for breeding purposes. Have a veterinarian perform this operation. A colt may be castrated when only a few days old, but most horsemen prefer to delay the operation until the animal is about a year old. While there is less real danger to the animal and much less setback with early altering, it results in imperfect development of the foreparts. Delaying castration for a time results in more muscular, bolder features and better carriage of the foreparts.

Weather and management conditions permitting, the time of altering should be determined by the development of the individual. Underdeveloped colts may be left uncastrated six months or even a year longer than overdeveloped ones.

Breeders of Thoroughbred horses usually prefer to race them first as uncastrated animals.

There is less danger of infection if colts are castrated in the spring soon after they are turned out on clean pasture and before hot weather and "fly time" arrive. This is extremely important in the southern states because of the danger of screwworm infestation.

BREAKING

A foal will not need "breaking" if it has been trained properly. When a young horse can be saddled or harnessed with satisfactory ease, it is because the proper training program has been followed. Saddling and harnessing are just additional steps. A good time to harness and work the horse for the first time is during the winter as a rising two-year-old.

ARTIFICIAL INSEMINATION

Artificial insemination is, by definition, the deposition of spermatozoa in the female genitalia by artificial rather than by natural means.

Today, there is renewed interest in artificial insemination of horses, as a result of a successful method of freezing stallion semen. Stallion semen is now being collected, processed, and frozen, but the fertility level of frozen semen has been low.

Figure 5.18 The first registered foal in the U.S. to be produced by artificial insemination with frozen stallion semen. (Courtesy, R. M. Taylor, M.D., Little River, California)

Mares are inseminated by (1) using a syringe and catheter arrangement with a speculum, (2) placing a gelatin capsule, holding 10 to 25 milliliters of extended semen, in the uterus by hand, or (3) introducing a rubber catheter by hand through the cervix and into the uterus and injecting the semen by means of a syringe attached to the opposite end of the tube.

Among the advantages of artificial insemination, in comparison with natural service, are the following:

- It increases the use of outstanding sires for breeding.
- It alleviates the danger and bother of keeping a sire.
- It makes it possible to overcome certain physical handicaps to mating.
- It lessens the sire costs.
- It reduces the likelihood of costly delays through using infertile sires.
- It makes it feasible to prove more sires.
- It creates large families of animals.
- It increases pride of ownership, when a better stallion can be used.
- It may lessen and control certain diseases.
- It increases profits.
- It allows sires to compete during the breeding season.
- It avoids the risk and expense of shipping mares for breeding and stabling them away from home.

But there are limitations to artificial insemination, among which are the following:

- It must conform to physiological principles.
- It requires skilled technicians.
- It takes considerable capital to initiate and operate an A.I. breeding service.
- It is not always possible to obtain the services of a given sire.
- It may accentuate the damage of a poor sire.
- It may restrict the sire market.
- It may increase the spread of disease.
- It may be subject to certain abuses.

Until recently, stallion semen could not be stored for any length of time. It is viable for only one to two days in the liquid state. However, stallion semen has now been cooled and frozen successfully, and its use will grow. This development may write a new chapter in horse breeding, especially in breeding grade mares.

But before wide-scale use can be made of artificial insemination of horses, solutions to additional problems must be found. These include the following needs:

- The ability to breed more mares per stallion.
- The ability to detect when mares are ready for breeding.
- The ability to bring mares in heat at will.
- The ability to freeze and store stallion semen in such manner that a higher fertility level will be obtained.

REGISTRATION OF FOALS PRODUCED THROUGH ARTIFICIAL INSEMINATION OR EMBRYO TRANSFER

Although artificial insemination (A.I.) was first practiced with horses, some American registry associations frown upon or forbid the practice. Moreover, there is little unanimity of opinion so far as their rules apply to the practice. Table 5.1 summarizes the horse association rules relative to registering young produced by A.I. or Embryo Transfer.

BLOOD TYPING OF HORSES

Blood typing was developed at the University of Wisconsin during the decade 1940–50. It involves a study of the components of the blood, which are inherited according to strict genetic rules that have been established in the research laboratory. By determining the genetic

Table 5.1 HORSE ASSOCIATION RULES RELATIVE TO REGISTERING YOUNG
PRODUCED BY A.I. OR EMBRYO TRANSFER[1]

Breed	Present Rules or Attitude of Registry Association Relative to A.I. or Embryo Transfer
Light Horses and Ponies:	
American Bashkir Curly	A.I. and embryo transfer are not sanctioned.
American Creme Horse	A.I. accepted, but must have signed statement of insemination.
American Gotland Horse	No rules.
American Mustang	Accepted provided certified authentication is provided by the attending veterinarian of both mare and stallion. Embryo transfer is not accepted.
American Part-blooded Horse Registry	Accepted provided customary proof of breeding is provided.
American Saddlebred	Accepted provided A.I. takes place (1) on premises where stallion is standing, and (2) in presence of owner or party authorized to sign certificate of breeding. Embryo transfer accepted on two foals per year per donor mare, but all animals involved must be blood typed.
American Walking Pony	Accepted only if (1) stallion and mare are on same premises and insemination is done by licensed veterinarian, or (2) same veterinarian collects, transports, and inseminates if sire and dam are on different premises. No rules on embryo transfer.
American White Horse	A.I. accepted, but must have signed statement of insemination.
Andalusian	The International Association does not register foals produced by A.I. or by embryo transfer. The American Andalusian Horse Association permits A.I., but has not addressed embryo transfer.
Anglo-Arab and Half-Arabian	Accepted provided (1) stallion has been licensed by Arabian Horse Registry for A.I., and (2) registration certificate is stamped to show animal was A.I. produced.
Appaloosa	Accepted provided (1) stallion's blood type is filed with the ApHC, and (2) semen is not stored, shipped, or transported from premises where the stallion is standing. Embryo transfer accepted, but limited to one foal per donor mare per year, unless there are twins.
Arabian	A.I. accepted provided (1) collection of semen from stallion and insemination of mare with this semen take place on the same premises, and (2) all semen

Breed	*Present Rules or Attitude of Registry Association Relative to A.I. or Embryo Transfer*
	is used immediately after collection. Embryo transfer accepted, but limited to registration of one foal per calendar year from one donor mare.
Buckskin	International Buckskin Horse Association, Inc. accepts A.I. and embryo transfer.
Chickasaw	No rules.
Connemara	Accepted provided (1) fresh semen is used, and (2) signed letters are on file from stallion owner, mare owner, the veterinarian who collected the semen, and the veterinarian who did the inseminating.
Galiceno	Accepted, without rules or restrictions.
Hackney	Accepted provided insemination takes place on premises where stallion is standing and in presence of owner or party authorized to sign certificate of breeding for stallion.
Half-Saddlebred	Accepted provided insemination takes place on premises where stallion is standing and in presence of owner.
Hanoverian	A.I. is accepted.
Lipizzan	A.I. and embryo transfer accepted.
Missouri Fox Trotting Horse	No rules. No horses registered by A.I. to date.
Morab	A.I. not permitted.
Morgan	A.I. and embryo transfer permitted, with stipulations.
National Appaloosa Pony	No rules.
National Show Horse	A.I. and embryo transfer allowed, with stipulations.
National Spotted Saddle Horse	A.I. is accepted.
Norwegian Fjord Horse	Neither A.I. nor embryo transfer allowed.
Paint Horse	Accepted only if semen is used (1) within 24 hours of collection, and (2) on premises of collection. Embryo transfer accepted provided stipulated conditions are met.
Palomino	As "color registries" both Palomino associations recognize the A.I. and embryo transfer rules of the other registry associations in which Palomino horses are registered.

Table 5.1 HORSE ASSOCIATION RULES RELATIVE TO REGISTERING YOUNG PRODUCED BY A.I. OR EMBRYO TRANSFER (*cont.*)

Breed	*Present Rules or Attitude of Registry Association Relative to A.I. or Embryo Transfer*
Paso Fino	A.I. and embryo transfer accepted, according to rules detailed by the registry association.
Peruvian Paso	A.I. and embryo transfer accepted under stipulated rules of each registry association.
Pinto	Accepted provided (1) intent of each A.I. breeding requested in letter to registrar; (2) a veterinarian (not necessarily the same one for each step) certifies to collection of semen, insemination of mare, and birth of foal; and (3) blood type evidence of parentage, along with foaling date, is furnished.
Pony of the Americas	A.I. on the farm where the stallion is located is approved. But mailing of semen is not allowed. No rules regarding embryo transfer.
Quarter Horse	A.I. permitted provided insemination (1) is immediately following collection, and (2) is at the place or premises of collection. Embryo transfer is permitted, but only one genetic offspring per mare per calendar year shall be eligible for registration, unless both foals are the result of the fertilization of one ovum and both foals are carried by one recipient mare following a single implantation.
Rangerbred	No rules. No request to use A.I.
Shetland Pony	No ruling on A.I. or embryo transplant.
Spanish-Barb	A.I. permitted, but (1) must have prior written approval of the Board, (2) both stallion and mare must be blood-typed, and (3) semen must be used within 48 hours. Embryo transfer accepted, but (1) must have prior written approval of the Board and (2) only one embryo transfer will be allowed for a mare in one calendar year.
Spanish Mustang	A.I. accepted, but limited to 100 foals per year. Embryo transfer accepted, but each mare limited to 3 embryo transplants per year.
Standardbred	Accepted provided (1) fresh semen is used (frozen or dessicated semen not permitted), and (2) insemination takes place on same day and same premises where semen was produced.
Tennessee Walking Horse	Accepted provided insemination (1) is done on premises where stallion is standing, and (2) takes place in presence of owner or party authorized to

Breed	*Present Rules or Attitude of Registry Association Relative to A.I. or Embryo Transfer*
	sign certificate of breeding for the stallion used. Embryo transfer is allowed on the basis of one foal per mare per year.
Thoroughbred	Natural service only. But the immediate A.I. reinforcement of the stallion's service with a portion of the ejaculate produced by the stallion during such cover is permitted. Embryo transfer not eligible for registration.
Trakehner	Accepted provided (1) there is prior approval by the Association, (2) semen is used immediately following collection and at the place or premises of collection, and (3) insemination is under supervision of licensed veterinarian. Embryo transfer accepted on the basis of one foal per mare per year, or twins.
Trottingbred	Neither A.I. nor embryo transfer are allowed.
Welsh Pony and Cob	A.I. accepted as stipulated.
Draft Horses:	
American Cream	No rules.
Belgian	Accepted provided stallion and mare were on the same farm at the time mare was bred.
Clydesdale	No rules.
Percheron	Accepted provided (1) semen is obtained from member of Percheron Horse Association of America, or from reputable A.I. establishment; (2) blood type of stallion is on file with the Association; (3) authentication is furnished by owner of stallion, owner of mare, and veterinarian who implanted; and (4) application for registry of A.I.-produced foal is filed before June 1 of the year following date of foaling.
Shire	A.I. and embryo transfer accepted under certain rules.
Suffolk	No rules, but favorable toward A.I.
Jacks and Donkeys:	
Donkeys	American Donkey and Mule Society, Inc.: No rules. Miniature Donkey Registry of the U.S.: No rules.
Jacks and Jennets	Eligible for registration. No stipulations.

[1] The A.I. and embryo transfer regulations of breed registries change from time to time. So, anyone wishing to apply these practices should first secure the latest rules from the intended registry.

"markers" in each sample and then applying the rules of inheritance, parentage can be determined. To qualify as the offspring of a given mare and stallion, an animal must not possess any genetic markers not present in its alleged parents. If it does, it constitutes ground for illegitimacy.

Blood typing is used for the following purposes.

- *To verify parentage* — The test is used in instances where the offspring may bear some unusual color or markings or carry some undesirable recessive characteristic. It may also be used to verify a registration certificate. There is need to use blood typing much more extensively as a bulwark of breed integrity. Through blood typing, parentage can be verified with 90 percent accuracy.[1]

  Although this means that 10 percent of the cases cannot be settled, it is not possible to do any better than that in human blood typing.

- *To determine which of two stallions* — When a mare has been served by two or more stallions during one breeding season, blood typing can identify the sire.

- *To provide a permanent blood type record for identification purposes* — Two samples of blood are required for each animal to be studied; and the samples must be taken in tubes and in keeping with detailed instructions provided by the laboratory. In parentage cases, this calls for blood samples from the foal and both parents; in paternity cases, samples must be taken from the foal, the mare, and all the stallions.

- *To substitute for fingerprinting* — Much attention is now being given to the idea of utilizing blood typing as a positive means of identification of stolen animals, through proving their parentage.

  The following laboratories are capable of determining equine parentage:

IN THE U.S.

Department of Veterinary Sciences, University of Kentucky, 102 Animal Pathology Building, Lexington, Kentucky 40546.

Serology Laboratory, School of Veterinary Medicine, University of California, Davis, California 95616.

Stormont Laboratories, Inc., 1237 E. Beamer St., Suite D, Woodland, California 95695.

IN CANADA

Mann Equitest, Inc., 550 McAdam Road, Mississauga, Ontario, L4Z IPI.

---

[1] In a personal communication to the author, Dr. Clyde Stormont, Professor Emeritus, University of California at Davis and owner of Stormont Laboratories, Inc., 1237 E. Beamer St., Suite D, Woodland, California 95695, reported that they have been able to solve approximately 91 percent of all the parentage cases.

FEEDING HORSES

Figure 6.1 Bright eyed and bushy tailed — signs of a well-fed foal. (Courtesy, The American Morgan Horse Association, Shelburne, Vermont)

Feed is the most important influence in the environment of the horse. Unless properly fed, the horse cannot achieve its maximum potential in reproduction, growth, body form, speed, endurance, style, and attractiveness. Also, feed constitutes the greatest single cost item in the horse business.

Feeding practices vary from one locality to another and among horsemen. The size of individual horses, the use to which they are put, and the size of the enterprise also make for differences.

Fundamentally, the nature of horses remains the same. For this reason, successful feeding in one stable is not much different from successful feeding in another stable.

Skill and good judgment are essential in feeding horses. Horsemen may secure widely different results under similar conditions. The horses may be in the best of condition in one stable and have ani-

149

mation, nerve, speed, and endurance. In another stable, listless animals with dull eyes and rough coats testify to lack of judgment in their feeding and management. The unsatisfactory condition in the latter stable may not mean that the owner tried to economize; horsemen who feed their animals most economically may have the best horses.

Unfortunately, altogether too many horse feeds are based on fads, foibles, and trade secrets, rather than on sound, scientific facts. Worse yet, some concoctions contain ingredients that aren't needed or that are in excess; some of them actually produce harmful imbalances, and all of them cost money.

HORSE FEEDS AND FEEDING FACTS

The following facts relative to horse feeds and feeding are noteworthy:

- *Grass hay and farm grains are inadequate* in quantity and quality proteins, in certain minerals and vitamins, and in unidentified factors; this is especially so during the critical periods (growth, reproduction, lactation, and when under stress) of the horse. It is also noteworthy that in the country of its origin the Arabian never had oats or timothy hay.

- *Horses differ* from other farm animals because (1) they are kept for recreation, sport, and work, instead of for meat, milk, or wool production; (2) they are fed for a longer life of usefulness than meat animals — the latter are usually marketed for slaughter at an early age; (3) they have a smaller digestive tract, which does not permit as much use of bulk as is possible with ruminants; (4) they should not carry surplus body weight; and (5) they are fed for nerve, mettle, animation, and character of muscle, rather than tenderness and flavor.

- *Artificial conditions have been created* for horses, more so than for any other class of livestock. In the wild state, they roamed the plains in bands, with plenty of outdoor exercise on natural footing, fed on feeds derived from unleached soils, and were in unforced production. Today, many horses are stall-fed all or a large part of the year (some horses spend up to 95 percent of their time in a stall); feeds are often produced on depleted soils; and young stock are forced for early growth and use (as in racing two-year-olds). Under these unnatural conditions, (1) unsoundnesses, (2) breeding problems, and (3) nutritional diseases and ailments have become increasingly common.

- *Feed storage and labor costs have spiraled,* with the result that, for reasons of economy, storage space for feed, and labor for feeding and cleanup, should be held to a minimum — factors which favor the use of pelleted feeds.

THE DIGESTIVE SYSTEM

The alimentary canal includes the entire tube extending from the mouth to the rectum. Table 6.1 and Figure 6.2 show the comparative structures and sizes of the digestive tracts of farm animals. As noted, the digestive tract of the horse is anatomically and physiologically quite different from that of the ruminant; and it is much smaller, with the result that horses cannot eat as much roughage as cattle. Also, the primary seats of microbial activity in ruminants and horses occupy different locations in the digestive system in relation to the small intestine. In cows and sheep, the rumen precedes the small intestine; in horses, the cecum follows it.

Both the amount of bacterial synthesis and the efficiency of absorption of nutrients synthesized by the microorganisms are likely to be lower in a horse than in a ruminant. In comparison to a cow, therefore, a horse should be fed less roughage, more and higher quality protein (no urea), and added B vitamins. Actually, the nutrient requirements of a horse appear more nearly parallel to those of a pig than a cow.

STOMACH OF HORSE VS. STOMACH OF COW

Some basic differences between the stomach of the horse and the stomach of the cow are:

- The cow has four compartments (rumen, reticulum, omasum, and the abomasum or true stomach), whereas the horse has one.
- The stomach capacity of the horse is smaller — 8 to 16 quarts for the mature horse (but it functions best at two-thirds capacity) as opposed to about 200 quarts for the mature cow. Because of its small stomach, if a horse is fed too much roughage, labored breathing and quick

Table 6.1 CAPACITIES OF DIGESTIVE TRACTS OF HORSE, COW, AND PIG [1]

Parts of Digestive Tract	Horse (quarts)	Cow (quarts)	Pig (quarts)
Stomach	8 to 16	(200)	6 to 8
Rumen (paunch)		160	
Reticulum (honeycomb)		10	
Omasum (manyplies)		15	
Abomasum (true stomach of cow)		15	
Small intestine	48	62	9
Cecum	28 to 32		
Large intestine	80	40	10

[1] Values are for average-size horses of 1,000 to 1,200 lb.

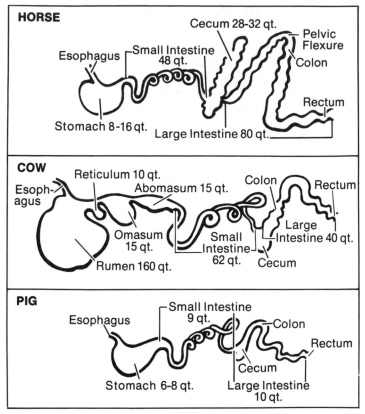

Figure 6.2 Digestive tracts of the horse, cow, and pig.

tiring may result. Actually the horse's stomach is designed for almost constant intake of small quantities of feed (such as happens when a horse is out grazing on grass), rather than large amounts at one time.

- Without feed, the horse's stomach will empty completely in 24 hours, whereas it takes about 72 hours (three times as long) for the cow's stomach to empty. At the time of eating, feed passes through the horse's stomach very rapidly — so much so that the feed eaten at the beginning of the meal passes into the intestine before the last part of the meal is completed.

- There is comparatively little microbial action in the stomach of the horse, but much such action in the stomach (rumen) of the cow.

CECUM SYNTHESIS GIVES ONLY LIMITED ASSIST

In the case of ruminants (cattle and sheep), there is tremendous bacterial action in the paunch. These bacteria build body proteins of high quality from sources of inorganic nitrogen, but nonruminants (humans, rats, swine, poultry, and dogs) cannot do this. Further on in the digestive tract, the ruminant digests the bacteria and obtains good proteins therefrom. Although the horse is not a ruminant, apparently the same bacterial process occurs to a limited extent in the cecum — that greatly enlarged blind pouch of the large intestine of the horse. However, it is much more limited than in ruminants, and the cecum is located beyond the small intestine, the main area for digestion and absorption of nutrients. This points up the fallacy of relying on cecum synthesis in the horse; above all, it must be remembered that little cecum synthesis exists in young equines.

In recognition of the more limited bacterial action in the horse, most state laws forbid the use of such nonprotein nitrogen sources as urea in horse rations. For such an animal, high quality proteins in the diet are requisite to normal development.

The limited protein synthesis in the horse (limited when compared with ruminants), and the lack of efficiency of absorption due to the cecum being on the lower end of the gut (thereby not giving the small intestine a chance at the ingesta after it leaves the cecum), clearly indicate that horse rations should contain high quality proteins, adequate in amino acids.

FUNCTIONS OF FEEDS

The feed consumed by horses is used for a number of different purposes, the exact usage varying somewhat with the class, age, and productivity of the animal. A certain part of the feed is used for the maintenance of bodily functions aside from any useful production. This is known as the maintenance requirement. In addition, feed is used to take care of the functions for which horses are kept. Thus, young growing equines need nutrients suitable for building muscle tissue and bone; horses being readied for show or sale need a surplus of energy feeds for formation of fat; broodmares require feed for the development of their fetuses, and, following parturition, for the production of milk; whereas work animals (horses in heavy use or training, like racehorses) use feed to supply energy for work.

NUTRIENT REQUIREMENTS AND ALLOWANCES

In ration formulation, two words are commonly used — "requirements" and "allowances." Requirements do not provide for margins of safety. Thus, to feed a horse on the basis of meeting the bare requirements would not be unlike building a bridge without providing margins of safety for heavier than average loads or for floods. No competent engineer would be so foolish as to design such a bridge. Likewise, knowledgeable horse nutritionists provide for margins of safety — they provide for the necessary nutritive allowances. They allow for variations in feed composition; possible losses during storage and processing; day to day, and period to period, differences in needs of animals; age and size of animal; stage of gestation and lactation; the kind and degree of activity; the amount of stress; the system of management; the health, condition and temperament of the animal; and the kind, quality, and amount of feed — all of which exert a powerful influence in determining nutritive needs.

RECOMMENDED NUTRIENT ALLOWANCES

Presently available information indicates that the recommended nutrient allowances given in Table 6.2 will meet the minimum requirements for horses and provide reasonable margins of safety. A margin of safety is important, to compensate for (1) variations in feed composition because of the soil on which it was grown, stage of maturity when it was harvested, amount of weathering, and losses in processing and storage; and (2) differences in environment and individual animals.

STRESS AND NUTRITIVE REQUIREMENTS

Stress may be caused by excitement, temperament, fatigue, number of horses together, previous nutrition, breed, age, and management. Race and show horses are always under stress; and the more tired they become and the greater the speed, the greater the stress. Thus, the ration for race and show horses should be scientifically formulated, rather than based on fads, foibles, and trade secrets. The greater the stress, the more exacting the nutritive requirements.

SPECIFIC NUTRIENT NEEDS

To supply all the needs — maintenance, growth, fitting (fattening), reproduction, lactation, and work — the different classes of horses must receive sufficient feed to furnish the necessary quantity of energy (carbohydrates and fats), protein, minerals, and vitamins, plus water.

ENERGY NEEDS

The energy needs of horses vary with the individuality and size of animals, and the kind, amount, and severity of work performed. The energy requirements of a horse when racing may be up to 100 times greater than at rest.

It is common knowledge that a ration must contain proteins, fats, and carbohydrates. Although each of these has specific functions in main-

Figure 6.3 When racing, a horse's energy requirements may be 100 times greater than when he is at rest. (Courtesy, American Quarter Horse Association, Amarillo, Texas)

taining a normal body, they can all be used to provide energy for maintenance, for work, or for fattening. From the standpoint of supplying the normal energy needs of horses, however, the carbohydrates are by far the most important, more of them being consumed than any other compound, whereas the fats are next in importance for energy purposes. In comparison with fats, carbohydrates are usually more abundant and cheaper, and they are very easily digested, absorbed, and transformed into body fat. Besides, carbohydrate feeds may be more easily stored in warm weather and for longer periods of time, whereas feeds high in fat content are likely to become rancid, and rancid feed is unpalatable, if not actually injurious in some instances.

Two methods of measuring energy are used in this country — the total digestible nutrient system (TDN), and the calorie system. The TDN is the sum of the digestible protein, digestible fiber, digestible nitrogen-free extract, and digestible fat, × 2.25. One calorie is the amount of heat required to raise the temperature of one gram of water 1° C (precisely, from 14.5° C to 15.5° C).

Generally, increased energy for horses is met by increasing the grain and decreasing the roughage. Young equines and working (or running) horses must have rations in which a large part of the carbohydrate content of the ration is low in fiber, and in the form of nitrogen-free extract.

A lack of energy may cause slow and stunted growth in foals, and loss of weight, poor condition, and excessive fatigue in mature horses.

Table 6.2 Recommended Nutrient Allowances for Horses (Total Ration/As-Fed Basis)[1]

		Idle Horses/ Light Work/ Moderate Work (1,000 lb. Wt.)	Heavy Training/ Heavy Work (1,000 lb. Wt.)	Stallions in Breeding Season (1,000 lb. Wt.)	Mares, Last 90 Days Gestation (1,000 lb. Wt.)	Mares, Peak of Lactation (1,000 lb. Wt.
Digestible Energy:						
TDN[2]	(%)	55	62.50	75	62.50	75
Mcal per	(lb)	0.8	1.2	1.0	0.90	1.10
Mcal per	(kg)[3]	1.80	2.55	2.15	2.0	2.35
Crude Protein	(%)	9.0	11.0	14.0	13.0	14.0
Lysine	(%)	0.25	0.36	0.30	0.32	0.41
Major or Macrominerals:						
Salt	(%)	0.75	0.75	0.75	0.75	0.75
Calcium	(%)	0.21	0.31	0.26	0.29	0.47
Phosphorus	(%)	0.15	0.23	0.19	0.30	0.30
Magnesium	(%)	0.08	0.12	0.10	0.10	0.09
Potassium	(%)	0.27	0.39	0.33	0.33	0.38
Sulfur	(%)	0.15	0.15	0.15	0.15	0.15
Trace or Microminerals:						
Cobalt	(ppm)[4]	0.11	0.11	0.11	0.11	0.11
Copper	(ppm)	25	25	25	25	30
Iodine	(ppm)	0.11	0.11	0.11	0.11	0.11
Iron	(ppm)	40	60	90	90	90
Manganese	(ppm)	46	46	46	46	46
Selenium	(ppm)	0.11	0.11	0.11	0.11	0.11
Zinc	(ppm)	80	90	90	100	100
		(/lb.)	(/lb.)	(/lb.)	(/lb.)	(/lb.)
Fat-soluble Vitamins in Feed:						
Vitamin A	(IU)	1,045	1,045	1,045	1,569	1,569
Vitamin D	(IU)	156	156	156	314	314
Vitamin E	(IU)	26	41	41	41	41
Vitamin K	(mg)	0.32	0.32	0.32	0.32	0.32
Water-soluble Vitamins in Feed:						
Biotin	(mg)	0.1	0.1	0.1	0.1	0.1
Choline	(mg)	20	30	30	30	30
Folacin	(mg)	0.8	1.2	1.2	1.2	1.2
Niacin	(mg)	10	20.8	10	10	10
Pantothenic acid	(mg)	10	20.8	10	10	10
Riboflavin	(mg)	1.6	1.6	1.6	1.6	1.6
Thiamin (B-1)	(mg)	1.57	2.61	1.57	1.57	1.57
Vitamin B-6	(mg)	1.0	1.0	1.0	1.0	1.0
Vitamin B-12	(mg)	0.005	0.006	0.006	0.006	0.006
Vitamin C (Ascorbic acid)	(mg)	2.4	4.0	4.0	4.0	4.0

Mature Horses (Consuming 25 lb. feed/horse/day. Idle horses require less feed and/or consume more roughage than heavily worked horses or lactating mares.)

[1] Where hay is fed separately, double the amounts shown in this table should be added to the concentrate.
[2] 1 lb TDN (total digestible nutrients) = 2 Mcal or 2,000 Kcal.
[3] 1 kg = 2.2 lb or 1,000 g.
[4] 1 ppm (part per million) = 1 mg/kg.

Young Horses
(Based on Mature Weight 1,000 lb.)

Creep Feed (250 lb. Body Wt./11 lb. Feed Daily)	Weanlings (450 lb. Body Wt./12 lb. Feed Daily)	Yearlings (650 lb. Body Wt./13 lb. Feed Daily)	2-Yr-Olds & 3-Yr-Olds (800 lb. Body Wt./14 lb. Feed Daily)	2-Yr-Olds in Light Training (800 lb. Body Wt./15 lb. Feed Daily)
75	75	70	60	65
1.25	1.25	1.15	1.00	1.10
2.60	2.60	2.50	2.20	2.40
18.0	16.0	14.0	13.0	13.0
0.54	0.55	0.48	0.38	0.41
0.75	0.75	0.75	0.75	0.75
0.62	0.55	0.40	0.28	0.31
0.34	0.30	0.22	0.15	0.17
0.07	0.07	0.07	0.08	0.09
0.27	0.27	0.27	0.27	0.29
0.15	0.15	0.15	0.15	0.15
0.11	0.11	0.11	0.11	0.11
40	40	30	25	25
0.11	0.11	0.11	0.11	0.11
90	80	60	60	60
46	46	46	46	46
0.11	0.11	0.11	0.11	0.11
100	100	100	90	90
(/lb.)	(/lb.)	(/lb.)	(/lb.)	(/lb.)
1,045	1,045	1,045	1,045	1,045
419	419	419	419	419
41	41	41	41	41
0.30	0.30	0.30	0.30	0.30
0.1	0.1	0.1	0.1	0.1
62.5	62.5	62.5	62.5	62.5
3.0	3.0	3.0	3.0	3.0
10	10	10	10	10
10	10	10	10	10
1.6	1.6	1.6	1.6	1.6
1.57	1.57	1.57	1.57	1.57
0.5	0.5	0.5	0.5	0.5
0.007	0.007	0.007	0.007	0.007
3.75	3.75	3.75	3.75	3.75

PROTEIN NEEDS

Proteins are complex organic compounds made up chiefly of amino acids, which are present in characteristic proportions for each specific protein. This nutrient always contains carbon, hydrogen, oxygen, and nitrogen; and, in addition, it usually contains sulfur and frequently phosphorus. Proteins are essential in all plant and animal life as components of the active protoplasm of each living cell.

Crude protein is determined by finding the nitrogen content of a product, then multiplying the result by 6.25 (100 ÷ 16 = 6.25), because protein contains 16% nitrogen. Digestible protein is ingested food protein which is absorbed.

In plants, the protein is largely concentrated in the actively growing portions, especially the leaves and seeds. Legumes also have the ability to synthesize their own proteins from such relatively simple soil and air compounds as carbon dioxide, water, nitrates, and sulfates. Thus, plants, together with some bacteria that are able to synthesize these products, are the original sources of all proteins.

In animals, proteins are much more widely distributed than in plants. Thus, the proteins of the animal body are primary constituents of many structural and protective tissues, such as bones, ligaments, hair, hoofs, skin, and the soft tissues, which include the organs and muscles. The total protein content of a horse's body ranges from about 10 percent in very fat mature horses to 20 percent in thin young foals. By way of further contrast, it is also interesting to note that, except for the limited bacterial action in the cecum, horses lack the ability of the plant to synthesize proteins from simple materials. They must depend upon plants as a source of dietary protein. In brief, except for the proteins built by the bacterial action in the cecum, they must have amino acids or more complete protein compounds in the ration.

Horses of all ages and kinds require adequate amounts of protein of suitable quality, for maintenance, growth, fattening, reproduction, and work. Of course, the protein requirements for growth and reproduction are the greatest and most critical.

A deficiency of proteins in the horse may result in the following deficiency symptoms: depressed appetite, poor growth, loss of weight, reduced milk production, irregular estrus, lowered foal crops, loss of condition, and lack of stamina.

Since the vast majority of protein requirements given in feeding standards meet minimum needs only, the allowances for race, show, breeding, and young animals should be higher. *Caution:* Increasing the protein in foal rations to stimulate growth without providing adequate levels of minerals may cause skeletal deformities and leg weaknesses which cannot be reversed.

Quality of Protein

In addition to supplying an adequate quantity of proteins, it is essential that the character of proteins be thoroughly understood. Proteins are very complex compounds with each molecule made up of hundreds of thousands of amino acids combined with each other. The amino acids, of which some 23 are known, are sometimes referred to as the building blocks of proteins. Certain of these amino acids can be made by the animal's body to satisfy its needs. Others cannot be formed fast enough to supply the body's needs, and therefore are known as essential (or indispensable) amino acids. These must be supplied in the feed. Thus, rations that furnish an insufficient amount of any of the essential amino acids are said to have proteins of poor quality, whereas those which provide the proper proportions of the various necessary amino acids are said to supply proteins of good quality. In general, proteins of plant origin (linseed meal, cottonseed meal, and soybean meal) are not of as good quality as proteins of animal origin and their by-products.

The necessity of each amino acid in the diet of the experimental rat has been thoroughly tested, but less is known about the requirements of large animals or even of humans. According to our present knowledge, based largely on work with the rat, the following division of amino acids as indispensable and dispensable seems proper:

Indispensable (essential): arginine, histidine, isoleucine, leucine, lysine, methionine, phenylalanine, threonine, tryptophan, valine.

Dispensable (not essential): alanine, aspartic acid, citrulline, cysteine, cystine, glutamic acid, glycine, hydroxyglutamic acid, hydroxyproline, norleucine, proline, serine, tyrosine.

In recognition that lysine is the first limiting amino acid of horses (the amino acid in a protein that is first to limit production because of its insufficiency) and is thus an indicator of protein quality, the recommended lysine allowance for horses is given in Table 6.2.

Fortunately, the amino acid content of proteins from various sources varies. Thus, the deficiencies of one protein may be improved by combining it with another, and the mixture of the two proteins often will have a higher feeding value than either one alone. It is for this reason, along with added palatability, that a considerable variety of feeds in the horse ration is desirable.

The feed proteins are broken down into amino acids by digestion. They are then absorbed and distributed by the bloodstream to the body cells, which rebuild these amino acids into body proteins.

Protein Poisoning

Some opinions to the contrary, protein poisoning as such has never been documented. There is no proof that heavy feeding of high protein feeds to horses is harmful, provided (1) the ration is balanced out in all other respects, (2) the animal's kidneys are normal and healthy (a large excess of protein in terms of body needs increases the work of the kidneys for the excretion of the urea), (3) any ration change to high protein feed is made gradually, as is recommended for any change in feed, and (4) there is adequate exercise and normal metabolism.

Some horses do appear to be allergic to certain proteins or to excesses of specific amino acids, as a result of which they may develop "protein bumps."

Metabolic bone disease (MBD) — In recent years, there has been a great increase in metabolic bone disease in growing horses, especially epi-physitis, contracted tendons, and osteochondritis dissecans (OCD). A brief description of each of these conditions follows:

1. *Epiphysitis.* This is an inflammation of the growth plate of the long bones, primarily found at the lower end of the radius above the knee, but it may be noticeable at the distal tibial and the distal metacarpal and metatarsal bones. Epiphysitis results in a firm and painful swelling.

2. *Contracted tendons.* This involves a shortening of the flexor tendons, causing the heels to be raised and the pasterns to be straight or, in severe cases, to knuckle forward with the horse walking on its toe. Contracted tendons may be present at birth, or they may be acquired during growth.

3. *Osteochondritis dissecans (OCD).* This is a condition in which the cartilage in a growing foal does not properly convert into bone. It may appear in either of two forms: (a) the form in which it is localized in one or a few joints (most commonly the stifle and hock joints, although any joint may be involved), usually without any clinical signs; and (b) the second and less common form, which usually affects the more distal limb joints such as the pastern and fetlock, although it may affect any joint, including those of the back.

At this time, the cause of the increase in the incidence of the above bone diseases is not entirely clear. However, it appears that the major factors are: (1) rapid growth and excess weight, (2) injury to the epi-physis, (3) nutritional imbalances, (4) genetic predisposition, (5) limited forced exercise, (6) exercise on hard ground, and (7) faulty conformation.

Based on experiments and experiences to date, the author recommends (1) that breeders continue to feed a legume hay to pregnant mares and growing horses, and (2) that the levels of calcium, phosphorus, copper, iron, manganese, and zinc be in keeping with the recommendations given in Table 6.2 of this book.

It is recognized that protein in excess of what the body can use tends to be wasted insofar as its specific functions are concerned, since it cannot be stored in any but very limited amounts and must be catabolized. Nevertheless, some wastage of protein in terms of its known functions may be both physiologically and economically desirable in order to (1) maintain the protein reserves, (2) provide an adequate protein-calorie ratio for efficient energy utilization, and (3) assure that protein quality needs are met, despite the marked difference of quality among commonly fed rations. Generally speaking, high protein feeds are more expensive than high energy feeds (feeds high in carbohydrates and fats), with the result that there is the temptation to feed too little of them.

MINERALS

When we think of minerals for the horse, we instinctively think of bones and unsoundnesses. This is so because (1) a horse's skeleton is very large, weighing 100 lb. or more in a full-grown horse, of which more than half consists of organic matter or minerals, and (2) experienced trainers estimate that one-third of the horses in training require treatments for unsoundnesses, in one form or another. But in addition to furnishing structural material for the growth of bones, teeth, and tissues, minerals regulate many of the life processes.

The classical horse ration of grass hay and farm grains is usually deficient in calcium, but adequate in phosphorus. Also, salt is almost always deficient; and many horse rations do not contain sufficient iodine and certain other trace elements. Thus, horses usually need special mineral supplements. But they should not be fed either more or less minerals than needed.

In an amazingly short time after birth, a healthy foal can run almost as fast as its mother — and on legs almost as long. In fact, the cannon bones (the lower leg bones extending from the knees and hocks to the fetlocks) are as long at the time of birth as they ever will be. This indicates that important development of the skeleton takes place in the fetus, before the foal is born. It is evident, therefore, that adequate minerals must be provided the broodmare if the bones of her offspring are to be sound.

Although acute mineral-deficiency diseases and actual death losses are relatively rare, inadequate supplies of any one of the 18 essential mineral elements may result in lack of thrift, poor gains, inefficient feed utilization, lowered reproduction, and decreased performance in racing, showing, riding, or whatnot.

The 18 mineral elements which have been shown to be essential for at least some animal species are: calcium, chlorine, chromium, cobalt, copper, fluorine, iodine, iron, magnesium, manganese, molybdenum, phosphorus, potassium, selenium, silicon, sodium, sulfur, and zinc. This does not mean that all 18 of these minerals must always be included in horse mineral supplements. Rather, only the specific minerals that are deficient in the ration — and in the quantities necessary — should be supplied. *Excesses and mineral imbalances are to be avoided.*

Major Minerals

The major minerals are: salt (sodium chloride), calcium/phosphorus, magnesium, potassium, and sulfur.

Salt (Sodium Chloride) — Salt, which serves as both a condiment and a nutrient, is needed by all classes of animals, but more especially by herbivores (grass-eating animals). It may be provided in the form of granulated, rock, or block salt. In general, the form selected is determined by price and availability. It is to be pointed out, however, that it is difficult for horses to eat very hard block and rock salt. This often results in inadequate consumption. Also, if there is much competition for the salt block in a pasture, the more timid animals may not get their requirements. Individual salt bricks can be placed in each horse's stall.

Iodized salt should be provided in iodine-deficient areas. Trace-mineralized salt is recommended, because it is a simple, safe means of providing iodine and other trace minerals at only slightly greater cost than common salt.

Both sodium and chlorine are essential to animal life. They are necessary in maintaining the osmotic presssure of body cells (thereby assisting in the transfer of nutrients to the cells and the removal of waste materials). Also, sodium is important as one of the main body buffers and in making bile, which aids in the digestion of fats and carbohydrates. Chlorine is required for the formation of the hydrochloric acid in the gastric juice, so vital to protein digestion. The blood contains 0.25 percent chlorine, 0.22 percent sodium, and 0.02 to 0.22 percent potassium; thus, the chlorine content is higher than that of any other mineral in the blood. The salt requirement is greatly increased under conditions which cause heavy sweating, thereby resulting in large losses of this mineral from the body. Unless it is replaced, fatigue will result. For this reason, when engaged in hard work and perspiring profusely, horses should receive liberal allowances of salt.

On the average, a horse needs about 3 ounces of salt daily, or 1⅓ lb. per week, although salt requirements vary with work and temperature. Salt can be fed free choice to horses, provided they have not been salt-starved. That is, if the animals have not previously been fed salt for a considerable length of time, they may overeat, resulting in digestive disturbances and even death. Salt-starved animals should first be hand-fed salt, and the daily allowance should be increased gradually until they start leaving a little in the mineral box. When this point is reached, self-feeding may be followed. The Indians and the pioneers of this country handed down many legendary stories about the large numbers of buffalo and deer that killed themselves simply by gorging at a newly found salt lick after having been salt-starved for long periods of time.

When added to the concentrate ration, salt should be added at a level of 0.5 to 1.0 percent.

Calcium and Phosphorus — Horses are more apt to suffer from a lack of calcium and phosphorus than from any of the other minerals except salt. These two minerals comprise about three-quarters of the ash of the skeleton and from one-third to one-half of the minerals of milk.

Knowledge of the following general characteristics of feeds in regard to calcium and phosphorus is important in rationing horses.

- The cereal grains and their by-products and straws, dried mature grasses, and protein supplements of plant origin are low in calcium.
- The protein supplements of animal origin and legume forage are rich in calcium.
- The cereal grains and their by-products are fairly high or even rich in phosphorus, but a large portion of the phosphorus is not readily available.
- Almost all protein-rich supplements are high in phosphorus. But, here again, plant sources of phosphorus contain much of this element in a bound form.
- Beet by-products and dried, mature nonleguminous forages (such as grass hays and fodders) are likely to be low in phosphorus.
- The calcium and phosphorus content of plants can be increased through fertilizing the soil upon which they are grown.

The availability to the horse of calcium and phosphorus in common feedstuffs is unknown. But the availability of calcium is assumed to be 55 to 75 percent, and the availability of phosphorus is assumed to be 35 to 55 percent. Several factors account for this poor absorption, including the calcium-phosphorus ratio, level of intake, source of calcium and phosphorus, and the presence of organic inhibitors such as oxalate and phytate. Also, aged animals (animals over 20 years of age) tend to utilize calcium and phosphorus poorly, so their requirements for these minerals are higher than for younger animals.

In considering the calcium and phosphorus requirements of horses, it is important to realize that the proper utilization of these minerals by the body is dependent upon three factors: (1) an adequate supply of calcium and phosphorus in an available form; (2) a suitable ratio between the two minerals; and (3) sufficient vitamin D to make possible the assimilation and utilization of the calcium and phosphorus. If plenty of vitamin D is present (as provided either by sunlight or through the ration), the ratio of calcium to phosphorus becomes less important. Also, less vitamin D is needed when there is a desirable calcium-phosphorus ratio.

Normally, the calcium to phosphorus ratio should be about 1.1:1. However, the ratio varies according to age. For example, older horses can have a calcium-phosphorus ratio of 2:1. Provided adequate phosphorus is fed, weanling foals will *tolerate* a 3:1 ratio and mature horses a 5:1 ratio. It is important, however, to have more calcium than phosphorus — but not too much calcium. Feeding excessive calcium interferes with the utilization of magnesium, manganese, and iron, and perhaps with the utilization of zinc. For guidance relative to the proper amounts of calcium and phosphorus in the ration, and the correct ratio of the two minerals, horsemen may follow the recommendations given in Table 6.2 of this book, and seek the counsel of their nutritionist or veterinarian.

Lack of either or both calcium and phosphorus can result in bone disorders, with the type and severity of the disorder dependent upon the age of the animal and the degree and duration of the deficiency. Deficiency in young horses is generally characterized by poorly formed, soft bones, which may bend or bow; and deficiency in older animals, by porous, fragile bones. Because these conditions are not completely reversible, prevention is imperative.

A deficiency of either calcium or phosphorus will cause rickets in foals. Also, there is substantial evidence that lack of calcium and phosphorus, along with deficiencies of copper and zinc, cause epiphysitis, contracted tendons, and osteochondritis dissecans (OCD) in young horses.

Bone disturbances (called osteodystrophia febrosa, nutritional secondary hyperparathyroidism, osteomalacia, osteoporosis, and Miller's disease) develop in adult horses fed rations containing limited calcium and high phosphorus. The disease develops when rations with a calcium-phosphorus ratio of 0.8:1 are fed for 6 to 12 months, and it progresses rapidly when the ratio is 0.6:1.

Generally speaking, legume forages, such as alfalfa or clover mix hay or pasture, are rich in calcium; cereal grains and their by-products — oats, corn, barley, and wheat bran — are fair to good sources of phosphorus; and the protein supplements — linseed meal, soybean meal, and dried skim milk — are good sources of both calcium and phosphorus. So, by selecting and combining the common horse feeds properly, the maintenance needs of most horses can be met.

Where both calcium and phosphorus are needed, the author favors the use of high-quality steamed bone meal for horses, because bone meal contains many ingredients in addition to calcium and phosphorus. It is a good source of iron, manganese, and zinc, and it contains such trace minerals as copper and cobalt. However, it is increasingly difficult to get good bone meal. Some of the imported products are high in fat, rancid, and/or odorous and unpalatable. Where good bone meal is not available, dicalcium phosphate is generally recommended.

When calcium alone is needed, ground limestone or oystershell flour are commonly used.

Where phosphorus alone is needed, defluorinated rock phosphate, sodium monophosphate, or sodium polyphosphate are the minerals of choice. Sodium monophosphate and sodium polyphosphate are not palatable, hence it is important that they be combined with more palatable products.

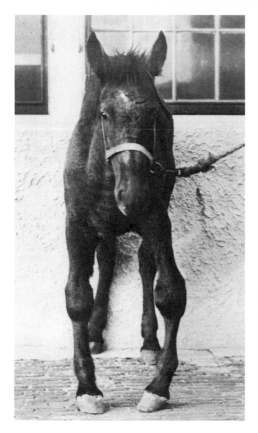

Figure 6.4 Foal with severe rickets, showing the enlarged joints and crooked legs. Rickets may be caused by a lack of calcium, phosphorus, or vitamin D, or by an incorrect ratio of the two minerals. (Courtesy, College of Veterinary Medicine, University of Illinois, Urbana)

Magnesium — Rations containing 50 percent forage will likely contain sufficient magnesium for unstressed horses, unless the forage is known to be deficient in magnesium. But horses at hard work (as in racing and showing) consume more grain (which is low in magnesium) and less forage. Also, horses being raced or shown, or otherwise stressed, are frequently keyed up, high-strung, and jumpy, showing a nervousness similar to the behavior of animals and humans known to be suffering from a magnesium deficiency.

In view of the above, it would appear prudent that one-half to two-thirds of the recommended daily magnesium allowance of the horse be added to the ration.

Potassium — Forage-consuming animals generally require about 0.3 percent of potassium in their rations. A ration that contains at least 50 percent forage can be expected to meet potassium requirements. However, a horse ration that does not contain roughage, molasses, or oil meals may be deficient in potassium.

Significant amounts of potassium are lost during heavy sweating.

A reduced appetite is an early sign of a potassium deficiency. A severe deficiency may cause muscle tremors and erratic heartbeat.

Sulfur — If the protein requirement of the ration is met, the sulfur intake will usually be at least 0.15 percent, which appears to be adequate.

Trace Minerals

The need for trace minerals may be inferred from the many reports on the value of blackstrap molasses (a good source of trace minerals) for horses fed low quality hays.

Trace minerals may be supplied (1) as part of either the concentrate or complete ration, and/or (2) in a trace-mineralized (TM) salt. When incorporated in the concentrate mix, TM salt should be added at the rate of 1 percent. When TM salt is fed free choice, it may be in either loose or block form, which should be placed in a conveniently located covered mineral box in amounts that will be consumed in not more than one to two weeks. When remaining in a mineral box longer than this period of time, it may become unpalatable and there may be losses of some elements.

A discussion of each of the trace minerals follows.

Cobalt — Cobalt is required for the synthesis of vitamin B-12 in the intestinal tract of the horse. A lack of cobalt and/or B-12 will result in anemia. Also, it is noteworthy that an anemia in horses has responded to vitamin B-12 treatment; and, of course, B-12 contains cobalt in the molecular structure. Thus, inclusion of cobalt in the ration of horses is in the nature of good insurance.

Copper — A copper deficiency has been reported in Australia in horses grazing on pastures low in copper. Also, mare's milk (along with milk from all species) is low in copper, and its copper concentration decreases greatly during the first weeks of lactation. The presence of 5 to 25 ppm (parts per million) of molybdenum in forages causes disturbances in copper utilization in horses.

Copper is of special interest to horsemen because, in addition to its effect on iron metabolism, it is closely associated with normal bone development in young growing animals of all species. Abnormal bone development has been reported in foals on low copper rations.

There are wide species differences in tolerance to copper. Horses are very tolerant of copper, whereas sheep are very sensitive to it. The maximum tolerable levels of copper for growing animals in parts per million (ppm), according to the National Academy of Sciences, are: horses, 800 ppm; chicken, 300 ppm; swine, 250 ppm; cattle, 100 ppm; and sheep, 25 ppm.

The author's recommended copper allowances are: 30 ppm of the total ration for lactating mares, and 40 ppm for young horses. (See Table 6.2.)

In high-molybdenum areas, it is recommended that the copper level for horses be about five times higher than the normal level.

Iodine — Pregnant mares are very susceptible to iodine deficiency. Where such a deficiency exists, the foals are usually stillborn or so weak that they cannot stand and suck. There is also some evidence to indicate that the incidence of navel ill in foals may be lessened by feeding iodine to broodmares.

More than half of the total iodine content of the body is located in the thyroid gland of the neck. Iodine, which is secreted by the thyroid gland in the form of thyroxin (an iodine-containing hormone), controls the rate of metabolism of the body.

If the soil — and the water and feed crops coming therefrom — is low in iodine, the body is likely to show deficiency symptoms in the form of simple goiter, unless an adequate source of iodine is provided artificially. A goiter is simply an enlargement of the thyroid gland, which is nature's way of trying to make enough thyroxin when there is insufficient iodine in the feed. However, iodine-deficiency symptoms are not always evidenced by the appearance of goiter, although this is the most common characteristic of such deficiency. In foals, the only symptom may be extreme weakness at birth, resulting in an inability to stand and suck.

Iodine deficiencies are worldwide. In the United States, the northwestern states, the Pacific Coast, and the Great Lakes region are classed as goiter areas.

The simplest method of supplying iodine in deficient areas is through use of salt containing (a) 0.01 percent potassium iodide (0.0076 percent iodine), or (b) calcium iodate. Most of the salt companies now manufacture stabilized iodized salt. If iodized salt is fed, additional iodine supplementation is unnecessary. Organic iodine supplements, such as kelp, are not any better than iodized salt.

Iodized salt should always be kept in a dry place and it should be kept fresh. It should also be provided in such form and quantities as to ensure an adequate intake of iodine.

Iron — If horses are fed diets that are too low in iron, or in iron and copper, nutritional anemia results.

The National Academy of Sciences estimates the maintenance requirements of the horse for iron at 40 ppm, and the requirements of foals at 50 ppm. However, it has been reported that horses which are subjected to stresses from racing, showing, or other heavy use, require higher levels of iron.

To be on the safe side, approximately one-half of the iron requirement of the horse should be added to the ration, and it should be in a biologically available form, such as ferric chloride (iron oxide should not be used as a source of iron for horses because it is poorly absorbed).

Manganese — Feeds containing 60 to 70 ppm of manganese are recommended, with the higher levels fed to foals, stressed horses, and breeding animals.

Since most natural feedstuffs are rich in manganese, it can be assumed that part of the requirement for this element will be met by the normal ration.

Selenium — Selenium is an essential mineral for horses. Deficient animals have muscle disorders and lowered serum selenium.

It is recommended that horse rations contain 0.1 ppm of selenium in the complete feed. Excess selenium above 5 ppm results in selenium poisoning, or alkali disease.

Zinc — A level of 80 to 100 ppm of zinc is recommended, with young and highly stressed animals receiving the upper level.

Zinc is necessary for the maintenance and development of skin and hair. Since beautiful hair coats are important in horses, fortifying the daily ration with zinc will prevent any possibility of a zinc deficiency; and if the zinc in the feed is on the low side, the supplement should improve the hair coat.

Chelated Trace Minerals

The word chelate is derived from the Greek *chelae,* meaning a claw or pincerlike organ. Those selling chelated minerals generally recommend a smaller quantity of them (but at a higher price per pound) and extol their "fenced-in" properties.

When it comes to synthetic chelating agents, much needs to be learned about their selectivity toward minerals, the kind and quantity most effective, their mode of action, and their effects upon different species of animals with varying rations.

It is possible that use of chelated minerals may actually create a mineral imbalance. These answers, and more, should be forthcoming through carefully controlled experiments.

Mineral Imbalances

Having the right balance and forms of minerals can be very important. The more calcium you feed, the more phosphorus you need. The more copper you feed, the more manganese you need.

Also, minerals can be fed in several different forms. For example, iron can be fed as an oxide, sulfite, sulfate, or as a proteinate. Oxides may be absorbed at about 2 to 5 percent, while sulfites may be absorbed at up to 10 percent, and sulfates at 25 percent.

Thus, the requirements of any mineral may be modified (1) by another mineral which enhances or interferes with its utilization, or (2) by the form of the mineral.

From the above, it is apparent that excess fortification of the horse's ration with one or more mineral elements may prove more detrimental than helpful. Thus, caretakers who know and care will avoid harmful imbalances; they will provide minerals on the basis of *recommended al-*

lowances (see Table 6.2). Also, when fortifying rations with minerals, consideration should be given to the minerals provided by the ingredients of the normal ration, for it is the total composition of the feed that counts.

Feeding Minerals

With the exception of sodium, the self-feeding of the major minerals cannot be relied upon to meet the needs of horses. This is so because horses consume such supplements on the basis of palatability, rather than because of dietary need. As a result, the free-choice intake of minerals among individual horses will vary from too little to too much. Sometimes minerals are incorporated in a salt mix, but salt consumption is erratic and variable according to the sodium content of the feedstuffs being fed. So, the only way to ensure that each horse receives the needed major minerals is to incorporate the proper amounts in the animal's feed and/or water.

Trace minerals may be added to the ration and/or incorporated in the salt. In either case, the amounts and proportions of trace minerals should be selected with care because the improper use of trace minerals can lead to induced deficiencies. Theoretically, the total ration (grain plus forage) should be balanced in trace mineral content, with the trace mineral mix providing only the minerals needed and with each one in the right amount. Of course, this isn't practical. Therefore, a trace mineral mix must contain an array of minerals in adequate levels to meet a wide variety of conditions. Fortunately, the horse is tolerant of most trace mineral excesses.

When horses are on pasture and no grain or protein supplement is being fed, minerals may be self-fed, usually as either a commercially manufactured mineral block or as a mineral mixture. A suitable home-mixed mineral for horses on pasture may be prepared as follows:

1. *Where the pasture is primarily grass.* Prepare a mixture containing two parts of calcium to one part of phosphorus.

2. *Where the pasture is primarily a legume.* Prepare a mixture containing one part of calcium to one part of phosphorus.

To each of the above mixes, add one-third trace-mineralized salt to provide the microminerals and improve the palatability.

VITAMINS[1]

The lack of vitamins in a horse ration may, under certain conditions, be more serious than a short supply of feed. Deficiencies may lead to

---

[1] In this section, when reference is made to a National Academy of Science recommendation, the following source is cited: *Nutrient Requirements of Horses,* No. 6, 5th rev. ed., National Academy of Sciences, 1989.

failure in growth or reproduction, poor health, and even characteristic disorders known as deficiency diseases.

Unfortunately, there are no warning signals to tell a caretaker when a horse is not getting enough of certain vitamins. But a continuing inadequate supply of any one of several vitamins can produce illness which is very hard to diagnose until it becomes severe, at which time it is difficult and expensive — if not too late — to treat. The important thing, therefore, is to insure against such deficiencies occurring. But caretakers should not shower a horse with mistaken kindness through using shotgun-type vitamin preparations. Instead, the quantity to be fed of each vitamin should be based on available scientific knowledge.

It has long been known that the vitamin content of feeds varies considerably according to soil, climatic conditions, and curing and storing.

Deficiencies may occur during periods (1) of extended drought or in other conditions of restriction in diet, (2) when production is being forced, or during stress, (3) when large quantities of highly refined feeds are being fed, or (4) when low quality forages are utilized.

Certain vitamins are necessary for the growth, development, health, and reproduction of horses. Deficiencies of vitamins A and D are sometimes encountered. Also, indications are that vitamin E and some of the B vitamins are required by horses. Further, it is recognized that single, uncomplicated vitamin deficiencies are the exception rather than the rule.

High quality, leafy, green forages plus plenty of sunshine generally give horses most of the vitamins they need. Horses get carotene (which they can convert to vitamin A) and riboflavin from green pasture and green hay not over a year old, and they get vitamin D from sunlight and sun-cured hay. If plenty of green forage and sunlight are not available, the caretaker should get the advice of a nutritionist or veterinarian on the use of vitamin additives to the feed.

Table 6.2 lists the vitamins most commonly involved in horse nutrition and gives recommended allowances for each of them.

Fat-soluble Vitamins

The fat-soluble vitamins, which are stored in the body in appreciable quantities, are vitamin A (carotene), vitamin D, vitamin E, and vitamin K.

Vitamin A — Vitamin A is strictly a product of animal metabolism, no vitamin A being found in plants. The counterpart in plants is known as carotene, which is the precursor of vitamin A. Because the animal body can transform carotene into vitamin A, this compound is often spoken of as *provitamin A.*

Carotene is the yellow-colored, fat-soluble substance that gives the characteristic color to carrots and to butterfat (vitamin A is nearly a colorless substance). Carotene derives its name from the carrot, from which it was first isolated over 100 years ago. Though the yellow color

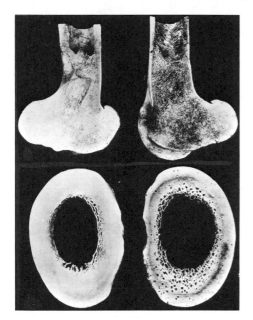

Figure 6.5 Vitamin A made the difference! *Upper row:* On the right is the sagittal section of the distal end of the femur of a vitamin A-deficient horse, compared to normal bone (left). *Lower row:* Cross section of the cannon bone from a vitamin A-deficient horse (on the right), compared to normal bone (left). (Courtesy, University of California, Agricultural Experiment Station, Davis)

is masked by the green chlorophyll, the green parts of plants are rich in carotene and have a high vitamin A value. Also, the degree of greenness in a roughage is a good index of its carotene content, provided it has not been stored too long. Early cut, leafy green hays are very high in carotene.

Vitamin A is not synthesized in the cecum. Thus, it must be provided in the feed, either (1) as vitamin A, or (2) as carotene, the precursor of vitamin A. For horses, 1 mg of beta-carotene is equivalent to 400 IU of vitamin A.

Aside from yellow corn, practically all of the cereal grains used in horse feeding have little carotene or vitamin A value. Even yellow corn has only about one-tenth as much carotene as well-cured hay. Dried peas of the green and yellow varieties and carrots are also valuable sources of carotene.

Severe deficiency of vitamin A may cause night blindness (impaired adaptation to darkness), lacrimation (tears), keratinization of the cornea and skin, reproductive difficulties, poor or uneven hoof development, difficulty in breathing, incoordination, convulsive seizures, progressive weakness, and poor appetite. There is also some evidence that deficiency of this vitamin may cause or contribute to certain leg bone weaknesses. When vitamin A deficiency symptoms appear, the horseman should add a stabilized vitamin A product to the ration.

A considerable margin of safety in vitamin A and carotene is provided in the recommended allowances in Table 6.2, since these materials tend to be lost through oxidation in feeds during storage. But, it is wasteful to feed more vitamin A than is needed. Also, feeding exceedingly high levels of vitamin A over an extended period of time may cause bone fragility, hyperostosis, and exfoliated epithelium. When fed as directed, the vast majority of horse feeds won't provide excesses of vitamin A.

Fortunately, horses are able to store vitamin A, primarily in the liver, during periods of abundance to tide them through periods of scarcity. Thus, horses that have been consuming green forage for 4 to 6 weeks usually store sufficient vitamin A in the liver to maintain adequate levels of plasma vitamin A for 3 to 6 months.

It is noteworthy (1) that the absorption of vitamin A is adversely affected by the presence of parasites in the intestinal tract, and (2) that the presence of enough protein of good quality enhances the conversion of carotene to vitamin A.

It is generally believed that stressed horses have a higher vitamin A requirement than those not under stress. Among such stress factors are: racing, showing, fatigue, hot weather, confinement, excitement, and number of animals run together.

The vitamin A requirements for gestating mares may be five times the minimum maintenance requirements. Therefore, unless properly fed, broodmares may become almost depleted of their vitamin A reserves by the end of winter — at a time when a vitamin A deficiency could be critical to the rapid development of the fetus.

Vitamin D — For horses, both D-2 (the plant form) and D-3 (the animal form) are equally effective, so there is no need to use some of each.

Foals sometimes develop rickets because of insufficient vitamin D, calcium, or phosphorus. Rickets is characterized by reduced bone calcification, stiff and swollen joints, stiffness of gait, irritability, and reduction in serum calcium and phosphorus (see p. 228). It can be prevented by exposing the animal to direct sunlight as much as possible, by allowing free access to a suitable mineral mixture, or by providing good quality sun-cured hay or luxuriant pasture grown on well-fertilized soil. In northern areas that do not have adequate sunshine, many horsemen provide the foal with a vitamin D supplement.

With vitamin D, as with vitamin A, there is need for adequacy without harmful excesses. Too much vitamin D may harm a horse. Vitamin D toxicity is characterized by calcification of the blood vessels, heart, and other soft tissues, and by bone abnormalities. Also, there is general weakness and loss of body weight. Although the toxic level of vitamin D in the horse has not been established, a level 50 times the requirement may be harmful.

The vitamin D requirement is lower when a proper balance of calcium and phosphorus exists in the ration.

Of all the known vitamins, vitamin D has the most limited distribution in common feeds. Very little of this factor is contained in the cereal grains and their by-products, in roots and tubers, in feeds of animal origin, or in growing pasture grasses. The only important natural

Figure 6.6 Osteomalacia of the facial bones in a Hackney. This deficiency disease in mature horses may be caused by (1) a lack of vitamin D, (2) a lack of calcium or phosphorus, or (3) an incorrect ratio of calcium to phosphorus. (Courtesy, College of Veterinary Medicine, University of Illinois, Urbana)

sources of vitamin D are sun-cured hay and other roughages. The chief vitamin-D-rich concentrates include vitamin D-2, vitamin D-3, sun-cured hay, cod and certain other fish liver oils, irradiated cholesterol and ergosterol, and irradiated yeast.

The effectiveness of sunlight is determined by the lengths and intensity of the ultraviolet rays which reach the body. It is more potent in the tropics than elsewhere, more potent at noon than earlier or later in the day, more potent in the summer than in the winter, and more potent at high altitudes. The ultraviolet rays are largely screened out by clothing, window glass, clouds, smoke, or dust. Also, some biochemists theorize that the color of the skin of humans is nature's way of regulating the manufacture of vitamin D — that the dark skin of races near the equator filters out excess ultraviolet light. Perhaps color of hair and skin in horses exercises a similar control, although this is not known.

Vitamin E — Vitamin E, or tocopherol, is asssociated with reproduction. Also, it prevents and corrects anhidrosis, a condition characterized by a dry, dull hair coat, elevated temperature, high blood pressure, and labored breathing. Anhidrosis has been successfully treated by the oral administration of 1,000 to 3,000 IU of vitamin E daily for 1 month.

Most practical rations contain liberal quantities of vitamin E, perhaps enough except under conditions of work, stress, or reproduction, or where there is interference with its utilization. Green forages, especially alfalfa, are good sources.

The requirements for vitamin E are influenced by interrelationships with other essential nutrients — increased by the presence of interfering substances, and spared by the presence of other substances that may be protective or that may assume part of its functions. The recommended allowances of vitamin E are given in Table 6.2.

Vitamin K — When vitamin K is deficient, the coagulation time of the blood is increased and the prothrombin level is decreased. This is the main justification for adding this vitamin to the ration of the horse. Also, vitamin K has value in veterinary medicine as an aid in controlling hemorrhage.

Water-soluble Vitamins

The large amounts of water which pass through the horse's body daily tend to carry out the water-soluble vitamins, thereby depleting the supply. Thus, they must be supplied in the horse's ration on a day-to-day basis. All of the water-soluble vitamins except vitamin C are known as B vitamins.

Vitamins of the B-complex, particularly biotin, choline, folacin (folic acid), niacin, pantothenic acid, riboflavin, thiamin (B-1), vitamin B-6 (pyridoxine), and vitamin B-12, may be essential, especially for (1) young horses before the synthesis of the B-complex vitamins by the microflora begins, and (2) horses that are under stress, as in racing and showing.

Healthy horses usually get enough of the B-complex vitamins, either in natural rations or by synthesis in the intestinal tract. However, when neither green pasture nor high quality dry forage is available, it may be in the nature of good insurance to provide them, especially for horses that are under stress.

Although some of the B vitamins and unidentified factors are synthesized in the cecum of the horse, it is doubtful that microbial activity is sufficient to meet the needs during the critical periods — growth, reproduction, and when animals are subjected to great stress as in showing or racing. Also, there is reason to question the efficacy of absorption this far down the digestive tract; for, in comparison with that of humans and other animals, the cecum is on the wrong end of the digestive tract, after the small intestine. Moreover, it is known that horses fed thiamin-deficient rations lose weight, become nervous, and show incoordination in the hindquarters; then, when thiamin is added to the ration, this condition is cured. For these reasons, in valuable horses it is not wise to rely solely on bacterial synthesis. The B vitamins, along with unidentified factors, may be provided by adding to the ration such ingredients as distillers' dried solubles, dried brewers' yeast, dried fish solubles, or animal liver meal, usually available in a reputable commercial pelleted feed.

Biotin — Ordinary equine rations probably contain ample biotin, or horses synthesize all they need. But, in recognition that biotin is required by all species, and that it plays an important role in the metabolism of carbohydrates, fats, and proteins, it is possible that adding biotin to the ration of the horse may assure maximum performance. Also, there is indication that biotin is essential for sound hoofs, but it should not be concluded that all hoof problems are due to biotin deficiency. They are not. Actually, several nutrients are known to influence hoof growth — biotin among them. Studies indicate that a complete balanced ration is essential for proper hoof growth. Without doubt, heredity is also a factor.

Choline — Choline is a metabolic essential for building and maintaining cell structure and in the transmission of nerve impulses.

The dietary requirement for choline depends on the level of methionine (an amino acid) in the ration. Also, it is noteworthy that all naturally occurring fats contain some choline; however, normal horse feeds are low in fat. Hence, the recommended allowances are as given in Table 6.2.

Folacin (Folic Acid) — Folacin is widely distributed in horse feeds. Also, it is synthesized in the lower digestive tract of the horse. Hence, it is unlikely that a dietary source is required, although a small amount may be in the nature of cheap insurance.

Niacin (Nicotinic Acid, Nicotinamide) — Some evidence indicates that niacin is synthesized by the horse. Also, the horse can convert the essential amino acid tryptophan into niacin. Hence, it is important to make certain that the ration is adequate in niacin; otherwise, the horse will use tryptophan to supply niacin needs. Niacin is widely distributed in feeds; fermentation solubles, yeast (brewers', torula), and certain oil meals are especially good sources. Only a modest addition of niacin to the ration is indicated.

Pantothenic Acid (Vitamin B-3) — Intestinal synthesis of pantothenic acid has been found to occur in all animal species studied. In the case of the horse, such synthesis appears to be sufficiently extensive to meet body needs, at least in part. However, of all the B vitamins, pantothenic acid is most likely to be deficient when horses are stabled (confined). As indicated in Table 6.2, a daily allowance of 250 mg of pantothenic acid is recommended for a 1,000-lb. gestating or lactating mare.

Riboflavin (Vitamin B-2) — A deficiency of riboflavin may cause periodic ophthalmia (moon blindness), characterized by catarrhal conjunctivitis in one or both eyes, accompanied by photophobia, and lacrimation. Repeated attacks affect the retina, lens, and ocular fluids and cause impaired vision or blindness. But it is known that lack of this vitamin is not the only factor causing this condition. Sometimes moon blindness follows leptospirosis in horses, and it may be caused by a localized hypersensitivity or allergic reaction. Periodic ophthalmia caused by lack of riboflavin may be prevented by feeding green hay and green pasture, supplying feeds high in riboflavin, or by adding crystalline riboflavin to the ration.

Two properties of riboflavin lend support to riboflavin supplementation for the horse: (1) it is destroyed by light, and it is destroyed by heat in an alkaline solution; and (2) body storage is very limited, so day-to-day needs must be provided in the ration.

Thiamin (Vitamin B-1) — Vitamin B-1 is synthesized in the lower gut of the horse by bacterial action, but there is some doubt as to its sufficiency and as to the amount absorbed always meeting the full requirements.

A thiamin deficiency has been produced experimentally. It is characterized by loss of appetite, loss of weight, anemia, incoordination (especially of the hind legs), lower blood thiamin, elevated blood pyruvic acid, and dilated and hypertrophied heart.

Vitamin B-1 is required for normal carbohydrate metabolism. Since carbohydrate metabolism is increased during physical exertion, it is important that B-1 be available in quantity at such times.

Vitamin B-6 (Pyridoxine, Pyridoxal, Pyridoxamine) — There is no evidence that deficiencies of vitamin B-6 occur in horses on commonly fed rations; and it is not expected that deficiencies should occur in view of the widespread distribution of vitamin B-6 in feedstuffs and the probable synthesis of B-6 in the cecum. Yet, these sources may not be adequate to assure maximum performance of the horse. So, the daily supplementation of 25 mg of vitamin B-6 per horse may be in the nature of cheap insurance, especially because of the important role of the vitamin.

Vitamin B-6, in its coenzyme forms, is involved in a large number of physiologic functions, particularly the metabolism of protein, carbohydrate, and fat. Also, it is involved in clinical problems, including (1) anemia that does not respond to iron supplements, (2) kidney stones, and (3) the physiologic demands of pregnancy.

Vitamin B-12 (Cobalamins) — It has been reported that horses in poor nutritional condition showing anemia respond to the administration of vitamin B-12. An allowance of 0.084 mg of B-12 per day is recommended for weanlings.

Vitamin B-12 injections are frequently given to horses to improve performance and to prevent or cure anemia. There is no experimental evidence that such shots are either helpful or harmful.

Vitamin C (Ascorbic Acid, Dehydroascorbic Acid) — A dietary need for ascorbic acid is limited to humans, monkeys, guinea pigs, fruit-eating bats, and bulbul birds. However, the vitamin is probably required by all other species, including the horse, but is synthesized adequately in the body. It is conjectured that heavily stressed horses may not be able to synthesize enough vitamin C for maximum performance; hence, adding the vitamin to the ration may provide added assurance that levels are sufficient.

Vitamin Imbalances

Experiments have shown that the amounts needed of certain vitamins may be affected by the supply of another vitamin or of some other nutritive essential. Also, it is known that excess fortification of the horse's ration with certain vitamins may prove more detrimental than helpful. Thus, caretakers should avoid harmful imbalances; they should provide vitamins on the basis of recommended allowances. Also, when fortifying with vitamins, consideration should be given to the vitamins provided by the ingredients of the normal ration, for it is the total composition of the feed that counts.

Unidentified Factors

Since the U.S. foal crop is only around 50 percent, and since horses under stress (racing, showing, etc.) frequently become temperamental in their eating habits, it is obvious that there is room for improvement in the ration somewhere along the line. Perhaps unidentified factors are involved.

Unidentified factors include those vitamins which the chemist has not yet isolated and identified. For this reason, they are sometimes referred to as the vitamins of the future. There is mounting evidence of the importance of unidentified factors for animals, including humans. Among other things, they lower the incidence of ulcers in humans and swine. For horses, they appear to increase growth and improve feed efficiency and breeding performance when added to rations thought to be complete with regard to known nutrients. The anatomical and physiological mechanism of the digestive system of the horse, plus the stresses and strains to which modern horses are subjected, would indicate the wisdom of adding unidentified factor sources to the ration of the horse. Unidentified factors appear to be of special importance during breeding, gestation, lactation, and growth.

Three highly regarded unidentified-factor sources are dried whey product, corn fermentation solubles, and dehydrated alfalfa meal.

WATER

Water is essential for the various physiological processes of the horse, such as the production of saliva. Hence, horses should have access to ample quantities of clean, fresh water at all times. They will drink 10 to 12 gallons daily; the amount depends on weather, amount of work done (sweating), rations fed, and size of horse.

Free access to water is desirable. When this is not possible, horses should be watered at approximately the same times daily. Opinions vary among horsemen as to the proper times and methods of watering horses. All agree, however, that regularity and frequency are desirable. Most horsemen agree that water may be given before, during, or after feeding.

Frequent small waterings between feedings are desirable during warm weather or when the animal is being put to hard use. Do not allow a horse to drink heavily when he is hot, because he may founder; and do not allow a horse to drink heavily just before being put to work.

Water should be available in both stalls and corrals. All waterers should have drains for easy cleaning and should be heated to 40° to 45° F during the winter months in cold regions.

FEEDS

More than one kind of hay makes for appetite appeal. In season, any good pasture can replace part or all of the hay unless work or training conditions make substitution impractical.

Good quality oats and timothy hay always have been considered standard feeds for light horses. However, feeds of similar nutritive properties can be interchanged in the ration as price relationships warrant. Some of these feeds are grains (oats, corn, barley, wheat, and sorghum), protein supplements (linseed meal, soybean meal, cottonseed, canola (rapeseed), and sunflower meal), and hays of many varieties. Feed substitution makes it possible to obtain a balanced ration at lowest cost.

During winter months, it is well to add a few sliced carrots to the ration, an occasional bran mash, or a small amount of linseed meal. Also, use bran mash or linseed meal to regulate the bowels.

The proportion of concentrates must be increased and the roughages decreased as energy needs rise with the greater amount, severity, or speed of work. A horse that works at a trot needs considerably more feed than one that works at a walk. For this reason, riding horses in medium to light use require somewhat less grain and more hay in proportion to body weight than light horses that are racing. Also, from an esthetic standpoint, large, paunchy stomachs are objectionable on horses that are used for recreation and sport.

HAY

Through mistaken kindness or carelessness, horses are often fed too much hay or other roughage, with the result that they breathe laboriously and tire quickly. With cattle and sheep, on the other hand, it is usually well to feed considerable roughage. This difference between horses and ruminants is due primarily to the relatively small size of the simple stomach of the horse in comparison with the four-fold stomach of the ruminant.

When limiting the allowance of roughage, it is sometimes necessary to muzzle greedy horses (gluttons) to prevent them from eating the bedding.

Usually, young horses and idle horses can be provided with an unlimited allowance of hay. In fact, much good will result from feeding young and idle horses more roughage and less grain. But one should gradually increase the grain and decrease the hay as work or training begins.

The hay should be early cut, leafy, green, well cured, and free from dust and mold. Hay native to the locality is usually fed. However, horsemen everywhere prefer good quality timothy. With young stock and breeding animals especially, it is desirable that a sweet grass-legume mixture of alfalfa hay be fed. The legume provides a source of high quality proteins and certain minerals and vitamins.

Horses like variety. Therefore, if at all possible, it is wise to have more than one kind of hay in the stable. For example, timothy may be provided at one feeding and a grass-legume mixed hay at the other feeding. Good horsemen often vary the amount of alfalfa fed, for increased amounts of alfalfa in the ration will increase urination and give a softer consistency to the bowel movements. This means that elimination from kidneys and bowels can be carefully regulated by the amount and frequency of alfalfa feedings. Naturally, such regulation becomes more necessary with irregular use and idleness. On the other hand, in some areas alfalfa is fed as the sole roughage with good results.

Timothy

Timothy is the hay preferred by most horsemen. Although it may be grown alone, it is commonly seeded in mixtures with medium red or alsike clover.

Timothy is easy to harvest and cure. However, in comparison with hay made from the legumes, it is low in crude protein and minerals, particularly calcium.

As with all other forages, the feeding value of timothy is affected by the stage of growth of the plants at the time of cutting. With increasing maturity, (1) the percentage of crude protein decreases, (2) the percentage of crude fiber increases, (3) the hay becomes less palatable, and (4) the digestibility decreases. However, delaying cutting until timothy has reached the full bloom stage, or later, usually results in the highest yields. When both yield and quality are considered, the best results are obtained when timothy is cut for hay at the early bloom stage.

Alfalfa (Lucerne)

Alfalfa is an important, perennial, leguminous forage plant with trifoliate leaves and bluish-purple flowers. It is grown widely, principally for hay. Alfalfa is capable of surviving dry periods because of its extraordinarily long root system, and it is adapted to widely varying conditions of climate and soil. It yields the highest tonnage per acre and has the highest protein content of the legume hays.

Good quality alfalfa hay is excellent for horses. It averages 15.3 percent protein, which is of high quality; and it is a good source of certain minerals and vitamins. In addition to being used as a hay, alfalfa is an ingredient of most all-pelleted feeds.

Hay Quality

The easily recognizable characteristics of hay of high quality are:

1. It is made from plants cut at an early stage of maturity, thus assuring the maximum content of protein, minerals, and vitamins, and the highest digestibility.
2. It is leafy, thus giving assurance of high protein content.
3. It is bright green in color, thus indicating proper curing, a high carotene or provitamin A content (provided it is not over a year old), and palatability.
4. It is free from foreign material, such as weeds and stubble.
5. It is free from must or mold and dust.
6. It is fine-stemmed and pliable — not coarse, stiff, and woody.
7. It has a pleasing, fragrant aroma; it "smells good enough to eat."

Forage Substitutions

Forages of similar nutritive properties may be interchanged in the ration as availability and price relationships warrant, thereby making it possible at all times to obtain a balanced ration at the lowest cost. Table 6.3 presents, in summary form, some roughage substitution guidelines.

CONCENTRATES

Of all the concentrates, heavy oats most nearly meet the need of horses; and, because of the uniformly good results obtained from their use, they have always been recognized as the leading grain for horses. Corn is also widely used as a horse feed, particularly in the central states. Despite occasional prejudice to the contrary, barley is a good horse feed. As proof of the latter assertion, it is noteworthy that the Arab — who was a good horseman — fed barley almost exclusively. Also, wheat, wheat bran, and commercial mixed feeds are extensively used. It is to be emphasized, therefore, that careful attention should be given to the prevailing price of feeds available locally, for many feeds are well suited to horses. Often substitutions can be made that will result in a marked saving without affecting the nutritive value of the ration. When corn or other heavy grains are fed, it is important that a little linseed meal or wheat bran be used, in order to regulate the bowels.

Oats

Oats are the leading U.S. horse feed. They normally weigh 32 lb. per bushel, but the best horse oats are heavier. The feeding value varies according to the hull content and test weight per bushel.

Because of their bulky nature, oats form a desirable loose mass in the stomach, which prevents impaction.

Table 6.3 FORAGE SUBSTITUTION TABLE

Forage	Value Compared to Timothy Hay, Which Is Designated as Equal to 100	Maximum Percentage of Timothy Hay Which It Can Replace
Timothy hay	100	100
Alfalfa hay	133⅓	100
Corn silage	45–55 (wet basis)	33⅓–50
Oat hay	100	100
Prairie hay	100	100
Sorghum fodder	100	50

Oats may be rolled, crimped, or fed whole. Hulled oats are particularly valuable in the ration for young foals.

Barley

Barley is the leading horse grain in the western U.S.

Compared with corn, barley contains somewhat more protein (crude protein: barley 13 percent; corn 10 percent) and fiber (due to the hulls) and somewhat less carbohydrate and fat. Like oats, barley is quite variable in feeding value, due to the wide spread in test weight per bushel. Most horsemen feel that it is preferable to feed barley along with more bulky feeds; for example, 25 percent oats or 15 percent wheat bran.

When fed to horses, barley should always be steam rolled or ground coarsely.

Corn (Maize)

Corn ranks second to oats as a horse feed. It is palatable, nutritious, and rich in energy-producing carbohydrate and fat, but it has certain very definite limitations. It lacks quality (being especially low in the amino acids lysine and tryptophan) and quantity of proteins (it runs about 9 percent), and it is deficient in minerals, particularly calcium.

Corn may be fed to horses on the cob, shelled, cracked, as corn-and-cob meal, or flaked.

Certain types of molds or fungi, sometimes found on corn and other feeds, have caused death in horses and other animal species. So, moldy feed should not be fed to horses.

Wheat Bran

Wheat bran is the coarse outer covering of the wheat kernel. It contains a fair amount of protein (averaging about 16 percent), a good amount of phosphorus, and is laxative in action. Bran is valuable for horses because of its bulky nature and laxative properties. Also, it is very palatable.

Bran Mash — Feeding a bran mash is the traditional way of regulating the bowels of horses on idle days and at such other times as required.

The mash is prepared by filling a 2- to 2½-gallon bucket with wheat bran, pouring enough boiling hot water over it to make it the consistency of breakfast oatmeal, covering the bucket with a blanket or towel and allowing it to steam until cool, then feeding a quantity of it to the horse according to size and appetite.

Occasionally, when a horse is offered a bran mash for the first time, he may refuse to eat it. When this occurs, the animal may be enticed to eat the mash by either (1) introducing him to a little of it by hand, or (2) sprinkling some sugar, or some other well-liked feed, over it.

Molasses (Cane or Beet)

Molasses is a by-product of sugar factories, with cane molasses coming from sugarcane and beet molasses coming from sugar beets. Cane molasses is slightly preferred to beet molasses for horses, although either is satisfactory.

For horses, molasses is 80 to 95 percent as valuable as oats, pound for pound. However, molasses is used primarily as an appetizer.

In hot, humid areas, molasses should be limited to 5 percent of the ration; otherwise, mold may develop. Where mustiness is a problem, add calcium propionate to the feed according to the manufacturer's directions.

Grain Substitutions

Table 6.4, Grain Substitution Table, shows the value for horses of certain cereal grains compared to oats.

PROTEIN SUPPLEMENTS

Grass hays and farm grains are low in quality and quantity of proteins. Hence, they must be supplemented with other sources of protein.

In practical horse feeding, foals should be provided with some protein feeds of animal origin in order to supplement the proteins found in grains and forages. In feeding mature horses, a safe plan to follow is to provide plant protein from several sources.

In general, feeds of high protein content are more expensive than those high in carbohydrates or fats. Accordingly, there is a temptation to feed too little protein. On the other hand, when protein feeds are the cheapest — as is often true of cull peas in certain sections of the West — excess quantities of them may be fed as energy feeds without harm, provided the ration is balanced in all other respects. Any amino acids that are left over, after the protein requirements have been met, are

Table 6.4 Grain Substitution Table

Energy Feeds	Relative Value Compared to Oats, Which Is Designated as Equal to 100	Maximum Percentage of Oats Which It Can Replace
Oats	100	100
Barley	110	100
Corn	115	100
Milo (sorghum)	110–115	85
Molasses	80–95	10
Wheat	115	50

deaminated or broken down in the body. In this process, a part of each amino acid is turned into energy, and the remainder is excreted via the kidneys.

Milk By-Products

The superior nutritive value of milk by-products are due to their high quality proteins, vitamins, a good mineral balance, and the beneficial effect of the milk sugar, lactose. In addition, these products are palatable and highly digestible. They are an ideal feed for young equines and for balancing out the deficiencies of the cereal grains. Most foal rations contain one or more milk by-products, primarily dried skim milk, with some dried whey and dried buttermilk included at times. The chief limitation to their wider use is price.

Linseed Meal

Linseed meal is a by-product of flaxseed following oil extraction by either of two processes: (1) the mechanical process (known as the "old process"); or (2) the solvent process ("new process"). If the meal is solvent-extracted, it must be so designated. Horsemen prefer the mechanical process, for the remaining meal is more palatable, has a higher fat content, and imparts more gloss to the hair coat.

Linseed meal averages about 35 percent protein content. For horses, the proteins of linseed meal do not effectively make good the deficiencies of the cereal grains — linseed meal being low in the amino acids lysine and tryptophan. Also, linseed meal is lacking in carotene and vitamin D and is only fair in calcium and the B vitamins. Because of its deficiencies, linseed meal should not be fed to horses as the sole protein supplement.

Because of its laxative nature, linseed meal in limited quantities is a valuable addition to the ration of horses. Also, it imparts a desirable "bloom" to the hair of show and sale animals.

Soybean Meal

Soybean meal, processed from the soybean, is the most widely used protein supplement in the United States. It is the ground residue (soybean oil cake or soybean oil chips) remaining after the removal of most of the oil from soybeans. The oil is extracted by one of three processes: (1) the expeller process; (2) the hydraulic process; or (3) the solvent process. Although a name descriptive of the extraction process must be used in the brand name, well-cooked soybean meal produced by each of the extraction processes is of approximately the same feeding value.

Soybean meal normally contains 41, 44, or 50 percent protein, according to the amount of hull removed; and the proteins are of better quality than the other protein-rich supplements of plant origin. It is low in calcium, phosphorus, carotene, and vitamin D.

Soybean meal is satisfactory as the only protein supplement to grain for mature horses, providing a high quality ground legume (such as alfalfa or clover) is incorporated in the ration and adequate sources of calcium and phosphorus are provided. For foals, it is best that a dried milk by-product be included.

Cottonseed Meal

Among the oilseed meals, cottonseed meal ranks second to soybean meal in tonnage used in the U.S.

The protein content of cottonseed meal can vary from about 22 percent in meal made from undecorticated (unhulled) seed to 60 percent in flour made from seed from which the hulls have been removed completely. Thus, in screening out the residual hulls, which are low in protein and high in fiber, the processor is able to make a cottonseed meal of the protein content desired — usually 41, 44, or 50 percent.

Cottonseed meal is low in lysine and tryptophan and deficient in vitamin D, carotene (vitamin A value), and calcium. Also, unless glandless seed is used, it contains a toxic substance known as gossypol, varying in amounts with the seed and the processing. But it is rich in phosphorus.

Some prejudices to the contrary, good grade cottonseed meal is satisfactory for horses. It may be fed in the amounts necessary to balance ordinary rations.

Rapeseed Meal (Canola Meal)

Rape is adapted to cold climates; it grows in northern Europe and Asia, Canada, and the northern U.S.

In common with other plants in the *Brassica* (wild mustard) group, rapeseed contains goitrogenic (goiter-inducing) compounds called glucosinolates. Fortunately, selected cultivars of rape have been developed which are low in glucosinolates. In Canada, the low-glucosinate cultivars that they developed are called canola.

Solvent-extracted rapeseed (canola) meal runs about 41–43 percent protein on a moisture-free basis. It is used as a protein supplement for all animal species, including horses.

Sunflower Meal

The development of high oil-yielding varieties by Russian scientists has stirred worldwide interest in the use of sunflowers as an oilseed crop. Some of these varieties yield over 50 percent oil.

Sunflower meal (41 percent protein or better) can be used as a protein supplement for horses provided (1) it is good quality, and (2) care is taken to supply adequate lysine, for sunflower meal is low in this amino acid. When incorporated in well-balanced rations, properly processed sunflower meal of good quality may supply up to one-third of the protein supplement of horses.

Urea for the Horse

It is recognized that horses frequently consume urea-containing cubes and blocks intended for cattle and sheep, particularly on the western range. Moreover, it appears that mature horses are able to do so without untoward effects. The latter observation was confirmed in one limited experiment[2] in which four horses consumed an average of 4.57 lb. per day of a urea-containing supplement, or 0.55 lb./head/day of feed urea (262 percent), for 5 months. Also, the Louisiana Station[3] did not find urea detrimental or toxic to horses when it constituted up to 5 percent of the grain ration, with up to 0.5 lb. per day of urea consumed. There are reports, however, of urea toxicity in foals, in which bacterial action in the digestive tract is more limited than in older horses. Also, most state feed-control laws limit the sale of urea-containing feeds to ruminants.

SPECIAL FEEDS AND ADDITIVES

Special feeds may be needed from time to time for imparting bloom or gloss to the hair and for promoting growth of young stock.

Feeds that Impart Bloom or Gloss

Bloom or gloss is important in horses. But sometimes they lack this desired quality — their hair is dull and dry. Feeding a well-balanced ration will usually rectify this situation. Also, feeding either of the following products will make for an attractive, shiny coat:

1. *Corn oil* — Feed at the rate of one tablespoon per horse per day.

[2] *Veterinary Medicine*, vol. 58, no. 12, Dec. 1963.

[3] "Non-Toxicity of Urea Feeding to Horses," *Veterinary Medicine/Small Animal Clinician*, Nov. 1965.

2. *Whole flaxseed soaked* — Put a handful of whole flaxseed in a teacup, cover it with water, let it stand overnight, then pour it over the morning feed. Repeat twice each week.

Unless the horse is afflicted with lice, mange, or some other ailment, either of the above treatments will impart bloom or gloss to the coat.

Milk Replacer

As indicated by the name, a milk replacer is a replacement for milk. Such replacers generally contain the following composition: animal or vegetable fat, 17–20 percent; crude soybean lecithin, 1–2 percent; skimmed milk solids, 78–82 percent (10–15 percent dried whey powder can be included in place of an equivalent amount of skimmed milk solids); plus fortification with minerals and vitamins.

Foals suckling their dams generally develop very satisfactorily up to weaning time. But the most critical period in the entire life of a horse is that space from weaning time (about six months of age) until one year of age. This is especially so in the case of young horses being fitted for shows or sales, where condition is so important. Thus, where valuable weanlings or yearlings are to be shown or sold, the use of a milk replacer may be practical.

Lysine

Protein quality is important for horses. Because amino acid synthesis is more limited in the horse than in ruminants, plus the fact that the cecum is located beyond the small intestine — the main area for digestion and absorption of nutrients — it is generally recommended that high quality protein rations, adequate in amino acids, be fed to equines. This is especially important for young equines, because cecal synthesis is very limited in early life.

Fortunately, the amino acid content of proteins from various sources varies. Thus, the deficiencies of one protein may be improved by combining it with another, and the mixture of the two proteins often will have a higher feeding value than either one alone. It is for this reason, along with added palatability, that a considerable variety of feeds in the horse ration is desirable.

Cornell University reported that the addition of lysine to the diet of growing horses increased weight gains, feed consumption, and feed efficiency.

In recognition that lysine is the first limiting amino acid (the amino acid in a protein test which is first to limit production because of its insufficiency) of horses and is thus an indicator of the quality of protein which horses require, the recommended lysine allowance for horses is given in Table 6.2.

Antibiotics

Antibiotics are not nutrients; they're drugs. They are a chemical substance, produced by molds or bacteria, which has the ability to inhibit the growth of or to destroy other microorganisms.

Certain antibiotics, at stipulated levels, are approved by FDA for growth promotion and for the improvement of feed efficiency of young equines up to one year of age. Unless there is a disease level, however, there is no evidence to warrant the continuous feeding of antibiotics to mature horses. Such practice may even be harmful. *Note:* Bovatec and Rumensin, two antibiotics, can be toxic to horses, so they should not be fed to horses. Hence, where antibiotics are needed for therapeutic purposes, it is best to seek the advice of a veterinarian.

TREATS FOR THE HORSE

Horses are fed a great variety of treats. On a government horse-breeding establishment in Brazil, the author saw a large and well-manicured vegetable garden, growing everything from carrots to melons, just for horses. Also, trainers recognize that most racehorses, which are the prima donnas of the equine world, don't "eat like a horse"; they eat like people — and sometimes they're just as finicky. Their menus may include a choice of carrots or other roots, fruits, pumpkins, squashes, melons, molasses, sugar, honey, or innumerable other goodies.

Ask the average horseman why he feeds treats to his horse and you'll get a variety of answers. However, high on the list of reasons will be (1) as appetizers, (2) as a source of nutrients and conditioners, (3) as rewards, (4) as a means of alleviating obesity (dieting the horse), or (5) folklore.

Treats as Appetizers

If a horse doesn't eat his feed, it won't do him any good. Hence, feed consumption is important.

Sooner or later, a horseman is bound to get one of those exasperating equines that just refuses to clean up his feed. Perhaps he'll eat a few bites, then stop; or maybe he won't even touch the "stuff." Sometimes this happens to race and show horses that started training in great physical shape, only to lose appetite and have to be taken out of training for rest.

Lots of things can cause finicky eaters, among them, (1) stress and nervousness, (2) an unpalatable and monotonous ration, (3) nutritional deficiencies, (4) poor health, and (5) lack of exercise. Whatever the cause, the condition(s) making for poor feed consumption should be rectified — if it can be determined, and if it is within the power of the caretaker to correct it. Additionally, there should be incorporated in the ration something that the horse really likes, such as carrots or other roots; molasses, sugar, or honey; or sliced fruit.

But treats can be overdone. Hence a horse should not be permitted to eat too much of any treat simply because he likes it. In this respect, horses are like boys and girls. If given a choice between candy and a well-balanced diet, most youngsters will take the candy. Yet, few parents or doctors would be so foolish as to permit a child to eat unlimited candy.

Treats as a Source of Nutrients

Sometimes folks, and even nutritionists, overlook the fact that, when evaluated on a dry-matter basis, high-water-content tubers, fruits, and melons have almost the same nutrient value as the cereal grains. This becomes apparent in Table 6.5, which gives the energy value on a moisture-free basis of several horse treats compared with barley, corn, oats, and timothy.

Generally speaking, horse treats are not fed because they're considered to be a good buy when evaluated on a cost-per-unit of nutrient content (protein, energy, etc.) basis. This becomes obvious when it is realized that it takes nearly 7 lb. of carrots to equal 1 lb. of oats in energy value. Occasionally, such products as carrots are in surplus or of low quality. At such times, they may be available for as little as $3 to $4 per ton, in which case they are a good buy in comparison with grains. Even

Table 6.5 COMPARATIVE ENERGY VALUE, DRY BASIS, OF SOME COMMON HORSE FEEDS AND TREATS

| | | Energy Value (TDN)[1] | | Dry Matter |
Feed	Water (%)	Dry Matter (%)	As Fed (%)	Basis (%)
Barley	10	90	77	85
Corn	10	90	80	90
Oats	11	89	68	76
Timothy hay, mature	14	86	41	48
Apples	82	18	13	74
Carrots	88	12	10	82
Melons	94	6	5	80
Potatoes	79	21	18	85
Sugar beets	87	13	10	77

[1] Total digestible nutrients. This is a method of measuring energy. For further explanation of TDN, see the section earlier in this chapter headed "Energy Needs."

then, it is best that they not replace more than 10 to 20 percent of the normal grain ration. For the most part, however, treats are fed to horses because they possess qualities not revealed by a chemical analysis — because of their values as appetizers, in aiding digestion, and as conditioners.

Treats as Rewards

The training of horses is based on a system of rewards and punishments. This doesn't mean that the horse is fed a tidbit each time he obeys, or that he is beaten when he refuses or does something wrong.

But horses are big and strong; hence, it's best that they want to do something, rather than have to be forced. Also, too frequent or improper use of such artificial aids as whips, spurs, reins, and bits makes them less effective; worse yet, it will likely make for a mean horse.

Horses appreciate a pat on the shoulder or a word of praise. However, better results may be obtained by working on an equine's greediness — his fondness for such things as carrots or a sugar cube. Also, treats may be used effectively as rewards to teach some specific thing such as posing, or to cure a vice like moving while the rider is mounting; but this should not be overdone.

Treats to Alleviate Obesity

Horses are equine athletes; hence, they should be lean and hard rather than fat and soft. Obese horses should be avoided because (1) they lack agility, (2) excessive weight puts a strain on the musculoskeletal system, (3) fertility is lowered in broodmares and stallions, (4) fat horses are prone to founder, and (5) overweight horses are more susceptible to azoturia (tying up).

Such watery feeds as carrots and melons are filling, but low in calories. This becomes obvious when it's realized that (1) it takes more than 8 lb. of fresh carrots to produce 1 lb. of dried product, and (2) it takes nearly 7 lb. of carrots or over 13 lb. of melons to furnish as much energy as 1 lb. of oats. Thus, when used as a "salad" for the horse, carrots or melons are as effective as slenderizers for equines as they are for humans.

Treats for Folklore Reasons

Among the bagful of horsemen's secrets, sometimes the claim is made that apple cider will prolong life, increase vigor, and improve sex drive, fertility, and reproduction. However, there isn't a shred of evidence, based on studies conducted by a reputable experiment station, to substantiate such claims. Of course, it's good to have faith in something; and, too, nature is a wonderful thing. It is estimated that 70 to 80 percent of all horses with afflictions would recover even without treatment.

Carrots and Other Roots

Carrots are relished by horses. Additionally, they're succulent, and high in carotene and minerals. Carotene, known as the precursor of vitamin A because the animal body can convert it into the vitamin, derives its name from the carrot, from which it was first isolated over 100 years ago. Carotene is the yellow-colored substance that imparts the characteristic yellow color to carrots. Each pound of fresh carrots contains 48 milligrams of carotene, which can be converted into 26,640 IU of vitamin A by the young equine, sufficient vitamin A to meet the daily requirement of a 1,000-lb. horse. By contrast, 1 lb. of timothy hay (mature) provides only 2.1 milligrams of carotene, or 1,165 IU, which is only ¹⁄₂₆th of the daily vitamin A requirement for a 1,000-lb. horse. Also, carrots are a good source of minerals; on a dry basis 1 lb. contains 0.42 percent calcium and 0.34 percent phosphorus, whereas mature timothy hay as fed contains 0.17 percent and 0.15 percent of these elements, respectively. Additionally, carrots are high in sugar; on a dry basis they contain 40 percent sugar (invert), which explains their sweetness.

Horsemen have long fed carrots, especially during the winter months when green feeds are not available and to horses that are stabled much of the time. They report that 1 to 2 lb. of carrots per horse per day will stimulate the appetite, increase growth, assist in reproduction, make for normal vision, and improve the health, coat, and attractiveness of the animal.

Carrots should be cleaned, sliced from end to end in small strips, so as to avoid choking, then mixed with the grain.

Other roots such as parsnips, rutabagas, turnips, potatoes, and sugar beets may be fed to horses in small amounts, provided they are first cut finely enough to avoid choking.

Pumpkins, Squashes, and Melons

Pumpkins, squashes, and melons are sometimes used as relish for horses. They contain only 6–10 percent dry matter; hence, their nutritive value on a wet basis is low in comparison with cereal grains. When fed in the usual amounts, their seeds are not harmful to horses, some opinions to the contrary. However, an entire ration of seeds alone is apt to cause indigestion, because of their high fat content.

Apples and Other Fruits

An apple a day is good for a horse, especially when used as a tidbit or reward. They are very palatable because of their sugar content. However, the feeding of apples can be overdone; many a case of colic, or even death, has resulted from old dobbin's stolen visit to the orchard.

Also, peaches, plums, and pears are occasionally used as treats for the horse. The seeds of stone fruits should always be removed prior to feeding.

Molasses, Sugar, and Honey

The horse has a "sweet tooth"; or at least he readily cultivates a taste for sweets. Hence, when added to the ration, molasses, sugar, and honey make for a "sweet feed," or appetizer. For this reason, small amounts (usually about 5 percent) of molasses, sugar, or honey are sometimes added to the concentrate mixtures of racehorses, show horses, and other finicky eaters. Once a horse becomes accustomed to a sweet feed, it is difficult to eliminate it from the ration; in fact, if the sweets are suddenly deleted, the horse may refuse to eat altogether. Thus, if for any reason sweets must be taken out of the ration, the change should be very gradual.

Also, sugar cubes are a good and convenient reward, providing too many of them are not used and the tendency of nipping or biting is avoided.

PALATABILITY OF FEED

Palatability is important, for horses must eat their feed if it's to do them any good. But many horses are finicky simply because they're spoiled. For the latter, stepping up the exercise and halving the ration will usually effect a miraculous cure.

Also, it seems possible that well-liked feeds are digested somewhat better than those which are equally nutritious, but less palatable.

Palatability is particularly important when feeding horses that are being used hard, as in racing or showing. Unless the ration is consumed, such horses will not obtain sufficient nutrients to permit maximum performance. For this reason, lower quality feeds, such as straw or stemmy hay, should be fed to idle horses.

Familiarity and habit are important factors concerned with the palatability of horse feeds. For example, horses have to learn to eat pellets, and very frequently they will back away from feeds with new and unfamiliar odors. For this reason, any change in feeds should be made gradually.

Occasionally, the failure of horses to eat a normal amount of feed is due to a serious nutritive deficiency. For example, if horses are fed a ration made up of palatable feeds, but deficient in one or more required vitamins or minerals, they may eat normal amounts for a time. Then when the body reserves of the lacking nutrient(s) are exhausted, they will usually consume much less feed, due to an impairment of their health and consequent lack of appetite. If the deficiency is not continued so long that the horses are injured permanently, they will usually recover their appetites if some feed is added which supplies the nutritive lack and makes the ration complete.

Palatability of the Protein Supplement

Where a protein supplement lacks palatability, the situation can usually be corrected by increasing the salt content of the supplement to 3.0 percent. The reasoning behind increasing the salt is this: whatever the cause of the unpalatability in a supplement may be (particularly if it is one of the ingredients), it's apt to show up more in the supplement than in other feeds, simply because it is more concentrated. The high salt content usually overcomes the unpalatability and adequate consumption follows. Of course, one should not go higher than 2.0 percent in a concentrate or in an all-pelleted ration because higher levels of salt are unpalatable, but up to 3.0 percent salt in a supplement fed at a level of 1 to 2 lb. per horse per day will usually work wonders.

Palatability Checklist

Here is a checklist, along with the author's comments, where there appears to be a palatability problem with a horse feed.

☐ 1. *Quality of feeds* — Make very certain on this point. It's almost impossible to detect through a chemical analysis many factors that may lower quality, such as "heated grain" and poor quality hay.

☐ 2. *Mustiness* — Again, check with care. Remember that horses can detect mustiness more quickly and easily than people.

☐ 3. *Hard pellets* — If pellets are too hard, horses will spit them out.

☐ 4. *Flavors* — In some cases, flavors will help in overcoming the lack of palatability due to poor quality feeds, but they will do little to enhance good quality feeds.

☐ 5. *Your premix* — Check on the "carrier" and premix ingredients which your feed manufacturer is using in his horse feeds. The author recalls one incident where dried fish meal was being used in a premix as a source of unidentified factors, and an unpalatable ration resulted because of the poor quality of the fish meal in the premix.

☐ 6. *The formulation* — Of course, some feeds are more palatable to horses than others. Among the well-liked feeds are wheat bran and molasses, both of which are usually incorporated in horse rations.

DISTANCE LENDS ENCHANTMENT TO FEEDS

Distance lends enchantment! Many horsemen not only believe that there is something magical about certain horse feeds, but they think that they must be grown in a specific area. For example, timothy hay and oats are frequently extolled on the basis that they are grown in certain "name" areas; they are even referred to as "racehorse oats" or "racehorse timothy hay." Such specialty areas may produce superior products, but their feeding value is generally exaggerated far beyond their price, with much of their added cost going for hundreds of miles of transportation and for middlemen.

FEED PREPARATION

The physical preparation of cereal grains for horses has been practiced by horsemen for a very long time. Basically, grain is either soaked, cooked, ground, or rolled (wet or dry), and hay is either fed long, pelleted, or cubed.

A summary relative to each of the common methods of feed preparation for horses follows.

FLAKING

Flaking, which is the modification of steam rolling in which the grain is subjected to steam for a longer period of time, is the preferred method of processing grains for horses. It produces light, fluffy particles, which result in fewer digestive disturbances than any other method of feed preparation.

The flaking process varies according to the grain. For example, corn is usually steamed for approximately 20 minutes at a temperature of 200° F, to a moisture content of about 18 percent. The grain that responds the most to flaking is milo, which is generally flaked as follows: the grain is subjected to 20 lb. of steam pressure for 20 to 25 minutes, at approximately 205° F; then, at 18 to 20 percent moisture content, it is run through large rollers operated at one-third to one-half capacity and rolled to thin flakes. The end product has a distinct and pleasant aroma, resembling cooked cereal.

STEAM ROLLING

If properly done, steam rolling of grains is preferred to grinding for horses. However, there is great variation in steam rolling. Altogether too much steam rolling consists of exposing the grain to steam for 3 to 5 minutes, using a temperature of about 180° F, and adding an unknown amount of moisture. Such processing is little better than dry rolling.

Desirable steam processing, which is generally called *steam flaking*, may be achieved by either of the following procedures:

1. By subjecting the grain to steam under atmospheric conditions for 15 to 20 minutes, followed by rolling into flat flakes with 16 to 20 percent moisture.
2. By subjecting the grain to steam under pressure for a short time

(such as 50 psi for 1 to 2 minutes) and a temperature approaching 300° F, then cooling below 200° F and drying below 20 percent moisture, followed by rolling.

DRY ROLLING, CRIMPING, AND GRINDING

These methods can be and are used in preparing horse feeds. The important thing is to keep the grain as coarse as possible and to avoid fines.

PELLETING

Currently, horsemen are much interested in complete, all-pelleted feed, in which the hay and grain are combined. Pelleted feeds may be prepared from concentrates alone, forage alone, or concentrates and roughage combined in a complete ration.

Compared to conventional long hay and grain concentrate fed separately, all-pelleted feed has the following advantages:

1. It is less bulky and easier to store and handle, thus lessening transportation, building, and labor costs. Pelleted roughage requires one-fifth to one-third as much space as is required by the same roughage in loose or chopped form.
2. Pelleting prevents horses from selectively refusing ingredients likely to be high in certain dietary essentials; each bite is a balanced feed.
3. Pelleting practically eliminates waste; therefore, less pelleted feed is required. Horses may waste up to 20 percent of long hay. Waste of conventional feed is highest where low quality hay is fed or feed containers are poorly designed.
4. Pelleting eliminates dustiness and lessens the likelihood of heaves.
5. Pellet-fed horses are trimmer in the middle and more attractive because they consume less bulk.
6. Pellets lessen pollution. Feeding pellets lessens the manure by about 25 percent, simply because of less wastage and lower feed consumption; hence, it lessens pollution. Since a 1,000-lb. horse normally produces about 8 tons of manure, free of bedding, per year, this is an important consideration in the present environment-conscious era. Thus, an all-pelleted ration will result in about 2 tons less manure per horse per year.

The following points are pertinent to the proper understanding and use of all-pelleted rations.

1. One-half-inch pellets are preferred for mature horses, and ¼-inch pellets for weanlings and short yearlings. Also, very hard pellets should be avoided; if horses cannot chew them, they will not eat them.

2. The ratio of roughage to concentrates should be higher in all-pelleted rations than when long hay is fed. For most horses, the ratio may range from 60.5 percent roughage to 39.5 percent concentrate up to 69 percent roughage to 31 percent concentrate.

3. Any horse feed should form a loose mass in the stomach to assure ease of digestion, fewer digestive disturbances, and less impaction. To this end, in a complete all-pelleted ration, such feeds as oats and barley should be crimped or steam rolled but not finely ground. The roughage should be ¼-inch chop or coarser. Otherwise, a couple of pounds of long hay may be fed daily to each horse.

4. Young horses and horses at heavy work need more energy. They should be fed less roughage and more concentrate.

5. When less roughage and more concentrate is fed, horses are likely to be overfed and get too fat if they are idle or at light to medium work. But if the total feed consumption is limited too severely to keep the weight down, the problem of wood chewing is increased because of a lack of physical filling of the digestive tract.

6. When the roughage consists of high quality legume (alfalfa or clover mix) hay, a higher percentage of roughage may be used than when all or part of the roughage is grass or other nonlegumes.

7. If more energy is needed for racing or young stock on an all-pelleted ration, it can be provided either by increasing the daily allowance of the all-pelleted ration, and/or replacing a portion of the all-pelleted ration with a suitable concentrate or supplement.

8. Because waste is eliminated, less all-pelleted feed is required than conventional feed. For a horse at light work, give 14 to 18 lb. of all-pelleted feed daily per 1,000 lb. of body weight. Use a feed that contains 51 to 58 percent total digestible nutrients (TDN). Increase the feed allowance with the severity of work.

9. As with any change in feed, the switch to an all-pelleted ration should be made gradually; otherwise, such vices as wood chewing and bolting (eating feed too rapidly) may be induced. At first, continue to offer all the long hay the horse wants and slowly replace the grain portion of the conventional ration with the complete pelleted feed. Increase the pelleted feed by 1 to 2 lb. daily and begin gradually reducing the amount of hay. After a few days, the horse usually will stop eating the hay and it can be removed completely from the ration.

10. The feces of pellet-fed horses are softer than the feces of those not fed pellets.

   Among many horsemen, the feeling persists that horses fed all-pelleted rations are more likely to chew wood than those fed long hay. This may be true to some degree. But some horses will chew wood regardless of what they are fed. (See section on "Pica; Wood Chewing" on page 206.)

HAY CUBES

This refers to the practice of compressing long or coarsely cut hay into cubes or wafers, which are larger and coarser than pellets. Most cubes are about 1¼ inch square and 2 inches long, with a bulk density of 30 to 32 lb. per cubic foot. Cubing costs about $5.00 per ton more than baling.

This method of haymaking is increasing, because it (1) simplifies haymaking, (2) facilitates automation, (3) lessens transportation costs and storage space — cubed roughages require about one-third as much space as when the forage is baled and stacked — and (4) decreases nutrient losses.

From a nutrition standpoint, hay cubes are as satisfactory as hay in any other form (long or baled). However, some horsemen report occasional choking from feeding cubes. Just as it is a good idea to crack open and inspect a flake of hay, it is also wise to check hay cubes for possible contaminants.

RATIONS

Correctly speaking, a ration is the amount of feed given to a horse in a day, or a 24-hour period. To most horsemen, however, the word implies the feeds given to an animal without any time limitation.

To supply all the needs — maintenance, growth, reproduction and lactation, and work (running) — horses must receive feeds in quality and quantity to furnish the necessary energy (carbohydrates and fats), proteins, minerals, vitamins, and perhaps unknown factors and additives. Such rations are said to be balanced. Moreover, the feed must be palatable — horses must like it. The rations listed in Table 6.6 meet these standards. Also, liberal margins of safety have been provided to compensate for variations in feed composition, environment, possible losses of nutrients during storage, and differences in individual animals.

HOME-MIXED FEEDS

A horse feeding guide is given in Table 6.6. In selecting rations, compare them with commercial feeds. If only small quantities are required or little storage space is available, it may be more satisfactory to buy ready-mixed feeds.

When home-mixed feeds are used, feeds of similar nutritive properties can be interchanged in the ration as price relationships warrant. This makes it possible to obtain a balanced ration at lowest cost.

The quantities of feeds recommended in Table 6.6 are intended as guides only. Increase the feed, especially the concentrates, when the horse is too thin and decrease the feed if he gets too fat.

Avoid sudden changes in diet, especially when changing from a less concentrated ration to a more concentrated one. When this rule of feeding is ignored, digestive disturbances result and the horse goes "off feed." In either adding or omitting one or more ingredients, the change should be made gradually. Likewise, caution should be exercised in turning horses to pasture or in transferring them to more lush grazing.

In general, horses may be given as much nonlegume roughage as they will eat. But they must be accustomed gradually to legumes because legumes may be laxative.

In feeding horses, as with other classes of livestock, it is recognized that nutritional deficiencies (especially deficiencies of certain vitamins and minerals) may not be of sufficient proportions to cause clear-cut deficiency symptoms. Yet, such deficiencies without outward signs may cause great economic losses because they go unnoticed and unrectified. Accordingly, sufficient additives (especially minerals and vitamins) should always be present, but care should be taken to avoid imbalances.

Suggested Rations

Several suggested rations are given in Table 6.6 (See pp. 198–199).

Amount of Roughage for a Horse

Actually, a horse does not need any hay. Also, more horses receive too much roughage rather than not enough, as evidenced by hay bellies (distended digestive tracts), quick tiring, and labored breathing.

Under most conditions, the roughage requirement of horses ranges from 0.5 percent to 1.0 percent of body weight, or from 5 to 10 lb. of roughage daily for a 1,000 lb. horse.

Racehorses should receive a minimum of roughage, since they need a maximum of energy. Sometimes it is necessary to muzzle greedy horses to keep them from eating bedding when their roughage allowance is limited.

COMMERCIAL FEEDS

Commercial feeds are feeds mixed by manufacturers who specialize in the feed business. Today, more than 100 million tons of commercial feeds are marketed each year.

Commercial feed manufacturers are able to purchase feed in quantity lots, making possible price advantages and the scientific control of quality. Many horsemen have found that because of the small quantities of feed usually involved, and the complexities of horse rations, they have

Table 6.6 Light Horse Feeding Guide

Age, Sex, and Use	Daily Allowance	Kind of Hay
Stallions in breeding season (weighing 900 to 1,400 lb.)	¾ to 1½ lb. grain per 100 lb. body weight, together with a quantity of hay within same range.	Grass-legume mixed; or ⅓ to ½ legume hay, with remainder grass hay.
Pregnant mares (weighing 900 to 1,400 lb.)	¾ to 1½ lb. grain per 100 lb. body weight, together with a quantity of hay within same range.	Grass-legume mixed; or ⅓ to ½ legume hay, with remainder grass hay. (Straight grass hay may be used first half of pregnancy.)
Foals before weaning (weighing 100 to 350 lb. with projected mature weights of 900 to 1,400 lb.)	½ to ¾ lb. grain per 100 lb. body weight, together with a quantity of hay within same range.	Legume hay.
Weanlings (weighing 350 to 450 lb.)	1 to 1½ lb. grain and 1½ to 2 lb. hay per 100 lb. body weight.	Grass-legume mixed; or ½ legume hay, with remainder grass hay.
Yearlings, second summer (weighing 450 to 700 lb.)	Good, luxuriant pasture. (If in training or for other reasons without access to pasture, the ration should be intermediate between the adjacent upper and lower groups.)	
Yearlings, or rising two-year-olds, second winter (weighing 700 to 1,000 lb.)	½ to 1 lb. grain and 1 to 1½ lb. hay per 100 lb. body weight.	Grass-legume mixed; or ⅓ to ½ legume hay, with remainder grass hay.
Light horses at work; riding, driving, and racing (weighing 900 to 1,400 lb.)	**Hard use** — 1¼ to 1⅓ lb. grain and 1 to 1¼ lb. hay per 100 lb. body weight. **Medium use** — ¾ to 1 lb. grain and 1 to 1¼ lb. hay per 100 lb. body weight. **Light use** — ⅖ to ½ lb. grain and 1¼ to 1½ lb. hay per 100 lb. body weight.	Grass hay.
Mature idle horses; stallions, mares, and geldings (weighing 900 to 1,400 lb.)	1½ to 1¾ lb. hay per 100 lb. body weight.	Pasture in season; or grass-legume mixed hay.

Note — With all rations and for all classes and ages of horses, provide free access to a mineral box as follows: (1) Where the pasture or hay is primarily a grass, use a mixture containing 2 parts of calcium to 1 part of phosphorus; and (2) where the pasture or hay is primarily a legume, use a

Suggested Grain Rations

Rations No. 1 (lb.)	Rations No. 2 (lb.)	Rations No. 3 (lb.)
Oats-55 Wheat-20 Wheat bran-20 Linseed meal-5	Corn-35 Oats-35 Wheat-15 Wheat bran-15	Oats-100
Oats-80 Wheat bran-20	Barley-45 Oats-45 Wheat bran-10	Oats-95 Linseed meal-5
Oats-50 Wheat bran-40 Linseed meal-10	Oats-30 Barley-30 Wheat bran-30 Linseed meal-10	Oats-80 Wheat bran-20

Rations balanced on basis of following assumption: Mares of mature weights of 600, 800, 1,000, and 1,200 lb. may produce 36, 42, 44, and 49 lb. of milk daily.

Rations No. 1 (lb.)	Rations No. 2 (lb.)	Rations No. 3 (lb.)
Oats-30 Barley-30 Wheat bran-30 Linseed meal-10	Oats-70 Wheat bran-15 Linseed meal-15	Oats-80 Linseed meal-20
Oats-80 Wheat bran-20	Barley-35 Oats-35 Bran-15 Linseed meal-15	Oats-100
Oats-100	Oats-70 Corn-30	Oats-70 Barley-30

(With grass hay, add ¾ lb. of a high-protein supplement daily.)

mixture containing 1 part of calcium to 1 part of phosphorus. To each of these mixes, add ⅓ salt (trace mineralized) to improve acceptability. If preferred, a good commercial mineral mix may be used. Self-feed salt separately.

more reason to rely on good commercial feeds than do owners of other classes of farm animals.

The nutritive requirements of horses vary according to age, weight, use or demands, growth, stage of gestation or lactation, and environment. Also, part of the horse ration may be homegrown. It would appear, therefore, that the commercial feeds shown in Table 6.7 are necessary if one is to meet most horse needs.

"Sweet feed" refers to a feed to which has been added one or more ingredients that are sweet. Most commonly, it contains considerable molasses (approximately 10 percent); although brown sugar (about 5 percent) is sometimes used, and occasionally honey.

The horse has a "sweet tooth"; hence, it's not easy to switch him from a sweet feed to what may be a more nutritious ration. Of course, the manufacturer of the sweet feed would have it that way. Also, it must be remembered that sweet feeds are a way in which a feed manufacturer may make poor quality feed ingredients more appetizing. Remember, too, that most boys and girls would rather eat candy than foods that are more nutritious. But doctors and mothers know best!

How to Evaluate a Commercial Feed

There is a difference in commercial feeds! That is, there is a difference from the standpoint of what a horseman can purchase with his feed dollars. The smart horseman will know how to determine what constitutes the best in commercial feeds for his specific needs. He will not rely solely on how the feed looks and smells. The most important factors to consider or look for in buying a commercial feed are

1. *The reputation of the manufacturer* — This may be determined by conferring with other horsemen who have used the particular product and checking on whether or not the commercial feed under consideration has consistently met its guarantees. The latter can be determined by reading the bulletins or reports published by the respective state departments in charge of enforcing feed laws.

2. *The specific needs* — Feed needs vary according to (a) the class, age, and productivity of horses, and (b) whether animals are fed primarily for maintenance, growth, fattening (or show-ring fitting), reproduction, lactation, or work (running). The wise operator will buy different formula feeds for different needs.

3. *Flexible formulas* — Feeds with flexible formulas are usually the best buy. This is because the price of feed ingredients in different source feeds varies considerably from time to time. Thus, a good feed manufacturer will shift his formulas as prices change, in order to give the horseman the most for his money. This is as it should be, for (a) there is no one best ingredient, and (b) if substitutions are made wisely, the price of the feed can be kept down, and the horseman will continue to get equally good results.

Table 6.7 COMMERCIAL HORSE FEEDS AND NEEDS

Needed Horse Feeds	Prevailing Conditions	Crude Protein (%)	Used for
Complete (hay and grain combined in a pellet)	For the horseman who must buy all feeds.	13	All horses 10 months or older.
Concentrate	For the horseman who has satisfactory hay and/or pasture.	14	All horses 10 months or older.
Protein supplement	For supplementing available hay and grain.	25	All horses 10 months or older.
Foal ration	For creep feeding.	18	2 weeks to 10 months of age.
Protein-salt block	For free-choice feeding in corral or on pasture.	20	All horses 10 months of age or older.
Enriched vitamin-trace mineral-unidentified factor supplement	For the horseman who has hay and grain that meet all needs except vitamin-trace mineral-unidentified factors.	. . .	All horses not receiving any of the above feeds.

4. *What's on the tag?* — Horsemen should be able to study and interpret what's on the feed tag. The information that follows was taken from a foal ration:

GUARANTEED ANALYSIS

Crude Protein, not less than	21.00%
Crude Fat, not less than	2.00%
Crude Fiber, not more than	9.00%
Ash, not more than	9.00%
Added Mineral, not more than	3.00%
Calcium, not less than	1.00%
Phosphorus, not less than	.75%
Salt, not more than	.50%
Iodine, not less than	.00035%
TDN, not less than	68.00%

Ingredients: Rolled Oats, Dried Whey, Soybean Meal, Cottonseed Meal, Linseed Meal, Dehydrated Alfalfa Meal, Wheat Bran, Wheat Shorts, Wheat Flour, Cane Molasses, Bone Meal, Iodized Salt, Distiller's Dried Grains with Solubles, Alfalfa Leaf Meal, Condensed Fish Solubles (Dried), Brewer's Dried Yeast, Streptomycin Mycelia Meal, Vitamin A Palmitate with Increased Stability, Fleischmann's Irradiated Dry Yeast (source of Vitamin D-2), d-Alpha-Tocopherol Acetate (source of Vitamin E), Choline Chloride, Ferrous Carbonate, Niacin, Calcium Pantothenate (source of d-Pantothenic Acid), Riboflavin Supplement, Copper Oxide, Manganous Oxide, Thiamin, Sulfur, Menadione Sodium Bisulfate (source of Vitamin K), Calcium Iodate, Folic Acid, Cobalt Carbonate, Vitamin B-12 Supplement. Preserved with Ethoxyquin (1, 2-dihydro-6-ethoxy-2, 2, 4-trimethylquinoline), Anise.

An analysis of the above tag reveals the following:

a. The guaranteed analysis, each stated in percent, in minimum crude protein and crude fat; maximum crude fiber, ash, and mineral; minimum calcium and phosphorus; maximum salt; and minimum iodine and TDN (total digestible nutrients). But guaranteed analysis, within itself, will not suffice. For example, on the basis of chemical composition, soft coal (9.06 percent crude protein) and coffee grounds (11.23 percent crude protein) are comparable in protein content to many commonly used grains.

b. The ingredients (the constituent material making up the feed) listed in descending order of amounts, by weight. This type of listing aids in making decisions as to the possible quality of the feed. For example, if feather meal, which contains 85 percent protein by analysis, were listed (which it is not in the above feed), you could conclude that the horse would obtain little nutritional advantage from this type of ration component. All ingredients listed in the above ration are good, and each one appears to contribute needed nutrients.

Many states differ slightly in feed labeling requirements from the tag just analyzed. Some require both the minimum and maximum percentage of calcium and salt.

By studying the feed tag, a knowledgeable user can readily and easily see what's in the feed and determine if it will meet the requirements of the horse to which it is to be fed.

RATION FORMULATION BY IMITATION

Sometimes horse trainers pattern their ration after what some great horse is getting — they get some of the same "stuff."

Of course, it is difficult to argue with success. Also, it is well known that horsemen as a whole are great imitators. The author has known them to pay $50 for a gallon of a mysterious concoction, in a green jug, made in a little hamlet in Kentucky. Of course, the fallacy of such imitation — of feeding what the "great horse" got — is that the "name" horse might have been even greater had he been fed properly, and that there must be a reason why there are so few truly great horses. Also, the following searching question might well be asked: Why do many horses start training in great physical shape, only to slow down and lose appetite, and be taken out of training for some rest?

RESULTS MORE IMPORTANT THAN COST PER BAG

As is true when buying anything — whether it be a suit of clothes, a dinner, or whatnot — horse feed should be bought on a quality basis, rather than what is cheapest. Results are more important than cost per bag. If this were not so, one might well buy and feed many cheap products, including sawdust.

Consideration should be given to meeting the specific needs of the horse, with special attention given to providing adequate quantity and quality proteins, minerals, vitamins, unidentified factors, and palatability.

HOW TO FEED

Feeding horses is both an art and a science. The art is knowing how to feed and how to take care of each horse's individual requirements. The science is meeting the nutritive requirements with the right combination of ingredients.

AMOUNT TO FEED

Because the horse has a limited digestive capacity, the amount of concentrates must be increased and the roughages decreased when the energy needs rise with more work. The following general guides may be used for the daily ration of horses under usual conditions.

Horses at light work (1 to 3 hours per day of riding or driving) — Allow ⅖ to ½ lb. of grain and 1¼ to 1½ lb. of hay per day per 100 lb. of body weight.

Horses at medium work (3 to 5 hours per day of riding or driving) — Allow about ¾ lb. of grain and 1 to 1¼ lb. of hay per 100 lb. of body weight.

Horses at hard work (5 to 8 hours per day of riding and driving) — Allow about 1¼ to 1⅓ lb. of grain and 1 to 1¼ lb. of hay per 100 lb. of body weight.

As will be noted from these recommendations, the total allowance of both concentrates and hay should be about 2 to 2½ lb. daily per 100 lb. of body weight.

The recommended feed allowances on the basis of animal weight are equally applicable to equines of all sizes, including ponies and donkeys;

simply vary as necessary according to the work performed and the individuality of the animal.

About 6 to 12 lb. of grain daily is an average grain ration for a light horse at medium or light work. Racehorses in training usually consume 10 to 16 lb. of grain per day; the exact amount varies with the individual requirements and the amount of work. The hay allowance averages about 1 to 1¼ lb. daily per 100 lb. of body weight, but it is restricted as the grain allowance is increased. Light feeders should not be over-worked.

Horses differ just as people do, in feed required and tendency to put on weight. Moreover, the age and degree of activity of horses are quite important factors; the amount of feed should be increased in keeping with the amount, severity, and speed of work. Also, feed requirements are influenced by weather — for example, under ideal fall weather conditions, a horse may require 14 lb. of 60 percent TDN feed daily, whereas in the same area the same horse may require 16 lb. daily of the same feed in July and August, and 20 lb. in the winter.

The quantities of feeds recommended are intended as guides only. The allowance, especially the concentrates, should be increased when the horse is too thin and decreased when the horse is too fat.

Overfeeding

Overfeeding may result in two consequences: if done suddenly it may cause founder (laminitis); if prolonged it will likely result in obesity (too fat). Both are bad.

The main qualities desired in horses are trimness, action, spirit, and endurance. These qualities cannot be obtained in horses that are overfed and fat. The latter is especially true with horses used for racing, where the carrying of any surplus body weight must be avoided.

Self-Feeding

A few caretakers do self-feed high energy rations, but, sooner or later, those who do usually founder a valuable horse. Except for the use of reasonably hard salt-protein blocks, salt-feed mixes in meal form (never in pellet form), or high roughage rations, the self-feeding of horses is not recommended.

STARTING HORSES ON FEED

Horses must be accustomed to changes in feed gradually. In general, they may be given as much nonlegume roughage as they will consume. But they must be accustomed gradually to high quality legumes, which may be very laxative. This can be done by slowly replacing the non-legume roughage with greater quantities of legumes. Also, as the grain ration is increased, the roughage is decreased.

Starting horses on grain requires care and good judgment. Usually it is advisable first to accustom them to a bulky type of ration; a starting ration with considerable rolled oats is excellent for this purpose.

The keenness of the appetite and the consistency of the droppings are an excellent index of a horse's capacity to take more feed. In all instances, scouring (diarrhea) should be avoided.

FREQUENCY, REGULARITY, AND ORDER OF FEEDING

The grain ration usually is divided into three equal feeds given morning, noon, and night. Because a digestive tract distended with hay is a hindrance in hard work, most of the hay should be fed at night. The common practice is to feed one-quarter of the daily hay allowance at both the morning and noon feedings and the remaining half at night, when the animals have plenty of time to eat leisurely.

Usually the grain ration is fed first and then the roughage. This way, the animals can eat the bulky roughages more leisurely.

Horses learn to anticipate their feed. Accordingly, they should be fed at the same time each day. During warm weather, they will eat better if the feeding hours are early and late, in the cool of the day.

AVOID SUDDEN CHANGES

Sudden changes in diet should be avoided, especially when changing from a less concentrated ration to a more concentrated one. If this rule of feeding is ignored, horses have digestive disturbances and go "off feed." When ingredients are added or omitted, the change should be made gradually. Likewise, caution should be exercised in turning horses to pasture or in transferring them to more lush grazing.

ATTENTION TO DETAILS

A successful horseman pays great attention to details. In addition to maintaining the health and comfort of his animals, he also considers their individual likes and temperaments. Nervousness and inefficient use of feed are caused by excessive exercise to the point of undue fatigue and stress, rough treatment, noise, and excitement.

BOLTING FEED

Horses that eat too rapidly are said to be bolting their feed. It can be lessened by spreading the concentrate thinly over the bottom of a large grain box, so that the horse cannot get a large mouthful; or by placing in the grain box a few smooth stones about the size of baseballs, so that the horse has to work to get feed.

EATING BEDDING

Sometimes gluttonous animals eat their bedding. This is undesirable because (1) most bedding materials are low in nutritional value, and (2) feces-soiled bedding adds to the parasite problem.

PICA; WOOD CHEWING

Horses, particularly those confined to stalls or lots, sometimes consume such materials as dirt, hair, bones, or feces. Such depraved appetites are known as "pica." This condition is usually caused by one or more of the following conditions:

1. *Boredom,* because they have nothing to do. The more limited the exercise, and the more quickly they consume their feed, the greater the unoccupied time available and the consequent boredom.

    By contrast, little *Eohippus* (the dawn horse of 58 million years ago) was a denizen of the swamp. Later, through evolution, he became a creature of the prairies. Although his natural habitat shifted during this long predomestication period, until man confined him he gleaned the feeds provided by nature. Inevitably, this occupied his time and provided exercise.

2. *Nutritional inadequacies,* which may be due to (a) a deficiency of one or more nutrients, (b) an imbalance between certain nutrients, or (c) objection to the physical form of the ration — for example, it may be ground too finely.

3. *Psychological stress and habit,* which contribute to the behavior of horses, and which have been accentuated by the unnatural environment to which man has subjected them.

Whatever the reason(s) for pica, the suspected causative factor(s) should first be rectified. When and where needed, the exercise should be stepped up; the eating time should be prolonged, and the interval between feedings shortened; nutritional deficiencies, imbalances, and physical form of ration should be corrected; and stress should be minimized. Even after these conditions have been rectified, it may be disconcerting to find that wood chewing, and perhaps various other forms of pica, persist among certain horses — perhaps due to habit. In the final analysis, there is only one foolproof way in which to prevent wood chewing, namely, to have no wood on which they can chew — to use metal, vinyl, or other similar materials, for fences and barns. Of course, this isn't always practical. So you can lessen, although you cannot entirely prevent, wood chewing through one or more of the following practices:

1. Stepping up the exercise.

2. Feeding three times a day, rather than twice a day, even though the total daily feed allowance remains the same.

3. Spreading out the feed in a larger feed container, and/or placing a few large stones about the size of a baseball in the feed container, thereby making the horse work harder and longer to obtain his feed.

4. Providing 2 to 4 lb. of straw or coarse grass hay per animal per day, thereby giving the horse something to nibble on during his spare time.

GENERAL FEEDING RULES

Observance of the following rules will help avoid some of the common difficulties that result from poor feeding practices.

1. Know the approximate weight and age of each animal.

2. Feed by weight of feed, not by volume (volume as determined by a coffee can or marked scoop). Horses do not require a certain volume of feed; rather, they require a certain amount of nutrients based on their body weight.

3. Avoid sudden changes in the ration.

4. Never feed moldy, musty, dusty, or frozen feed.

5. Feed regularly. Horses anticipate their feed.

6. Look for problems at feeding time; don't just dump the feed and run. Look for injuries and abnormalities.

7. Check the feces. Any change in quantity, odor, color, or composition may presage trouble.

8. Inspect the feedbox frequently to see if the horse goes off feed. Feed refusal means (1) the horse was overfed, (2) something is wrong with the feed, or (3) the horse is sick.

9. Keep the feed and water containers clean. Scrub them periodically to insure proper sanitation.

10. Do not overfeed. Some horses suffer from obesity, while others suffer from deficiency. Fat horses not receiving adequate exercise are predisposed to colic and founder. An old Arab proverb cautions: "The two greatest enemies of horses are fat and rest."

11. Force aggressive eaters to slow down. Some horses may bolt their feed when fed in deep narrow feed boxes. Their eating may be slowed by scattering the feed in a larger box, or by placing large round stones, bricks, or salt blocks in the feed container.

12. Accord timid eaters solitude to eat. Feed them where it is quiet and they will not be disturbed.

13. Do not feed from the hand; this can lead to *nibbling*.

14. Exercise stalled horses daily. It improves their appetite, digestion, and overall well being. This may be accomplished by riding, longeing, walking, ponying, swimming, or treadmilling.

15. Avoid excessive exercise (to the point of fatigue and stress), rough treatment, noise, and excitement.

16. Do not feed concentrates 1 hour before or within 1 hour after hard work.

17. Feed horses as individuals; consider their likes and temperaments. Learn the peculiarities and desires of each animal because each one is different.

18. Gradually decrease the condition of horses that have been fitted for show or sale. Many caretakers accomplish this difficult task, and yet retain strong vigorous animals, by cutting down gradually on the feed and increasing the exercise.

19. Prevent wood chewing. This habit usually results from boredom, lack of exercise, lack of adequate roughage, or lack of phosphorus, so alleviate the causes.

20. Make certain that the horse's teeth are sound.

21. Know the signs of a well-fed, healthy horse, any departure from which constitutes a warning signal.

SIGNS OF A WELL-FED, HEALTHY HORSE

The signs of a well-fed, healthy horse are:

Contentment — The horse looks completely unworried when resting.

Alertness — The horse is "bright eyed and bushy tailed," and he will perk up his ears at the slightest provocation.

Good appetite — The appetite is good, as indicated by neighing and pawing before he is fed and attacking the feed with relish.

Sleek coat and pliable, elastic skin — A sleek coat and a pliable, elastic skin characterize a healthy horse. When the hair loses its luster and the skin becomes dry, scurfy, and hidebound, usually trouble is ahead.

Pink eye membranes — The eye membranes, which can be seen when the lower lid is pulled down, should be pink and moist.

Normal feces and urine — The consistency of the feces varies with the diet. For example, lush pasture usually causes looseness, and pellets generally cause moist feces. Neither extreme dryness nor scouring should exist. Both the feces and urine should be passed without effort and free of blood, mucus, or pus.

Normal temperature, pulse, and breathing — The average rectal temperature of horses is 100.5° F, with a range of 99 to 100.8° F. The normal pulse rate is 32 to 44 beats per minute, and the normal breathing rate is 8 to 16 breaths per minute. In general, any marked and persistent deviations from these normal vital signs are signs of ill health.

FEEDING PLEASURE HORSES

Keeping pleasure horses — horses used for recreation and sport — in peak condition makes for greater satisfaction when they're used.

It is difficult to feed pleasure horses properly because their use is often irregular. Sometimes they're used moderately; at other times they're idle; at still other times they're worked hard over the weekend or on a trail ride.

Most horses used for pleasure are worked lightly, perhaps 1 to 3 hours of riding per day. Others are worked medium hard, as when ridden 3 to 5 hours per day. Still others are worked very hard, as when raced or when ridden 5 to 8 hours per day. The recommended daily feed allowance per 100 lb. body weight of pleasure horses in light, medium, and hard use follows:

Lb. Daily/100 lb. Weight of Horse	Light Use	Medium Use	Hard Use
Hay	1¼–1½	1–1¼	1–1¼
Grain	²⁄₅–½	¾–1	1¼–1⅓

Figure 6.7   Well-fed pleasure horse, in peak condition and animated. (Courtesy, Paso Fino Owners and Breeders Association, Columbus, North Carolina)

As shown above, the roughage content of the ration decreases and the concentrate content increases as the amount of work increases. This is because the digestibility and the efficiency of conversion are greater for high energy concentrates than for roughages.

Of course, horses differ in temperament and in ease of keeping. Also, no two horses will perform the same amount of work with an equal expenditure of energy, and no two horsemen will get the same amount of work out of the same horse. So, the feed allowance should be increased if the horse fails to maintain condition, and it should be decreased if the animal becomes too fat.

In season, pasture may replace hay, all or in part, according to the quality of the pasture. But the concentrate allowance of the working horse should remain about the same on pasture as in the stable or dry corral. There is a tendency of the pastured working horse to sweat and tire more easily (be "soft"), probably due to the high water content of green forage.

In addition to forage and grain, pleasure horses should have access to salt and a suitable mineral mix, fed free choice. The mineral requirements of the working horse differ from the idle horse mainly in the salt requirements, due to the loss of salt in perspiration.

The vitamin requirements of working horses are approximately the same as those of idle horses, except for the increase in the B-complex requirements due to the greater carbohydrate metabolism of the working horse.

FEEDING HORSES IN TRAINING

Horses in heavy training for specific purposes — such as training for racing, cutting, roping, jumping, or hunting — have a higher nutritional requirement than most pleasure horses. And the younger the animal in training, the higher the level of nutrition needed in order to develop and maintain sound legs and build a strong frame and body. Therefore, the level of work, the temperament of the individual, and the age of the horse determine the nutritional needs. For this reason, horses in training should be fed as individuals.

Horses in training will eat about 1½ lb. of grain and 1 lb. of hay per 100 lb. liveweight.

FEEDING RACEHORSES

Racehorses are equine athletes whose nutritive requirements are the most exacting, but the most poorly met, of all animals. This statement may be shocking to some, but it's true, because racehorses are commonly

- Started in training very shortly past 12 months of age, which is comparable to an adolescent boy or girl doing sweatshop labor.
- Moved from track to track under all sorts of conditions.
- Trained the year around, raced innumerable times each year, and forced to run when fatigued.
- Outdoors only a short time each day — usually before sunup, with the result that the sun's rays have little chance to produce vitamin D from the cholesterol in the skin.
- Without opportunity for even a few mouthfuls of grass — a rich, natural source of the B vitamins and unidentified factors.
- Fed oats, grass hay, and possibly bran — all produced in unknown areas and on soils of unknown composition. Such an oats-grass hay-bran ration is almost always deficient in vitamins A and D and the B vitamins, and lopsided and low in calcium and phosphorus.
- Given a potion of some concoction of questionable value — if not downright harmful.

By contrast, human athletes — college football teams and participants in the Olympics, for example — are usually required to eat at a special training table, supervised by nutrition experts. They are fed the best diet that science can formulate and technology can prepare. It's high in protein, rich in readily available energy, and fortified and balanced in vitamins and minerals.

It's small wonder, therefore, that so many equine athletes go unsound, whereas most human athletes compete year after year until overtaken by age.

Indeed, high-strung and highly stressed racehorses need special rations, just as human athletes do — and for the same reasons; and the younger the age, the more acute the need. This calls for rations high in protein, rich in readily available energy, fortified with vitamins, minerals, and unidentified factors — and with all nutrients in proper balance.

A racehorse is asked to develop a large amount of horsepower in a period of 1 to 3 minutes. The oxidations that occur in a racehorse's body are at a higher pitch than in an idle horse, and, therefore, more vitamins are required. In this connection, it is noteworthy that the late Clyde Beatty, great animal trainer of the circus, sweated off a pound under the stress of every 18-minute performance.

Also, racehorses are the prima donnas of the equine world; most of them are temperamental, and no two of them can be fed alike. They vary in rapidity of eating, in the quantity of feed that they will consume, in the proportion of concentrate to roughage that they will take, and in response to different caretakers. Thus, for best results, they must be fed as individuals.

Figure 6.8   Broodmare and foal; well fed, heads up.

Most racehorse rations are deplorably deficient in protein, simply because they are based on the minimum requirements of little-stressed, slow, plodding horses.

During the racing season, the hay of a racehorse should be limited to 7 or 8 pounds, whereas the concentrate allowance may range up to 16 pounds. Heavy roughage eaters may have to be muzzled, to keep them from eating their bedding. A bran mash is commonly fed once a week.

FEEDING BROODMARES

Regular and normal reproduction is the basis for profit on any horse breeding establishment. However, only 40 to 60 percent of mares bred produce foals. There are many causes of reproductive failure, but inadequate nutrition is a major one. The following pointers are pertinent to feeding a broodmare properly.

1. Condition the mare for breeding by providing adequate and proper feed and the right amount of exercise prior to the breeding season.

2. See that adequate proteins, minerals, and vitamins are available during the last third of pregnancy, when the fetus grows most rapidly.

3. Feed and water with care immediately before and after foaling. For the first 24 hours after parturition, the mare may have a little hay

and a limited amount of water from which the chill has been taken. A light feed of bran or a wet bran mash is suitable for the first feed and the following meal may consist of oats or a mixture of oats and bran. A reasonably generous allowance of good quality hay is permissible after the first day. If confined to the stable, as may be necessary in inclement weather, the mare should be kept on a limited and light grain and hay ration for about 10 days after foaling. Feeding too much grain at this time is likely to produce digestive disturbances in the mare and, even more hazardous, it may make her produce too much milk, which may cause indigestion in the foal. If weather conditions are favorable and it is possible to allow the mare to foal on a clean, lush pasture, she will regulate her own feed needs most admirably.

4. Provide adequate nutrition during lactation, because the requirements during this period are more rigorous than the requirements during pregnancy.

5. Make sure that young growing mares receive adequate nutrients; otherwise, the fetus will not develop properly or the dam will not produce milk except at the expense of her body tissues.

FEEDING STALLIONS

The ration exerts a powerful effect on sperm production and semen quality. Successful breeders adhere to the following stallion feeding rules.

1. Feed a balanced ration, giving particular attention to proteins, minerals, and vitamins.

2. Regulate the feed allowance, because the stallion can become infertile if he gets too fat. Also, increase the exercise when the stallion is not a sure breeder.

3. Provide pasture in season as a source of both nutrients and exercise.

FEEDING FOALS

Growth is the very foundation of horse production. This is so because horses cannot perform properly, or possess the necessary speed and endurance if their growth has been stunted or their skeletons have been injured by inadequate rations during early age. Naturally, these requirements become increasingly acute when horses are forced for early use, such as the training and racing of the two-year-old. Also, unless foals are rather liberally fed when young, they never attain the much-desired body form, even if they are well fed later in life; this point is especially important where young stock is sold or shown.

Figure 6.9 Stallion in breeding condition. (Courtesy, *The Quarter Horse Journal*, Amarillo, Texas)

The foal should be provided with a low-built grain box, or with a creep (a separate enclosure away from the dam) if on pasture.

The following pointers are pertinent to proper feeding of foals.

1. Start on feed early, which means at 10 days to 3 weeks of age. Rolled oats and wheat bran, to which a little brown sugar has been added, is especially palatable as a starting ration. Crushed or ground oats, cracked or ground corn, wheat bran, and a little linseed meal may be provided later with good results. Or a good commercial ration may be fed if desired and available.

2. Use a scientifically formulated ration even though it seems expensive, for usually it will represent a wise investment. Supplemental feeding also affords a convenient way in which to improve upon milk, by reinforcing it with certain minerals (for example, milk is low in iron and copper), vitamins, and additives.

   Provide a good hay, preferably a legume, or pasture, in addition to the foal's grain ration.

3. Allow about ½ lb. of grain daily per 100 lb. of body weight at 4 to 5 weeks of age. This ration should be increased by weaning time to about ¾ lb. or more per 100 lb. of body weight. The exact amount of the ration will vary with the individual, the type of feed, and the development desired.

4. Obtain growth with durability and soundness, which calls for expert care and particular emphasis on the kind of ration, feed allowance, and exercise.

5. Simplify weaning and setback by feeding foals so that they rely less upon their mothers.

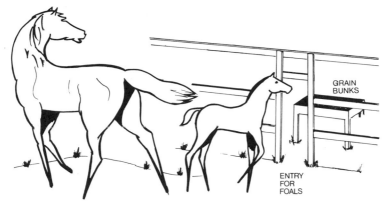

GRAIN
BUNKS

ENTRY
FOR
FOALS

Figure 6.10   A foal creep. With this arrangement the foal can be fed separately from the dam.

FEEDING WEANLINGS

The most critical period in the entire life of a horse is that interval from weaning time (about six months of age) until one year of age. Foals suckling their dams and receiving no grain may develop very satisfactorily up to weaning time. However, lack of preparation prior to weaning and neglect following the separation from the dam may prevent the animal from gaining proper size and shape. The primary objective in the breeding of horses is the economical production of a well-developed, sound individual at maturity. To achieve this result requires good care and management of weanlings.

No great setback or disturbances will be encountered at weaning time provided that the foals have developed a certain independence from proper grain feedings during the suckling period. Generally, weanlings should receive 1 to 1½ lb. of grain and 1½ to 2 lb. of hay daily per each 100 lb. of liveweight. The amount of feed will vary somewhat with the individual animal, the quality of roughage, available pastures, the price of feeds, and whether the weanling is being developed for show, race, or sale. Naturally, animals being developed for early use or sale should be fed more liberally, although it is equally important to retain clean, sound joints, legs, and feet — a condition which cannot be obtained so easily in heavily fitted animals.

Because of the rapid development of bone and muscle in weanlings, it is important that, in addition to ample quantity of feed, the ration also provides quality of proteins, and adequate minerals and vitamins.

FEEDING YEARLINGS

If young animals have been fed and cared for so that they are well grown and thrifty as yearlings, usually little difficulty will be experienced at any later date.

When on pasture, yearlings that are being grown for show or sale should receive grain in addition to grass. They should be confined to their stalls in the daytime during the hot days and turned out at night (because of not being exposed to sunshine, adequate vitamin D must be provided). This point needs to be emphasized when forced development is desired; for, good as pastures may be, they are roughages rather than concentrates.

The winter feeding program for the rising two-year-olds should be such as to produce plenty of bone and muscle rather than fat. From ½ to 1 lb. of grain and 1 to 1½ lb. of hay should be fed for each 100 lb. of liveweight. The quantity will vary with the quality of the roughage, the individuality of the animal, and the use for which the animal is produced. In producing for sale, more liberal feeding may be economical. Access to salt and to a mineral mixture should be provided at all times; or the minerals should be incorporated in the ration. An abundance of fresh, pure water must be available.

FEEDING TWO- AND THREE-YEAR-OLDS

Except for the fact that the two- and three-year-olds will be larger, and therefore will require more feed, a description of their proper care and management would be merely a repetition of the principles that have already been discussed for the yearling.

FITTING FOR SHOW OR SALE

Each year, many horses are fitted for shows or sales. In both cases, a fattening process is involved, but exercise is doubly essential.

For horses that are being fitted for shows, the conditioning process is also a matter of hardening, and the horses are used daily in harness or under saddle. Regardless of whether a sale or a show is the major objective, fleshing should be obtained without sacrificing action or soundness and without causing filling of the legs and hocks.

In fattening horses, the animals should be brought to full feed rather gradually, until the ration reaches a maximum of about 2 lb. of grain daily for each 100 lb. of liveweight. When on full feed, horses make surprising gains. Daily weight gains of 4 to 5 lb. are not uncommon. Such animals soon become fat, sleek, and attractive. This is probably the basis for the statement that "fat will cover up a multitude of sins in a horse."

Although exercise is desirable from the standpoint of keeping the animals sound, it is estimated that such activity decreases the daily rate of gains by as much as 20 percent. Because of the greater cost of gains and the expense involved in bringing about forced exercise, most feeders of sale horses limit the exercise to that obtained naturally from running in a paddock.

In comparison with finishing cattle or sheep, there is more risk in fattening horses. Heavily fed horses kept in idleness are likely to become blemished and injured through playfulness, and there are more sicknesses among liberally fed horses than in other classes of stock handled in a similar manner.

In fitting show horses, the finish must remain firm and hard, the action superb, and the soundness unquestioned. Thus, they must be carefully fed, groomed, and exercised to bring them to proper bloom.

Horsemen who fit and sell yearlings or younger animals may feed a palatable milk replacer or commercial feed to advantage.

CHEMICAL ANALYSIS OF FEEDS

Feed composition tables ("book values"), or average analysis, should be considered only as guides, because of wide variations in the composition of feeds. For example, the protein and moisture content of milo and hay are quite variable. Wherever possible, especially with large operations, it is best to take a representative sample of each major feed ingredient and have a chemical analysis made of it for the more common constituents — protein, fat, fiber, nitrogen-free extract, and moisture; and often calcium, phosphorus, and carotene. Such ingredients as oil meals and prepared supplements, which must meet specific standards, need not be analyzed so often, except as quality control measures.

Despite the recognized value of a chemical analysis, it is not the total answer. It does not provide information on the availability of nutrients to the animal; it varies from sample to sample, because feeds vary and a representative sample is not always easily obtained; and it does not tell anything about the associated effect of feedstuffs. Nor does a chemical analysis tell anything about taste, palatability, texture, undesirable physiological effects such as digestive disturbances and laxativeness. Thus, one cannot buy feed for horses on the basis of chemical analysis alone, as is substantiated by the example that follows.

Example: Based on chemical analysis and price, which of the following would you choose?

	#1	#2	#3	#4
Crude protein %	9.06	11.23	7.4	9.8
Fat %		13.59		9.1
Sugar %		0.43	51.2	
Fiber %		16.5		0.3
Moisture %		0.63		5.9

	#1	#2	#3	#4
Nitrogen-free extract* %				72.8
Price/ton $	60.00	100.00	40.00	80.00
Cost/cwt $	3.00	5.00	2.00	4.00
Cost/lb. protein $	0.33	.445	0.27	0.41

Here's the identity of the samples:

Sample #1   soft coal

Sample #2   coffee grounds

Sample #3   candy

Sample #4   crackers

---

* *Note:* NFE is determined by subtracting the sum of the percentages of moisture, crude protein, crude fat, crude fiber, and ash from 100.

However, a chemical analysis does give a solid foundation on which to start in evaluating feeds. Also, with chemical analysis at hand, and bearing in mind that it's the composition of the total feed (the finished ration) that counts, the person formulating the ration can more intelligently determine the quantity of protein to buy, and the kind and amounts of minerals and vitamins to add.

TERMS USED IN FEED ANALYSES AND GUARANTEES

Knowledge of the following terms is requisite to understanding feed analyses and guarantees.

Dry matter is found by determining the percentage of water and subtracting the water content from 100 percent.

Crude protein is used to designate the nitrogenous constituents of a feed. The percentage is obtained by multiplying the percentage of total nitrogen by the factor 6.25. The nitrogen is derived chiefly from complex chemical compounds called amino acids.

Crude fat is the material that is extracted from moisture-free feeds by ether. It consists largely of fats and oils with small amounts of waxes, resins, and coloring matter. In calculating the heat and energy value of the feeds, the fat is considered 2.25 times that of either nitrogen-free extract or protein.

Crude fiber is the relatively insoluble carbohydrate portion of a feed consisting chiefly of cellulose. It is determined by its insolubility in dilute acids and alkalis.

Ash is the mineral matter of a feed. It is the residue remaining after complete burning of the organic matter.

Nitrogen-free extract consists principally of sugars, starches, pentoses and non-nitrogenous organic acids. The percentage is determined by subtracting the sum of the percentages of moisture, crude protein, crude fat, crude fiber, and ash from 100.

Carbohydrates represent the sum of the crude fiber and nitrogen-free extract.

Calcium and phosphorus are essential mineral elements that are present in feeds in varying quantities. Mineral feeds are usually high in source materials of these elements.

TDN — The digestible nutrients of any ingredient are obtained by multiplying the percentage of each nutrient by the digestion coefficient. For example, dent corn contains 8.9 percent protein, of which 77 percent is digestible. Therefore, the percent of digestible protein is 6.9. The value given for TDN is the sum of all the digestible organic nutrients — protein, fiber, nitrogen-free extract, and fat (the latter multiplied by 2.25).

SOIL ANALYSIS

For the horseman who produces his own hay, a soil analysis can be very helpful; for example, (1) the phosphorus content of soils affects plant composition, (2) soils high in molybdenum and selenium affect the composition of the feeds produced, (3) iodine-deficient areas are important in horse nutrition, and (4) other similar soil-plant-animal relationships are important.

No analysis is any better than the sample taken, so make sure that you get a representative sample of soil. Ask your county agent (farm

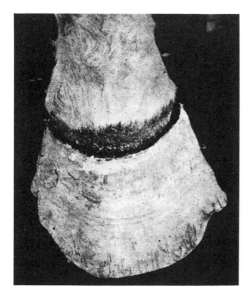

Figure 6.11 Separation of the hoof from the foot of a horse due to selenium poisoning, caused by consuming certain plants grown on soils containing selenium. (Courtesy, A. L. Moxon, South Dakota State University, Brookings, South Dakota)

advisor) how to take the samples and where to send them. Some colleges of agriculture make soil analyses at nominal cost.

NUTRITIONAL DISEASES AND AILMENTS

Nutritional deficiencies may be brought about either by (1) too little feed, or (2) rations that are too low in one or more nutrients. Also, forced production (such as racing two-year-olds) and the feeding of forages and grains which are often produced on leached or depleted soils have created many problems in nutrition. This condition has been further aggravated through the increased confinement of horses, many animals being confined to stalls or lots all or a large part of the year. Under these unnatural conditions, nutritional diseases and ailments have become increasingly common.

Table 6.8 NUTRITIONAL DISEASES AND AILMENTS OF HORSES

Disease	Species Affected	Cause	Symptoms (and Age or Group Most Affected)	Distribution and Losses Caused by
Anemia, nutritional	All warm-blooded animals and man.	Commonly an iron deficiency, but may be caused by a deficiency of copper, cobalt, and/or certain vitamins — especially B-12.	Loss of appetite, poor performance, progressive emaciation and death. Most prevalent in suckling young.	Worldwide. Losses consist of retarded growth and deaths.
Azoturia (Hemoglobinuria, Monday morning disease, Blackwater, tying up)	Horses	Associated with faulty carbohydrate metabolism, and with work following a period of idleness in the stall on full rations. Thought to be caused by excess glycogen stored in the muscle.	Profuse sweating, abdominal distress, wine-colored urine, stiff gait, reluctance to move, and lameness. Finally, animal assumes a sitting position, and eventually falls prostrate on the side.	Worldwide, but the disease is seldom seen in horses at pasture and rarely in horses at constant work.

Although the cause, prevention, and treatment of most equine nutritional diseases and ailments are known, they continue to reduce profits in the livestock industry simply because the available knowledge is not put into practice. Moreover, those widespread nutritional deficiencies which are not of sufficient proportions to produce clear-cut deficiency symptoms cause even greater economic losses because they go unnoticed and unrectified.

Unfortunately, there are no warning signals to tell a caretaker when a horse is not getting enough of a certain nutrient. A continuing inadequate supply of any one of several nutrients can produce illness which is very hard to diagnose until it becomes severe, at which time it is difficult and expensive — if not too late — to treat. The important thing, therefore, is to insure against such deficiencies occurring. But horsemen should not shower a horse with mistaken kindness through using shotgun-type vitamin preparations. Instead, the quantity of each nutrient should be based on available scientific knowledge.

Table 6.8 contains a summary of the important nutritional diseases and ailments affecting horses.

Treatment	Control and Eradication	Prevention	Remarks
Provide dietary sources of the nutrient or nutrients known to cause the condition.	When nutritional anemia is encountered, it can usually be brought under control by supplying dietary sources of the nutrient or nutrients known to cause the condition.	Supply dietary sources of iron, copper, cobalt, and certain vitamins. Keep suckling animals confined to a minimum and provide supplemental feeds at an early age.	Anemia is a condition in which the blood is either deficient in quality or quantity (a deficient quality refers to a deficiency in hemoglobin and/or red cells). Levels of iron in most feeds believed to be ample, since most feeds contain 40 to 400 milligrams/lb.
Absolute rest and quiet. While awaiting the veterinarian, apply heated cloths or blankets, or hot-water bottles to the swollen and hardened muscles. The veterinarian should determine the treatment.	Azoturia is noncontagious. When trouble is encountered, decrease the ration and increase the exercise on idle days.	Restrict the ration and provide daily exercise when the animal is idle. Give a wet bran mash the evening before an idle day or turn the idle horses to pasture. Some horsemen feel that a diuretic or increased B vitamins will prevent azoturia.	The chances of recovery are good for horses that remain standing, are not forced to move after the signs are noticed, and whose pulses return to normal within 24 hours.

(cont.)

Table 6.8 NUTRITIONAL DISEASES AND AILMENTS OF HORSES (cont.)

Disease	Species Affected	Cause	Symptoms (and Age or Group Most Affected)	Distribution and Losses Caused by
Colic	Horses	Internal parasites are the number one cause of colic. Additional causes are improper feeding, working, or watering.	Excruciating pain; and depending on the type of colic, other symptoms are: The horse looking at his belly, distended abdomen, increased intestinal rumbling, violent rolling and kicking, profuse sweating, constipation, and refusal of feed and water.	Worldwide. Colic is the most common ailment among horses and is the leading cause of death.
Fescue Foot	Horses, cattle, sheep.	The fungus, *Acyemonium coenophialum*, which lives in the leaves, stems, and seeds of tall fescue.	Decrease or absence of milk production, prolonged gestation, abortion, and thickened placenta.	Wherever tall fescue is grown.
Fluorine poisoning (Fluorosis)	All farm animals, poultry, and man.	Ingesting excessive quantities of fluorine through the feed, water, or air, or a combination of these.	Abnormal teeth (especially mottled enamel) and bones, stiffness of joints, loss of appetite, emaciation, reduction in milk flow, diarrhea, and salt hunger.	The water in parts of Arkansas, California, South Carolina, and Texas has been reported to contain excess fluorine. Occasionally throughout the U.S. high fluorine phosphates are used in mineral mixtures. Areas near certain industries which heat earthy materials or burn high-fluoride coal may be a problem.

Treatment	Control and Eradication	Prevention	Remarks
Call a veterinarian. To keep the horse from injuring itself, (1) place it in a large, well-bedded stall, or (2) take it for a slow walk. Most veterinarians use the stomach tube in the treatment of colic.	Proper feeding, working, and watering.	Parasite control, proper feeding, working, and watering.	Colic is also a symptom of abdominal pain that can be caused by a number of different conditions. For example, bloodworms cause a colic due to damage to the walls of blood vessels.
There is no effective treatment.		Seeding of fungus-free fescue seed. Where fescue foot is a problem, gestating mares should be removed from fescue pastures the last 2 to 3 months of pregnancy.	
Any damage may be permanent, but animals which have not developed severe symptoms may be helped to some extent, if the sources of excess fluorine are eliminated.	Discontinue the use of feeds, water, or mineral supplements containing excessive fluorine.	Avoid the use of feeds, water, or mineral supplements containing excessive fluorine. Not more than 60 ppm fluorine should be present in dry matter of rations when rock phosphate is fed.	Fluorine is a cumulative poison.

(cont.)

Table 6.8 NUTRITIONAL DISEASES AND AILMENTS OF HORSES (*cont.*)

Disease	Species Affected	Cause	Symptoms (and Age or Group Most Affected)	Distribution and Losses Caused by
Founder (Laminitis)	Horses, cattle, sheep, goats.	Overeating (grain; or lush legume or grass, known as "grass founder"), over-drinking, or inflammation of the uterus following par-turition. Also intestinal inflam-mation. Too rapid change in the ration.	Extreme pain, fever (103° to 106° F) and reluctance to move. If neglected, chronic laminitis will de-velop, resulting in a dropping of the hoof soles and a turning up of the toe walls.	Worldwide. Actual death losses from founder are not very great, but use-fulness may be af-fected.
Heaves	Horses, mules.	Exact cause un-known, but it is known that the condition is often associated with the feeding of damaged, dusty, or moldy hay. It often follows severe respira-tory infections such as strangles. Probably an allergy.	Difficulty in forcing air out of the lungs, resulting in a jerking of flanks (double flank action) and coughing. The nostrils are often slightly dilated and there is a nasal discharge.	Worldwide. Losses are negligible.
Iodine Deficiency (Goiter)	All farm animals and man.	A failure of the body to obtain sufficient iodine from which the thyroid gland can form thyrox-in (an iodine-containing compound).	Foals may be weak.	Northwestern U.S. and the Great Lakes region. Also, goiter areas are scattered all over the world.

Treatment	Control and Eradication	Prevention	Remarks
Pending arrival of the veterinarian, the attendant should stand the animal's feet in a cold-water bath. Antihistamines, restricting the diet, use of diuretics, and anti-inflammatory agents, such as corticosteroids or phenylbutazone, may speed up recovery and alleviate serious aftereffects.	Alleviate the causes; namely, (1) overeating, (2) overdrinking, and/or (3) inflammation of the uterus following parturition.	Avoid overeating and overdrinking (especially when hot). Seek veterinary attention if mares retain the afterbirth longer than 12 hours.	Unless foundered animals are quite valuable, it is usually desirable to dispose of them following a case of severe founder.
No satisfactory treatment, although affected animals are less bothered if turned to pasture, if used only at light work, or if the hay is sprinkled lightly with water at feeding.	(See Prevention.)	Avoid the use of damaged feeds. Feed an all-pelleted ration, thereby alleviating dust.	Unlike a human, a horse cannot breathe through its mouth. Basically, heaves is a rupture of some of the alveoli in the lungs, of which the specific cause is unknown. Heaves in horses is similar to emphysema in people.
Once the iodine-deficiency symptoms appear in farm animals, no treatment is very effective.	At the first signs of iodine deficiency, an iodized salt should be fed to all farm animals.	In iodine-deficient areas, feed iodized salt to all farm animals throughout the year. Salt containing 0.01% potassium iodide is recommended.	The enlarged thyroid gland (goiter) is nature's way of attempting to make sufficient thyroxin under conditions where a deficiency exists. Large excesses of iodine may cause abortions.

(cont.)

Table 6.8 NUTRITIONAL DISEASES AND AILMENTS OF HORSES (*cont.*)

Disease	Species Affected	Cause	Symptoms (and Age or Group Most Affected)	Distribution and Losses Caused by
Night Blindness (Nyctalopia)	All farm animals and humans.	Deficiency of Vitamin A.	Slow dark adaptation, progressing to blindness.	Worldwide. Especially prevalent during an extended drought, or in winter when feeding bleached grass/hay.
Nitrate Poisoning (oat-hay poisoning; cornstalk poisoning)	It may affect horses and sheep, but primarily horses.	Forages of most grain crops, sudan grass, and numerous weeds. Inorganic nitrate or nitrite salts, or nitrate fertilizer. Ponds or shallow wells with runoff water from barnyards or well-fertilized soils.	Rapid breathing and pulse rate, diarrhea, frequent urination, staggering gait. Blue color of the mucous membranes and muzzle due to lack of oxygen. Blood is a brown color due to formation of methemoglobin.	Nitrate poisoning increases wherever more nitrogen fertilizers are used.
Osteomalacia	All farm animals.	Inadequate phosphorus, sometimes inadequate calcium, and sometimes inadequate intake of both calcium and phosphorus. Lack of vitamin D. Incorrect ratio of calcium and phosphorus.	Phosphorus deficiency symptoms are: depraved appetite (gnawing on bones, wood, or other objects, or eating dirt); lack of appetite, stiffness of joints, failure to breed regularly, decreased milk production, and an emaciated appearance. Calcium deficiency symptoms are fragile bones, reproductive failures, and lowered lactations. Mature animals most affected. Most of the acute cases occur during pregnancy and lactation.	Southwestern U.S. is classed as a phosphorus-deficient area, whereas calcium-deficient areas have been reported in parts of Florida, Louisiana, Nebraska, Virginia, and W. Virginia.

Treatment	Control and Eradication	Prevention	Remarks
Correcting the vitamin A deficiency.	Provide adequate carotene and/or vitamin A.	Provide good sources of carotene in the ration or add vitamin A.	High levels of nitrates interfere with the conversion of carotene to vitamin A.
A 4% solution of methylene blue administered by a veterinarian intravenously at the rate of 100 cc/ 1,000 lb. body weight.	When nitrate trouble is expected or encountered, contact the veterinarian or county agent. Do not feed large amounts of high-nitrate or high-nitrite feeds.	Nitrate toxicity may be reduced by (1) feeding high levels of grain and other high-energy feeds and vitamin A, (2) limiting the amount of high-nitrate feeds, and (3) ensiling forages that are high in nitrates.	During digestion, nitrates are reduced to nitrites, which are 10 to 15 times more toxic than nitrates to horses.
Increase the calcium and phosphorus content of feeds through fertilizing the soils. Select natural feeds that contain sufficient quantities of calcium and phosphorus. Feed a special mineral supplement or supplements. If the disease is far advanced, treatment will not be successful.	(See Treatment.)	Feed balanced rations, and allow animals free access to a suitable phosphorus and calcium supplement.	Calcium deficiencies are much more rare than phosphorus deficiencies in horses.

(cont.)

Table 6.8 Nutritional Diseases and Ailments of Horses (cont.)

Disease	Species Affected	Cause	Symptoms (and Age or Group Most Affected)	Distribution and Losses Caused by
Periodic Ophthalmia (Moon Blindness)	Horses, mules, asses.	It may be due to deficiency of riboflavin in the ration. However, it may be caused by autoimmune reaction; allergic reaction; genetics; leptospirosis, brucellosis, or strangles; parasites; or fungi.	Periods of cloudy vision, in one or both eyes, which may last for a few days to a week or two and then clear up; but it recurs at intervals, eventually culminating in blindness in one or both eyes.	In many parts of the world. In the U.S., it occurs most frequently in the states east of the Missouri River.
Rickets	All farm animals and man.	Lack of calcium, phosphorus, or vitamin D, or an incorrect ratio of the two minerals.	Enlargement of the knee and hock joints, and the animal may exhibit great pain when moving about. Irregular bulges (beaded ribs) at juncture of ribs with breastbone, and bowed legs. Rickets is a disease of young animals, including foals.	Worldwide. It is seldom fatal.
Salt Deficiency	All farm animals and man.	Lack of salt (sodium chloride).	Loss of appetite, retarded growth, loss of weight, a rough coat, lowered production of milk, and a ravenous appetite for salt.	Worldwide, especially among grass-eating animals and the pig.

Treatment	Control and Eradication	Prevention	Remarks
Antibiotics or corticosteroids administered promptly are helpful. Immediately (1) change to greener hay or grass, or (2) add riboflavin at the rate of 40 mg per horse per day.	If symptoms of moon blindness are observed, immediately (1) change to greener hay or grass, or (2) add riboflavin to the ration at the rate of 40 mg per horse per day.	Feed high-riboflavin green grass or well-cured green leafy hays; or Add riboflavin to the ration at the rate of 40 mg per horse per day.	Lack of riboflavin is not the only factor causing periodic ophthalmia. Sometimes it follows leptospirosis in horses, and it may be caused by a localized hypersensitivity; allergic reaction; genetics; leptospirosis, brucellosis, or strangles; or fungi. This disease has been known to exist for at least 2,000 years.
If the disease has not advanced too far, treatment may be successful by supplying adequate amounts of vitamin D, calcium, and phosphorus, and/ or adjusting the ratio of calcium to phosphorus.	(See Prevention.)	Provide (1) sufficient calcium, phosphorus, and vitamin D, and (2) a correct ratio of the two minerals. Expose the animal to direct sunlight as much as possible, allow it free access to a suitable mineral mixture, and provide good quality sun-cured hay or pasture grown on well-fertilized soil.	Rickets is characterized by a failure of growing bone to ossify or harden properly.
Salt-starved animals should be gradually accustomed to salt; slowly increase the hand-fed allowance until the animals may be safely allowed free access to it.	(See Treatment and Prevention.)	Provide plenty of salt at all times, preferably by free-choice feeding.	Common salt is one of the most essential minerals for grass-eating animals and one of the easiest and cheapest to provide. Excess salt intake can result in toxicity.

(cont.)

Table 6.8 Nutritional Diseases and Ailments of Horses (*cont.*)

Disease	Species Affected	Cause	Symptoms (and Age or Group Most Affected)	Distribution and Losses Caused by
Salt Poisoning	All farm animals, including horses, but swine and sheep most frequently affected.	When excess salt is fed after a period of salt starvation. When salt is improperly used to govern self-feeding of concentrates.	Extreme nervousness, muscle twitching, tremors, staggering, blindness, normal temperature, rapid pulse, diarrhea, followed by death.	Salt poisoning is relatively rare.
Selenium Poisoning (Alkali disease)	All farm animals and man.	Consumption of plants grown on soils containing high levels of selenium.	Loss of hair from the mane and tail in horses. In severe cases, the hoofs slough off, lameness occurs, food consumption decreases, and death may occur by starvation.	In certain regions of western U.S. — especially certain areas in South Dakota, Montana, Wyoming, Nebraska, Kansas, and perhaps areas in other states in the Great Plains and Rocky Mountains. Also in Canada.
Urinary Calculi (Gravel, Stones, Water Belly)	Horses, cattle, sheep, goats, mink, man.	Unknown, but there is a higher incidence when there is: a higher phosphorus than calcium intake, a high potassium intake, a high proportion of beet pulp or grain sorghum in the ration.	Frequent attempts to urinate, dribbling or stoppage of the urine, pain and renal colic. Usually only males affected, the females being able to pass the concretions. Bladder may rupture, with death following. Otherwise, uremic poisoning may set in.	Worldwide. Affected animals seldom recover completely.

Treatment	Control and Eradication	Prevention	Remarks
Provide large amounts of fresh water. The veterinarian may give water by stomach tube to those that cannot or will not drink.	Provide adequate salt at all times.	When animals have been salt-starved, limit feed salt and increase gradually.	Wild animals that are salt-starved may gorge themselves when they come upon a new salt lick.
Although arsenic has been shown to counteract the effects of selenium toxicity, there appears to be no practical method of treating other than removal of animals from affected areas.	(See Prevention.)	Abandon areas where soils contain selenium, because crops produced on such soils constitute a menace to both animals and man.	Chronic cases of selenium poisoning occur when animals consume feeds containing 8.5 ppm of selenium over an extended period; acute cases occur on 500 to 1,000 ppm. The toxic levels of selenium are in the range of 2.27–4.54 mg/lb. of feed. The maximum level of selenium recommended by FDA is 2 ppm.
Once calculi develop, dietary treatment appears to be of little value. In horses, bladder calculi must be removed surgically.	Avoid high phosphorus and low calcium. Keep the Ca:P ratio between 2:1 and 1:1.	Good feed and management appear to lessen the incidence, but no sure preventive is known. 1 to 3% salt in the concentrate ration may help (using the higher levels in the winter when water consumption is normally lower).	Calculi are stone-like concretions in the urinary tract which almost always originate in the kidneys. These stones block the passage of urine.

(cont.)

Table 6.8 NUTRITIONAL DISEASES AND AILMENTS OF HORSES (*cont.*)

Disease	Species Affected	Cause	Symptoms (and Age or Group Most Affected)	Distribution and Losses Caused by
Vitamin A Deficiency (Night Blindness and Xerophthalmia)	All farm animals and man.	Vitamin A deficiency.	Night blindness, the first symptom of vitamin A deficiency, is characterized by faulty vision, especially noticeable when the affected animal is forced to move about in twilight in strange surroundings. Xerophthalmia develops in the advanced stages of vitamin A deficiency. The eyes become severely affected, and blindness may follow. Also, a severe deficiency of vitamin A may cause reproductive difficulties, poor or uneven hoof development, certain leg bone weaknesses, difficulty in breathing, incoordination, and poor appetite.	Worldwide.

Treatment	Control and Eradication	Prevention	Remarks
Add stabilized vitamin A to the ration.	(See Treatment and Prevention.)	Provide good sources of carotene (vitamin A) through green, leafy hays; silage; lush, green pastures; yellow corn or green and yellow peas; whole milk; fish oil; or add stabilized vitamin A to the ration.	

PASTURES

Figure 7.1 Good horsemen, good horses, and good pastures go together. (Photo by Ernst Peterson, Hamilton, Montana)

The great horse-breeding centers of the world — Kentucky, Ireland, and New Zealand, to name three of them — are characterized by good pastures. Yet, it is becoming difficult to provide good pasture for horses, especially in suburban areas. Also, it is recognized that many horsemen are prone to overrate the quality of their grass.

In season and when available, good pastures — pastures that are more than mere gymnasiums for horses — should be provided, especially for idle horses, broodmares, and young stock. In fact, pastures have a very definite place for all horses, with the possible exception of animals at heavy work or in training. Even with the latter, pastures may be used with discretion. Horses in heavy use may be turned to pasture at night or over the weekend. Certainly, the total benefits derived from pasture are to the good, although lush vegetation may have some laxative effects and produce a greater tendency to sweat.

The use of a temporary or seeded pasture grown in regular crop rotation is recommended instead of a permanent pasture that may become infested with parasites. However, the parasites in horse pastures can be reduced dramatically by picking up the manure twice a week. An Ohio State University study showed that a pasture routinely cleaned in this manner had 18 times fewer parasites than an uncleaned pasture. Manure can be removed manually or mechanically. In England, a power sweeper is available, consisting of a small tractor fitted with a vacuum pump powered by a tractor or small engine.

Horse pastures should be well drained and not too rough or stony. All dangerous places such as pits, stumps, poles, and tanks should be guarded. Shade, water, and suitable minerals should be available in all pastures.

Most horse pastures can be improved by seeding new and better varieties of grasses and legumes and by fertilizing and management. Also, horsemen need to give attention to supplementing some pastures with additional feed. Pastures early in the season have a high water content and lack energy. Mature, weathered grass is almost always deficient in protein, with as little as three percent or less, and low in carotene, the precursor of vitamin A. However, these deficiencies can be corrected by proper supplemental feeding.

In addition to the nutritive value of the grass, pasture provides invaluable exercise on natural footing, with plenty of sunshine, fresh air, and lowered feeding costs as added benefits. Feeding on pasture is the ideal existence for young stock and breeding animals.

But pastures should not be taken for granted. Again and again, scientists and practical horsemen have demonstrated that the following desired goals in pasture production are well within the realm of possibility:

- To produce higher yields of palatable and nutritious forage.
- To extend the grazing season from as early in the spring to as late in the fall as possible.
- To provide a fairly uniform supply of feed throughout the entire season.

KINDS OF PASTURE

Broadly speaking, all horse pastures may be classified as either (1) permanent pastures, or (2) seeded or temporary pastures.

1. *Permanent pastures* — Those which, with proper care, last for many years. They are most commonly found on land that cannot be used profitably for cultivated crops, mainly because of topography, moisture, or fertility. The vast majority of U.S. farms have one or

Figure 7.2 Broodmares on permanent pastures on a western range. (Photo by Ernst Peterson, Hamilton, Montana)

more permanent pastures, and most range areas come under this classification.

2. *Seeded or temporary pastures* — Seeded pastures are used as part of the established crop rotation. They are generally used for two to seven years before plowing.

LEGUMES AND GRASSES ADAPTED TO 10 AREAS OF THE 48 CONTIGUOUS STATES

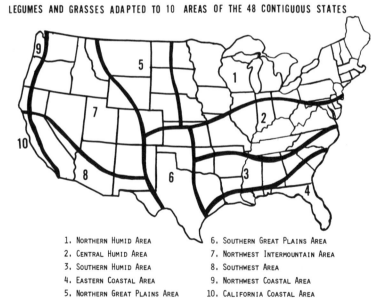

1. NORTHERN HUMID AREA	6. SOUTHERN GREAT PLAINS AREA
2. CENTRAL HUMID AREA	7. NORTHWEST INTERMOUNTAIN AREA
3. SOUTHERN HUMID AREA	8. SOUTHWEST AREA
4. EASTERN COASTAL AREA	9. NORTHWEST COASTAL AREA
5. NORTHERN GREAT PLAINS AREA	10. CALIFORNIA COASTAL AREA

Figure 7.3 The ten generally recognized pasture areas in the U.S. Different grasses are recommended for different areas; see Table 7.1.

Temporary pastures are those that are used for a short period — like rye, wheat, or oat pasture. They are seeded for the purpose of providing supplemental grazing during the season when the regular permanent or seeded pastures are relatively unproductive.

ADAPTED VARIETIES AND SUITABLE MIXTURES

The specific grass or grass-legume mixture will vary from area to area, according to differences in soil, temperature, and rainfall. A complete listing of all adapted and recommended grasses and legumes for horse pastures would be too lengthy for this book. However, Table 7.1 shows the most important ones for each of the 10 generally recognized U.S. pasture areas (see map). In using Table 7.1, bear in mind that many species of forages have wide geographic adaption, but subspecies or varieties often have rather specific adaptation. Thus, alfalfa, for example, is represented by many varieties, which give this species adaptation to nearly all states. Variety then, within species, makes many forages adapted to widely varying climates and geographic areas. The county agricultural agent or state agricultural college can furnish recommendations for the area that they serve.

Five grass species — orchardgrass, reed canary grass, fescue, smooth bromegrass, and Bermuda grass — account for the major portion of seeded grasses in the U.S. The leading legumes are alfalfa, trefoil, lupine, sweet clover, kudzu, and clover.

Sudan and hybrid Sudans in the growing stage should never be grazed by horses, because of the hazard of cystitis. This disease, which occurs more frequently in mares than in stallions or geldings, is characterized by continuous urination, mares appearing to be constantly in heat, and incoordination in the gait. Animals seldom recover after either the incoordination or the dribbling of urine becomes evident. Apparently hay from Sudan or from hybrid Sudans will not produce this malady.

SUPPLEMENTING PASTURES

Except for idle horses, it is generally advisable to provide supplemental feed for horses that are on pasture. This is so because (1) horses are usually subjected to considerable stress; (2) show, sale, and pleasure horses should have eye appeal — sleek, bloomy hair coats that attract judges, buyers, and all who see them; and (3) young animals are usually forced for early development. Further, it is important not to jeopardize soundness or lower the reproductive ability of breeding animals. Consequently, the nutritive requirements of horses are generally more critical than can be met by pasture alone.

Table 7.1 ADAPTED GRASSES AND LEGUMES (INCLUDING BROWSE AND FORBS) FOR HORSE PASTURES, BY TEN GEOGRAPHICAL AREAS OF THE U.S.[1] (SEE MAP)

	Areas of the United States									
	1	2	3	4	5	6	7	8	9	10
Grasses, shrubs, forbs:										
Alfileria (filaree)								X	X	
Bahiagrass (a paspalum)			X	X						
Beardgrass (a bluestem)								X		
Bentgrass	X	X								
Bermudagrass		X	X	X		X		X		X
Bluegrass	X	X			X		X	X		
Bluestem	X	X			X	X		X		
Bristlegrass (a millet)								X		
Bromegrass	X	X			X		X	X	X	
Buckwheat (wild)								X		
Buffalograss					X	X				
Buffelgrass						X				
Chamiza (fourwing saltbush)								X		
Cottontop								X		
Curly mesquite (a Hilaria)						X		X		
Dallisgrass (a paspalum)			X	X						
Dropseed						X		X		
Fescue, tall	X	X	X				X	X	X	X
Foxtail							X	X	X	
Galleta (a Hilaria)						X		X		
Grama grass	X				X	X		X		
Hardinggrass									X	X
Indiangrass	X	X			X	X				
Indian ricegrass								X		
Indianwheat								X		
Johnsongrass (a sorghum)			X	X		X				
Junegrass					X	X		X		
Kleingrass						X				
Lovegrass	X	X				X		X		
Mesquite (vine, a panicum)						X		X		
Millet	X	X	X	X		X				
Mormon tea (ephedra, jointfir)								X		
Muhly								X		
Needlegrass (needle-and-thread)					X		X			
Oatgrass									X	
Oats	X	X	X	X	X	X		X	X	X
Orchardgrass	X	X	X	X	X		X	X	X	X
Pangola digitgrass			X	X						
Panicgrass (a panicum)						X		X		
Paragrass (malojillo)				X						

	Areas of the United States									
	1	*2*	*3*	*4*	*5*	*6*	*7*	*8*	*9*	*10*
Pea bush								X		
Pearlmillet		X	X	X		X				
Ratany								X		
Redtop	X						X		X	
Reed canarygrass	X	X			X		X		X	
Rescuegrass			X	X					X	
Rhodesgrass			X	X						
Rye	X	X	X	X	X	X		X	X	X
Ryegrass, annual		X	X	X		X			X	
Ryegrass, perennial	X	X	X						X	
Sacaton								X		
St. Augustine grass			X							
Stargrass			X							
Switchgrass (a panicum)	X	X	X		X	X				
Three-awn (wiregrass)						X		X		
Timothy	X	X					X		X	
Tobosa (a Hilaria)						X				
Wheat	X	X	X	X	X	X	X	X	X	X
Wheatgrass						X	X	X	X	
Wild-rye						X	X	X		
Winterfat (white sage)								X		
Wintergrass, Texas						X				
Legumes:										
Alfalfa (lucerne)	X	X	X	X	X	X	X	X	X	X
Alyceclover			X	X						
Black medic (yellow trefoil)			X			X		X		
Bur-clover		X						X		X
Cicer milkvetch	X				X		X			
Clover, alsike	X	X			X		X	X	X	
Clover, arrowleaf		X	X							
Clover, crimson		X	X							
Clover, Hubam (white sweet clover)	X	X						X	X	
Clover, Kura	X	X			X		X		X	
Clover, Ladino	X	X	X	X			X	X	X	X
Clover, prairie						X		X		
Clover, red	X	X	X	X			X	X	X	
Clover, strawberry					X		X	X		X
Clover, subterranean			X	X				X	X	X
Clover, white	X	X	X	X			X	X	X	X
Cowpeas			X	X						
Crown vetch	X	X								
Field pea			X	X			X			
Hairy indigo			X							

Table 7.1 Adapted Grasses and Legumes (including Browse and Forbs) for Horse Pastures, by Ten Geographical Areas of the U.S. (*cont.*)

	\multicolumn{10}{c}{Areas of the United States}									
	1	2	3	4	5	6	7	8	9	10
Lespedeza (annual)		X	X	X						
Lespedeza (perennial, sericea)		X	X	X						
Peas (flat)									X	
Soybeans	X	X	X	X			X			
Sweet clover	X	X			X	X	X	X	X	
Trefoil, birdsfoot	X	X	X				X		X	X
Velvet beans		X	X							
Vetch		X	X	X	X	X		X	X	

[1] Authoritative recommendations for this chart were made by the following agronomists: J. E. Baylor, Ph.D., Professor Emeritus of Agronomy Extension, The Pennsylvania State University, State College; R. A. Forsberg, Ph.D., *et al.*, Department of Agronomy, University of Wisconsin, Madison; J. R. Forwood, Ph.D., Research Agronomist, USDA-ARS, University of Missouri, Columbia; S. C. Fransen, Ph.D., Forage Agronomist, Western Washington Research and Extension Center, Washington State University, Puyallup; C. S. Hoveland, Ph.D., Professor of Agronomy, Department of Agronomy, The University of Georgia, Athens; W. E. McMurphy, Ph.D., Professor, Department of Agronomy, Oklahoma State University, Stillwater; D. A. Miller, Ph.D., Professor, Department of Agronomy, University of Illinois, Urbana; R. R. Smith, Ph.D., Professor, Department of Agronomy, University of Wisconsin, Madison.

SUPPLEMENTING EARLY SPRING GRASS

Turning horses on pasture when the first sprigs of green grass appear will usually make for a temporary deficiency of energy, due to (1) washy (high water content) grasses, and (2) inadequate forage for animals to consume. As a result, owners are often disappointed in the poor condition of horses.

If there is good reason why grazing cannot be delayed until there is adequate spring growth, it is recommended that early pastures be supplemented with grass hay or straw (a legume hay will accentuate looseness, which usually exists under such circumstances), preferably placed in a rack; perhaps with a high energy concentrate provided, also.

SUPPLEMENTING DRY PASTURE

Dry, mature, weathered, bleached grass characterizes (1) drought periods, and (2) fall-winter pastures. Such cured-on-the-stalk grasses are low in energy, in protein (as low as 3 percent or less), in carotene (the precursor of vitamin A), and in phosphorus and perhaps certain other minerals. These deficiencies become more acute following frost and increase in severity as winter advances. This explains the often severe loss in condition of horses following the first fall freeze.

In addition to the deficiencies which normally characterize whatever plants are available, dry pasture may be plagued by a short supply of feed.

Generally speaking, a concentrate or supplement is best used during droughts or on fall-winter pastures. However, when there is an acute shortage of forage, hay or other roughage should be added, also.

PASTURE SUPPLEMENTS

Horsemen face the question of what pasture supplement to use, when to feed it, and how much of it to feed.

In supplying a supplement to horses on pasture, the following guides should be observed:

- It should balance the diet of the horses to which it is fed, which means that it should supply all the nutrients missing in the forage.

- It should be fed in such a way that each horse gets its proper proportion, which generally means (1) the use of salt blocks, (2) tying up horses during concentrate feeding when more than one animal is fed in a given pasture, or (3) taking them to their stalls at feeding time.

- The daily allowance of the supplement should be determined by (1) the available pasture (quantity and quality), and (2) the condition of the horse.

  The results from the use of the supplement, rather than cost per bag, should determine the choice of supplement.

MANAGEMENT OF HORSE PASTURES

Many good horse pastures have been established only to be lost through careless management. Good pasture management involves the practices that follow.

CONTROLLED GRAZING

Nothing contributes more to good pasture management than controlled grazing. At its best, it embraces the following:

1. *Protection of first-year seedings* — first-year seedings should be grazed lightly or not at all in order that they may get a good start. Where practical, instead of grazing, it is preferable to mow a new first-year seeding about 3 inches above the ground and to utilize it as hay, provided there is sufficient growth to justify this procedure.

2. *Rotation or alternate grazing* — Rotation or alternate grazing is accomplished by dividing a pasture into fields (usually two to four) of approximately equal size, so that one field can be grazed while

Figure 7.4 Broodmares and foals on a well-managed pasture at Walmac International, Lexington, Kentucky. (Courtesy, Thoroughbred Publications, Inc., Lexington, Kentucky)

the others are allowed to make new growth. This results in increased pasture yields, more uniform grazing, and higher quality forage.

Generally speaking, rotation or alternate grazing is (a) more practical and profitable on seeded and temporary pastures than on permanent pastures, and (b) more beneficial where parasite infestations are heavy than where few or no problems with parasites are involved.

3. *Shifting the location of salt, shade, and water* — Where portable salt containers are used, more uniform grazing and scattering of the droppings may be obtained simply by the practice of shifting the location of the salt to the less-grazed areas of the pasture. Where possible and practical, the shade and the water should be shifted likewise.

4. *Deferred spring grazing* — Allow 6 to 8 inches of growth before turning horses out to pasture in the spring, thereby giving grass a needed start. Anyway, the early spring growth of pastures is high in moisture and washy.

5. *Avoiding close late fall grazing* — Pastures that are grazed closely late in the fall start late in the spring. With most pastures, 3 to 5 inches of growth should be left for winter cover.

6. *Avoiding overgrazing* — Never graze more closely than 2 to 3 inches during the pasture season. Continued close grazing reduces the yield, weakens the plants, allows weeds to invade, and increases soil erosion. The use of temporary and supplemental pastures may "spell off" regular pastures through seasons of drought and other pasture shortages and thus alleviate overgrazing.

7. *Avoiding undergrazing* — Undergrazing seeded pastures should also be avoided, because (a) mature forage is unpalatable and of low nutritive value, (b) tall-growing grasses may drive out low-growing plants due to shading, and (c) weeds, brush, and coarse grasses are more apt to gain a foothold when the pasture is grazed insufficiently. It is a good rule, therefore, to graze the pasture fairly close at least once each year.

CLIPPING PASTURES AND CONTROLLING WEEDS

Pastures should be clipped at such intervals as necessary to control weeds (and brush) and to get rid of uneaten clumps and other unpalatable coarse growth left after incomplete grazing. Pastures that are grazed continuously may be clipped at, or just preceding, the usual haymaking time; rotated pastures may be clipped at the close of the grazing period.

FERTILIZING

Like animals, for best results grasses and legumes must be "fed" properly throughout a lifetime. It is not sufficient that they be fertilized (and limed if necessary) at or prior to seeding time. In addition, in most areas it is desirable and profitable to topdress pastures with fertilizer annually, and, at less-frequent intervals, with lime (lime to maintain a pH of about 6.5). Such treatments should be based on soil tests, and are usually applied in the spring or fall.

Improper fertilization of pasture or hayland can result in an imbalance of the mineral content of the forage, which, in turn, will affect the animal. But when soil samples are properly taken and analyzed, then used as a guide for fertilizer application, the mineral content of the forage will be improved.

Remember that it is the total mineral intake of the horse that counts. This calls for (1) soil testing, with the fertilizer application based thereon, (2) forage testing, and (3) ration testing, with the mineral supplement balancing out the needs of the horse.

CLEANING PASTURES

The parasites in a pasture can be reduced dramatically by picking up the manure twice a week. Manure can be removed manually or me-

Table 7.2 GUIDE FOR CARING FOR HORSE PASTURES AND RECREATIONAL AREAS

For	When	How to Do It
Pasture maintenance	Twice a week.	Pick up manure from pasture, using a shovel or a mechanically powered vacuum.
	When it's hot and dry.	Use a chain-type tine harrow to 1. Tear out the old, dead material. 2. Stimulate growth through gentle cultivating action. 3. Prevent a sod-bound condition. 4. Increase moisture penetration. 5. Scatter horse feces and expose larvae to death by drying, *only in hot, dry weather*.
Pasture renovation	Spring or fall.	Use a chain-type tine harrow to work the fertilizer and seed into the soil, and yet destroy a minimum of the existing sod.
Preparing new pasture seedbed	Spring or fall.	Use a chain-type tine harrow to 1. Level. 2. Smooth down. 3. Pack.
Racetracks; show rings	Whenever the track or ring becomes bedded.	Set a chain-type tine harrow for maximum or light penetration, depending on the condition of the ring or track.
	Just before the race or show; and between races or show events.	Use a chain-type tine harrow as a drag mat to smooth and fill holes.
Bridle paths; farm lanes; dirt roads	Whenever they become rough or uneven.	Use maximum penetration of chain-type tine harrow to put in shape; then turn harrow over to level and fill up holes.

chanically; by using a muscle-powered shovel, or by using a vacuum pump powered by a tractor or small engine. In wet or damp conditions, however, a harrow should not be used to break up the manure; it will merely spread the parasite larvae into the grazing area. If pasture harrowing is done in hot, dry weather, it will effectively break up feces and expose larvae to death by desiccation.

Comments

Researchers at Ohio State reported that twice a week cleaning of pastures resulted in 18 times fewer parasites than uncleaned pastures.

Altogether too many horse pastures are merely gymnasiums or exercising grounds. This need not be so. Through improved pasture maintenance, caretakers can:
1. Produce higher yields of nutritious forage.
2. Extend the grazing season from early in the spring to late in the fall.
3. Provide a fairly uniform supply of feed throughout the entire season.

Run-down pastures can be brought back into production without plowing and reseeding.

When properly prepared, a seedbed should be so firm that you barely leave a footprint when you walk across it. The firmer the better from the standpoint of moisture conservation and small seeds.

Good racetracks and show rings must be firm, yet resilient.

Because it's flexible, this harrow can be pulled at good speed, as is necessary between races or show events, and yet do an excellent job of smoothing and filling holes.

GRAZING BY MORE THAN ONE CLASS OF ANIMALS

Grazing by two or more classes of animals makes for more uniform pasture utilization and fewer weeds and parasites, provided the area is not overstocked. Different kinds of livestock have different habits of grazing; they show preference for different plants and graze to different heights. Also, with the exception of the small stomach worm, horse parasites die in cattle and sheep. For these reasons, horses and cattle are commonly grazed on the same pastures in the great horse breeding centers of the world.

IRRIGATING WHERE PRACTICAL AND FEASIBLE

Where irrigation is practical and feasible, it alleviates the necessity of depending on the weather.

SUPPLEMENTING TO PROVIDE NEEDED NUTRIENTS

Although the horse ration should be as economical as possible, condition and results in show, sale, and use are the primary objectives, even at somewhat added expense. Generally, this calls for supplemented feeding on pasture — for providing added energy, protein, minerals, and vitamins.

EXTENDING THE GRAZING SEASON

In the South and in Hawaii, year-round grazing is a reality on many a successful horse establishment. By careful planning and by selecting the proper combination of crops, other areas can approach this desired goal.

Figure 7.5 The use of seeded or temporary pastures and picking up pasture manure twice a week will reduce parasites dramatically. Manure may be removed with a hand shovel or by using a vacuum pump powered by a tractor or engine. (Courtesy, California Thoroughbred Breeders Association, Arcadia, California)

In addition to lengthening the grazing season through the selection of species, earlier spring pastures can be secured by avoiding grazing too late in the fall and by the application of a nitrogen fertilizer in the fall or early spring. Nitrogen fertilizers will often stimulate the growth of grass so that it will be ready for grazing 10 days to 2 weeks earlier than unfertilized areas.

POINTERS ON HORSE PASTURES AND RECREATIONAL AREAS

There is a paucity of information on the care of horse pastures and recreational areas. Few college courses even mention them, and precious little authoritative literature has been published on the subject.

Table 7.2 tells how successful operators maintain, renovate, and seed horse pastures, and how they care for racetracks, show rings, bridle paths, and other like areas. These areas can no longer be taken for granted. They're big and important — and they'll get bigger. Hence, they merit the combined best recommendations of scientists and practical operators.

MANAGEMENT

Figure 8.1   A horse auction in progress. Management begins with buying your first horse. (Courtesy, *Thoroughbred Record,* Lexington, Kentucky)

Horse management practices vary between areas and individual horsemen. In general, however, the principles of good management are the same everywhere, and they apply whether one horse or many horses are involved.

STABLE MANAGEMENT

The following stable management practices are recommended:

1. Remove the top layer of clay floors yearly; replace with fresh clay, then level and tamp. Keep the stable floor higher than the surrounding area so the floor will stay dry.
2. Keep stalls well lighted.

3. Use properly constructed hayracks to lessen waste and contamination of hay. Do not have hayracks in maternity stalls.

4. Scrub concentrate containers as often as necessary and always after feeding a wet mash.

5. Remove excrement and wet or soiled material from the bedding daily, and provide fresh bedding.

6. Practice strict stable sanitation to prevent fecal contamination of feed and water.

7. Lead foals when taking them from the stall to the paddock and back as a way to further their training.

8. Restrict the ration when horses are idle, and provide either a wet bran mash the evening before an idle day or turn idle horses to pasture.

9. Provide proper ventilation at all times by means of open doors, windows that open inwardly from the top, or stall partitions slatted at the top.

10. Keep stables in repair at all times to lessen injury hazards.

BEDDING, KIND AND AMOUNT

The term "bedding" refers to materials used to make a bed for animals. The horseman should select bedding material according to availability and price, absorptive capacity, and potential value as a fertilizer. Bedding should not be dusty, too coarse, or too easily kicked aside. Cereal grain (wheat, barley, or oats), straw or wood shavings generally make the best bedding materials for horses.

A soft, comfortable bed will insure proper rest. Also, horses are much easier to groom if their bedding is kept clean. Table 8.1 shows that bedding materials differ considerably in their relative capacities to absorb liquid. Other facts of importance, relative to certain bedding materials and bedding uses, are:

1. *Wood products (sawdust, shavings, tree bark, chips, etc.)* — The suspicion that wood products will hurt the land is rather widespread but unfounded. It is true that shavings and sawdust decompose slowly, but this process can be expedited by the addition of nitrogen fertilizers. Also, when plowed under, they increase soil acidity, but the change is both small and temporary.

   Softwood (on a weight basis) is about twice as absorptive as hardwood, and green wood has only 50 percent the absorptive capacity of dried wood.

   Caution: Beware of black walnut sawdust, chips, or shavings. Although the black walnut (*Juglans nigra*) is the aristocrat of U.S. hardwoods for making furniture, numerous cases of laminitis in horses exposed to black walnut sawdust, chips, or shavings have been reported. The laminitis occurs within 12 to 24 hours of contact with fresh bedding containing black walnut shavings or sawdust. Skin contact will trigger the onset of laminitis; horses need not eat the bedding. Swelling of the fetlocks and hocks have been reported in some cases — and there have been some deaths. Although the toxic element has not been identified, some researchers are studying a chemical component unique to black walnut known as *juglone.*

2. *Cut straw* — Cut straw will absorb more liquid than long straw; cut oats or wheat straw will take up about 25 percent more water than long straw from comparable material. But there are disadvantages to chopping: chopped straws may be dusty.

From the standpoint of the value of plant food nutrients per ton of air-dry material, peat moss is the most valuable bedding when recycled as fertilizer and wood products the least valuable.

The minimum desirable amount of bedding to use is the amount necessary to absorb completely the liquids in manure. For 24-hour confinement, the minimum daily bedding requirements of horses, based on uncut wheat or oat straw, is 10 to 15 lb. With other bedding materials, these quantities will vary according to their respective absorptive capacities (see Table 8.1). Also, more than minimum quantities of bedding may be desirable where cleanliness and comfort of the horse are important.

In most areas, bedding materials are becoming scarcer and higher in price, primarily because (1) geneticists are breeding plants with shorter straws and stalks, (2) there are more competitive and numerous uses for some of the materials, and (3) the current trend toward more confinement rearing of livestock requires more bedding.

Horsemen may reduce bedding needs and costs as follows:

- *Chop bedding* — Chopped straw, waste hay, fodder, or cobs will go further and do a better job of keeping horses dry than long materials.
- *Ventilate quarters properly* — Proper ventilation lowers the humidity and keeps the bedding dry.
- *Provide exercise area* — Where possible and practical, provide for exercise in well-drained, dry pastures or corrals, without confining horses to stalls more than necessary.

HORSE MANURE

The term manure refers to a mixture of animal excrements (consisting of undigested feeds plus certain body wastes) and bedding.

The rise in light horse numbers, along with the shift of much of the horse population from the nation's farms and ranches to stables and

Table 8.1 WATER ABSORPTION OF BEDDING MATERIALS

Material	Lb. of Water Absorbed per CWT of Air-Dry Bedding
Barley straw	210
Cocoa shells	270
Corn stover (shredded)	250
Corncobs (crushed or ground)	210
Cottonseed hulls	250
Flax straw	260
Hay (mature, chopped)	300
Leaves (broadleaf)	200
Pine needles	100
Oat hulls	200
Oat straw (long)	280
(chopped)	375
Peanut hulls	250
Peat moss	1,000
Rye straw	210
Sand	25
Sawdust (top quality pine)	250
(run-of-the-mill hardwood)[1]	150
Sugarcane bagasse	220
Tree bark (dry, fine)	250
(from tanneries)	400
Vermiculite[2]	350
Wheat straw (long)	220
(chopped)	295
Wood chips (top quality pine)	300
(run-of-the-mill hardwood)[1]	150
Wood shavings (top quality pine)	200
(run-of-the-mill hardwood)[1]	150

[1] *Caution:* Do not use black walnut sawdust, chips, or shavings. They may cause acute laminitis — and even death.

[2] This is a mica-like mineral mined chiefly in South Carolina and Montana.

small enclosures in suburban areas, has made for manure disposal problems.

From the standpoint of soils and crops, barnyard manure contains the following valuable ingredients:

- *Organic matter* — Manure supplies valuable organic matter which cannot be secured in chemical fertilizers. Organic matter — which constitutes 3 to 6 percent, by weight, of most soils — improves soil tilth, increases water-holding capacity, lessens water and wind erosion, improves aeration, and has a beneficial effect on soil microorganisms and plants. It is the "lifeblood" of the land.

- *Plant food* — It supplies plant food or fertility — especially nitrogen, phosphorus, and potassium. In addition to these three nutrients, manure contains calcium, and trace elements such as boron, manganese, copper, and zinc. A ton of well-preserved horse manure, free of bedding, contains plant food nutrients equal to about 100 lb. of 13-2-12 fertilizer (see Table 8.2). Thus, spreading manure at the rate of 8 tons per acre supplies the same amounts of nutrients as 800 lb. of a 13-2-12 commercial fertilizer.

The quantity, composition, and value of horse manure produced vary according to weight of animal, kind and amount of feed, and kind and amount of bedding. The author's computations in Table 8.2 are on fresh manure (exclusive of bedding) basis and per 1,000 lb. liveweight. As indicated, a 1,000-lb. horse will produce about 8 tons of manure, free of bedding, per year.

The data in Table 8.2 are based on animals confined to stalls the year around. Actually, the manure recovered and available to spread where desired is considerably less than indicated because (1) animals are kept on pasture and along roads and lanes much of the year, where the manure is dropped, and (2) losses in weight often run as high as 60 percent when manure is exposed to the weather for a considerable time.

About 75 percent of the nitrogen, 80 percent of the phosphorus, and 85 percent of the potassium contained in horse feeds are returned as manure. In addition, about 40 percent of the organic matter in feeds is excreted as manure. As a rule of thumb, it is commonly estimated that 80 percent of the total nutrients in feeds are excreted by horses as manure.

The urine makes up 20 percent of the total weight of the excrement of horses. Yet the urine, or liquid manure, contains nearly 50 percent of the nitrogen, 60 percent of the phosphorus, and 60 percent of the potassium of average manure; roughly one-half of the total plant food of manure. Also, it is noteworthy that the nutrients in liquid manure are more readily available to plants than the nutrients in the solid excrement. These are the reasons why it is important to conserve the urine.

Horsemen sometimes fail to recognize the value of this barnyard "crop" because (1) it is produced whether or not it is wanted, and (2) it is available without cost.

Clay floors cannot be cleaned by flushing with water, and hard stable floors of concrete, asphalt, or wood require considerable bedding to provide softness and comfort. These conditions make it impractical to handle horse manure as a liquid. But horse manure is relatively dry and well adapted to handling as a solid.

In large horse establishments, the use of automatic gutter cleaners can eliminate much of the hand labor in handling manure as a solid. Automatic gutter cleaners may be (1) located in the alleyway or immediately outside the barn, (2) covered except for trapdoors, and (3) de-

Table 8.2 QUANTITY, COMPOSITION, AND VALUE OF FRESH HORSE
MANURE (FREE OF BEDDING) EXCRETED PER 1,000 POUNDS LIVEWEIGHT

Tons Excreted/ Year/1,000 lb. Liveweight[1]	Excrement	Composition and Value of Manure on a Tonnage Basis[2]					
		Lb./ Ton[3]	Water (%)	N (lb.)	P[4] (lb.)	K[4] (lb.)	Value/ Ton[5] ($)
8	Liquid	400					
	Solid	1,600					
	Total	2,000	60	13.8	2.0	12.0	5.05

[1] *Manure is Worth Money — It Deserves Good Care,* University of Illinois Circ. 595, 1953, p. 4.
[2] Last 5 columns on the right from *Farm Manures,* University of Kentucky Circ. 593, 1964, p. 5, Table 2.
[3] From Reference Material for 1951 Saddle and Sirloin Essay Contest, p. 43, compiled by M. E. Ensminger, data from *Fertilizers and Crop Production,* by Van Slyke, published by Orange Judd Publishing Co.
[4] Phosphorus (P) can be converted to P_2O_5 by multiplying the figure given above by 2.29, and potassium (K) can be converted to K_2O by multiplying by 1.2.
[5] Calculated on the assumption that nitrogen (N) retails at 25 cents, phosphorus (P) at 20 cents, and potassium (K) at 10 cents per pound in commercial fertilizers.

signed to carry the manure from the gutter directly into a spreader.

Some large establishments fork the manure from the stalls into the alley and then load it by means of a scraper or power loader. But this method is more messy and less convenient than an automatic gutter cleaner.

Both small and large horse establishments face the problem of what to do with horse manure after it is removed from the stable. Because the feces of horses are the primary source of infection by internal parasites, fresh horse manure should never be spread on pastures grazed by horses.

The alternatives for the handling of horse manure are as follows:

1. Spread fresh manure on fields that will be plowed and cropped (not grazed) if there is sufficient land and this is feasible.

2. Contract with a nearby vegetable grower to remove the manure.

3. Store the manure in a tightly constructed pit for a few weeks before spreading it; this allows the spontaneously generated heat to destroy the parasites.

4. Compost the manure in an area where it will neither pollute a stream nor offend the neighbors; then spread it on the land.

5. Remove manure manually or mechanically from horse pastures twice a week.

Despite the recognized value of horse manure, it does possess the following objectionable features:

1. It may propagate insects.
2. It may spread diseases and parasites.
3. It may produce undesirable odors.
4. It may scatter weed seeds.

GROOMING

Proper grooming is necessary to keep a horse attractive and help maintain his good health and condition. Grooming cleans the hair, helps keep the skin functioning normally, lessens skin diseases and parasites, and improves the condition and fitness of the muscles.

In the wild state, horses cleaned (groomed) themselves by rolling and taking dust baths. They do the same thing when turned into a corral.

Grooming should be rapid and thorough but not so severe that it makes the horse nervous or irritates his skin. Horses that are kept in stables or small corrals should be groomed thoroughly at least once a day. When horses are worked or exercised, they should be groomed both before and after the work or exercise.

Wet or sweating animals should be handled as follows:

1. Remove the tack as fast as possible, wipe it off, and put it away.
2. Remove excess water from the horse with a sweat scraper and then rub him briskly with a grooming or drying cloth to dry his coat partially.
3. Cover the horse with a blanket and walk him until he is cool.
4. Allow the horse to drink two or three swallows of water every few minutes while he is cooling and drying.

GROOMING EQUIPMENT

The following articles of grooming equipment are commonly used:

1. A hoof pick to clean the feet.
2. A rubber, plastic, or metal curry comb to groom horses that have long thick coats and to loosen scurf and dirt in the hair. Horses with shorter coats can be groomed with a flexible rubber mitt that has a network of small bumps on the surface.
3. A body brush to brush the body. This is the principal tool used in grooming.
4. A dandy brush to remove light dirt from the skin and to brush the mane and tail. The dandy brush is made of stiff fiber, usually about 2 inches long.

Curry Comb

Body Brush

Dandy Brush

Mane & Tail Comb

Sweat Scraper

Hoof Pick
(or hook)

Grooming Cloth

Figure 8.2 Grooming equipment.

5. A mane and tail comb to comb out a matted mane and tail.

6. A sweat scraper to remove excess water from wet or sweating animals.

7. A grooming cloth to wipe and polish the coat and for other miscellaneous cleaning. The grooming cloth can be made from old towels or blankets. It should be about 18 to 24 inches square.

HOW TO GROOM A HORSE

To assure that the horse is groomed thoroughly and that no body parts are missed, follow a definite order of grooming. This may vary according to individual preference, but the following order is most common.

The feet — Use a hoof pick to clean the feet. Work from the heel toward the toe. Thoroughly clean the depressions between the frog and the bars. Inspect the feet for thrush and loose shoes.

The body — To groom the body, hold the curry comb in the right hand and the brush in the left hand. Start on the left side of the horse and follow this order: neck, breast, withers, shoulders, foreleg down to the knee, back, side, belly, croup, and hindleg down to the hock.

At frequent intervals, clean the dust and hair from the brush with the curry comb. Knock the curry comb against some solid object to free it of dirt.

Curry gently and in small circular strokes, but brush vigorously. Do not use the metal curry comb below the knees or hocks, about the head, or over body prominences. Also, the metal curry comb should not be used on horses that have been clipped recently or that have a thin coat of hair. Horses with fine coats and sensitive skin should be groomed with a flexible rubber mitt.

Brush the hair in the direction it grows. Brush with care in the regions of the flanks, between the fore and hindlegs, at the point of elbows, and in the fetlocks.

After grooming the left side of the horse, transfer the brush to the right hand and the curry comb to the left hand and groom the right side.

The head, mane, and tail — Brush the head, and comb and brush the mane and tail. Use the body brush on the head; be careful to avoid the eyes. Brush the mane and tail downward, using either the body brush or the dandy brush.

Clean the tail by combing upward with a mane and tail comb, cleaning a few strands of hair at a time, or by picking and separating a few hairs at a time by hand. Wash the mane and tail occasionally with warm water and soap.

Miscellaneous cleaning — Use the grooming cloth to wipe about the ears, face, eyes, nostrils, lips, sheath, and dock; to give a final polish to the coat; and to dry or ruffle the coat before it is brushed.

Checking the grooming — Rub the fingertips against the natural lay of the hair. If the coat and skin are not clean, the fingers will get dirty and gray lines will show on the coat where the fingers passed. Inspect the cleanliness of the ears, face, eyes, nostrils, lips, sheath, and dock.

Cleaning the grooming equipment — Wash the grooming equipment with warm water and soap often enough to keep it clean. Disinfect it as a precaution against the spread of disease.

Clipping and shearing — Besides routine grooming, horses should be clipped as often as needed. Clip the long hairs from the head, the inside of the ears, on the jaw, and around the fetlocks. A wad of cotton may be put in the horse's ears to cut down on noise from the clippers and to prevent hair from falling in his ears.

HOW TO SHAMPOO A HORSE

Shampooing will make the horse look better and feel better. Horses like to be clean.

Shampooing (1) cleans the animal — it removes the dirt, stains, and sweat that cannot be removed by grooming; (2) makes for a fine hair coat with a good sheen; and (3) keeps the skin smooth and mellow.

Figure 8.3 Following strenuous exercise, the horse should receive a welcome and refreshing bath. The caretaker sponges him all over with water, removing the dust and sweat. Next, the horse is scraped off and brushed almost to dryness and is covered with a blanket (a cooler). Then he is led around and around, as his tension subsides and he relaxes. This is the cooling-out process, designed to prevent stiff muscles. (Courtesy, *From Dawn to Destiny*, by Frank Jennings and Allen F. Brewer, Jr., published by The Thoroughbred Press, Lexington, Kentucky)

Formerly, there was strong prejudice against washing horses; perhaps stemming from the use of old-fashioned, harsh detergents and strong soaps, followed by poor rinsing. But "baths" are good for horses, just as they are good for people; and horses like to be shampooed.

Shampoo the horse as frequently as necessary, as determined by soiling, work, and weather conditions. For example, always wash him following use on a sloppy, muddy ring, trail, or track — when he comes back covered with mud from head to tail; or after using him when it's hot and muggy, and he's all lathered up with sweat.

In preparation for shampooing, (1) groom the horse carefully, (2) secure the animal for washing either by having someone hold him by the shank or by tying, and (3) have shampoo concentrate, warm water, buckets, and sponges available.

Step 1 — Wet the animal thoroughly all over with water alone. For this purpose, fill one bucket with warm water (and refill it as necessary), then apply the water to the horse by means of a large sponge, which may be dipped into the bucket as fast and frequently as desired.

To assure that the horse will be washed thoroughly and that no body parts will be missed, follow a definite order. This may differ somewhat according to individual preference, but the following procedure is most common: Start with the head, wetting between the ears and on the foretop (but do not get water in the ears; either hold them down or shut them off with the hand as the head is washed), over the face and cheeks, and all around the eyes, muzzle, and nostrils.

Next, proceed to the left side. While carrying the bucket in your left hand and holding the sponge in your right hand, with long strokes wet the neck, withers, shoulder, back, side, and croup. Return to the front, and with sponge in left hand, wash the chest. Return the sponge to the right hand and wash under the elbow and down the foreleg. Then, take the sponge in the left hand, set the bucket down as near as possible, and sponge the belly thoroughly. Hold onto the hind leg on the outside above the hock (this precaution will keep a restive horse from pawing, kicking, or stepping on your foot) while sponging the sheath (for stallions and geldings) and the inside of the hind leg down to the hoof.

Station yourself to the left of the horse near the hind leg, facing to the rear. Set the bucket nearby. Take the sponge in the right hand and wash behind the hind legs and in the groove between the thighs. Since many horses fuss about this operation, be careful to avoid getting kicked or stepped on.

Hold up the tail with the left hand and wash under it with the right hand. The tail is best washed by sponging with plenty of water at the tailhead, then putting the full length of the tail into the bucket of water, lifting the bucket to the bone and sloshing the tail around in the water. Set the bucket down, grip the tail near the top and draw the squeezed sponge down the full length of the hair; then give the tail a snap from side to side to swish out the water that is left.

After wetting the near (left) side and the rear end, get a bucket of fresh water. Then, while holding the bucket in your right hand and the sponge in your left hand, wet the off (right) side of the horse in the same order as described above, starting with the neck.

Step 2 — Shampoo the horse. Put in a bucket or other suitable container shampoo concentrate and water in the amounts and proportions recommended on the shampoo label, then stir it vigorously with your hand to form suds. Sponge the shampoo solution over the animal, following exactly the same procedure and order as outlined for wetting. Scrub against the hair with the sponge and your hands until a rich, thick lather covers all parts.

Step 3 — Rinse the horse with warm water, using either a bucket and sponge or a hose (if the horse is used to the latter), following the procedure and order given in Step 1. Rinse thoroughly.

Step 4 — Scrape with a "sweat scraper" held snugly against the hair to remove excess water, using long sweeping strokes and following the procedure and order given in Step 1, except do not scrape the head and legs.

Step 5 — Dry with a clean dry sponge or coarse towel, squeezing it out at intervals, following the procedure and order given in Step 1.

Step 6 — Blanket the horse and walk him until he is completely dry.
Step 7 — Apply a coat dressing if desired.

COAT DRESSING

"Trifles make perfection, but perfection is no trifle," is an old and well-known adage among horsemen. This philosophy prompts experienced caretakers to use a good coat dressing to achieve the all-important "bloom" or eye appeal in show, parade, and sale animals. Also, they use a coat dressing because they take pride in the everyday appearance of their charges, for how the horses look is indicative of the kind of caretakers back of them.

A coat dressing will not take the place of the natural conditioning of the horse, which can be achieved only through proper feeding, health, grooming, and shampooing.

Proper grooming should always precede the use of coat dressing. Coat dressing is best applied by means of a heavy cloth (preferably terry cloth). Moisten the rag with the dressing and rub the coat vigorously in the direction of the natural lay of the hair; then brush to bring out the bloom.

Coat dressing should always be used following washing, and for show, parade, or sale. It is best to apply a heavier application of coat dressing 12 to 24 hours ahead of the event, then go over the horse with a lightly dressed rag immediately before the event. Be careful not to apply a silicone-based coat dressing in the saddle area, or your saddle will slip.

EXERCISE

Horses should exercise as much as possible on pasture. They will develop strong, sound feet and legs from outdoor exercise. If no pasture is available, exercise mature animals for an hour or two a day under saddle or in harness.

Horses with bad feet frequently cannot exercise on roads. Those with faulty tendons may not be able to exercise under saddle. Allow these animals to exercise in a large paddock, or by longeing on a 30- to 40-foot rope, by leading, or by using a mechanical walker.

CARE OF THE FEET

Nature didn't intend that the horse be used on hard surfaces and have a person on his back. Thus, when man domesticated the horse, he assumed certain responsibilities for his care in an unnatural environment — including trimming and shoeing his feet.

Figure 8.4 A horseshoer at work. (Courtesy, *Sunset Magazine*)

To the end that sound feet shall prevail, good caretakers (1) keep the feet clean, (2) prevent them from drying out, (3) trim them to retain proper shape and length, and (4) shoe them correctly, when shoes are needed. But they (or their horseshoer) never rasp off the periople, the shiny covering of the hoof, which is nature's means of keeping moisture within the foot.

The feet of horses that are shod, stabled, or worked should be cleaned each day. A hoof pick is used for this purpose. The caretaker should work from the heel toward the toe, making sure to clean out the depressions in the underside of the feet. While cleaning the feet, he should also inspect for loose shoes and thrush.

Thrush is a disease of the foot characterized by a pungent odor. It causes a deterioration of tissue in the cleft of the frog or in the junction between the frog and bars. This disease produces lameness and, if not treated, can be serious.

When it is realized that the horse has been transplanted from his natural roving environment and soft, mother-earth footing to be used in carrying and drawing loads over hard, dry-surfaced topography by day and then stabled on hard, dry floors at night, it is not surprising that foot troubles are commonplace. Nor are these troubles new. The Greeks alluded to them in the age-old axiom, "No foot, no horse."

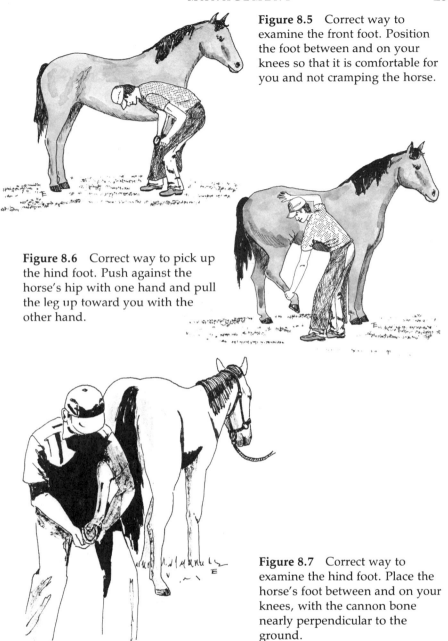

Figure 8.5 Correct way to examine the front foot. Position the foot between and on your knees so that it is comfortable for you and not cramping the horse.

Figure 8.6 Correct way to pick up the hind foot. Push against the horse's hip with one hand and pull the leg up toward you with the other hand.

Figure 8.7 Correct way to examine the hind foot. Place the horse's foot between and on your knees, with the cannon bone nearly perpendicular to the ground.

PARTS OF THE FOOT

In order to lessen foot troubles, and to permit intelligent shoeing, knowledge of the anatomy of the horses's foot is necessary (see Table 8.3 and the illustration on p. 264).

Table 8.3 Parts of the Hoof

The Part	*What It Is*	
The Four Major Parts:	They are:	
The bones	Long pastern bone	Coffin bone
	Short pastern bone	Navicular bone
The elastic structure	Consists of:	
	Lateral cartilages	Planter cushion
The sensitive structure called the corium or pododerm	Consists of:	
	Coronary band	Sensitive sole
	Perioplic ring	Sensitive frog
	Sensitive laminae	
The horny wall	The outer horny covering.	
The Exterior of the Hoof:		
The horny wall	The basic shell and wearing surface of the foot.	
The perioplic ring	The seat where periople is produced.	
The white line	The juncture of the wall and horny sole. It is about ⅛ in. wide.	
The horny frog	The V-shaped pad in the middle of the sol	
The commissures	The deep grooves on both sides of the frog	
The horny sole	The bottom of the foot. It is a thick (about ⅜ in.) plate or horn which grows out from the fleshy sole.	
The perimeter sections: Inside and outside toe The quarters The heel	The horny protrusions that lie along the frog between the commissures and the sol	

Its Functions	*Comments*
To provide framework of the foot and facilitate locomotion.	Long pastern bone lies entirely above the hoof. Only lower end of short pastern bone is within hoof.
To overcome concussion or jar when the foot strikes the ground.	Normally, heel expands about $\frac{1}{16}$ in. on each side of foot.
To furnish nutrition to corresponding part of hoof.	All five parts are highly sensitive and vascular.
To enclose and protect the sensitive parts beneath.	

To protect; there is no feeling in the wall of the foot until the area of the coronary band is reached.	The horny wall extends vertically from the edge of the hair around the front and sides of the foot; then turns in upon itself at the heel, forming the bar which extends forward toward the center.
To produce periople, the varnishlike substance that covers the outer surface of the wall and seals it from excess drying.	The wall of a normal foot consists of about $\frac{1}{4}$ water, by weight.
The horseman's "red light," beyond (toward the inside of the foot) which nails should not go.	A nail past the white line may either enter the sensitive structure or produce pressure, with resulting lameness.
Compresses under weight, and transmits pressure to the elastic structures. Aids blood circulation, absorbs concussion, and prevents slippage.	Without this normal pressure, the hoof has a tendency to shrink and become dormant, with contracted feet and unsoundness resulting.
To give elasticity.	Thrush is often found in the commissures.
Protects the foot from the bottom. Nature didn't intend that the horny sole should carry weight; for it is convex in shape so that most of the weight rests on the wall and frog area.	The sensitive sole is directly under the horny sole. Pressure on the horny sole area will usually produce lameness.
Helps support the foot and keep it open at the heels.	

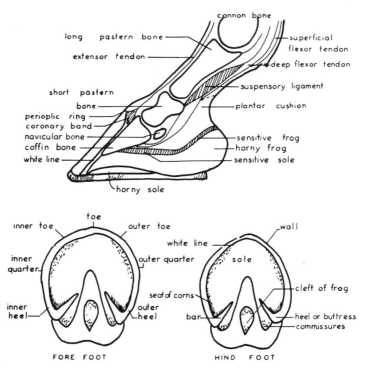

Figure 8.8　Parts of the foot.

TRIMMING THE HOOF

The hoof grows downward and forward. A complex system of arteries, veins, and nerves inside the outer structure provides for its growth. The average rate of growth of the horny portions of the hoof (wall, sole, and frog) is about ⅜ inch per month.

Before trimming the hoof, a horseman should be able to recognize proper and faulty conformation. The illustration on the next page shows the proper posture of the hoof and incorrect postures caused by hoofs grown too long either in toe or heel. The slope is considered normal when the toe of the hoof and the pastern have the same direction. This angle should be kept in mind and changed only as a corrective measure. If it should become necessary to correct uneven wear of the hoof, correct gradually over a period of several trimmings.

Before the feet are trimmed, the horse should be inspected while standing squarely on a level, hard surface. Then he should be seen at both the walk and the trot.

The hoofs should be trimmed every month or six weeks whether the animal is shod or not. If shoes are left on too long, the hoofs grow out of proportion. This may throw the horse off balance and put extra stress on the tendons. Always keep the hoofs at proper length and correct posture. Trim the hoofs near the level of the sole; otherwise they will split off if the horse remains unshod. Trim the frog carefully and remove only ragged edges that allow filth to accumulate in the crevices. Trim the sole very sparingly, if at all, and never rasp the wall of the hoof.

CORRECTING FAULTS BY TRIMMING

Before trimming the feet or shoeing a horse, it is important to know what constitutes both proper and faulty conformation (see Chapter 3, pp. 78–83).

The following list describes the common faults of the foot and tells how to correct them by proper trimming.

Splayfoot — The front toes are turned out and the heels are turned in. Trim the outer half of the foot.

Pigeon-toe — The front toes are turned in and the heels are turned out, the opposite of splayfoot. Trim the inner half of the foot more heavily; leave the outer half relatively long.

Quarter crack — A vertical crack appears on the side of the hoof. Keep the hoof moist. Shorten the toe of the hoof and use a corrective shoe with quarter clips to keep the crack from spreading.

Cocked ankles — The horse stands with the fetlocks bent forward, most frequently the hind ones. Although raising the heels will give the horse immediate comfort, they should be lowered in order to correct the condition.

Contracted heels — The heels are contracted or shrunken. Lower the heels and allow the frog to carry more of the weight. This tends to spread the heels apart.

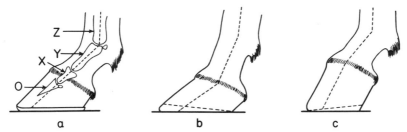

Figure 8.9 (A) Properly trimmed hoof with normal foot axis: O, coffin bone; X, short pastern bone; Y, long pastern bone; Z, cannon bone. (B) Toe too long, which breaks the foot axis backward. Horizontal dotted line shows how hoof should be trimmed to restore normal posture. (C) Heel too long, which breaks the foot axis forward. Horizontal dotted line shows how trimming will restore the correct posture.

TREATMENT OF HOOFS

In the wild state, horses roved over the prairies and moistened their hoofs frequently as they drank deep from the streams and lakes. But man changed all this. Today, the vast majority of horses spend much of their time in a dry stall or corral; stand dry-footed as they drink water from a bucket, fountain, or tank; are shod; and are exercised on a hard, dry surface — conditions which make for dry, brittle hoofs. With the domestication of the horse, therefore, man entered into an unwritten contract with him — to replace nature's way of keeping the hoofs moist.

When hoofs become dry and brittle, they sometimes split and cause lameness. The frogs lose their elasticity and are no longer effective shock absorbers. If the dryness is prolonged, the frogs shrink and the heels contract.

Dry hoofs usually can be prevented by keeping the ground wet around the watering tank, attaching wet burlap sacks around the hoofs, or applying a hoof dressing.

Hoof Dressing — A good hoof dressing will restore and maintain necessary flexibility and elasticity of the hoof. It will (1) penetrate the hoof structure readily, (2) allow the hoof to "breathe," (3) regulate the absorption and evaporation of moisture, and (4) accentuate the natural luster of the hoof; without leaving a sticky residue or sealing off the hoof wall. When applied daily, a hoof dressing will provide added moisture which will penetrate the hoof and prevent evaporation of the moisture that is already within the hoof, thereby imparting suppleness (elasticity).

When it comes to preventing dry hoofs, "an ounce of prevention is worth a pound of cure" — and then some. Each day, the feet of shod horses that are confined to a stable (or corral) should be cleaned thoroughly, then treated with hoof dressing. By means of a brush or cloth, apply the hoof dressing to the coronet, the wall, and the bottom surface (including the frog), of freshly cleaned feet. Do not put too much dressing around the nail holes. Because most of the moisture within the hoof rises through the sole (as sap rises in a tree), be sure to apply plenty of hoof dressing to the bottom area. Let it soak in before you return the horse to his stall.

The telltale symptoms of too-dry feet are: hardness and drying of the horny frog, contracted heels, corns, brittle hoofs, and sometimes cracks and lameness. When any one of these conditions prevails, good nursing and first-aid treatment are essential. The first step is to correct any errors in shoeing and trimming, and the second is to restore and maintain the normal moisture content of the horn. Treating the wall and bottom of the feet daily with hoof dressing will accomplish the latter.

Hoof dressing is not designed to take the place of proper trimming and shoeing by an experienced farrier; rather, it should go hand in hand with them.

Use of Gelatin — Although it is true that the major protein in the hoofs of horses is gelatin, the author is not aware of any experimental evidence that the feeding of gelatin as such will improve the structure, toughness, and moisture of the hoof.

Hoof tissue is synthesized in the body primarily from the amino acids contained in the bloodstream, and these can be derived from any good source of protein for horses, such as linseed meal and soybean meal. Of course, a deficiency of protein in the horse's ration would tend to produce poor hoofs, but this protein can be furnished from sources other than gelatin and the same results obtained.

From the standpoint of other tissues in the body, gelatin is a rather incomplete protein, notably deficient in the amino acids lysine and tryptophan. From an overall metabolism standpoint, therefore, gelatin would appear to be a poorer source of protein than the oilseed proteins — linseed, soybean, cottonseed, and peanut meal.

For the above reasons, before buying and feeding gelatin instead of one of the oilseed proteins, the horseman is admonished to see research data, conducted by a reputable independent research laboratory, in support of the "gelatin theory."

Use of Biotin — Biotin is essential for sound hoofs, so it should be included in a well-balanced ration. (See Chapter 6 of this book, section on "Biotin".)

SHOEING

Horseshoeing is a time-honored profession. In the Golden Age of the horse, which extended from the Gay Nineties to the mechanization of American agriculture, every schoolboy knew and respected the village blacksmith who plied his trade "under the spreading chestnut tree."

Horses should be shod when they are used on hard surfaces for any length of time. Also, shoes may be used to change gaits and action; correct faulty hoof structure or growth; protect the hoof from such conditions as corns, contractions, or cracks; and aid in gripping the track. Shoes should be made to fit the foot and not the foot to fit the shoes. Reshoe or reset at four- to six-week intervals.

A good horseman should be knowledgeable relative to (1) anatomy and nomenclature of the foot, (2) what constitutes proper stance and motions, and how to correct some faults through trimming, (3) kinds of shoes, (4) the basic horseshoeing tools and how to use them, (5) how to recognize good and faulty shoeing, and (6) treatment of dry hoofs.

HORSESHOES

A number of factors should be considered when selecting the shoes for a given horse; among them:

The Old Standard Shoe (size)	Multi-Product Shoe (size)
00	3
0	4
1	5
Half Size	6
2	7
Half Size	8
3	9

1. *The proper size* — The shoe should fit the foot, rather than any attempt made to trim the hoof to fit the shoe. Shoes come in sizes. A comparison of the old sizes and sizes available in the Multi-Product shoe (a popular Japanese-made shoe), which is widely used in the U.S., is given above.[3]

2. *Front vs. hind shoes* — Front shoes are more circular and wider at the heels than hind shoes. Thus, when buying shoes, it is important to specify front or hind shoes, because they are different.

3. *The individual horse* — His weight, the shape and texture of his hoof, and the set of his legs.

4. *The use to which the horse is put, and the kind of ground* — A plain shoe or a rim shoe is satisfactory for most horses used for pleasure, cutting, roping, barrel racing, polo, and jumping; whereas racing plates, to aid in gripping the track, are needed on running horses. Also, there are many corrective shoes, a few of which are listed in the accompanying table (see Table 8.4).

Shoes may be either handmade or ready-made (factory-made). The latter are becoming increasingly popular because they (1) require a minimum of work, and (2) are ideal for the do-it-yourselfer. Both steel and aluminum shoes are available.

Some common kinds of corrective shoes are described in Table 8.4, and some common kinds of shoes are pictured on the next page.

HORSESHOEING TOOLS AND HOW TO USE THEM

Horses are shod to protect the foot from breaking and wearing away faster than the growth of the horn. When properly done, shoes should interfere as little as possible with the physiological functions of the different structures of the foot or with the gaits of the horse.

Just as do-it-yourself wood workers, mechanics, and whatnot, usually have a shop and some tools, so the horseman should have certain basic

[3] Several good brands of shoes are available from which selections may be made.

Table 8.4 SOME CORRECTIVE SHOES AND THEIR USE

Kinds of Corrective Shoes	Purpose or Use
The bar shoe	To apply pressure to the frog of the foot, or to relieve pressure on any part of it.
The rocker toe shoe	For use on horses that stumble, forge, or have ringbone or sidebone.
The squared-toe shoe with trailer	For cow-hocked horses.
The lateral extension toed shoe	For horses that either toe out or toe in.

horseshoeing tools, *if* he has been taught how to use them properly by a knowledgeable farrier. Table 8.5 may be used as a guide in selecting tools.

Figure 8.10 (5 parts):

Ready-made shoes, recommended for use on most riding and driving horses.

Rim shoes, recommended for horses used for riding, cutting, roping, barrel racing, polo, and jumping.

Hot shoes, recommended for use by professional farriers and experienced horsemen who ply the trade.

Training plates, recommended for the purpose implied by the name — training.

Racing plates, recommended for racehorses. They're lightweight, with a toe grab that is easily shaped.

Table 8.5 HORSESHOEING TOOLS AND THEIR USE

Tool	Use
Anvil 	As a block to shape shoes, and as the farrier's workbench.
Forge 	Used to heat steel or shoes in preparation for shaping them for the horse being shod.
Vise 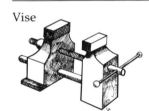	To finish shoes, and to hold metal.
Hoof knife 	To remove dirt and trim excess frog and sole from the foot. The hook on the end is used to trim the frog and clean the crevice between the bar and frog.
Nippers or parers 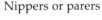	There is hardly any limit to the sizes and descriptions of these items: some are one-sided, others are two-sided. But all of them are used to trim the wall of the hoof and other parts that are too hard for the knife.
Hoof level 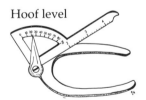	This device is used to determine the angle of the hoof relative to the ground surface.
Clinch cutter 	Used to cut clinches prior to pulling shoes.

Tool	Use
Rasp 	Used to level the foot after trimming; one side is coarse, and the other side fine.
Driving hammer 	Used to drive nails into hoof.
Hardy 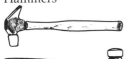	As a wedge in the anvil hole, in cutting steel of the desired length, and in cutting off shoes.
Hammers  	Various kinds of hammers may be used to shape shoes.
Tongs	Used to hold hot metal.
Nails	Assorted sizes of nails are available for different types of horseshoes. The old and the new nail sizes, side by side, follow:

The Old Standard Nail (size)	The Multi-Product Nail (size)
3½	1
4	2
4½	3
5	4
Half Size	5
6	6

Tool	Use
Apron 	Protects the horseshoer from sparks, from cuts that might otherwise be inflicted by slips of the knife or rasp, and from possible nail injury by nervous horses.

HOW TO RECOGNIZE GOOD AND FAULTY SHOEING

It is not necessary that horse owners and managers be expert farriers. But they should know how to recognize good and faulty shoeing.

The following checklist may be used as a means through which to evaluate a shoeing job, whether plied by yourself or a professional farrier:

Yes No

1. *As viewed from the front —*
☐ ☐ Are the front feet the same size, the toes the same length, and the heels the same height?

☐ ☐ Is the foot in balance in relation to the leg?

☐ ☐ Is the foot directly under the leg; is the axis of the foot in prolongation to the axis of the upper leg bones; and is the weight of the body equally distributed over the foot structures?

2. *As viewed from the side —*
☐ ☐ Does the axis of the foot coincide with the axis of the pastern?

☐ ☐ Does the slope of the wall from the coronet to the lower border parallel the slope of the pastern?

☐ ☐ Has the lower outer border of the wall been rasped?

☐ ☐ Does the conformation of the foot and the type of shoe used warrant the amount of rasping done?

3. *As the height and strength of nailing are inspected closely —*
☐ ☐ Do the nails come out of the wall at the proper height and in sound horn?

☐ ☐ Are the nails driven to a greater height in the wall than necessary?

☐ ☐ Is the size of the nail used best suited for the size and condition of the foot and the weight of the shoe?

☐ ☐ Are the clinches of sufficient thickness where the nail comes out of the wall to ensure strength?

☐ ☐ Are the clinches smooth and not projecting above the surface of the wall?

4. *As the outline and size of the shoe are scrutinized —*
☐ ☐ Is the toe of the shoe fitted with sufficient fullness to give lateral support to the foot at the moment of breaking over and leaving the ground?

☐ ☐ Are the branches of the shoe from the bend of the quarter to the heel fitted fuller than the outline of the wall to provide for expansion of the foot and normal growth of horn between shoeing periods?

☐ ☐ Are the heels of the shoe of sufficient length and width to cover the buttresses?

☐ ☐ Are the heels finished without sharp edges?

☐ ☐ Does the shoe rest evenly on the bearing surface of the hoof, covering the lower border of the wall, white line, and buttresses?

☐ ☐ Is the shoe concaved so that it does not rest upon the horny sole?

☐ ☐ Are the nail heads properly seated?

☐ ☐ Is the shoe the correct size for the foot?

☐ ☐ Will the weight of the shoe provide reasonable wear and protection to the foot?

☐ ☐ Have the ragged particles of the horny frog been removed?

MARKING OR IDENTIFYING HORSES

Until the 16th century (and even later in some parts of England), the ears of horses were cut in various ways as a means of identification. For example, a "bitted" ear was bitten (a piece was cut out) from the inner edge, and a cropped ear was cut straight across halfway down the ear. Eventually, cropped ears became fashionable, much as they are with certain breeds of dogs today, with the result that the practice persisted into the 18th century. This explains why early paintings of horses frequently showed the animals with tiny ears, scarcely 2 inches long.

In racehorses, an infallible means of identification is necessary to prevent a "ringer" — the name once given to a horse that was falsely identified, with the idea of entering him in a race with slower horses where he was almost certain to win. In the early 1920s, the most common camouflage for a ringer was a coat of paint; hence, the terms "dark horse" and "horse of another color." Formerly, the ringer's nemesis was rain; today, it is the lip-tattoo system or the photographs of his chestnuts. Through these the public is guaranteed the identity of each and every horse running in major races. The lip tattoo consists of branding, with forgery-proof dye, the registry number under the upper lip of the horse, with a prefix number added to denote age. The process is both simple and painless.

Pinkertons, and others, have "fingerprinted" the horse's chestnuts or night-eyes — the horny growth on the inside of each of the four legs. Studies have revealed that the chestnuts of no two horses are alike, and that, from the yearling stage on, these protrusions retain their distinctive sizes and shapes. The chestnuts are photographed, and then classified according to size and distinctive pattern.

On the western range, hide branding is primarily a method of establishing ownership. Also, it is a powerful deterrent to rustling (stealing).

In purebred horses, identification is necessary as a means of ascertaining ancestry or pedigree. Among the marks used for identifying registered horses are: (1) the lip tattoo, (2) hot iron brands, and (3) cold brands.

Figure 8.11 A drawing showing the lip tattoo under the upper lip of a Thoroughbred that has been on the track. The prefix letter denotes the age of the horse, and the numbers denote the Jockey Club registry number.

Until recently, the hot iron was the preferred method of branding. In this method, the irons are heated to a temperature that will burn sufficiently deep to make a scab peel, but which will not leave deep scar tissue.

Today, a new method of cold branding (freeze marking), developed by the USDA at Washington State University, is popular. The Arabian Horse Registry has adopted this method for permanent identification, using a series of right angles to replace Arabic numerals. This system is illustrated at the top of the next page.

Freeze marking is a permanent, painless, unalterable means of identification. On colored horses, it alters the pigment-producing cells so as to leave a mark of white hair. On a gray horse, a depilated, hairless mark is left in the area of contact.

The Arabian Horse Registry has designated the side of the neck under the mane as the official site of application. The mark is applied approximately 2 inches below the eruption of the mane and about midway between the poll and withers. An area approximately 2" × 7" is clipped close to the skin, then washed with alcohol. In the meantime, the marking iron is submerged in a bath of dry ice and alcohol until it reaches a temperature of about −80° C. The iron is then removed from the bath, dried, and applied to the clipped area of the neck. The contact time on the horse is dependent upon the color of the animal.

TRANSPORTING HORSES

Horses are transported via trailer, van, truck, rail, boat, and plane. Regardless of the method, the objectives are: to move them safely, with the maximum of comfort, and as economically as possible. To this end, selection of the equipment is the first requisite. But equipment alone, no matter how good, will not suffice.

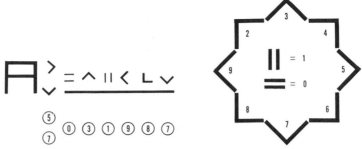

Figure 8.12 The series of right angles developed to replace the Arabic numerals. The number that each angle represents is written inside the angle. This is a freeze brand as it would actually appear under the mane of a horse. The encircled numbers do not appear in the brand; they are included here to decipher the symbols. The first symbol, the capital A, denotes that the horse is a purebred Arabian. The stacked symbols in the second position indicate the year of birth of the horse. The remaining symbols are the horse's registration number: 031987.

The trip must be preceded by proper preparation, including conditioning of horses; and horses must receive proper care, including smooth driving en route.

Most horses are transported in trailers, which have the distinct advantage of door-to-door transportation.

The requisites of good transportation are:

- *Provide good footing* — The floor of the vehicle should be covered with heavy coco matting made for the purpose, sand covered with straw

Figure 8.13 Cold- (freeze-) branded horses. Note the numbers on their right shoulders. (Courtesy, Louisiana State University)

Figure 8.14   Air travel for horses. These horses are in special stalls provided by the airline to avoid injury in flight. (Courtesy, United Air Lines)

or other suitable bedding material, or rubber mats. Clean the floor covering at frequent intervals while in transit to avoid ammonia and heat.

- *Drive carefully* — Drive at a moderate, constant speed, as distinguished from fast or jerky driving, which causes added stress and tiring. If weather conditions make the roads unsafe, the vehicle should be stopped.

- *Make nurse stops* — Nurse stops should be made at about three-hour intervals when mares and foals are transported together.

- *Provide proper ventilation* — Provide plenty of fresh air without drafts.

- *Teach horses to load early in life* — When horses will be transported later in life, they should be accustomed to transportation as youngsters before they get too big and strong. This can be done by moving them from one part of the farm to another.

- *Provide health certificate and statement of ownership* — A health certificate signed by a licensed veterinarian is required for most interstate shipments. Foreign shipments must be accompanied by a health certificate that has been approved by a government veterinarian. This takes several days. Branded horses must be accompanied by a brand certificate. All horses should be accompanied by a statement of ownership and a negative Coggins test certificate.

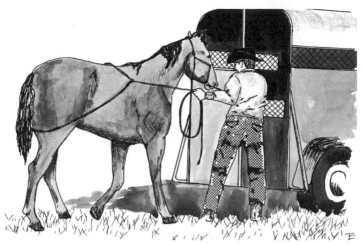

Figure 8.15   Easy does it! This is an easy way in which to load a green horse into a trailer.

- *Schedule properly* — Schedule the transportation so that animals will arrive on time. Show, sale, and race animals should arrive a few days early.
- *Have the horses relaxed* — Horses ship best if they are relaxed and not overtired before they are moved.
- *Clean and disinfect public conveyance* — Before using any type of public conveyance, thoroughly clean and disinfect it. Steam is excellent for this purpose. Remove nails or other hazards that might cause injury.
- *Have a competent caretaker accompany horses* — Valuable horses should not be shipped in the care of an inexperienced person.
- *Use shanks except on stallions* — When animals are tied, use a ⅝-inch cotton rope shank that is 5 feet long and has a big swivel snap at the end. Short nylon trailer ties with quick-release snaps are handy, but chain shanks are too noisy. Tie the shank short enough so the horse cannot get it over his neck. Always tie the shank with a knot that can easily and quickly be released in case of an emergency.
- *Feed lightly* — Allow horses only a half feed of grain before they are loaded for shipment and at the first feed after they reach their destination. In transit, horses should be given all the good quality hay they will eat, preferably alfalfa, to keep the bowels open, but no concentrates should be fed. Commercial hay nets or homemade burlap containers may be used to hold the hay in transit, but they should not be placed too high.
- *Water liberally* — When transporting horses, give them all the fresh,

clean water they will drink at frequent intervals unless the weather is extremely hot and there is danger of gorging. A tiny bit of molasses or grape juice may be added to each pail of water, beginning about a week before the horses are shipped, and the addition of molasses or juice to the water may be continued in transit. This prevents any taste change in the water.

- *Pad the stalls* — Many experienced shippers favor padding the inside of the vehicle to lessen the likelihood of injury, especially when a valuable animal is shipped. Coco matting or a sack of straw properly placed may save the horse's hocks from injury.

- *Take along tools and supplies* — The following tools and supplies should be taken along in a suitable box: pinch bar, hammer, hatchet, saw, nails, pliers, flashlight, extra halters and shanks, twitch, canvas slapper or short piece of hose, pair of gloves, fork and broom, fire extinguisher, and medicine for colic and shipping fever provided by a veterinarian.

- *Check shoes, blankets, and bandages* — Whenever possible, ship horses barefoot. Never allow them to wear calked shoes during a long shipment. They may wear smooth shoes. In cool weather, horses may be blanketed if an attendant is present in case a horse gets entangled. The legs of racehorses or show horses in training should be bandaged to keep the ankles from getting scuffed or the tendons or coronet bands bruised. Bandages are not necessary on breeding stock except for valuable stallions and young animals. When bandages are used, they should be reset often.

- *Be calm when loading and unloading* — In loading and unloading horses, always be patient and never show anger. Try kindness first; pat the horse and speak to him to reassure him. If this fails, it may be necessary to use one of the following techniques:

  1. Sometimes the use of the twitch at the right time is desirable, especially if the horse is tossing his head about.
  2. When a horse must be disciplined, a canvas slapper or a short rubber hose can be used effectively; these make noise without causing much hurt.
  3. If a horse gets very excited and is about to break out, dash a bucket of water in his face; usually he will back off and calm down.
  4. A nervous, excitable horse may be calmed by a tranquilizer, which should be administered by a veterinarian.
  5. If a horse will not move or is kicking, grab his tail and push it over his back. In this position, he cannot kick but can be pushed along.

- *Control insects* — In season, flies and other insects molest animals in transit. When necessary, use a reliable insecticide to control insects. Follow directions on the container label.

STRAY HORSES ON HIGHWAYS

Although state, county, and township laws vary, and it is not possible to predict with accuracy what damages, if any, may be recovered in particular instances, the following general rules apply:

- If a horse owner is negligent in maintaining his fences and allows his horse(s) to get on the road, he can be held liable for damage resulting to persons using the highway.

- If a horse owner has good fences that are well maintained, but has a horse(s) which he knows is in the habit of breaking out, he may be held liable for damages caused by such horse(s).

- If a horse(s) gets onto the highway, despite the facts that there are both good fences and the horse(s) is not known habitually to get out, the owner may be held liable for any damage inflicted provided he knew that the horse(s) was out and made no reasonable effort to get him in.

- If the horse owner is not negligent in any way, he may or may not be judged liable for the damage inflicted by his horse(s), depending on the state law and other circumstances.

- If a horseman is driving a horse(s) along or across a highway, he is not likely to suffer liability for any damage unless it can be proved that he was negligent. Stock-crossing signs usually increase the caution exercised by motorists, but do not excuse a horse owner from exercising due care.

- In some states, laws provide that a horse owner may, under supervision of and with varying amounts of assistance from highway authorities, construct an underpass for his horse(s) and for general farm use.

BUSINESS ASPECTS

In addition to being able to handle money matters, most horsemen — big and little — need a working knowledge of one or more of the following business aspects: boarding agreement, syndicated horses, incentive basis for the help, and taxes.

BOARDING AGREEMENT

Today's tough zoning laws and antipollution campaigns are making it increasingly difficult to keep horses in towns and suburban areas. As a result, more and more horses are being stabled and cared for in boarding establishments out in the country, to which owners commute. This prompts the need for an agreement.

Boarding agreements should always be in writing, rather than verbal, "gentlemen's agreements." From a legal standpoint, a boarding agreement is binding to the parties whose signatures are affixed thereto. Thus, it is important that the agreement be carefully filled out, read and fully understood before signing. A sample boarding agreement is shown on the next page.

SYNDICATED HORSES

Reduced to simple terms, a syndicated horse is one that is owned by several people. Most commonly, it's a stallion, although an expensive yearling or broodmare is sometimes syndicated. Also, any number of people can form a syndicate. However, there is a tendency to use the term "partnership" where two to four owners are involved, and to confine the word "syndicate" to a larger group of owners.

Each member of the syndicate owns a certain number of "shares," depending on how much he purchased or contributed. It's much like a stock market investor, who may own one or several shares in General Electric, IBM, or some other company. Sometimes one person may own as much as half-interest in a horse. Occasionally, half-shares are sold.

Generally speaking, the number of shares in a stallion is limited to the number of mares that may reasonably be bred to him in one season — usually 30 to 35 with Thoroughbred stallions.

Owners of stallions that have raced successfully usually have the opportunity to choose between: (1) continuing as sole owner of the horse, and standing him for service privately or publicly; or (2) syndicating him. In recent years, more and more owners of top stallions have elected to syndicate. The most common reasons given for so doing are:

1. The stallion owner does not have a breeding farm or an extensive band of broodmares.

2. The owner's belief that the stallion under consideration may not nick well with many of his mares, or perhaps because the stallion is closely related to them.

3. The owner's need for immediate income. Moreover, the profit, according to a tax court ruling, is subject to the frequently advantageous capital-gains treatment on income tax. By contrast, if sole ownership is retained, considerable promotional and advertising expenses will be involved for approximately three years until the stallion's get make their debut on the tracks; and, in the meantime, practically no income can be expected until about a year from entering stud, at which time the usual "live foal" guarantee is met — a live foal condition is fulfilled, and stud fees that are collected are generally held in escrow, as protection if they should have to be returned.

BOARDING AGREEMENT

(To be executed in duplicate; one copy to be retained by each party.)

This agreement made and entered into by and between _____

_____ (owner of horse)

_____, hereinafter designated "Horse Owner,"
_____ (address)

and _____, _____,
_____ (owner of stable) _____ (address)

hereinafter designated, "Stable Owner." This agreement covers the horse described as follows:

_____	_____	_____	_____
(Name)	(Sex)	(Age)	(Color)

Stable Owner agrees that —

1. He will keep the horse in a stall and/or paddock described as follows: _____

_____

_____

2. He will feed, water, and care for the horse in a good and husbandlike manner; feeding horse as follows:

	Amount of Feed		
Kind of Feed	Morning	Noon	Night
	(lb.)	(lb.)	(lb.)

3. He will perform the following additional services:

   a. Grooming (specify): _____

   b. Exercising (specify): _____

   c. Parasite treatments (specify): _____

_____

_____

   d. Others (list): _____

_____

_____

Horse Owner agrees that —

1. He will make all arrangements for the periodic shoeing of the horse, and assume the cost thereof. Any exception to this shoeing arrangement shall be given in the space that follows:

2. He will pay Stable Owner (a) for the foregoing facilities, feed, and services the sum of $_____ per month, payable on the _____ day of each month in advance; and (b) for drugs and medications, at cost, the first of each month following invoicing.

3. Stable Owner shall be entitled to a lien against the boarded horse for the value of services rendered, and shall be entitled to enforce said lien according to the appropriate laws of the state, *provided* (a) Stable Owner performs the services herein specified, and (b) Horse Owner fails to make a scheduled payment.

Horse Owner and Stable Owner mutually agree that —

1. In the event the horse shall require the services of a veterinarian, Stable Owner will immediately contact Horse Owner. In the event Horse Owner cannot be reached, Stable Owner is hereby authorized, as agent for Horse Owner, (a) to call Dr. _____, DVM; and, should he be unavailable, (b) to call any other licensed veterinarian of his choice. All fees charged by said veterinarian shall be the sole and exclusive responsibility of the Horse Owner, with no liability whatsoever on the part of the Stable Owner for such fees.

2. This document constitutes the entire agreement between the parties and there are no other agreements between them except as noted below.

_____	_____
(Signature of Horse Owner)	(date)

_____	_____
(Signature of Stable Owner)	(date)

Figure 8.16 Boarding agreement.

4. It spreads the risk, should the stallion get injured or die, or prove unsuccessful as a sire.

The owner may arrange the syndication himself, usually with competent legal advice; or, if preferred, the syndication can be turned over to a professional manager, who will generally take a free share as his organization fee.

INCENTIVE BASIS FOR HELP

On horse-breeding establishments there is need for some system which will encourage caretakers to (1) get a high conception rate, (2) be good nursemaids to newborn foals, though it may mean the loss of sleep, and (3) develop and sell surplus animals advantageously.

From the standpoint of the owner of a horse-breeding establishment, production expenses remain practically unchanged regardless of the efficiency of the operation. Thus, the investment in land, buildings and equipment, stallion and broodmares, feed, and labor differs very little with a change (up or down) in the percent foal crop; and income above the break-even point is largely net profit. Yet, it must be remembered that owners take all the risks; hence, they should benefit most from profits.

On a breeding establishment, the author recommends that profits beyond the break-even point (after deducting all expenses, including the salary of the owner) be split on an 80:20 basis. This means that every dollar made above a certain level is split, with the owner taking 80 cents and the employees getting 20 cents. Also, there is merit in an escalator arrangement; with the split changed to 70:30, for example, when a certain plateau of efficiency is reached. Moreover, that which goes to the employees should be divided on the basis of their respective contributions, all the way down the line; for example, 25 percent of it might go to the manager, 25 percent might be divided among the foremen, and 50 percent of it divided among the rest of the help; or that which goes to the employees may be divided on a prorata of salary basis.

Gross income in horse-breeding operations is determined primarily by (1) percent conception on mares bred, (2) percent foal crop, and (3) prices on horses sold. The first two factors can easily be determined. Usually, enough horses are sold to establish prices or values; otherwise, the going price can be used.

The incentive basis proposed in Table 8.6 for horse-breeding operations is simple, direct, and easily applied. As noted, it is based on the number and price of yearlings sold.

Break-Even Points

Whenever possible, the break-even point on a horse establishment — the dollars gross necessary in order to break even — should be arrived at from the actual records accumulated by the specific horse establish-

Table 8.6 A Proposed Incentive Basis for a Breeder Who Sells Yearlings

Yearling Crop Sold Based on 100 Mares Bred to Produce (No. of yearlings sold)	Price of Yearlings ($)	Here's How It Works
30	400	On this particular establishment, 100 mares are bred annually, and each year 15 top fillies are retained as herd replacements. Over and above this, the break-even point is 50 yearlings marketed annually. Thus, if 100 mares were bred in 1990, to break even there would have to be 65 yearlings in 1991, out of which 15 would be kept and 50 marketed.
35	600	
40	800	
45	1,000	
50 ←break-even→	1,200	
55	1,400	
60	1,600	
65	1,800	
70	2,000	
75	2,200	
80	2,400	

Moreover, the historical records of this establishment show that $1,200/head is the break-even point, provided 50 yearlings are sold, or a total gross of $60,000.

The sale of each yearling in excess of 50 head involves only $600 expense, primarily for added feed.

Thus, if 60 yearlings are marketed at an average of $2,000, that's a gross of $120,000. The break-even point is $60,000 (50 yearlings @ $1,200), plus the added cost of $6,000 to produce 10 more yearlings (10 × $600), or a total of $66,000. Hence, the net is $54,000. With an escalator arrangement, there might be an 80:20 split on a net up to $54,000; a 70:30 split of a net from $54,000 to $80,000, and a 65:35 split of a net in excess of $80,000.

It is recommended that division among employees be on a prorata of salary basis.

ment, preferably over a period of years. Perhaps, too, they should be moving averages, based on 5 to 10 years, with older years dropped out and more recent years added from time to time; thereby reflecting improvements in efficiency due primarily to changing technology, rather than to the efforts of the caretakers.

With a new horse operation, on which there are no historical records from which to arrive at break-even points, it is recommended that the figures of other similar operations be used at the outset. These can be revised as actual records on the specific enterprise become available. It is important, however, that the new operation start an incentive basis, even though the break-even points must be arbitrarily assumed at the time.

HORSEMEN AND TAXES[4]

The recent rounds of tax legislation have made significant changes in the procedures horsemen must use in accounting, as well as in their approaches to financial and estate planning. More than ever, it is important that they consult competent tax authorities before embarking upon any business operation involving horses.

ACCOUNTING METHODS

Pertinent information relative to accounting methods follows:

- *Cash vs. accrual method* — Most horsemen have the choice of using either the cash method or the accrual method. If the accrual method is used, annual inventories must be kept, with taxes determined from increases in inventory and deduction given for decreases. Having elected a method, the horseman will not generally be allowed to change methods without the approval of the IRS. With the general trend towards requiring accrual accounting, there is likely to be more resistance toward shifting from accrual to cash accounting than the reverse.

- *Valuation of inventory* — A horseman using the accrual method can select any reasonable method to value inventory, such as the farm-price method, and the unit-livestock method. Under the *farm-price* method, inventories are valued at market price less direct costs of disposition, such as broker's commissions, freight, and handling charges. Under the *unit-livestock price* method, a standard unit price is assigned to each animal within a class of livestock. If a horseman determines that it costs approximately $1,000 to produce a foal, and $500 each year to raise the animal, then the classifications and unit prices would be as follows: foals, $1,000; yearlings, $1,500; two-year-olds, $2,000; mature animals, $2,500. The classifications and prices are subject to approval by the IRS upon audit.

- *Capitalization of inventory costs* — The Revenue Act of 1987 (RA '87) reduced the ability of many businesses to deduct expenses currently by requiring that a number of expenses associated with the produc-

[4] This section was prepared by the author's son, John J. Ensminger, Esq., attorney specializing in taxes and estate planning, New York, NY.

tion of inventory be capitalized. This applies to the direct costs of producing the inventory, as well as to certain indirect costs which are allowed to be allocated to the inventory. An exception allowing current deductions for expenses was provided for taxpayers with gross receipts of $10 million or less. Also, an exception was provided for any plant or animal which is produced in a farming business and which has a prereproductive period of two years or less. With the Technical and Miscellaneous Revenue Act of 1988 (TAMRA), Congress extended the exception so that only farms under the accrual method must use uniform capitalization. Because of the flux in this area, horsemen who decided on an accounting method prior to TAMRA should have their tax advisers reconsider these choices.

Horsemen using the unit-livestock method are permitted to elect a simplified production method for determining costs required to be capitalized.

Drought relief — After 1987, a farmer using the cash method who is forced to sell livestock as a result of drought conditions, can defer income on the excess sales to the following year. However, this deferral cannot be used for income from livestock held for draft, breeding, dairy, or sporting purposes.

HOBBY OR BUSINESS

If an activity is not engaged in for profit, deductions are generally not available for conduct of the activity except to the extent of income from it. (Actually, because the expenses of a hobby are limited to the extent of 2 percent of adjusted gross income, such expenses will not be fully deductible.) This requirement has frequently been applied when the IRS determines that a horse operation is actually a hobby. Though the problem will generally not apply to full-time horsemen, others who devote a smaller amount of their time to a horse operation may find their activity is classified by the IRS as a hobby.

The general presumption for activities is that if an activity is profitable for three of the five consecutive years before being audited, it will be presumed to be engaged in for profit. Recognizing that horse operations often depend on the success of a rare horse, in such an operation Congress has allowed the activity to be presumed to be engaged in for profit if only two of the seven years are profitable. The IRS has indicated that an activity cannot be considered as engaged in for profit until there is a profit year.

Horsemen can delay the determination of whether a horse operation is engaged in for profit until the seventh taxable year of the activity. This election also keeps open the statute of limitations for those years.

In determining whether a horse operation is a business or a hobby, the IRS will examine the following factors:

1. *The manner in which the horseman carries on the activity.* The more businesslike the conduct of the activity, the more likely it is to be recognized as a business. This includes the keeping of accurate records of income and expenses. If the operation is conducted in a manner similar to other profit-making horse operations, it is more likely to be recognized as a business. If operating methods and procedures are changed because of losses, the impression is enhanced that the operation is a business. If the horse operation is typical of other operations in the vicinity, it may indicate an attempt to fit into the horse industry.

2. *The expertise of the horseman and his employees.* A study of the industry and of other successful operations indicates a profit-making approach. If the horseman tends to ignore advice, he may have to establish that his expertise is even greater than that of his advisers.

3. *Time and effort spent in carrying out the operation.* The more time the horseman devotes to the activity as a business and not a recreational pursuit, the more likely the IRS will find that the operation is a business. If the horseman hires a full-time assistant to run day-to-day operations, he will be in a stronger position to argue that he is attempting to turn a profit. If the assistant is an inexperienced family member, the horseman's position may, on the other hand, be weakened. Proper and rigid culling of horses will enhance the evidence for business conduct.

4. *The expectation that assets used in the activity will appreciate in value.* Even if current operations do not produce much income, the investment in land and buildings may support an argument that the horseman has taken other businesslike factors into consideration. If a primary focus of the operation is breeding, it may take considerable time to get the necessary stock.

5. *Prior successes of the horseman.* The more experienced the horseman and the more successful his prior horse operations, the more he is likely to be seen as a serious businessman. It may be important that the horseman comes from a family of successful horsemen.

6. *The operation's history of income and losses.* If losses are due to unforeseen circumstances (drought, disease, fire, theft, weather damages or other involuntary conversions, or from depressed markets), it may be possible to argue that there was nevertheless a profit motive in the operation.

7. *Occasional profits.* An occasional profit may indicate a profit motive if the investment or the losses of other years are comparatively small. The more speculative the venture, the more the horseman may be able to show that the losses were not due to a lack of profit intent.

8. *Financial status of the horseman.* The more the horseman relies on his horse operation, the more likely he is to be able to justify it as a

business. If there are substantial profits from other sources, it may appear that the horse operation is nothing more than a private tax shelter. If this is the case, the horseman may also have to worry about the effect of the limits on passive activity losses (see below).

9. *Elements of recreation or pleasure.* Though having fun does not mean an operation is a hobby, the more the recreational element dominates the horseman's involvement, the more likely he is to have difficulty convincing the IRS that he is trying to make a profit. The presence of fishing holes, tennis courts, and guest houses may indicate that the horseman has his own country club (a different sort of business, but not a horse operation).

Passive Activity Losses

Perhaps the most complicated addition to tax law added by TRA '86 was the passive activity loss concept, a development which will take tax lawyers years to decipher, with untold questions yet to be answered. Under this concept, all income and losses are divided between passive and nonpassive activities. A passive activity is one which involves the conduct of a trade or business in which the horseman does *not* materially participate. Losses and credits from passive trade or business activities are disallowed to the extent they exceed aggregate passive income. Passive income does not include portfolio income (interest, dividends, or royalties). However, rental activities are (if within the definition provided in the Internal Revenue Code) always passive.

- *Material participation.* The IRS has provided seven exclusive tests for meeting the material participation requirement as to a particular activity:

  1. *The 500-hours test.* The horseman participates more than 500 hours in the horse operation during the year. Obviously, full-time horsemen will not have significant difficulties in meeting this requirement.

  2. *Substantially all test.* The horseman's participation constitutes substantially all participation in the activity. Given the requirements for the care of horses, it is unlikely that this test is even necessary for horsemen, as they would then satisfy the first test in any case.

  3. *The 100-hours test.* The individual participates for more than 100 hours and no other person participates for a greater number of hours. Again, this will not generally be relevant to horsemen.

  4. *The related-activities test.* The horseman participates in a group of activities for more than 500 hours, more than 100 hours in each. This may apply where a horseman has a number of operations, but only limited involvement in each.

  5. *The five of ten years test.* This allows a horseman who has

materially participated in his activity in the past to qualify as materially participating presently, even if his direct involvement has fallen off somewhat.

6. *Personal service activities.* This would apply to consultants involved in the horse industry, but not to horsemen running their own operations.

7. *Facts and circumstances test.* This test is essentially similar to the 100 hours test.

Also, certain retired horsemen will qualify in the event of death during the year. Though these requirements will have no effect on the full-time horseman, they are an important consideration in terms of investment planning for anyone who is considering investment in rental real estate activities and other ventures.

- *At-risk rules.* Another provision limits losses to the extent that a taxpayer is at risk with respect to a particular activity. This means generally that a taxpayer is limited to the amount of his personal investment and the amount as to which he is personally liable. This provision specifically applies to farming, which includes livestock activities. The provision was designed principally to preclude losses from tax shelters and other leveraged investments where there may be no real chance that the taxpayer will have to cover the losses. Thus, it will seldom affect horsemen whose credit is generally limited to the amount of collateral they can provide.

Feed Purchases

Purchasing feed for use in subsequent years by cash-basis horsemen is an effective means of reducing current income, but the IRS will contest the deduction if (1) the payment is, in fact, a deposit, (2) there was no business purpose for it, or (3) it distorts income. Acceptable business purposes include guaranteeing prices and making certain of supply.

- *Prepayments.* TRA '86 added a provision concerning *farming syndicates* which generally limited deductions for feed, seed, fertilizer, or similar supplies, to the taxable year in which the supplies are actually used or consumed. A farming syndicate is a partnership or other enterprise (but not a C corporation) engaged in the business of farming, including the feeding, training, and management of animals, if at any time any interest requiring federal or state registration has been offered for sale in the enterprise. It also includes an entity where more than 35 percent of the losses during any period are allocable to limited partners or limited entrepreneurs. The IRS has indicated that a farming syndicate can include a general or limited partnership, a sole proprietorship involving an agency relationship created by a management contract, a trust, a common trust fund, and a subchapter S corporation. In 1988, Congress determined that the effect of the provision requiring farming syndicates to expense feed in the year consumed was unnecessary as such entities must use the accrual method of accounting in any case.

Of more general application is a provision stating that, to the extent that prepaid farming supplies (feed, seed, fertilizer, or similar supplies) exceed 50 percent of other deductible farming expenses, the excess amounts can only be deducted as consumed. This includes interest and depreciation. A farmer whose principal residence is on the farm, whose principal occupation is farming, or who is a member of such a farmer's family, is excepted from this provision if the excess supplies are attributable to extraordinary circumstances. Such an individual is also excepted if he does not have excess prepaid farm supplies based on the prior three years' operations.

- *Deferred-payment contracts.* It is sometimes desirable to delay recognition of income from a sale of horses until a subsequent year. Though the IRS is prone to finding that income which has been earned has, in fact, been constructively received by a taxpayer, and thus includable in his income, there are certain procedures which can be used to delay recognition. The general procedure for such a deferral involves the receipt of the funds by a middle party, but not an agent. The horseman should not receive cash equivalents, such as negotiable notes or securities or letters of credit. If the horseman is to receive funds directly from the buyer, the contract should require a deferral of income. The contract should specify the terms under which the horseman will receive payment. In the typical escrow agreement, there must be conditions, enforceable by both buyer and seller, which preclude the horseman from receiving payment until a subsequent date. The horseman cannot receive any present beneficial interest from the receipt of the funds by the escrowee.

DEPRECIATION

Horses bought (but not raised) for breeding or racing purposes may be depreciated. Depreciation is not available for inventory, which would include horses held for sale to customers. Of course, depreciation is available for other property used in the trade or business, such as buildings (but not land) and equipment. After 1986, depreciable property is placed in specific classes. Race horses that are more than two years old at the time placed in service are considered to be in the three-year class. This class also includes other horses which are more than 12 years old at the time placed in service. Automobiles and pick-up trucks, as well as certain technological and research equipment, are in the five-year class. Single-purpose agricultural structures are generally in the ten-year class after 1988. Residential rental property is now in the 27.5-year class, and nonresidential real property is generally in the 31.5-year class.

For property in the three- five- seven- and ten-year classes, depreciation was, prior to 1989, calculated on the double declining balance method, switching to the straight-line method at the time where depreciation is maximized. For property in the fifteen- and twenty-year classes, the 150 percent declining balance method is used. For the 27.5 and 31.5 year classes, the straight line method is used. However, for personal property (i.e., non-real property) placed in service in a farming business after 1988, the 150 percent declining balance must be used regardless of the recovery period. A horseman can elect to depreciate a two-year-old race horse under the straight-line method provided the election is made for all property in the same class. Once the election is made it is irrevocable. Special provisions apply to property which is not placed in service at the beginning of the year. If property depreciated under certain methods is sold, the gain will be characterized as ordinary income, a factor which may become relevant if differential capital gains rates are re-introduced. For purchased animals, the price paid will generally determine the amount which can be depreciated. Inherited or gift horses can be depreciated. However, their value may have to be established by a qualified independent appraiser, if the IRS contests the horseman's valuation.

- *Annual expensing.* The annual expensing limitation is $10,000 for property placed in service after 1986. However, this election is not available for taxpayers whose aggregate cost of qualifying property exceeds $210,000 (reduced-dollar-for-dollar over $200,000). The amount which can be expensed is limited to taxable income derived from the trade or business. The repeal of the Investment Tax Credit and the longer recovery periods for most classes of property increases the value of this provision for horsemen.

- *Soil and water conservation.* Horsemen can deduct soil and water conservation expenditures only if the expenditures are consistent with a conservation plan approved by the USDA or a comparable state agency. Though land clearing expenses are no longer deductible, ordinary maintenance, including brush clearing, remains deductible. Costs of fertilizing and other conditioning of land remain deductible.

- *Education expenses.* Educational expenses, such as the cost of short courses, are deductible if they are taken to maintain or improve the skills of the horseman in conducting his operation, or, if the horseman is employed by a horse operation, and they are taken as a requirement of continuing that employment. However, if taken to allow the horseman to enter another trade or business, such expense will not be deductible. For instance, a physician who owns a few horses, who takes a course of study with the idea of eventually managing a horse operation, will not likely be able to deduct the education expenses.

ESTATE PLANNING

- *Special use valuation.* Owners of farms and small businesses have been granted an estate planning advantage by means of what is called *special use valuation*. Under this concept, a farm or ranch can escape valuation for estate tax purposes at the highest and best use. Thus, a farm located in an area undergoing development may be considerably more valuable to developers than it is as a farm. Nevertheless, if the family is willing to continue the farming or ranching use for ten years, the farm can be included in the estate at its value as a farm. The aggregate reduction in fair market value cannot exceed $750,000.

  In order to qualify for special use valuation, the decedent must have been a U.S. citizen or resident and the farm must be located in the U.S. The farm must have been used by the decedent or a family member at the date of the decedent's death. A lease to a nonfamily member, if not dependent on production, will not satisfy this requirement. At least 50 percent of the value of the decedent's estate must consist of the farm and more than 25 percent of the estate must consist of the farm real property. It may be possible to split up a farm and take the special valuation for only part of it, but this part must involve real property worth at least 25 percent of the estate.

  The property must be passed to a qualified heir, including ancestors of the decedent, his spouse and lineal descendants, lineal descendants of his spouse or parents, and the spouse of any lineal descendant. Aunts, uncles, and first cousins are excluded. Legally adopted children are included.

  The property must have been owned by the decedent or a family member for five of the eight years preceding the decedent's death and used as a farm in that period. The decedent or a family member must have participated in the farming operation for such a period prior to the decedent's death or disability.

- *Electing special use valuation.* Though the procedures are clear as to how special use valuation is elected, the frequency with which mistakes are made indicates the importance of having a competent tax attorney or CPA firm prepare the estate tax return. A procedural failure denying the estate the considerable savings that can be gained by the election may give sufficient grounds for a malpractice suit against the return preparer.

- *Recapture tax.* If the farm ceases to be operated by the heir or a family member within ten years, an additional estate tax will be imposed and the advantage of the election will be substantially lost. Partition among qualified heirs will not bring about recapture. When heirs granted oil leases on a family farm, the portion of the land devoted to the oil rigs was subject to recapture. A recent change allows the surviving spouse of the decedent to lease a farm on a net cash basis to a family member without being subject to the recapture tax.

- *Payment extension.* Estates eligible for special use valuation may often be able to defer the payment of estate taxes. Where more than 35 percent of an estate of a U.S. citizen or resident consists of a farm, the estate tax liability may be paid in up to ten annual installments beginning as late as five years from when the tax might otherwise be due. If any portion of the farm is disposed of before the final payment, a corresponding portion of the amount deferred will come due.

HORSE HEALTH: DISEASES
AND PARASITES

Figure 9.1 Sign of good health — a winner. (Courtesy, The Jockey Club, New York, New York)

H orses are generally quite valuable, and they must be in good health if they are to perform at their best. Thus, they merit well-informed and ever present friends to guard against a host of perils and ailments, from scratches to sniffles, from colic to worms.[1]

Today, with more rapid transportation and dense horse centers, the opportunities for animals to get diseases and parasites are greatly increased compared to a generation ago.

Table 9.1 gives the normal temperature, pulse rate, and breathing rate of horses. Any marked and persistent deviations from these normal ranges may be looked upon as a sign of ill health.

---

[1] The material presented in this chapter is based on factual information believed to be accurate, but it is not guaranteed. When the instructions and precautions given herein are in disagreement with those of competent local authorities or manufacturers, always follow the latter two.

Table 9.1 NORMAL TEMPERATURE, PULSE RATE, AND BREATHING RATE OF HORSES

Normal Rectal Temperature		Normal Pulse Rate	Normal Breathing Rate
Average	Range		
(degrees F)	(degrees F)	(rate/minute)	(rate/minute)
100.5	99–100.8	32–44	8–16

Every horseman should provide himself with an animal thermometer, which is heavier and more rugged than the ordinary human thermometer. The temperature is measured by inserting a thermometer (with a long string tied to the outside end) full length in the rectum; the pulse rate is taken either at the margin of the jaw where an artery winds around from the inner side, at the inside of the elbow, or under the tail; and the breathing rate can be determined by observing the rise and fall of the flank or the rhythmic flaring of the nostrils. In cool weather, you can watch the breath condense as it comes from the nostrils.

In general, infectious diseases are ushered in with a rise in body temperature, but it must be remembered that body temperature is affected by stable or outside temperature, exercise, excitement, age, feed, etc. It is lower in cold weather, in older animals, and at night. Also, the pulse rate increases with exercise, excitement, digestion, and high outside temperature; and respiration is accelerated by exercise, excitement, hot weather, and poorly ventilated buildings.

IMMUNITY

When an animal is immune to a certain disease, it means that it is not susceptible to that disease.

The animal body is remarkably equipped to fight disease. Chief among this equipment are large white blood cells, called phagocytes, which are able to overcome many invading organisms.

The body also has the ability, when properly stimulated by a given organism or toxin, to produce antibodies and/or antitoxins. When an animal has enough antibodies for overcoming particular disease-producing organisms, it is said to be immune to that disease.

When immunity to a disease is inherited, it is referred to as a natural immunity.

Acquired immunity or resistance is either active or passive. When the animal is stimulated in such manner as to cause it to produce antibodies, it is said to have acquired active immunity. On the other hand, if an animal is injected with the antibodies (or immune bodies) produced by an actively immunized animal, it is referred to as an acquired passive immunity. Such immunity is usually conferred by the injection of blood serum from immunized animals, the serum carrying with it the substances by which the protection is conferred. Passive immunization confers immunity upon its injection, but the immunity disappears within three to six weeks.

In active immunity, resistance is not developed until after one or two weeks, but it is far more lasting, for the animal apparently keeps on manufacturing antibodies. It can be said, therefore, that active immunity has a great advantage.

It is noteworthy that young suckling mammals secure a passive immunity from the colostrum that they obtain from the mother for the first few days following birth.

A PROGRAM OF HORSE HEALTH, DISEASE PREVENTION, AND PARASITE CONTROL

Although the exact program will and should vary according to the specific conditions existing on each individual horse establishment, the basic principles will remain the same. With this thought in mind, the following program of horse health, disease prevention, and parasite control is presented with the hope that the horseman will use it (1) as a yardstick with which to compare his existing program, and (2) as a guide so that he and his local veterinarian, and other advisers, may develop a similar and specific program for his own enterprise.

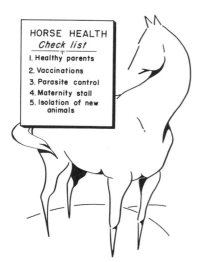

HORSE HEALTH
Check list
1. Healthy parents
2. Vaccinations
3. Parasite control
4. Maternity stall
5. Isolation of new animals

Figure 9.2 A horse health program.

GENERAL HEALTH PROGRAM

The following general, overall health program should be observed:

1. Avoid public feeding and watering facilities.
2. Read the sections in this book that discuss the diseases and parasites of horses; become familiar with symptoms and treatments.
3. When signs of infectious disease appear, isolate affected animals promptly, provide them with separate water and feed containers, and follow the instructions and prescribed treatment of a veterinarian.
4. Prevent or control parasites by adhering to the following program:
   a. Provide good sanitation and a high level of nutrition.
   b. Have adequate acreage. Use seeded pasture rather than permanent pasture, and practice rotation grazing.
   c. Pasture young animals on clean pastures. Never allow them to graze on an infested area unless the area has been either plowed or left idle for a year.
   d. Except during hot dry weather, do not spread fresh horse manure on pastures grazed by horses; either store the manure in a suitable pit for an extended period or spread it on fields that are to be plowed and cropped.
   e. Pick up the droppings from pastures and paddocks twice a week.
   f. Keep pastures mowed and harrowed. Use a chain harrow.
   g. Prevent fecal contamination of feed and water.
   h. Administer suitable vermifuges (dewormers) when internal parasites are present. Later, move horses to a clean area.
   i. Apply the proper insecticide when external parasites are present.
   j. If cattle and sheep are on the farm, alternate the use of pastures between them and horses because it will assist in the control of most parasites.
   k. Avoid overgrazing because more parasites are present on the bottom inch of grass.
5. As a disease preventive measure, arrange a scheduled yearly vaccination program with your veterinarian.

HEALTH PROGRAM FOR BREEDING AND FOALING

Reproduction is paramount in a horse-breeding program. To the end that there be superior conception followed by a high percent foal crop born and raised, the following reproductive disease-control program is recommended:

1. Mate only healthy mares to healthy stallions and observe scrupulous cleanliness at the time of service and examination. Never breed a mare that has any kind of discharge.

2. Provide plenty of exercise for the stallion and pregnant mare in harness, under saddle, or by turning them loose in a large pasture where plenty of shade and water are available.

3. Protect foals against the most common diseases (for example, influenza, rhinopneumonitis, and sleeping sickness; but rely on your veterinarian for advice) by immunizing pregnant mares about 30 days before foaling, thereby providing a high concentration of antibodies in the colostrum protecting foals.

4. During spring and fall when the weather is warm, allow the mare to foal in a clean, open pasture away from other livestock. During bad weather, keep the mare in a roomy, well-lighted, well-ventilated box stall that is provided with clean bedding. Before using the stall, thoroughly disinfect it with a lye solution made by adding 1 can lye to 12 to 15 gallons of water. After the foal is born, remove all wet, stained, or soiled bedding and dust the floor lightly with lime. Do not use too much lime because it irritates the eyes and nasal passages of foals. When the afterbirth has been completely discharged, it should be buried in lime or burned. The mare should be kept isolated until all discharges have stopped.

5. To lessen the danger of navel infection, promptly treat the navel cord of the newborn foal with tincture of iodine.

6. As a precaution against foaling diseases and other infections, a veterinarian may administer antibiotics to both the mare and foal on the day of foaling.

HEALTH PROGRAM FOR NEW HORSES AND VISITING MARES

New horses and visiting mares may bring in diseases and parasites. In order to minimize this hazard, the following program is recommended.

1. Isolate new animals for three weeks before adding them to the herd. During this period, a veterinarian may administer sleeping sickness vaccine in season and tetanus toxoid, and perhaps other vaccines; make a thorough general and parasitic examination; make a genital examination of breeding animals; and treat animals when necessary.

2. Make sure that mares brought in for breeding are accompanied by a health certificate issued by a veterinarian. Closely watch mares that have had trouble foaling or have lost foals.

3. If possible, saddle, bridle, or harness visiting mares near their own isolation quarters and use tack and equipment that is not used by mares kept on the establishment.

VACCINATION SCHEDULE

In no case should the vaccination program be used as a crutch for poor management. Likewise, no vaccination program is entirely successful without strict management practices to limit possible spread of infections.

For guidance purposes, a suggested vaccination program and schedule is given in Table 9.2 (see page 300).

DISEASES OF HORSES

It is intended that the summary of diseases that follows will (1) enhance the services of the veterinarian, (2) make for more rapid detection of trouble and improve nursing of sick horses, and (3) lessen the superstition, myth, and secret formulas so frequently used by horsemen.

ANTHRAX (Splenic Fever, Charbon)

An acute, infectious disease caused by *Bacillus anthracis*, a large, rod-shaped organism. It affects man, as well as horses. For this reason, a veterinarian should be summoned at the first sign of an outbreak.

Symptoms   This disease has a history of sudden deaths. Sick animals are feverish, excitable, and later depressed. They carry the head low, lag behind the herd, and breathe rapidly. Swellings appear over the body and around the neck regions. Milk secretions may turn bloody or stop entirely, and there may be a bloody discharge from all body openings.

Treatment   Isolate all sick animals. At the first sign of any of the above symptoms, a veterinarian should be called at once. The veterinarian may give large quantities of antibiotic (3 to 12 million units of penicillin or streptomycin). In the early stages of the disease, 50 to 100 milliliters (ml) of anti-anthrax serum may also be helpful. Provide good nursing care.

Control   Quarantine infected herds. All carcasses and contaminated material should be burned completely or buried deeply and covered with quicklime, preferably on the spot. Vaccinate all exposed but healthy animals, rotate pastures, and initiate a rigid sanitation program. Spray sick and healthy animals with an insecticide to avoid fly transmission of the infection.

Prevention   In infected areas, vaccination should be repeated each year, usually in the spring. Provide fly control by spraying animals during the insect season.

Discussion   The disease is general throughout the world in so-called anthrax districts. A farmer or rancher should never open the carcass of a dead animal suspected of having died from anthrax. Instead, a veterinarian should be summoned at the first sign of an outbreak. Control measures should be carried out under the supervision of a veterinarian. The bacillus that causes anthrax can survive for years in a spore stage, resisting all destructive agents.

DIARRHEA IN FOALS

Diarrhea is one of the most common disorders seen in foals, occurring in 70 to 80 percent of foals under six months of age.

Various factors may cause diarrhea, including the mare's first heat after foaling, dietary changes, parasites, and infectious agents such as bacteria or viruses. Recently, equine rotavirus has emerged as a significant cause of foal diarrhea. Most cases are mild and self-limiting, but the infectious diarrheas can be life-threatening and cause significant economic loss.

Symptoms   The symptoms and signs of foal diarrhea are depression, diarrhea, dehydration, and loss of appetite. In severe diarrhea, the foal may have fever and reddened mucous membranes.

Treatment   Diarrhea can most effectively be treated if discovered early. Treatment should be determined by the cause. If severe diarrhea persists for more than a day, fluids and electrolytes should be administered before the foal becomes too dehydrated. The veterinarian may also administer an antibiotic and/or a gut-soother such as Kaopectate.

Control   Isolation, sanitation, good nursing, and proper nutrition constitute the best control.

Prevention   Sanitation constitutes the best prevention. Foaling stalls should be thoroughly cleaned prior to each foaling, and the mare's udder should be washed. Staff hygiene should be strictly enforced. Foals should receive adequate colostrum. To date, no equine vaccine has been developed for the prevention of rotavirus.

Discussion   The most common diarrhea in foals occurs at about 7 to 12 days of age and coincides with the mare's first heat cycle. Usually, diarrhea is not serious, and the only treatment needed is to wash the feces off the buttocks and apply petroleum jelly to the area. The cause of foal-heat diarrhea at the time of the mare's first heat is not known; it is conjectured that it may be due to the changes in the mare's hormones at the time which affect the milk, or that it is caused by a change in the microorganisms in the foal's digestive tract. But the diarrhea is seldom

Table 9.2 EQUINE DISEASE VACCINATION PROGRAM AND SCHEDULE

Disease	Type
Encephalomyelitis: 1. Eastern (EEE) and Western (WEE)	Trivalent vaccine with EEE, WEE, and VEE, given intramuscularly.
2. Venezuelan (VEE)	Attenuated virus cell culture, given intramuscularly.
Equine Influenza (flu)	Bivalent inactivated vaccine.
Potomac Horse Fever — vaccinate if present in state or area.	Inactivated *Erlichia risticii*.
Rabies	Intramuscular vaccine. (High egg passage or inactivated tissue culture vaccines only.)
Strangles (distemper)	1. Bacterin. 2. M protein fractions extract. Both vaccines confer comparable immunity and have similar complications.
Tetanus (lockjaw)	Toxoid — horse builds immunity lasting for at least 6–18 months after vaccination. Antitoxin — for a horse that receives a puncture wound, produces passive immunity for only 7–14 days. Antitoxin (1,500 to 3,000 IU) — only effective for 10–20 days.
Viral rhinopneumonitis (virus abortion)	Killed vaccine Modified live virus

Initial Immunization		Booster	Age First Given to Foals
One month before mosquito season.	Repeat within the year if mosquito season is long.	Both injections should be repeated annually.	2–3 months.
One injection only. *Do not give to pregnant mares*		One annually.	3 months.
1st injection.	2nd injection — 4–12 weeks after the first.	One annually is usually sufficient. But every 60–90 days in highly susceptible horses.	3–4 months.
2 doses, 21 days apart.		One annually.	
1st injection.	2nd injection — 30 days after the first.	One annually.	3 months.
Vaccination lasts 6–12 months.		Every 6–12 months.	3 months.
1st injection — intramuscular	2nd injection — intramuscular, 2–4 weeks after 1st injection.	One annually.	2–3 months.
Given to injured animals that have not been previously immunized with tetanus toxoid.			
• Pregnant mares — 5th, 7th, and 9th month of pregnancy. • Young animals — 2 doses, 4–6 weeks apart.		Followed by booster vaccination at intervals of 6 months.	
• All horses except pregnant mares— 2 doses, 4–8 weeks apart.		Followed by booster vaccination at intervals of 6 months.	

serious, and it generally subsides a day or two after the end of the mare's first heat cycle.

ENCEPHALOMYELITIS (Sleeping Sickness; or Eastern, Western, or Venezuelan equine encephalomyelitis)

This virus, epizootic (epidemic) brain disease, which affects both horses and man, is known as equine encephalomyelitis, or sleeping sickness. Both horse and man are "dead-end" hosts, infected only by the mosquito.

Since 1930, the Eastern and Western types of the disease have assumed alarming proportions in the U.S. Then, in 1971, Venezuelan equine encephalomyelitis first occurred in the United States, when an outbreak was reported in Texas. The Venezuelan type was first diagnosed in Venezuela in 1936 and was reported in several South and Central American countries prior to appearing in the U.S. Equine encephalomyelitis is seasonal in character, extending from early summer until the first sharp frost of fall, when it invariably disappears.

The disease is caused by several distinct viruses. The three most active types in the U.S. are: Eastern equine encephalomyelitis, Western equine encephalomyelitis, and Venezuelan equine encephalomyelitis. All three viruses may be spread from animals to man, with mosquitoes serving as the primary means of transport. Wild birds, rodents, and wild animals in all areas of the country are reservoirs of the disease, which enters the body of a mosquito when it feeds on infected creatures. While in the mosquito, the virus multiplies and becomes highly concentrated in the salivary glands. The infected mosquito then transmits the virus to a horse or a man, whichever is handy at its next feeding. In the Venezuelan type, horses can spread the disease directly since the virus is present in their saliva and nasal discharges.

Symptoms   In early stages, animals walk aimlessly about, crashing into objects. Later they may appear sleepy and stand with a lowered head. Grinding of the teeth, inability to swallow, paralysis of the lips, and blindness may be noted. Paralysis may cause animals to fall. If affected animals do not recover, death occurs in 2 to 4 days.

In mild cases, the horse may merely yawn a few times; and this may be the only clinical sign of the disease.

Treatment   Treatment is not very effective, because of the rapid course of the disease. Since the Western type progresses more slowly and results in a lower mortality rate than the Eastern and Venezuelan types, it lends itself to more supportive treatment. Good nursing is perhaps the best and most important treatment. The maintenance of fluid and electrolyte balance is recommended. No specific therapeutic agent is known to influence the course of the disease.

Control   Control measures include the isolation of infected animals in screened cages or the application of insect repellent; prompt disposal of all infected carcasses; destruction, if possible, of insect breeding grounds; and discouragement of movement of animals from an epizootic area to a clean one. Fly and mosquito control seems to be very effective, since most outbreaks of the disease do not extend to racetracks and stables where insect control is practiced.

Prevention   Prevention entails vaccination of all horses. Monovalent, bivalent (EEE and WEE), and trivalent (EEE, WEE, VEE) vaccines are available. Monovalent VEE vaccine is an attenuated virus of cell-culture origin and should not be used in pregnant mares or young foals. The attenuated VEE vaccine has been largely replaced by a formalinized product incorporated into a trivalent vaccine with EEE and WEE antigens. Vaccine should be given about one month before the mosquito season and, where the mosquito season is long, should be repeated within the year. A veterinarian should administer the vaccine in keeping with the manufacturer's directions. (See Table 9.2.)

Discussion   The disease is widespread. Since 1930 nearly a million horses and mules have been affected in the U.S. Some animals make full recovery, but other survivors do not.

Generally speaking, mortality from the Western type does not exceed 50 percent, whereas that from the Eastern and Venezuelan types is 90 percent or higher.

Horses are considered to be dead-end hosts for WEE and sylvatic VEE viruses; with EEE virus, horses may develop viremia adequate to infect vectors, but probably do not contribute significantly to viral transmission or persistence.

EQUINE ABORTION (Premature Expulsion of the Fetus)

Abortion is the expulsion of the impregnated ovum at any period prior to the time that the foal can survive out of the uterus. If the foal is advanced enough to live, it is known as premature parturition, and in the mare this may occur as early as the tenth month.

It is estimated that 20 to 30 percent of all equine conceptions end in abortions.

Symptoms Equine abortion symptoms vary according to the cause. The causes of abortion in mares may be grouped into two types: (1) infectious agents, such as viruses, bacteria, and fungi; and (2) noninfectious abortions, such as twinning, hormonal deficiencies, congenital anomalies, and miscellaneous causes. Some of the more common causes are discussed in the sections that follow.

- *Infectious causes of abortion* — A discussion of each of the infectious abortions follows.

   1. *Virus abortion.* The most common cause of abortion in mares is due to infection by equine herpesvirus one (equine viral rhinopneumonitis). Most abortions due to this virus occur between the eighth and eleventh months of gestation, although they may occur as early as the fifth month; usually they are not associated with a respiratory infection. Sometimes the foal is born alive at term, but dies at two to three days of age due to infection by the virus. There is usually no mammary development; the fetal membranes are seldom retained; and the genital tract returns to normal as quickly as it does following normal parturition. The abortion rate may approach 100 percent in a herd of susceptible mares. An effective vaccine will prevent rhinopneumonitis and should be used in areas subject to the disease. Additionally, the following management practices should be followed on all farms regardless of size: (1) isolate all pregnant mares from all other horses, including foals and yearlings; (2) isolate all horses coming onto the premises; and (3) train all farm personnel in the application of sanitary practices.

      Equine viral arteritis may also cause abortion, but it is less frequent than equine herpesvirus abortion. However, it has become a problem in some areas. It produces more obvious signs of illness than equine rhinopneumonitis, including discharge from the eyes and nose, fever (102°–106° F), and filling (edema) of the limbs. A laboratory examination is necessary to establish conclusively the presence of the specific virus. Up to 50 percent of affected pregnant mares may abort. The name *"arteritis"* is derived from the particular type of arterial damage that this disease inflicts; it results in degeneration of the middle layer of arterial walls, especially in the small arteries. Treatment consists in absolute rest and good nursing, augmented by antibiotics to prevent or combat secondary bacterial infections. An effective vaccine is available and should be used in areas where the disease is a problem.

2. *Bacterial abortion.* Sporadic abortions in mares can be caused by bacterial infection of the placenta, acquired through the cervix. Several species of bacteria have been incriminated, including *S. zooepidemicus, E. coli, K. pneumonial,* and *Staphylococcus aureus.* They may cause abortion at any stage of pregnancy. Bacteria gain entrance to the reproductive tract at the time of foaling or breeding and thence travel to the uterus, where they cause infection of the fetal membranes and result in abortion. Bacterial abortion is often characterized by retention of the placenta, as well as by metritis or inflammation of the uterus. Treatment of the mare may be necessary before she can be rebred successfully. It is a good practice to culture mares before rebreeding, to determine if harmful bacteria are present in the vagina. The latter precaution is especially important where it is the intent to rebreed mares on the ninth day after foaling.

Adherence to the following program will materially reduce bacterial abortions:

   a. Breed mares only when the genital tract has returned to normal.
   b. Mate only healthy (bacteriologically clean) mares to healthy stallions and be scrupulously clean at the time of breeding.
   c. Give a mare that has foaled abnormally in any respect plenty of time to return to the normal state.
   d. Remember that infection is ever present in the filth of the external genitals of both the stallion and the mare.
   e. Suturing the lips of the vulva (Caslick's operation) will control this type of abortion in many mares. But this should be done by and on the advice of the veterinarian.

When a mare is found to have a severe genital infection, she should be treated properly and should have sexual rest for from six months to a year.

3. Mycotic abortions may result from infection of the placenta by various types of fungi, including *Mucor* and *Aspergillus* spp. Fungi probably enter the uterus during the heat period at which conception occurs, or soon after birth — in the case of foaling mares. Fungi do not attack the fetus directly; rather, they cause degeneration of the placenta so that the fetus has insufficient nourishment. For this reason, the aborted fetus is often small and only a fraction of the normal weight for its gestational age. If abortion does not occur, the foal may be carried to full term and be born in a reasonably vigorous, but undersized and undernourished, state. Most mycotic abortions occur during the second

half of pregnancy. There is no vaccine. Like bacterial abortions, mycotic abortions can be prevented by good breeding hygiene, treatment of genital disease prior to breeding, and corrective surgery (Caslick's operation).

- *Noninfectious causes of abortion* — The common noninfectious causes of abortion are:

  1. *Twinning* — The birth of healthy twin foals is unusual. The generally accepted theory relative to the inability of the mare to carry twin foals successfully to term is that it is due to placental insufficiency — meaning that there are not enough fetal membranes to accommodate and provide nutrition for two developing fetuses.

  2. *Hormone failure* — The hormone progesterone plays a dominant role in the maintenance of pregnancy, preparing the uterus for reception of the fertilized egg and the attachment of the placenta. It is responsible for the necessary changes in the uterus for the continuance of pregnancy and nourishment of the fetus. Other hormones, such as estrogen and cortisone, are also involved in the process and can contribute to abortion. Thus, the maintenance of pregnancy is a matter of hormone balance. Although there are many gaps in our knowledge of reproductive physiology, it appears that some abortions are caused by failure of the glands that control hormonal balance.

  3. *Congenital defects* — Early embryonic deaths, which may be mistaken for failure of conception or silent heats, frequently occur. Some of these are presumed to be due to genetic or chromosomal defects resulting in improper development of the embryo, followed by rejection by the dam.

  4. *Miscellaneous causes* — This embraces all cases of abortion that cannot be definitely classified in any of the categories discussed above — it includes abortions *not* caused by viruses, bacteria, fungi, twinning, hormonal deficiencies, or congenital anomalies. In the category of miscellaneous causes of abortions are nutritional deficiencies, certain drugs, accidents, and injury — such as a severe kick that disturbs the uterus, and noninfectious pathological lesions in the uterus of the mare. Causes of this type are so numerous and general that aside from good breeding, feeding, and management practices not much can be done to prevent them; but these three practices are vital in prevention of abortion as well as other diseases. The mare may abort from almost any cause that very profoundly disturbs the system.

Treatment   It is important to recognize an impending abortion as early as possible, for sometimes it may be prevented. When a pregnant mare shows any general indefinable illness, she should be examined closely for abortion indications. Any suggestive indications should prompt the horseman to call the veterinarian immediately. Treatment should be left to the veterinarian.

Control   When a case of abortion is encountered, the following procedure is recommended: (1) Gather up the fetus and afterbirth with great care and arrange through the local veterinarian for a diagnosis by the state diagnostic laboratory; (2) isolate the mare in a place where she can be kept in quarantine; (3) burn or bury the bedding; and (4) thoroughly disinfect the stall with a five-percent Lysol solution.

Prevention   Preventive measures embrace avoidance of all possible causes. It begins with mating only healthy mares to healthy stallions, and with being scrupulously clean at the time of breeding. New horses should always be isolated as a preventive measure, and aborting mares should be quarantined. Where abortions have occurred in the broodmare band, the special cause in the matter of feed, water, exposure to injuries, overwork, lack of exercise, and so forth may often be identified and removed. Avoid constipation, diarrhea, indigestion, bloating, violent purgatives or other potent medicines — including administering cortisones in late pregnancy — painful operations, and slippery roads.

The following points are pertinent in preventing and controlling abortion in a band of broodmares:

1. Prevent rhinopneumonitis by following a planned immunization program under the direction of a veterinarian. (See Table 9.2).
2. Prevent equine arteritis in areas where the disease is a problem by administering the vaccine.
3. Control and prevent bacterial and mycotic abortion by mating only healthy mares to healthy stallions and observing scrupulous cleanliness at the time of service and examination. Suture mares where necessary.
4. Keep broodmares healthy and in good flesh, and feed a ration that contains all the essential elements of nutrition.

One of the most important factors to remember about abortion is that a veterinarian should be called for diagnosis, prevention, control, and treatment.

To forget this is to invite trouble and to pave the way for possible spreading of the infection.

EQUINE INFECTIOUS ANEMIA — E.I.A. (Swamp Fever)

An infectious virus disease.

Symptoms   Symptoms of the disease vary, but usually they include some of the following: high and intermittent fever; depression; stiffness and weakness, especially in the hindquarters; anemia; jaundice; edema

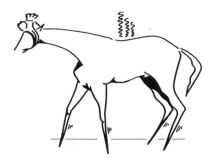

and swelling of the lower body and legs; unthriftiness; and loss of condition and weight, even though the appetite is good. Most affected animals die within two to four weeks.

- **Coggins Test** — The "Coggins test" for diagnosing E.I.A. is accurate — if properly used — fairly simple, and rather inexpensive. The test was developed by Dr. Leroy Coggins of the New York State Veterinary College, Cornell University; hence, the common name. Technically, the correct name for the blood test is the agar gel immunodiffusion (AGID) test. It is valid only if the blood sample is drawn by a veterinarian and submitted to a recognized laboratory. The AGID test is approved by the U.S. Department of Agriculture and is conducted in a number of laboratories.

The Coggins test is based on detection of antibodies (modified globulins) to E.I.A. virus. Infected horses become positive to this test two to four weeks after the onset of the initial infection and remain test positive the rest of their lives. Since foals receive large quantities of antibodies from their dams by way of colostrum, a nursing foal born of an E.I.A.-positive dam may be positive for the first four to six months of its life but not actively infected. Such foals can be considered free from the disease if they test negative at about seven months of age.

The test is usually repeated to confirm all positive reactions because horses are often destroyed on the basis of the test.

In 1976, the U.S. Department of Agriculture amended the animal import regulations to require that imported horses pass the Coggins test to assure that they are free of equine infectious anemia.

Treatment No successful treatment is known.

Control Segregate infected animals and have them use separate feeding and watering facilities. Kill sick animals and burn or bury their carcasses.

Prevention Use disposable hypodermic needles when horses are vaccinated against disease and sterilize all other skin-penetrating instruments by boiling them at least 15 minutes after each use. Practice good sanitation and eliminate or reduce biting insects as much as possible.

Watch for sick horses and get a diagnosis by a veterinarian if any are observed. Use separate tack equipment on each horse. Keep stalls, starting gates, and other facilities clean at racetracks and shows. This disease has existed in different sections of the U.S. for at least 50 years, but no preventive vaccination has been developed.

When a positive diagnosis has been made, a quarantine is imposed and slaughter of horses that test positive is advised. Compensation of $200 per horse is payable by the federal government in addition to any slaughter value for the animal. Infected mares or stallions should not be used for breeding purposes.

Discussion   Infected horses may be virus carriers for years and are a danger to susceptible horses.

After horse owners test and eliminate all infected animals from their herd, the Coggins test can be used to protect their stock from reinfection, (1) by buying horses only after they have been tested and found free from the disease, (2) by not allowing untested horses to be stabled or pastured with their own, and (3) by not bringing their horses to any assembly point (show, sale, racetrack, trail ride, etc.) where prior testing is not required.

EQUINE INFLUENZA

An infectious disease caused by a myxovirus that has properties of the Type A influenza viruses.

Symptoms   Young animals, except for very young foals that have immunity from the dam's milk, are particularly susceptible. Older animals are usually immune. Symptoms develop 2 to 10 days after exposure. The onset of the disease is marked by a rapidly rising temperature that may reach 106° F and persist for 2 to 10 days. Other symptoms include loss of appetite, extreme weakness and depression, rapid breathing, a dry cough, and a watery discharge from the eyes and nostrils that is followed by a white to yellow nasal discharge.

Treatment   Treatment should be handled by a veterinarian. Avoid exercising the animals during the period of elevated temperature. The use of antibiotics and/or sulfa drugs may prevent some of the complicated secondary conditions.

Control   Avoid transmission of the virus on contaminated feed, bedding, water, buckets, brooms, clothing and hands of attendants, and transportation facilities.

Prevention   Vaccinate with a killed virus. Use two doses; follow the manufacturer's directions on the time of the second dose. Also, give each animal a booster shot at intervals of about six months, or a booster when animals are exposed or when an epidemic occurs. Quarantine sick animals, and isolate all new animals to the premises for three weeks. (See Table 9.2.)

Discussion　　The disease is widespread throughout the world. It frequently appears where a number of horses are assembled, such as racetracks, sales, and shows. The death rate is low, but economic loss is high. The disease interrupts training, racing, and showing schedules, and it may force the withdrawal of animals from sales. Although horses, swine, and humans are subject to influenza and the symptoms are similar for each, there appears to be no transmission of the disease among them.

GLANDERS (Farcy)

An acute or chronic infectious disease caused by *Malleomyces mallei,* a bacterium.

Symptoms　　The chronic form most often attacks horses, affecting the lungs, skin, or nasal passages. There may be a nasal discharge that later becomes pus, and nodules and ulcers may appear in the skin. With the lung type, there generally is loss in condition, lack of endurance, bleeding and a mucus discharge from the nose, and coughing. The skin of the extremities may develop ulcers that exude a honeylike tenacious discharge.

The acute form more often attacks mules and donkeys. The symptoms are similar to the chronic form, but more severe. Death usually occurs in a week.

Treatment　　Sulfadiazine, given every 20 days, has proven fairly effective.

Control　　Use the "Mallein test" to detect infected animals or animals suspected of having the disease. Destroy infected animals and clean and disinfect contaminated equipment and premises.

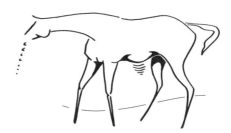

Prevention   Avoid inhalation or ingestion of the causative organism. Do not use public watering places.

No method of immunization is available.

Discussion   Glanders is prevalent in areas where horses still are used for transportation and work. The disease has largely disappeared from the mechanized areas of the world, including the U.S., but it has not been eradicated. Through the transport of animals, glanders can make its appearance anytime in any area.

LYME DISEASE

Lyme disease was first recognized in people in Old Lyme, Connecticut, in 1975, hence the name. At that time, the outbreak was traced to the bite of a small deer tick, *Ixodes dammini* (in California, the vector is the western black-legged tick, *Ixodes pacificus*). But Lyme disease can strike any mammal — horses, cattle, dogs, rodents, raccoons, opossums, and others. The first case in equines was diagnosed in a pony, in Wisconsin, in 1985.

In 1981, the disease agent (a spirochete) was isolated from the tick and named *Borrelia burgdorferi*.

Symptoms   The most common symptoms or signs in horses are lameness (arthritis), fever, muscle aches and pains, limb swelling, eye inflammation, hepatitis, nephritis, and abortion. A positive diagnosis of Lyme disease is based on clinical signs, opportunity for infection, antibody titers (revealed by a blood test), and response to treatment.

Treatment   Once diagnosed, Lyme disease is fairly simple to treat. Penicillin and tetracycline have been shown to be effective, particularly in the early stages of the disease; response to early treatment can be dramatic, often overnight. However, chronic cases may require treatment with antibiotics for a long time, up to six months.

Control   Control ticks and flies.

Prevention   The best prevention is a diligent tick and fly control program.

Discussion   Fervent research is in progress to develop a vaccine. In the meantime, control ticks and flies.

NAVEL INFECTION (Joint Ill, Navel Ill, Actinobacillosis, Streptococcus)

An infectious disease of newborn animals caused by several kinds of bacteria.

Symptoms   Infected animals have loss of appetite; swelling, soreness, and stiffness in the joints; general listlessness; and umbilical swelling and discharge.

Treatment   The standard treatment for infected joints is to wash out the joint cavity with fluid to remove the large number of pus cells and debris that accumulate from damaged surfaces. This is accomplished by forcing fluid through a needle into one part of the joint and draining it from another. Antibiotics, administered by injection, are used as an adjunct to this therapy. Also, antiinflammatory drugs, such as phenylbutazone, are given to relieve pain and restore some mobility to the affected part.

Control   See Prevention.

Prevention   Practice good sanitation and hygiene at mating and parturition. Feed iodized salt to pregnant mares in iodine-deficient areas. Soon after birth, treat the navel cord of newborn animals with tincture of iodine.

Discussion   The disease appears throughout the U.S. About 50 percent of infected foals die and many that survive have deformed joints. Providing clean quarters for the newborn and painting the navel cord with tincture of iodine are the best preventive measures.

POTOMAC HORSE FEVER

An acute, often fatal, diarrhea was first noticed in a number of horses in Montgomery County, Maryland, in the summer of 1979. At first the disorder was called *acute equine diarrhea syndrome,* but soon it became known as *Potomac Horse Fever,* after the region where it was first recognized.

The causative agent is named *Ehrlichia risticii,* after its discoverer. *E. risticii* is a member of the class of microorganisms called rickettsia, which are between bacteria and viruses in size.

Symptoms   Symptoms are: fever (102° to 108° F), depression, loss of appetite, colic, edema of the underline, and stocking up (filling) of the limbs. These symptoms are usually followed within 48 hours by the onset of diarrhea, which in severe cases is watery and explosive. A high percentage of horses with Potomac Horse Fever develop founder, or laminitis. The fatality rate approaches 30 percent, with death occurring primarily from dehydration and shock. A new rapid diagnostic test is available which is capable of giving a positive diagnosis in less than five minutes. The diagnostic test makes rapid treatment possible.

Treatment   Treatment consists of large volumes of intravenous fluids, tetracycline, and supportive treatment to control fever and reduce laminitis.

Control   Correct diagnosis is important in control since the symptoms of Potomac Horse Fever often mimic those of salmonellosis, yet the drug tetracycline, which is helpful against Potomac Horse Fever, can be deadly to horses with other diarrhea disorders.

Prevention   A successful vaccine is available, which is administered intramuscularly in two doses, repeated 21 days apart, followed by an annual booster shot. So, if Potomac Horse Fever is present in a state or area, all horses therein should be vaccinated against the disease.

Discussion   To date, researchers have not been able to determine how the disease is transmitted, but biting insects are strongly suspected, so insects should be controlled.

STRANGLES (Distemper)

A widespread contagious disease caused by *Streptococcus equi,* a bacterium.

Symptoms   Sick animals show depression, loss of appetite, high fever, and a discharge from the nose. By the third or fourth day of the disease, the glands under the jaw start to enlarge, become sensitive, and eventually break open and discharge pus. A cough is present.

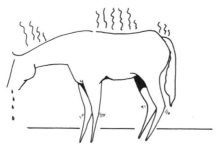

Treatment   Good nursing is the most important treatment. This includes clean, fresh water, good feed, uniform temperature, and shelter away from drafts. A veterinarian may prescribe one of the sulfas or antibiotics, or both. Early treatment is of the utmost importance in strangles.

Control   Put affected animals in strict quarantine. Clean and disinfect contaminated quarters and premises.

Prevention   Prevention consists of avoiding contact with infected animals or contaminated feeds, premises, and equipment.
     Two types of vaccines are available, both of which confer similar immunity and have similar complications. (See Table 9.2.)

Discussion   The disease is worldwide and it attacks animals of any age, but it is most common in young stock. Death losses are low. Affected animals are usually immune for the remainder of life.

TETANUS (Lockjaw)

Chiefly a wound-infection disease caused by a powerful toxin, more than 100 times as toxic as strychnine, that is liberated by the bacterium *Clostridium tetani,* an anaerobe.

Symptoms   This disease usually is associated with a wound. First sign of tetanus is a stiffness about the head. Animals often chew slowly and weakly and swallow awkwardly. The third or inner eyelid protrudes over the forward surface of the eyeball. The slightest noise or movement causes sick animals to have violent spasms. Usually sick animals remain standing until close to death. All ages are susceptible.

Treatment   Place sick animals under the care of a veterinarian and keep them quiet. Good nursing is important. If given early in the disease, massive doses of antitoxin, 100,000 to 200,000 units or more, may be effective. Also, tranquilizers will reduce the extent and severity of muscular spasms, and antibiotics will help.

Control   See Prevention.

Prevention   Under the direction of a veterinarian, give tetanus toxoid in two doses at six-week intervals, followed by a booster injection annually. If premises are unsanitary, all surgery should be accompanied with tetanus antitoxin.

Discussion   Tetanus is worldwide, but in the U.S. it occurs most frequently in the South. Death occurs in over half of the affected cases.

VESICULAR STOMATITIS

A contagious disease of the mouth caused by a virus.

Symptoms   Blisters and rawness appear mainly on the tongue but also on the inner surfaces of the lips, angles of the mouth, and the gums. There is considerable salivation. Symptoms appear in two to five days after exposure.

Treatment   Make the animal as comfortable as possible and provide plenty of water and soft feed.

Control   Control the movement of animals and disinfect transportation facilities.

Prevention   No vaccination is available in the U.S.

Discussion   When the disease strikes, it may affect 50 percent of the animals on the premises.

OTHER AILMENTS

Horses are subject to many other ailments; among them, colds, a discussion of which follows. (Also, see Chapter 6, Feeding Horses, for section on Nutritional Diseases and Ailments.)

Colds

Horses are subject to colds very similar to those in man. Colds are caused by a virus and, as in humans, there are various strains of the horse cold virus. The symptoms are: loss of appetite, shivering, a rise in temperature to 103° F or 104° F, and an increased pulse rate to around 50 or 60. Usually, a discharge develops, but the glands are not affected. Afflicted horses often develop a sore throat and a nasty cough.

Colds are highly contagious and can spread rapidly through an entire stable. Therefore, affected animals should be isolated immediately. A veterinarian should be called, who will generally administer an antibiotic to prevent secondary infection. Good nursing will help. The latter includes keeping the horse warm and dry in a well-ventilated but not drafty place and giving him a bran mash.

PARASITES OF HORSES

Parasites live in or on the bodies of host animals. Parasites kill some horses but the main damage is lowered efficiency. Attacks are insidious and can easily cause damage before the parasite is noticed.

Until the 1980s, parasite control programs were relatively standard-ized throughout the equine industry. But biotechnology changed all this! Even the parasites changed — some of them developed resistance to long-used chemicals. New drugs were developed; and the rotation of drug treatments, long held sacred, was challenged. And that was not all! Pollution, from whatever source, became a dirty word; and environ-mental control, sustainable agriculture, biological control of parasites, and animal behavior and welfare were in vogue. A basic understanding of all these forces is essential to establishing effective parasite control programs for the horses of tomorrow.

For guidance in the selection of an anthelmintic (dewormer) or insec-ticide, the user should seek the counsel of the veterinarian, county agent, extension entomologist, or agricultural consultant; and for in-struction on the use of an anthelmintic or insecticide, the user should follow the directions on the label.

INTERNAL PARASITES

Some 150 different kinds of internal parasites attack horses throughout the world, and probably no animal is ever entirely free of them.

Parasites may be located in practically every tissue and cavity of the body. However, most of them are in the alimentary tract, lungs, body cavity, or bloodstream. Those in the digestive system usually become localized there, but others travel throughout different parts of the body.

The general symptoms of parasitic infection in horses are weakness, unthriftiness, emaciation, tucked-up flanks, distended abdomen, rough coat, pale membranes in the eyes and mouth, stunted growth in young animals, and in some cases frequent colic and diarrhea. Affected ani-mals usually eat well and the temperature remains normal. But an in-fected animal always loses some efficiency as a working unit.

Preventive and Control Basics

Most parasitic infections of equines may be attributed to the fact that, under domestication, horses (as well all other animal species) have been forced to sleep and eat in close proximity to their own feces — being either confined and fed in a stall or fenced within limited grazing areas or pastures. By contrast, in the wild state animals roved over vast areas, seldom eating, watering, or sleeping in the same spot. As the feces of the horse are the primary source of infection by internal para-sites, it should be obvious that the most important requisite of success-ful control measures is that they be designed to separate the animal from its own excrement.

An effective program for the prevention and control of internal para-sites on all horse establishments, big or small and of whatever kind, calls for (1) good management, (2) superior sanitation, (3) periodic treat-ments with the proper anthelmintics, and (4) routine fecal examinations

Figure 9.3 Same horse before (*upper picture*) and after (*bottom picture*) treatment for internal parasites. Parasites retard the foal's development and lower the efficiency of mature horses. Also, feed is always too costly to give to parasites. (Courtesy, College of Veterinary Medicine, University of Illinois, Urbana)

conducted by a veterinarian or skilled technician to determine the numbers and types of parasites present. A brief discussion of some of the basics of internal parasite control programs follows.

Anthelmintic (Dewormer) Resistance

In recent years, many horse owners have noticed diminished effectiveness of certain anthelmintics (dewormers). This resistance is not due to a change in the drug itself; rather, it is due to biochemical and physiological adaptations by parasites to combat the action of the dewormer. Worms can achieve resistance by absorbing less drug, breaking it down with new enzymes, or bypassing chemical pathways that normally are blocked by a dewormer. Whatever biochemical mechanisms make for resistance, those traits become part of the successful parasite's genetic composition and are inherited in the offspring.

Once resistance has been demonstrated on a farm, these drugs should never be used there again. A complete history of anthelmintic use on a farm is essential to detect anthelmintic resistance.

Anthelmintics Abound

In the first half of the 20th century, the accepted means of deworming horses was with tobacco. Later, phenothiazine, piperazine, and carbon disulfide were added to the anthelmintic arsenal. In 1960, Drudge at the University of Kentucky recommended that anthelmintic treatment be administered every six to eight weeks to control strongyles, ascarids, and bots. Today, there is a great array of equine anthelmintics from which to choose.

Biological Control

There is little cross-infection of parasites between horses and ruminants, so either (1) mixed grazing of horses, cattle, and sheep, or (2) rotation grazing of horses, alternated with cattle or sheep, constitutes effective biological control, with one exception. The small stomach worm, *Trichostrongulus axei*, infects horses, cattle, and sheep.

Biological control with dung beetles is theoretically feasible, but to date it has been of little practical benefit.

Increasing use will be made of the biological control of parasites as an alternate to polluting the environment with pesticides.

Clean Pastures

Treating the horse while ignoring the pasture is of little value! The parasites in horse pastures can be reduced dramatically by picking up the manure twice a week. An Ohio State University study showed that a pasture routinely cleaned in this manner had 18 times fewer parasites than an uncleaned pasture. Manure can be removed manually or mechanically. In England, a power sweeper is available, consisting of a small trailer fitted with a vacuum pump powered by a tractor or small engine. A scoop shovel is just as effective.

In damp or wet conditions, a harrow should not be used to break up the manure; it will merely spread the parasite larvae into the grazing area. If pasture harrowing is done in hot dry weather, it will effectively break up feces and expose larvae to death by desiccation.

Typically, horses divide pastures into (1) defecating areas, and (2) grazing areas. However, if manure piles are completely removed from the pasture twice a week, either by hand or machine, horses will utilize the entire area for grazing.

Monitoring Control Programs

Monitoring the control program by fecal egg count is just as important as the choice of the anthelmintic and the timing of treatments. It enables the veterinarian to compare the efficacy of different anthelmintics, to detect the development of drug resistance, and to assess the effectiveness of the program in reducing pasture contamination.

Rotation of Anthelmintics

Until the mid-1980s, the rotation of dewormers was recommended as the best defense against resistance. Yet, those who rotate too frequently within the same drug class may be selecting, unwittingly, for resistance to more than one type of drug and further limiting the success of their deworming program.

Researchers are now recommending a less frequent rotation regimen, one that uses a single product for at least a year at a time. Also, it is very important that rotation be between drug classes; for example, rotation among the benzimidazoles (BZD) is not effectively combating resistance, because each wormer in this class works by the same mechanism.

Other Basics of an Internal Parasite Control Program

1. Make the program all inclusive (i.e., every horse on the farm that will share common ground should be treated simultaneously).

2. Isolate and treat newly added horses before allowing them to share pastures, paddocks, pens, or stalls with resident horses.

3. Control the parasites in the mare, thereby greatly reducing exposure of the foal.

4. Take periodic random fecal examinations to determine efficacy of therapeutic/treatment program and survey for potential parasite drug resistance. (Sample on day of treatment to compare to two-week post-treatment samples.)

5. Rotate drug therapy wisely and sparingly. Use a product for at least a year, then rotate between chemically unrelated drug classes — and *not within* drug classes.

6. Remember that route of administration plays no part in the success of the program, as long as the entire proper dose is consumed by each horse. Feed administration, paste preparations, stomach tubing, and injection are equally effective if the horse receives its recommended dose of the drug.

7. Read and follow all label directions explicitly; if there are any questions, call the veterinarian or the manufacturer for assistance.

8. Devise the program to suit your needs and desired goals.

9. Adjust the drug treatment interval to the environmental factors present in the area.

10. Eliminate the potential of repeated or recurrent reinfestation by sensible husbandry; avoid overcrowding, remove fecal contamination of stalls once or twice daily, avoid ground feeding, and remove manure from pastures twice a week.

11. Plan the program with flexibility to incorporate all age groups, yet be able to concentrate on the special concerns of each.

12. Remember that it costs less to maintain a routine and effective parasite control program on a year-round basis than it does to waste feed on a parasitized horse; the money spent on a routine program is better invested than money spent on life-saving treatment or surgery when the horse colics due to accumulated internal parasite damage.

13. Be a drum major for biological control, pollution and
environmental control, sustainable agriculture, and horse welfare.

COMMON INTERNAL PARASITES AND THEIR CONTROL

In North America horses are affected by more than 80 internal parasites, which inhabit nearly every organ. These parasites are so widespread that no horse escapes all of them.

Because there are so many kinds of internal parasites, only the most common and damaging ones are summarized in Table 9.3 and discussed at length in the narrative that follows. Strongyles, ascarids, and bots are generally the most injurious of internal parasites, although other kinds are capable of producing severe injury on occasion and generally contribute to the overall picture of parasitism wherever they occur.

Choice of drug (anthelmintic)   Knowing what internal parasites are present within a horse is the first requisite to the choice of the proper drug, or anthelmintic. Since no one drug is appropriate or economical for all conditions, the next requisite is to select the right one; the one which, when used according to directions, will be most effective and produce a minimum of side effects on the animal treated. So, coupled with knowledge of the kind of parasites present, an individual assessment of each animal is necessary. Among the factors to consider are age, pregnancy, other illnesses and medications, and the method by which the drug is to be administered. Some drugs characteristically put horses off performance for several days after treatment, whereas others have less tendency to do so. Some drugs are unnecessarily harsh or expensive for the problem at hand, whereas a safe, inexpensive alternative would be equally suitable.

Anthelmintics are constantly being improved, and new ones are becoming available. So, the horseman should consult his local veterinarian relative to the choice of drug to use on his horses at the time.

Program and schedule — Each horse establishment should, in cooperation with the local veterinarian and/or other advisers, evolve an internal parasite program and schedule. A general understanding of the life cycles of the various parasites is necessary in order to time the treatments to best advantage. Also, it is recommended that an equine practitioner or parasitology laboratory do periodic fecal examinations to help assess the effectiveness of the parasite control program.

Ascarids or Large Roundworms (Parascaris equorum)

The female varies from 6 to 22 inches long and the male from 5 to 13 inches. When full grown, both are about the diameter of a lead pencil.

Symptoms   The injury caused by ascarids ranges from light infections producing moderate effects to heavy infections that may cause death. Death usually is due to a ruptured intestine. Serious lung damage caused by migrating ascarid larvae may result in pneumonia. More common are retarded growth and development manifested by a potbelly, rough hair coat, and digestive disturbances. Ascarids affect foals and young animals, but rarely affect horses over five years old; older animals develop immunity from early infections.

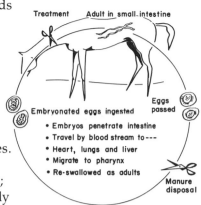

Treatment   The advice of the veterinarian should be sought relative to (1) the choice of drug(s) and (2) the treatment schedule for ascarid control.

Prevention and control   Keep the foaling barn and paddocks clean, store manure in a pit for two to three weeks, provide clean feed and water, and place young foals on clean pasture.

Discussion   Ascarids attack horses throughout the U.S. The presence of ascarids results in loss of feed to feeding worms, lowered work efficiency, retarded growth in young animals, lowered breeding efficiency, and death in severe infections.

Bots *(Gasterophilus* spp.)

Four species of bots have been found in the U.S., but only three are serious pests of horses.

Symptoms   Animals attacked by the botfly may toss their heads in the air, strike the ground with their front feet, and rub their noses on each other or any convenient object. Animals infected with bots may show frequent digestive upsets and even colic, lowered vitality and emaciation, and reduced work output. Bots may penetrate the stomach wall and cause death.

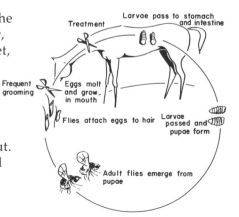

Table 9.3 INTERNAL PARASITES OF HORSES

Parasite	Where Found
Ascarids *(Parascaris)*, (Roundworms)	Small intestine.
Bots *(Gastrophilus)*	Larvae embedded in lining of mouth and tongue. Stomach.
Pinworm *(Oxyuris)*	Large intestine. Rectum.
Stomach worm *(Habronema* adult), *(Habronema* larvae)	Stomach, attached to wall or free.
Strongyles, large (Bloodworm)	Adult strongyles are found in large intestine, attached to walls or free. Larvae migrate extensively to various organs and arteries.
Strongyles, small *(Triodontophorus, Poteriostomum, Trichonema,* and others)	Large intestine and cecum, attached to walls and free.
Tapeworm *(Anoplocephala)*	Varies according to species: *A. magna* and *P. mamillana* in small intestine and stomach. *A. perfoliata* mostly in cecum.
Threadworm *(Strongyloides)*	Small intestine.

Treatment   Horsemen should seek the advice of their local veterinarian, county agent, extension entomologist, or consultant in arriving at the wormer of choice. Also, they are admonished to follow the label directions of the manufacturer.

Damage	Signs
Irritate intestinal wall, possible obstruction (impaction) and rupture of small intestine.	Digestive upsets (colic), diarrhea, weight loss, retarded growth, rough hair coat, potbelly, death (ruptured intestine), more common in young horses.
Irritation and nervousness during the botfly egg-laying season. Sore mouth and tongue. Inflammation, ulceration, perforation of stomach wall.	Excitement (caused by flies), evidence of pain when eating, digestive upsets (colic), retarded growth, poor condition, death (stomach rupture).
Irritation of anal region.	Rubbing of tail and anal regions, resulting in broken hairs and bare patches around tail and buttocks.
Stomach inflammation and colic. Larvae produce summer sores.	Gastritis, digestive disorders, and summer sores, which often heal spontaneously after first frost.
Adults suck blood, cause anemia, and produce ulcers on mucosa. Larvae interfere with blood flow to the intestine, damage arteries, and cause aneurisms, which may burst. Injury to the large intestine.	Anemia, rough hair coat, colic, loss of appetite, retarded growth, depression, soft feces with a foul odor. In large infestations, legs and abdomen swell. Anemia, loss of appetite, retarded growth, dark or black manure, soft feces with a foul odor. In large infestations, legs and abdomen swell.
Ulceration of mucosa in area of attachment.	Unthriftiness, digestive disturbances, and anemia.
Erosion of intestinal mucosa, enteritis.	Loss of appetite, loss of weight, diarrhea; worms disappear by time foals are 6 months old.

Prevention and control   Frequent grooming, washing, and clipping help prevent bot attacks. Prevention of reinfection is best assured through community campaigns in which all horses are treated. Fly nets and nose covers offer some relief from the attacks of botflies.

Figure 9.4 Bots attached to the stomach wall of a horse. At this stage they remain attached to the lining of the stomach and intestines for several months, feeding on blood until they are about ¾ inch in length, after which they release their hold and pass out with the feces. (Courtesy, Department of Veterinary Pathology and Hygiene, College of Veterinary Medicine, University of Illinois, Urbana)

Discussion   Bots are worldwide. The presence of bots results in loss of feed to feeding worms, itching and loss of tail hair from rubbing, lowered work efficiency, retarded growth of young animals, lowered breeding efficiency, and death in severe infections.

Figure 9.5 Washing to remove the eggs of adult botflies attached to the hairs of the horse. (Courtesy, U.S. Department of Agriculture)

Equine Piroplasmosis (Babesiasis)

Caused by *Babesia caballi* or *B. equi*, protozoan parasites that invade the red blood cells.

Symptoms   Equine piroplasmosis is similar to equine infectious anemia, but a positive diagnosis can be made by determining whether or not protozoa are in the red blood cells. Symptoms include a fever of 103° to 106° F, anemia, jaundice, depression, thirst, a discharge from the eyes, and swelling of the eyelids. Constipation and colic may occur and the urine is a yellow to reddish color. Symptoms appear one to three weeks after exposure.

Treatment   A number of treatments, some old, some new, may be used with success. The horseman should rely on his veterinarian in the choice of treatment.

Prevention and control   Prevention and control of equine piroplasmosis involves the control of the tropical horse tick. Methods of tick control are discussed in the section on external parasites. Practice rigid sanitation in the use of all syringes, needles, and medical instruments. Recovered animals remain carriers for ten months to four years and should be isolated.

Discussion   This infection is worldwide. In the U.S., it was first diagnosed in Florida in 1961. The death rate is from 10 to 15 percent of infected animals.

Lungworms (Dictyocaulus arnfieldi)

The equine lungworm is very rare in the U.S.

Symptoms   Donkeys seem to be able to carry large numbers of lungworms without showing any symptoms. They develop a tolerance. However, infected foals may become unthrifty and develop a cough. There is a rise in temperature with lungworm infection.

Prevention and control   Where lungworm infection is suspected, a fecal examination should be made. Infected burros should be kept away from foals.

Discussion   Lungworms may be found in the air passages of the horse and other equines. The male worm reaches a length of about 1 inch and the female may be about 2 inches long. The eggs are laid in the lungs and pass out of the horse's body through the intestine. They hatch into first-stage larvae that develop eventually into the third, or infective, stage. The infective larvae enter the body through the mouth, travel in the lymph vessels to the thoracic duct, then to the heart, and eventually to the lungs.

Pinworms (Rectal Worms; *Oxyuris equi,* *Probstmyria vivipara*)

Two species of pinworms, or rectal worms, frequently are found in horses. *Oxyuris equi* are whitish worms with long, slender tails. *Probstmyria vivipara* are so small they are scarcely visible to the eye.

Symptoms   The symptoms are irritation of the anus and tail rubbing. Heavy infections also may cause digestive disturbances and anemia. Large pinworms are most damaging to horses and may be seen in the feces of heavily infected animals.

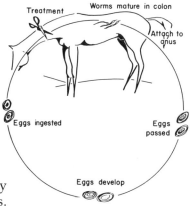

Treatment   The drug of choice should be administered in keeping with the label directions of the manufacturer. In case of severe itching, blue ointment may be applied around the tail beneath the anus.

Prevention and control   Provide good sanitation and keep animals separated from their own excrement.

Discussion   Pinworms attack horses throughout the U.S.

Stomach Worms (*Habronema* spp., *Trichostrongylus axei*)

A group of parasitic worms that produces inflammation of the stomach.

Symptoms   Horses suffer loss of condition and severe gastritis. Sometimes, the larvae of large stomach worms are partially responsible for the skin disease of horses called summer sores.

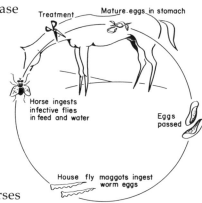

Treatment   Several wormers are effective when used according to manufacturers' directions.

Prevention and control   Provide good sanitation, proper manure disposal, and fly control.

Discussion   Stomach worms attack horses throughout the U.S. Wasted feed and lowered efficiency are the chief losses.

Strongyles, Large and Small (Bloodworms; *Strongylus* spp. and others)

There are about 40 species of strongyles. Three are large worms that grow up to 2 inches long. The rest are small and some are barely visible to the eye. Large strongyles are variously called bloodworms (*Strongylus vulgaris*), palisade worms, sclerostomes, and red worms.

Symptoms   Infected horses have lack of appetite, anemia, progressive emaciation, a rough hair coat, sunken eyes, digestive disturbances including colic, a tucked-up appearance, and sometimes posterior paralysis and death. Collectively these symptoms indicate the disease known as strongylosis. Harmful effects are greatest in young animals. One species of large strongyles (*Strongylus vulgaris*) may permanently damage the intestinal blood vessel wall and cause death at any age.

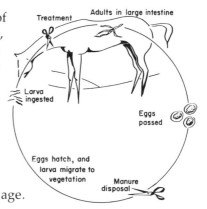

Treatment   Medication should supplement rather than replace wholesome feed and water and clean surroundings.

Prevention and control   Gather manure daily from pastures and barns and store it in a pit for two to three weeks. Rotate pastures and avoid moist pasture and overstocking.

Discussion   Strongyles attack horses throughout the U.S., wherever horses are pastured. Attacks of strongyles result in loss of feed to feeding worms, lowered work efficiency, retarded growth of young animals, lowered breeding efficiency, and death in severe infections.

Tapeworms (*Anoplocephala magna, A. perfoliata, Paranoplocephala mamillana*)

Anoplocephala perfoliata is the most common and most damaging.

Symptoms   Heavy infections may cause digestive disturbances, loss in weight, and anemia.

Treatment   Treatment is not ordinarily suggested, primarily because only light infections are encountered. However, pyrantel pamoate administered at twice the label dose is effective against tapeworms.

Prevention and control   Provide good sanitation and husbandry, proper manure disposal, and clean bedding.

Discussion   Tapeworms attack horses throughout the northern part of the U.S. Losses are primarily in wasted feed and retarded growth. Sometimes colic develops as a result of cecal impaction.

Threadworms *(Strongyloides westeri)*

Threadworms are also known as strongyloides.

Symptoms   Threadworms attack foals, causing diarrhea. The worms disappear by the time foals are six months old.

Treatment   Threadworms are self-limiting; they disappear by the time foals are six months of age.

Prevention and control   Provide good sanitation and clean, dry bedding.

Discussion   These worms are common where there is a concentration of foals. Losses are primarily in stunted growth and unthriftiness.

EXTERNAL PARASITES

Several kinds of external parasites attack horses. These pests lower the vitality of horses, damage the hair and skin, and produce a generally unthrifty condition.

External parasites also are responsible for the spread of several serious diseases of horses. Equine piroplasmosis (babesiasis) is transmitted by a tick, *Dermacentor nitens*. Mosquitoes *(Culicidae)* are vectors of equine infectious anemia (swamp fever) and equine encephalomyelitis (sleeping sickness).

The common measures used to prevent and control external parasites of horses are practicing good sanitation, good grooming, avoiding a too-heavy concentration of horses, and spraying or dusting with insecticides. Flies and lice are the most common external parasites of horses, but some of the others can produce more severe injury when they occur.

The cost of controlling external parasites on horses by using insecticides is usually very small compared to losses incurred when the infestations go uncontrolled. A good program for controlling external parasites of horses should (1) be initiated during the early stages of infestation, (2) include the use of good sanitation practices and manipulation of standing water in addition to the application of insecticides (not all external parasites can be controlled with insecticides), and (3) require use of insecticides in complete accordance with the labels and instructions.

COMMON EXTERNAL PARASITES AND THEIR CONTROL

The common external parasites of horses and recommended control measures follow. *Caution:* The choice of insecticides will vary because of (1) the diversity of environments and management practices under which they are used, (2) the varying restrictions on the use of insecticides from area to area, and (3) the fact that registered uses of insecticides change from time to time. Information about what insecticide is available and registered for use in a specific area can be obtained from the county agent, extension entomologist, agricultural consultant, or veterinarian.

Blowfly

The blowfly group consists of several species of flies that breed in animal flesh.

Damage inflicted; symptoms and signs of affected animals   The maggots of blowflies infest wounds and spread over the body, feeding on the skin surface, producing severe irritation, and destroying the ability of the skin to function. Infested animals rapidly become weak, fevered, and unthrifty.

Treatment   Insecticides should be considered supplementary to sanitation and management. The horseman should confer with local authorities relative to additional treatments.

Prevention and control   To control the blowfly, destroy dead animals by burning or deep burial and by using traps, poisoned baits, electrified screens, and repellents.

Discussion   Blowfly attacks are widespread but they present the greatest problem in the Pacific Northwest, the South, and the Southwest. Death losses are not large but work efficiency is lowered.

Flies and Mosquitoes

Flies and mosquitoes are probably the most important insect pests of horses. They lower the vitality of horses, mar the hair coat and skin, produce a general unthrifty condition, lower performance, and make

Figure 9.6 Blowfly. The blowfly group consists of a number of species of flies, all of which breed in necrotic animal flesh.

Figure 9.7   Horse fly and mosquito.

for hazards when riding or using horses. Also, they may temporarily or permanently impair the development of foals and young stock. Even more important, they can be the vector (carrier) of serious diseases. Because of their varying habits, along with different materials and methods required for their control, flies have been classed as either biting or nonbiting in the discussion that follows.

Biting Flies and Mosquitoes

Several species of biting (bloodsucking) flies and mosquitoes attack horses, but the following are the most common: horse flies (*Tabanus* spp.), deer flies (*Chrysops* spp.), stable flies *(Stomoxys calcitrans)*, horn flies *(Haematobia irritans)*, mosquitoes (species of the genera *Aedes, Anopheles, Culex,* and *Psorophora),* black flies (family Simuliidae), and biting midges (genus *Culicoides).* Because these flies suck blood, several of them may transmit such diseases as anthrax, encephalomyelitis (Eastern, Western, and Venezuelan), equine infectious anemia (swamp fever), vesicular stomatitis, and anaplasmosis. All of them are pests — that is, they cause considerable annoyance to horses.

Distribution: losses caused by biting flies and mosquitoes   Biting (bloodsucking) flies and mosquitoes are found wherever there are horses, with the highest population occurring during warm weather and where there is lack of sanitation. They annoy horses — on pastures, in stalls, and in paddocks. They cause pain and discomfort to the animals, and, at times, they make them unmanageable when they are being worked.

Horse and deer flies attack horses pastured in or near areas with a marsh, swamp, creek, or irrigation ditch.

Stable flies are found wherever there are horses, people, or other mammals — their usual victims.

Horn flies are found near cattle. So, horses are attacked when they are pastured with cattle, kept in areas near cattle, or ridden near cattle.

Mosquitoes cause special discomfort to horses, particularly during early spring and wet years.

Life history and habits   Horse flies and deer flies breed in standing water that is fairly shallow and has an abundance of organic matter.

Figure 9.8   Stable fly (*Stomaxys calcitrans*). (Courtesy, U.S. Department of Agriculture)

Stable flies breed in horse manure, soiled bedding, feed wastes, decomposed fruit and vegetable matter, and compost piles and clippings. Horn flies breed in single, fresh droppings of cow manure. Mosquitoes breed on water, in such places as water-holding low spots in corrals and paddocks, infrequently used drinking troughs, irrigated pastures, drainage ditches, natural flooded meadows, swamps, creeks, tree holes, leaf-choked rain gutters, and poorly covered septic tanks and drains.

Damage inflicted; symptoms and signs of affected animals   Horse flies and deer flies possess sharp, scissorlike mouthparts, which slice into the skin and make for a good flow of blood.

The stable fly sucks blood and is a vicious biter, especially in the early evening hours when the weather is warm and humid. Severe attacks irritate horses and cause restlessness and the stamping of feet. Because stable flies crawl over horse manure and then suck blood from the horse, they readily transmit stomach worms (*Habronema*).

Horn flies feed primarily on the back of the head, the sides of the neck, shoulders, withers, along the back, around the navel, and on the legs. They remain on the horse day and night.

In addition to their vicious biting habits, mosquitoes are of particular concern to horsemen because they transmit the viruses causing encephalomyelitis (Western, Eastern, and Venezuelan).

Treatment   Fly repellents which last 4 to 8 hours after application have been developed for the control of horse flies and deer flies on horses.

Prevention and control   Sanitation — the destruction of the breeding areas of the pests — is the key to the control of biting flies and mosqui-

Figure 9.9   Horn fly (*Haematobia irritans*).

toes. Do not allow manure or other breeding areas to accumulate. Remove manure from fields and paddocks every day or two. Control horse flies, deer flies, and mosquitoes by filling low spots in corrals or paddocks and draining all water-holding areas.

As a supplement to sanitation, use insecticide (of which there are several) according to manufacturer's directions. Treat manure piles and buildings for fly control; and treat wet areas that harbor mosquitoes.

Nonbiting Flies

Horses may be annoyed by the face fly *(Musca autumnalis)* and the house fly *(M. domestica)*, neither of which suck blood.

Distribution; losses caused by nonbiting flies   Face flies are serious pests of horses (and cattle) in the eastern, midwestern, and certain western states.

House flies are widely distributed throughout the world and are one of the principal pests around horse stables.

Life history and habits   The face fly breeds only in single, fresh animal droppings, and only from cattle on rangeland or pasture. The life cycle from egg to adult takes eight days during warm summer months and up to two to three weeks in cooler weather.

House flies are attracted to waste materials, where they feed and deposit their eggs. This includes stacked horse manure, soiled bedding, wet feed, and decomposed plant material (grass clippings, vegetable and fruit wastes). House flies do not normally develop in single manure droppings; rather, they use piles of manure or other organic matter. Under favorable conditions — warm weather and plenty of food — the usual life cycle from egg to adult fly is one week.

Damage inflicted; symptoms and signs of affected animals   Face flies congregate about the nose and eyes of horses, where they sponge up liquids. The feeding of face flies causes excessive flow of tears and saliva — and irritation. Infested horses usually stand about restlessly switching their tails and not grazing naturally. Almost complete freedom from face flies can be obtained by keeping horses confined to stables during the daytime.

The house fly, which feeds twice daily, regurgitates liquid through its proboscis while depositing fecal matter as it crawls over its food. In this manner, it can transmit human and animal diseases, and it transmits stomach worms *(Habronema)* to horses. The dark spots on walls, ceilings, corral fences, etc., are the characteristic "fly specks" of vomit or fecal material.

House flies are attracted to the moist areas of the horse's face.

Figure 9.10   Face fly (*Musca autumnalis*).

Treatment   Residual sprays will eliminate many house flies. Also, house flies are attracted to baits (insecticides mixed with sugar or other attractive material), which are effective house fly killers.

Prevention and control   Good face fly control is difficult to achieve. Pyrethrin repellents applied to the horse's face and head will repel nonbiting flies for 8 to 12 hours. A mask or net can be made and attached to the halter so that its movements protect the horse's eyes from face flies when on pasture. Residual sprays, when applied to the sunny surfaces of barns, shelters, and fences where face flies congregate, reduce populations.

Sanitation is the most efficient method of reducing populations of house flies. Sanitation may be additionally important if the horses are located near an urban area, in order to avoid complaints from neighbors.

Lice

These are small, flattened, wingless insect parasites. Horses are commonly infested by two species of lice; they are the common horse-biting louse, *Damalinia equi,* and the horse-sucking louse, *Haematopinas asini.*

Damage inflicted; symptoms and signs of affected animals   Symptoms include intense irritation, restlessness, and loss of condition. There may be severe itching and the animal may be seen scratching, rubbing, and gnawing the skin; scabs may be evident and the hair may be rough, thin, and without luster. Lice are likely to be most plentiful around the root of the tail, on the inside of the thighs, over the fetlock region, and along the neck and shoulders.

Figure 9.11   Sucking lice: female (*left*) and male (*right*).

Treatment   Lice are easily controlled by periodic applications, according to the directions on the label, of one of several suitable insecticides.

Prevention and control   Because of the close contact of horses during the winter, it is practically impossible to keep them from becoming infested with lice. For effective control, all horses should be treated with insecticides simultaneously at intervals as needed, especially in the fall about the time they are placed in winter quarters.

Discussion   Lice are widespread. They retard growth, lower work efficiency, and produce unthriftiness. They show up most commonly on neglected animals in winter.

Mites

These are very small parasites that cause mange (scabies, scab, and itch). The two chief forms of mange are sarcoptic mange caused by burrowing mites and psoroptic mange caused by mites that bite the skin and suck the serum and lymph but do not burrow. Mites also may cause chorioptic mange.

Damage inflicted; symptoms and signs of affected animals   Symptoms are irritation, itching, and scratching. The skin crusts over and becomes thick, tough, and wrinkled. Mange appears to spread most rapidly during the winter months.

Treatment   Lime-sulfur will meet federal regulations for the control of mites on horses, when used according to directions. *Where their use is permitted by FDA,* both lindane and toxaphene are effective for the control of mites, when used according to manufacturer's directions.

Prevention and control   Keep healthy horses away from diseased animals or infested premises. Spray infested animals with insecticides and quarantine affected herds.

Discussion   Mites are widespread. They retard growth, lower work efficiency, and produce unthriftiness. When sarcoptic and psoroptic mange appear, they must be reported to state or federal animal health agencies. Also, in many states, chorioptic mange must be reported.

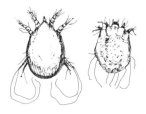

Figure 9.12   Psoroptic mange mite (*left*) and sarcoptic mange mite (*right*).

Figure 9.13 Ringworm.

Ringworm

This is a contagious infection of the outer layers of skin caused by an infestation of microscopic fungi.

Damage inflicted; symptoms and signs of affected animals Round, scaly areas almost devoid of hair appear mainly in the vicinity of eyes, ears, side of the neck, or root of the tail. Mild itching usually accompanies the infection.

Treatment Clip the hair from the infected skin areas. Soften skin crusts with warm soap and water and remove them if desired. Let infected areas dry and then paint them with weak tincture of iodine every three days or treat them with a mixture of one part salicylic acid and 10 parts alcohol every three days until the infection clears up.

Prevention and control Isolate infected animals. Disinfect everything that has been in contact with infected animals, including curry combs and brushes. Practice strict sanitation.

Discussion Ringworm attacks horses throughout the U.S., primarily as a stable infection. It is unsightly, and infected animals may have considerable discomfort, but economic losses are low.

Screwworm

Maggots of the screwworm fly require living flesh of animals on which to feed.

Damage inflicted; symptoms and signs of affected animals Symptoms include loss of appetite, unthriftiness, and lowered activity.

Figure 9.14 Screwworm. The screwworm fly (*left*) raises its maggots, or larvae (*right*), in the open wounds of animals.

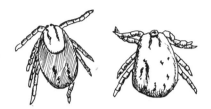

Figure 9.15 Ticks: female (*left*) and male (*right*).

Treatment   Screwworms in wounds can be killed by applying the type of normal dressing recommended by local authorities.

Prevention and control   Area-wide screwworm eradication by sterilizing pupal-stage screwworms with X-rays or gamma rays has been most effective. Try to keep animals from wounding themselves and protect any wounds that do occur. Schedule castrations in winter when flies are least numerous and active.

Discussion   The screwworm has been almost eliminated in the U.S. However, constant vigilance is necessary to detect a reinfestation and to eradicate it quickly before flies reproduce and spread.

Ticks

Several kinds may be found on horses. The most common ones are the winter tick, *Dermacentor albipictus;* the lone star tick, *Amblyomma americanum;* and the spinose ear tick, *Otobius megnini.*

Damage inflicted; symptoms and signs of affected animals   The symptoms are lowered vitality and itching; animals rub and scratch infested parts.

Treatment   The horseman should seek the advice of local authorities relative to the choice of an insecticide(s) for tick control.

Prevention and control   Treatment with insecticides will control ticks on horses and protect them against reinfestation for several weeks.

Discussion   Ticks appear mostly in the South and West. They reduce vitality of horses and may spread piroplasmosis, African horsesickness, and (in infested areas) Lyme disease.

FIRST AID FOR THE HORSE

Accidents do happen; horses are more injury prone and are subject to a more awesome variety of wounds than any other class of domestic animal. They are thin-skinned; and they cut, tear, and bruise easily. For this reason, maximum wound-preventative measures should be an integral part of horse management procedure. Such things as loose wire, sticks, sharp rocks, machinery, loose or broken boards, and trash have no place in horse pastures or corrals; and stables and trailers should be periodically examined for loose boards, protruding nails, or any sharp objects.

Despite all possible precautions, however, as long as there are horses, there will be such things as wire cuts, saddle galls, cinch sores, rope burns, and other abrasions. Hence, it is important that the horseman have on hand at all times a good first aid powder, as an aid in (1) stopping bleeding, (2) killing germs, (3) drying the wound (thereby speeding the healing process and discouraging flies and other insects from congregating around it), and (4) lessening proud flesh.

The horse, more than any other species of animal, must receive proper care and treatment of wounds. Mistreatment will result in slow healing, excessive scarring, blemishing, and sometimes unsoundness. Wounds below the knees and hocks are especially sensitive; hence, they require careful treatment, and sometimes bandaging, to prevent complications.

Liniment for the Horse   A good liniment, properly used, will hasten and assist nature in returning an injured part to normal and relieve fatigue, overexertion, and soreness.

Liniment is a mild stimulant. Its use, along with massage, stimulates circulation, assists the body in removing waste products of muscle metabolism, and hastens nature in returning an injured part to normal. Do not use it if heat is present in a leg, indicating acute inflammation.

The use of liniment is recommended for the following conditions: lameness, stiffness, soreness, strained tendons, sore shins, certain types of arthritis, and swellings, bumps, and bruises. It hastens recovery time and helps to prevent everyday injuries from turning into serious problems.

Also, liniment may be used, according to manufacturer's directions, as a body wash or brace after strenuous workouts or transportation, especially on the horse's legs, to relieve fatigue and overexertion, and to prevent soreness.

Wounds   Wounds take a variety of forms, sizes, and severity; and, in turn, these determine the treatment. Generally speaking, there are five classes of wounds: (1) *cut (incised) wounds* produced by sharp objects, such as glass or sharp metal, where there is a minimum of tissue damage and little bruising; (2) *torn (lacerated) wounds* produced by irregular objects, such as barbed wire and horn gores, characterized by extensive damage to underlying tissues; (3) *puncture (penetrating) wounds* produced by sharp objects, such as nails and pitchforks, characterized by small punctures and a considerable amount of deep injury; (4) *abrasions* caused by such things as rope burns and rubbing against a door or trailer, characterized by oozing of the serum and little bleeding; and (5) *bruises (contusions)* caused by a blow, such as a kick or fall, which do not break the skin but which cause bleeding and fluid loss deep down.

If the wound is serious, such as a deep puncture wound, or where the swelling or irritation persists, a veterinarian should be consulted. With minor wounds, however, the horseman may administer first aid. At the outset, it should be recognized that only nature can produce living cells and heal a wound; hence, man can merely aid the process.

Although wound treatment will vary according to form and severity, the following steps may be involved.

Step 1   *Stop the bleeding.* If it is severe, pressure may be applied by tight bandaging above and below the wound, or by placing a pad on the wound and bandaging over it. When a large artery is severed, as evidenced by bright red blood spurting with a pulsing action, it may be necessary to control the loss of blood by applying a tourniquet on the side of the wound nearest the heart, until the arrival of the veterinarian. A tourniquet must be released after about 20 minutes for a minute or two, but it can be reapplied.

Step 2   *Clean the wound* by washing it with cotton swabs soaked in warm sterile saline (salt) solution. Remove all foreign material (objects and dirt), hair, and torn tissue. Cleanliness is of great importance.

Step 3   *Clip or shave long hair* (it is often best not to remove short hair, because of the danger of contamination) from around the wound, to a distance of about ½ inch.

Step 4   *Apply first aid powder* according to the directions on the label.

Step 5   *Suture incised and lacerated wounds if necessary,* with this decision being left to, and the work done by, a veterinarian. Proper wound drainage should always be established.

Step 6   *Protect against tetanus* by administering (a) tetanus antitoxin if the animal is not already on a toxoid program, or (b) a toxoid booster when the horse has been immunized previously with this product. Also, the veterinarian may inject an antibiotic(s).

Step 7   *Switch from powder to salve.* As soon as a scab has formed over the wound, switch from first aid powder to first aid salve.

It should be recognized that poor nutrition of the horse will delay healing of a wound. Hence, poorly balanced or inadequate rations, bad teeth, and parasitism may contribute to delayed wound healing.

Some common problems which should receive first aid treatment follow.

- *Azoturia* — When the characteristic wine-colored urine, sweating, distress, and stiffness are noted, (1) stop all exercise, (2) rub the horse dry and blanket it, (3) apply hot-water bottles or heated blankets or cloths to the swollen and hardened muscles, and (4) secure professional help as quickly as possible. Use a trailer if necessary to move a horse that has severely tied up — do not force it to walk if it is "rooted to the ground."

- *Bleeders* — Bleeders are horses afflicted by blood flowing from their nostrils or bronchial tubes, but originating in the lungs following strenuous exercise. Furosemide, popularly known by the trade name Lasix, which reduces bleeding almost immediately, is approved by FDA as an equine medication, and is permitted as a raceday medication in most states.

- *Bruises and swellings* — Blows may produce hemorrhaging in the tissues under the skin. First aid for such injuries consists in (1) measures to stop the hemorrhages — cold applications together with firm, even pressure, (2) cold-water showers and cold-water bandages until the swelling stops, and (3) heat or liniment applied after the swelling has stopped.

- *Colic* — When colicky symptoms appear, keep the animal on its feet; walk it slowly and quietly, by leading; and apply heat to the abdomen. Seek a veterinarian's assistance promptly if the symptoms do not clear up right away. See also "Impaction"(below).

- *Founder (laminitis)* — Pending the arrival of the veterinarian, pull the shoes if the horse is shod, and stand the animal in a cold-water bath or apply cold bran poultices (preferably using ice water in either treatment).

- *Fractures* — In all cases of fracture, professional assistance should be secured as quickly as possible. Until help arrives, keep the horse as quiet as possible. With leg fractures, it may be necessary to splint the affected limb with wood or pipe to hold the break in place: then wrap it with towels or other padding.

- *Impaction* — Impaction is a form of colic caused by obstruction of the cecum or colon by fibrous feeds such as straw, cornstalks, or other coarse, high-fiber feeds, along with lack of water intake. Distention of the large colon with gas causes acute abdominal pain, accompanied by the usual signs described for colic. Medical treatments, which should be administered by a veterinarian, meet with variable success. Mineral oil or magnesium sulfate, administered by stomach tube, are popular treatments. An enema, made by mixing 1 quart of molasses with 3 quarts of milk, heated to body temperature and administered rectally, has been successful in some cases.

Common sense should always prevail when administering first aid; and the horseman should realize his limitations and consult a professional when unsure of his ability.

POISONS (TOXINS)

Horses are subject to many poisons (toxins). *A poison is a substance which in sufficient quantities and/or over a period of time kills or harms living things.* Many poisons are called toxins. *The study of poisons is called toxicology.* For most poisons, there is both a safe level and a poisonous level; and the severity of the effect depends upon (1) the amount taken, (2) the period of time over which the substance is taken (certain poisons are cumulative), and (3) the age and physical condition of the animal. This lends credence to the toxicological adage: "Only the dose makes the poison."

A list, along with a brief summary of each, of the most common potentially toxic substances to horses, both synthesized and naturally occurring, most of which are feed or stable related, follows:

- *Arsenic poisoning* — Arsenic is sometimes used to control insects and weeds, to defoliate crops, and as a feed additive for swine and poultry. When consumed in excess by horses, it may be toxic. Treatment should be handled by a veterinarian.

- *Black walnut toxicosis* — This malady is caused by black walnut shavings and sawdust used as bedding. Only skin contact is necessary; the material need not be eaten. Founder (laminitis) occurs within 12 to 24 hours after horses are exposed to black walnut shavings or sawdust bedding. Treatment consists in removing the black walnut bedding material. The veterinarian may administer medical treatment.

- *Botulism* — Botulism is a poisoning caused by ingestion of feed containing *Clostridium botulinum*. The toxins formed from these bacteria are the most potent poisons known — the most lethal being 10,000 times more deadly than cobra venom and millions of times more potent than strychnine or cyanide. Botulism may result in the death, usually due to nerve paralysis and respiratory or cardiac paralysis, of horses of all ages. Type B *Clostridium botulism* causes shaker foal syndrome, characterized by depression or lethargy; muscle weakness and trembling when standing (hence the term "shaker foal"); and inability to swallow, resulting in milk running out of the foal's mouth and nose. In the mid-1980's a safe and effective vaccine for preventing botulism in horses, and shaker foal syndrome in foals, and an antiserum that reverses the disease, were released. Prior to these developments, 90 percent of the horses that became ill because of botulism died. There are two problems with the antiserum: (1) the animal must live long enough for the new nerves to grow, which requires about six days; and (2) its high cost — a single dose costs more than $1,000 for a foal, and about $2,500 for an adult horse.

In Kentucky, it is commonly recommended that mares shipped into the state for foaling and breeding be vaccinated in three doses, one month apart, with the last dose administered four to six weeks prior to foaling; thereby giving the mare enough time to produce antibodies to the botulism vaccine and have a high titer of antibodies in the colostrum available for the newborn foal. Then, a yearly booster shot should follow.

- *Ergot poisoning (ergotism)* — Ergot poisoning is caused by a parasitic fungus which replaces the seeds in heads of grasses and cereal grains. Acute ergot poisoning, caused by consuming large quantities of ergot at one time, may produce paralysis of the limbs and tongue, disturbance of the gastrointestinal tract, and abortion. Chronic poisoning produces gangrene of the extremities, with subsequent sloughing off of the hoofs, ears, and tail. Treatment consists in removing the affected feed, administering tannin as an antidote, and giving a sedative, such as chloral hydrate, to nervous animals.

- *Fluorine poisoning (fluorosis)* — Fluorosis is caused by ingesting excessive quantities of fluorine through the feed, water, or air, or a combination of these. The symptoms and signs are: abnormal teeth (especially mottled enamel) and bones, roughened hair coat, stiffness of joints, loss of appetite, emaciation, reduction of milk flow, diarrhea, delayed maturity and salt hunger. Any damage may be permanent, but animals which have developed symptoms may be helped by eliminating the excess fluorine.

- *Mercury poisoning* — Mercury poisoning may be caused by the consumption of seed grains treated with fungicides that contain mercury, for the control of fungus diseases of oats, wheat, barley, and flax. Mercury poisoning in horses causes gastrointestinal, renal, and nervous disturbances, but it is impossible, on the basis of symptoms, to differentiate mercury from other poisons. Case history of horses consuming mercury-treated grains is the best evidence. Usually, treatment is not successful. Protein (milk, eggs, serum) may reduce gastrointestinal absorption, and selenium given at carefully controlled levels appears to be helpful.

- *Mycotoxins (toxin-producing fungi or molds)* — Certain molds which produce toxins are associated with cereals, hay, and grasses. The mold *Fusarium moniliforme* is of considerable concern to the horse industry. It produces brain damage. Affected horses wander aimlessly, walk in circles, and may press their heads against an obstacle such as a fence. Some affected horses may fall down and paddle, with death following soon thereafter. After the onset of signs, death may result within six hours, although 72 hours is considered the average survival time after the onset of signs.

- *Nitrate/nitrite poisoning (oat hay poisoning, cornstalk poisoning)* — Acute nitrate/nitrite poisoning is caused by the presence of nitrite in the blood at a level sufficient to cause anoxia (internal suffocation). Nitrate (NO_3) may be reduced to nitrite (NO_2) by microorganisms in the gastrointestinal tract of the horse at a rate which overwhelms the body's defense system. Nitrite combines with a hemoglobin of the red blood cells to form methemoglobin, which cannot transport oxygen to the body tissues. The three principal sources of nitrate are plants, water, and air. Nitrate poisoning of horses can result from ingesting plants or water high in nitrate content, commonly one or more of the following sources: (1) forages under stress (drought, insufficient sunlight, or after spraying with weed killer), or following heavy nitrate fertilization of soils; (2) inorganic nitrate or nitrite salts, or fertilizer, left where horses may consume them; or (3) pond or shallow well water from surface runoff from a barnyard or well-fertilized field. Death from nitrate/nitrite poisoning is usually sudden; few treated animals recover. The most common treatment is a 64-percent solution of methylene blue (in a 5-percent glucose or a 1.8-percent sodium sulfate solution), administered by a veterinarian intravenously at the rate of 100 cc per 1,000 lb. liveweight.

- *Pesticide poisoning* — Pesticides are chemicals used to destroy, prevent, or control pests, but they can also be toxic (poisonous) to horses and other animals. When properly used, pesticides are beneficial; when improperly used, they may be harmful. The symptoms and signs of pesticide poisoning vary with each pesticide. The first and most important precaution to observe when using any pesticide is to read and heed the directions on the label. In the event of an accident, the label becomes extremely important in remedial measures.

- *Phenylbutazone ("bute") toxicity* — Phenylbutazone is a safe, effective, and widely used analgesic (pain-killing) drug in horses when administered at recommended levels. However, it is relatively easy to produce toxicity with phenylbutazone if the dose is too large or the treatment prolonged. Signs of toxicity are loss of appetite, depression, ulceration in the mouth and gastrointestinal tract, ventral edema, diarrhea, and death. Once a horse is suspected of showing toxicity to phenylbutazone, administration of the drug should cease at once. The same precautions that apply to the use of phenylbutazone should be observed in the use of other pain-killing drugs to treat lameness in horses.

- *Poisonous plants* — Many plants are poisonous to horses. Some are deadly in small amounts; others are toxic only if the horse consumes large amounts. The list of poisonous plants is so extensive that no attempt is made herein to describe them in detail. Nevertheless, both equestrians and veterinarians should have a working knowledge of the principal poisonous species in the area in which they operate. Unfortunately, plant-poisoned horses are not generally discovered in sufficient time to avoid loss. So, prevention is decidedly superior to treatment. Following identification of the poisonous plant, treatment should be left to the veterinarian. Rapid and proper treatment may save an animal.

- *Salmonella (Salmonellosis)* — Salmonella is a bacteria (of which there are many species) found worldwide, which causes sickness in horses and other animals. The most common symptoms or signs in older horses are diarrhea, depression, dehydration, and fever, but it may be difficult to distinguish salmonellosis from colic. Foals may show lameness or stiffness in joints; these warning signs indicate that a veterinarian should be called immediately. Fatality rates among horses vary with the type of salmonella bacteria present and how aggressively the disease is treated. Treatment, which should be under the direction of a veterinarian, involves fluid therapy to correct the acid-base balance and dehydration, and antibacterial drugs. Prevention consists of the quarantine of new animals and avoiding contaminated feed.

- *Urea toxicity (ammonia toxicity)* — Ammonia is the actual toxic agent in urea poisoning. When urea is fed at excessive levels, large amounts of ammonia are liberated in the gastrointestinal tract, causing toxicity, evidenced by nervousness, excessive salivation, muscular tremors, respiratory difficulty, and tetanic spasms. Death occurs in ½ to 2½ hours. Young equines are more susceptible to urea toxicity than older horses. Mature horses can usually consume limited urea (if, for example, they have access to protein blocks containing urea); however, the efficiency of the nitrogen utilization from nonprotein nitrogen is considerably less than that of nitrogen from intake protein.

DISINFECTANTS

A disinfectant is a bactericidal or microbicidal agent that frees from infection (usually a chemical agent which destroys disease germs or other microorganisms, or inactivates viruses).

The high concentration of horses and continuous use of horse barns often results in a condition referred to as disease buildup. As disease-producing organisms — viruses, bacteria, fungi, and parasite eggs — accumulate in the environment, disease problems can become more severe and be transmitted to each succeeding group of horses raised on the same premises. Under these circumstances, cleaning and disinfection become extremely important in breaking the life cycle. Also, in the case of a disease outbreak, the premises must be disinfected.

Under ordinary conditions, proper cleaning of barns removes most of the microorganisms, along with the filth, thus eliminating the necessity of disinfection.

Effective disinfection depends on five things:

1. Thorough cleaning before application.
2. The phenol coefficient of the disinfectant, which indicates the killing strength of a disinfectant as compared to phenol (carbolic acid). It is determined by a standard laboratory test in which the typhoid fever germ often is used as the test organism.
3. The dilution at which the disinfectant is used.
4. The temperature; most disinfectants are much more effective if applied hot.
5. Thoroughness of application, and time of exposure.

Disinfection must in all cases be preceded by a very thorough cleaning, for organic matter serves to protect disease germs and otherwise interferes with the activity of the disinfecting agent.

Sunlight possesses disinfecting properties, but it is variable and superficial in its action. Heat and some of the chemical disinfectants are more effective.

The application of heat by steam, by hot water, by burning, or by boiling is an effective method of disinfection. In many cases, however, it may not be practical to use heat.

A good disinfectant should (1) have the power to kill disease-producing organisms, (2) remain stable in the presence of organic matter (manure, hair, soil), (3) dissolve readily in water and remain in solution, (4) be nontoxic to animals and humans, (5) penetrate organic matter rapidly, (6) remove dirt and grease, and (7) be economical to use.

The number of available disinfectants is large because the ideal universally applicable disinfectant does not exist. Table 9.4 gives a summary of the limitations, usefulness, and strength of some common disinfectants.

When using a disinfectant, *always read and follow the manufacturer's directions.*

Table 9.4 HANDY DISINFECTANT GUIDE

Kind of Disinfectant	Usefulness	Strength	Limitations and Comments
Alcohol (Ethyl/ethanol, isopropyl, methanol)	Primarily as skin disinfectants and for emergency purposes on instruments.	70% alcohol — the content usually found in rubbing alcohol.	Too costly for general disinfection. Alcohol is ineffective against bacterial spores.

Kind of Disinfectant	Usefulness	Strength	Limitations and Comments
Boric Acid [1]	As a wash for eyes, and other sensitive parts of the body.	1 oz. in 1 pt. water (about 6% solution).	It is a weak antiseptic. It may cause harm to the nervous system if absorbed into the body in large amounts. For this and other reasons, antibiotic solutions and saline solutions are fast replacing it.
Chlorines (Sodium hypochlorate, chlormine-T)	Used as deodorants. They will kill all kinds of bacteria, fungi, and viruses, providing the concentration is sufficiently high.	Generally used as a deodorant at about 200 ppm (parts per million).	They are corrosive to metals and neutralized by organic materials. Not effective against TB organisms or spores.
Cresols (Many commercial products available)	A generally reliable class of disinfectant. Effective against brucellosis, shipping fever, swine erysipelas, and tuberculosis.	Cresol is usually used as a 2 to 4% solution (1 cup to 2 gallons of water makes a 4% solution).	Cannot be used where odor may be absorbed, and therefore, not suited for use around milk and meat. Cresols give good results in foot baths.
Formaldehyde (Gaseous disinfectant)	In a 1 to 2% solution, formaldehyde will kill anthrax spores, TB organisms, and animal viruses. It is often used to disinfect buildings following a disease outbreak.	As a liquid disinfectant, it is usually used as a 1 to 2% solution. As a gaseous disinfectant (fumigant), use 1½ lb. of potassium permanganate plus 3 pt. of formaldehyde. Also, gas may be released by heating paraformaldehyde.	It has a disagreeable odor, destroys living tissue, and can be extremely poisonous. The bactericidal effectiveness of the gas is dependent upon having the proper relative humidity (above 75%) and temperature (above 86° F and preferably near 140° F).

Table 9.4 HANDY DISINFECTANT GUIDE (*cont.*)

Kind of Disinfectant	Usefulness	Strength	Limitations and Comments
Heat (By steam, hot water, burning, or boiling)	Very useful in the burning of rubbish or articles of little value, and in disposing of infected body discharges. The steam jenny is effective for disinfection *if properly employed*, particularly if used in conjunction with a phenolic germicide.	10 minutes exposure to boiling water is usually sufficient.	Exposure to boiling water will destroy all ordinary disease germs, but sometimes fails to kill the spores of such diseases as anthrax and tetanus. Moist heat is preferred to dry heat, and steam under pressure is the most effective. Heat may be impractical or too expensive.
Iodine[1] (Tincture)	Extensively used as skin disinfectant, for minor cuts and bruises.	Generally used as tincture of iodine, either 2% or 7%.	Never cover with a bandage. Clean skin before applying iodine. It is corrosive to metals.
Iodophore (Tamed iodine)	Effective against all bacteria (both gram-negative and gram-positive), fungi, and most viruses.	Usually used as disinfectants at concentrations of 50–75 ppm titratable iodine, and as sanitizers at levels of 12.5 to 25 ppm. At 12.5 ppm titratable iodine can be used as an antiseptic in drinking water.	Inhibited by organic matter and quite expensive. They should not be used near heat.
Lime (Quicklime; burnt lime; calcium oxide)	Used as a deodorant when sprinkled on manure and animal discharges; as a disinfectant when sprinkled on the floor, as a newly made "milk of lime," or as a whitewash.	Use as a dust, as "milk of lime," or as a whitewash, but use *fresh*.	Not effective against anthrax or tetanus spores. Wear goggles when adding water to quicklime.

Kind of Disinfectant	Usefulness	Strength	Limitations and Comments
Lye (Sodium hydroxide; caustic soda)	Useful on concrete floors, against the microorganisms of brucellosis and the viruses of foot-and-mouth disease, and vesicular exanthema. In strong solution (5%), effective against anthrax.	Lye is usually used as either a 2% or 5% solution. To prepare a 2% solution, add 1 can of lye to 5 gallons of water. To prepare a 5% solution, add 1 can of lye to 2 gallons of water. A 2% solution will destroy the organisms causing foot-and-mouth disease, but a 5% solution is necessary to destroy the spores of anthrax.	Damages fabrics, aluminum, and painted surfaces. Be careful, for it will burn the hands and face. Not effective against organism of TB or Johne's disease. Lye solutions are most effective when used hot. **Diluted vinegar can be used to neutralize lye.**
Lysol (The brand name of a product of cresol plus soap)	For disinfecting surgical instruments used in castrating and tattooing. Useful as a skin disinfectant before surgery, and for use on the hands before castrating.	0.5 to 2.0%.	Has a disagreeable odor. Does not mix well with hard water. Less costly than phenol.
Phenols (Carbolic acid): 1. Phenolics-coal tar derivatives 2. Synthetic phenols	They are ideal general-purpose disinfectants. Effective and inexpensive. They're very resistant to the inhibiting effects of organic residue; hence, they are suitable for barn disinfection and foot and wheel dip-baths.	Both phenolics (coal tar) and synthetic phenols vary widely in efficacy from one compound to another. So, note and follow manufacturer's directions. Generally used in a 5% solution.	They are corrosive, and they're toxic to animals and humans. Ineffective on fungi and viruses.

Table 9.4 HANDY DISINFECTANT GUIDE (*cont.*)

Kind of Disinfectant	Usefulness	Strength	Limitations and Comments
Quaternary Ammonium Compounds (QAC)	Very water soluble, ultra-rapid kill rate, effective deodorizing properties, and moderately priced. Good detergent characteristics and harmless to the skin.	Follow manufacturer's directions.	They can corrode metal. Not very potent in combating viruses. Adversely affected by organic matter.
Sal Soda	It may be used in place of lye against foot-and-mouth disease and vesicular exanthema.	10½% solution (13½ oz. to 1 gal. water).	
Sal Soda and Soda Ash (or sodium carbonate)	May be used in place of lye against foot-and-mouth disease and vesicular exanthema.	4% solution (1 lb. to 3 gal. water). Most effective in hot solution.	Commonly used as cleansing agent, but has disinfectant properties, especially when used as a hot solution.
Soap	Its power to kill germs is very limited. Greatest usefulness is in cleansing and dissolving coatings from various surfaces, including the skin, prior to application of a good disinfectant.	As commercially prepared.	Although indispensable for sanitizing surfaces, soaps should not be used as disinfectants. They are not regularly effective; staphylococci and the organisms which cause diarrheal diseases are resistant.

[1] Sometimes loosely classed as a disinfectant but actually an antiseptic and useful practically only on living tissue.

BUILDINGS AND EQUIPMENT

Figure 10.1   A two-stall horse barn. (Courtesy, *Sunset Magazine*)

Properly designed, constructed, and arranged horse buildings and equipment give increased animal comfort and performance, greater efficiency in the use of feed, and less expenditure of labor in the care of horses. Also, attractive barns add to the beauty of the landscape. In serving these purposes, buildings and equipment need not be elaborate or expensive.

SPACE REQUIREMENTS

One of the first and frequently one of the most difficult problems confronting the horseman who wishes to construct a building is that of arriving at the proper size or dimensions. Tables 10.1, 10.2, and 10.3 contain some conservative average figures giving the space requirements for (1) horse barns, (2) service passages, and (3) feed and bedding storage, respectively.

Table 10.1 SPACE REQUIREMENTS OF BUILDINGS FOR HORSES: KINDS AND PLANS

Kinds, Uses, and Purposes	Recommended Plan
Smaller Horse Establishments: Horse barns for pleasure horses, ponies, and/or raising a few foals.	12' × 12' stalls in a row; combination tack-feed room for 1- and 2-stall units; separate tack and feed rooms for 3-stall units or more. Generally, not more than a month's supply of feed is stored at a time. Use of all-pelleted rations (hay and grain combined) lessens feed-storage space requirements.
Larger Horse-breeding Establishments: The following specially designed buildings may be provided for different purposes:	
Broodmare and foaling barn	A rectangular building, either (1) with a central aisle, and a row of stalls along each side, or (2) of the "island" type, with two rows of stalls, back to back, surrounded by an alley or runway. Ample quarters for storage of hay, bedding, and grain. A record or office room, toilet facilities, hot water supply, veterinary supply room, and tack room are usually an integral part of a broodmare barn.
Stallion barn	Quarters for one or more stallions, with or without feed storage. A small tack and equipment room. Stallion paddocks, at least 300 ft. on a side, adjacent to or in close proximity.
Barren mare barn	An open shed or rectangular building, with a combination rack and trough down the center or along the wall. Storage space for ample hay, grain, and bedding.
Weanling or yearling quarters	Open shed or stalls. The same type of building is adapted to both weanlings and yearlings; but different ages and sex groups should be kept separate. When stalls are used, two weanlings or two yearlings may be placed together.
Breeding shed	A large, roofed enclosure with a high ceiling; should include laboratory for the veterinarian, hot water facilities, and stalls for preparing mares for breeding and holding foals.
Isolation (quarantine) quarters	Small barn, with feed and water facilities and adjacent paddock; for occupancy by new or sick animals.
For Riding Academies and Training and Boarding Stables	Either (1) stalls constructed back to back in the center of the barn, with an indoor ring around the outside; (2) stalls around the outside and a ring in the center; or (3) stalls on either side of a hallway or alleyway, and an outdoor ring.

Box Stalls or Shed Areas

Size	Height of Ceiling	Height of Doors	Width of Doors	Tie Stalls (Size)
Horses: 12′ × 12′ Ponies:[1] 10′ × 10′	8′–9′	8′	4′	5′ wide; 10′–12′ long
12′ × 12′ to 16′ × 16′	9′	8′	4′	
14′ × 14′	9′	8′	4′	
150 sq. ft. per animal	9′	8′	4′	
10′ × 10′	9′	8′	4′	
24′ × 24′	15′–20′	8′	9′	
12′ × 12′	9′	8′	4′	
12′ × 12′	9′	8′	4′	5′ wide; 10′–12′ long

[1] Even for ponies, a 12′ × 12′ stall is recommended since (1) it costs little more than a 10′ × 10′ and (2) it affords more flexibility—it can be used for bigger horses when and if the occasion demands.

Table 10.2 RECOMMENDED MINIMUM WIDTH FOR SERVICE PASSAGES

Kind of Passage	Use	Minimum Width
Feed Alley	For feed cart	4'
Driveway	For wagon, spreader, or truck	9'–12'
Doors and gate	Drive-through	8'–9'

TYPES AND SIZES OF HORSE BARNS

The primary reasons for having horse buildings are: (1) to provide a place in which to confine horses and store feed and tack; and (2) to modify the environment by controlling temperature, humidity, and other factors.

Needs for housing horses and storage of materials vary according to the intended use of the buildings. Broadly speaking, horse barns are designed to serve either (1) small horse establishments that have one to a few animals, (2) large horse-breeding establishments, or (3) riding, training, and boarding stables.

Various types and sizes of stalls and sheds are used in horse barns. However, in all types except the breeding shed, ceilings should be 9 feet high and doors should be 8 feet high and 4 feet wide. The breeding shed should have a ceiling of 15 to 20 feet high and a door wide enough to permit entrance of vehicles.

The recommended plans for different kinds of horse barns are as follows.

Figure 10.2   A three-stall horse barn.

Table 10.3 STORAGE SPACE REQUIREMENTS FOR FEED AND BEDDING

Kind of Feed or Bedding	Pounds per Cubic Feet (approx.)	Cubic Feet per Ton (approx.)	Pounds per Bushel of Grain	Cubic Feet per Bushel
Hay[1]				
Timothy, loose	3	625–640		
Wild hay, loose	3–4	450–600		
Alfalfa, loose	4	470–485		
Clover, loose	4	500–512		
Chopped hay	10	210–225		
Baled hay				
(closely stacked)	10	150–200		
Straw shavings				
Straw, baled	10	200		
Straw, loose[1]	2–3	600–1,000		
Shavings, baled	20	100		
Silage				
Corn or sorghum silage in tower silos	40	50		
Corn or sorghum silage in trench silos	35	57		
Mill feed				
Bran	13	154		
Middlings	25	80		
Linseed or soybean meal	35	57		
Grain				
Corn, shelled	45	45	56	1.25
Corn, ear	28	72	70	2.50
Corn, snapped	25	81	80	3.25
Oats	26	77	32	1.25
Barley	39	51	48	1.25
Wheat	48	42	60	1.25
Rye	45	44	56	1.25
Grain sorghum	45	44	56	1.25

[1] Under hay and loose straw, a range is given under the columns for "pounds per cubic feet," and "cubic feet per ton," the higher figures being for hay and loose straw settled 1 to 2 months, and the lower figures for hay or loose straw settled over 3 months.

SMALL HORSE ESTABLISHMENTS

These horse barns are for housing pleasure horses or ponies or raising a few foals. Box stalls should be 12 feet square and tie stalls should be 5 feet wide and 10 to 12 feet long.

Build the stalls in a row and provide a combination tack and feed room for units with one or two stalls. Use separate tack and feed rooms for units with three or more stalls. Generally, not more than a one-month supply of feed is stored at a time. The use of all-pelleted feed lessens storage space requirements.

Building plans for a small horse barn are shown in Figure 10.3.

Complete working drawings of small horse barns may be obtained through county agricultural agents or from extension agricultural engineers at most state agricultural colleges.

LARGE HORSE-BREEDING ESTABLISHMENTS

Large establishments need specially designed buildings for different purposes. They are as follows.

Broodmare and Foaling Barn — This can be a rectangular building either (1) with a central aisle and a row of stalls along each side, or (2) of the "island" type with two rows of stalls back to back surrounded by an alley or runway. Most broodmare stalls are 12 feet square, although they may be up to 16 feet square. A stall 16 feet square is desirable for foaling. A broodmare barn needs the following: (1) an office for records;

Figure 10.3   Riding horse barn (*left*) and floor plan (*below*). Barn has two box stalls, a feed room, and a tack room.

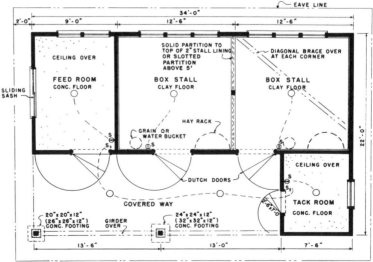

Figure 10.4 Barns at Gainesway Farm, Lexington, Kentucky — a masterly example of great beauty and elegance in horse barns. (Courtesy, Thoroughbred Publications, Inc., Lexington, Kentucky)

(2) toilet facilities; (3) hot water supply; (4) veterinary supply room; (5) tack room; and (6) storage space for hay, bedding, and grain.

Stallion Barn — This barn provides quarters for one or more stallions. It should have a small tack and equipment room, and it may or may not have feed storage. The stalls should be 14 feet square.

Provide a paddock near the barn or, if possible, adjacent to it. The paddock can be any shape but each side should be at least 300 feet long.

Barren Mare Barn — Use an open shed or rectangular building that has a combination rack and trough down the center or along the wall. Provide storage space for hay, grain, and bedding. Allow each animal 150 square feet of space.

Weanling and Yearling Quarters — Either an open shed or a barn with stalls may be used. Both weanlings and yearlings may be kept in the same building, but different age and sex groups should be kept apart. When stalls are used, two weanlings or two yearlings may be kept together. Stalls should be 10 feet square.

Breeding Shed — This should be a large, roofed enclosure that has a laboratory for the veterinarian, hot water facilities, and stalls for preparing mares for breeding and for holding foals. The shed should be 24 feet square.

Isolation Quarters — These quarters are for sick animals and animals new to the farm. Use a small barn that has feed and water facilities and an adjacent paddock. Stalls should be 12 feet square.

RIDING, TRAINING, AND BOARDING STABLES

For this purpose, the quarters may consist of (1) stalls constructed back to back in the center of the barn with an indoor ring around the stalls, (2) stalls built around the sides of the barn with the ring in the center, or (3) stalls on either side of a hallway or alleyway and the ring outdoors. Box stalls should be 10 to 12 feet square and tie stalls should be 5 feet wide and 10 to 12 feet long.

REQUISITES OF HORSE BARNS

Whether a new horse layout is built or an old one is altered, all buildings, fences, corrals, and trees should be placed according to a master plan, for, once established, they usually are difficult and expensive to move. The arrangement should make the best possible use of land and should require little walking by attendants when caring for horses.

All horse barns should meet the following requisites:

1. *Accessibility* — Barns should be on an all-weather roadway or lane to facilitate the use of horses, delivery of feed and bedding, and removal of manure.

2. *Dryness* — Barns should be on high ground so water will drain away from them.

3. *Expandable design* — Barns should be designed so they are easy to

Figure 10.5   Horse barn at Dixiana Farm, Lexington, Kentucky. (Courtesy, Thoroughbred Publications, Inc., Lexington, Kentucky)

expand if and when the time comes. Often a building can be lengthened provided no other structures or utilities interfere.

4. *Water and electricity* — Water and electricity should be available and convenient to use.

5. *Controlled environment* — Barns should be built to modify winter and summer temperatures, maintain acceptable humidity and ventilation, minimize stress on the horses' nerves, and protect horses from rain, snow, sun, and wind.

6. *Reasonable cost* — Initial cost is important but durability and maintenance should be considered, as well as such intangible values as pride and satisfaction in the buildings, and advertising value.

7. *Adequate space* — Too little space may jeopardize the health and well-being of horses, but too much space means unnecessary expense.

8. *Storage areas* — Storage space for feed, bedding, and tack should be provided in the building where they are used.

9. *Attractiveness* — An attractive horse barn increases the sale value of the property. A horse barn will have aesthetic value if it has good proportions and is in harmony with the natural surroundings.

10. *Minimum fire risk* — The use of fire-resistant materials gives added protection to horses. Also, fire-retarding paints and sprays may be used.

11. *Safety* — Projections that might injure horses should be removed. Feeding and watering equipment should be arranged so attendants need not walk behind horses.

12. *Labor-saving construction* — This requisite is a must in any commercial horse establishment. Also, where horses are kept for pleasure, unnecessary labor should be eliminated in feeding, cleaning, and handling.

13. *Healthful living conditions* — Healthy horses are better performers; therefore, barns should be easy to keep clean so they will provide healthful living conditions.

14. *Rodent and bird control* — Feed and tack storage areas should be rodent- and bird-proof.

15. *Suitable corrals and paddocks* — Horse barns should have well-drained, safe, fenced corrals or paddocks adjacent to them. If this is not possible, the corral or paddock should be nearby.

16. *Flexibility* — Possible changes in use make it desirable for horse barns to be as flexible as possible, even to the point that they can be cheaply and easily converted into cabins, garages, storage buildings, or buildings for other uses. Also, for suburbanites and renters, permanent, portable barns are advantageous.

STALLS

Stalls are of two general types: (1) box stalls; and (2) tie stalls. Most horsemen prefer box stalls because they allow the horse more liberty, either when standing or lying down. In addition to space requirement, the following features are important in stalls.

1. *Floors* — A raised clay floor covered with a good absorbent bedding, with proper drainage away from the building, is the most satisfactory flooring for horse stables. Clay floors are noiseless and springy, keep the hoofs moist, and afford firm natural footing unless wet; but they are difficult to keep clean and level. To lessen the latter problems, the top layer should be removed each year, replaced with fresh clay, and leveled. Also, a semicircular concrete apron extending into each stall at the doorway will prevent horses from digging a hole in a clay floor at this point. This arrangement is particularly desirable in barns for yearlings, as they are likely to fret around the door.

   Rough wooden floors furnish good traction for animals and are warm to lie upon; but they are absorbent and unsanitary, they often harbor rats and other rodents, and they lack durability.

   Concrete, asphalt, or brick floors are durable, impervious to moisture, easily cleaned, and sanitary; but they are rigid and without resilient qualities, slippery when wet, hazardous to horses, and cold to lie upon. It is noteworthy that concrete and asphalt, generously covered with bedding, are widely used for stable floors throughout Eastern and Western Europe.

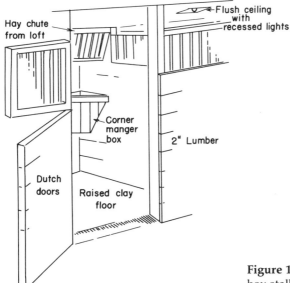

Figure 10.6 A satisfactory type of box stall for horses.

2. *Concrete footings* — Concrete footings and foundation walls are recommended as they are both durable and noncorrosive. The foundation should be a minimum of 8 inches high, so as to be above the manure level.

3. *Ceiling height* — A ceiling height of 8 to 9 feet is recommended, although there is no harm if it is higher.

4. *Walls* — The inside of the stall should be boarded up to a height of about 5 feet, using either (a) durable plywood of adequate thickness and strength, or (b) 2-inch, hard lumber, (such as oak) placed horizontally. Hollow concrete blocks encourage stall kicking; hence, when used, they should either be filled with concrete or lined with wood. About 5 feet, and extending up to a minimum of 7 feet (or even to the ceiling), stall partitions or fronts may be slatted, preferably with metal, to allow for air circulation and companionship with other horses.

5. *Doors* — Stall doors may be either (a) full sliding type suspended by overhead rollers or rails, or (b) the swinging Dutch type, with the top part swinging down or to the side.

6. *Weather protection over stall doors* — This is important. It can be easily and simply achieved by an overhanging roof.

TACK ROOM

A tack room is an essential part of any barn. With one- and two-stall units, a combination tack and feed room is usually used, for practical reasons. Good horsemen take pride in their tack and its arrangement in the tack room. Tack rooms should be floored, rodent- and bird-proof, and ceiled over.

ENVIRONMENTAL CONTROL

Animals perform better and require less feed if they are raised under ideal conditions of temperature, humidity, and ventilation. Environmental control is of particular importance in horse barn construction because many horses spend most of the time in a stall. The investment in environmental control facilities must be balanced against the expected increased returns because there is a point where further expenditures for environmental control will not increase returns sufficiently to justify added cost.

Before the building is designed, it is necessary to know how much heat and moisture a horse produces. Body heat production varies according to body weight, rate of feeding, environmental conditions, and degree of activity. Under average conditions, a 1,000-lb. horse produces about 1,790 British thermal units (Btu) per hour, and a 1,500-lb. horse about 2,450 Btu per hour.

Figure 10.7   A tack room, featuring a revolving saddle rack. (Photo by John H. Williamson, Arcadia, California. Courtesy, *Western Livestock Journal*)

A horse breathes into the air approximately 17.5 lb., or 2.1 gallons, of moisture per day. When it's cold and this moisture is not removed, it condenses and forms frost. The latter condition is indicative of lack of ventilation, and it may be indicative of insufficient insulation, also.

Until more experimental information is available, the following environmental control recommendations, based on confinement systems used for other classes of animals, may be followed.

- *Temperature* — A range of 45° to 75° F (7° to 24° C) is satisfactory, with 55° F (13° C) considered best. Until a newborn foal is dry, it should be warmed to 75° to 80° F (24° to 27° C). This can be done with a heat lamp.

- *Humidity* — A range of 50 to 75 percent relative humidity is acceptable, with 60 percent preferred.

- *Ventilation* — The barn should have as little moisture and odor as possible, and it should be free from drafts. In a properly ventilated barn, the ventilation system should provide 60 cubic feet per minute (cfm) for each 1,000 lb. of horse (1.7 m³/454 kg horse) in winter and 160 cfm per 1,000 lb. of horse (2.8 m³/454 kg horse) in summer. In summer, satisfactory ventilation usually can be achieved by opening barn doors and by installing hinged doors or panels near the ceiling that swing open.

- *Water temperature* — In the winter months, water for horses should be warmed to 40° to 45° F (4° to 7° C); in the summer, it should be within the range of 60° to 75° F (16° to 24° C).

MATERIALS

When building materials for horse barns are bought, the factors to be considered are initial cost, durability and maintenance, attractiveness, and fire resistance.

Some of the materials available and being used are wood, including plywood; metal; masonry, including concrete, concrete block, cinder, pumice block, brick, and stone; and plastics. Also, preengineered and prefabricated horse barns are being used more often, especially on smaller horse establishments.

SHEDS

In the wild state (as nature ordained it), the horse augmented his shaggy winter coat by seeking the protection afforded by hills, ravines, and trees. But man changed all this — and not always for the better. Diseases and unsoundnesses began with too close confinement and lack of exercise. Through mistaken kindness, horses are often subjected to lack of ventilation and high humidity.

For broodmares and horses not in constant use, an open shed, with access to a pasture or corral, is preferred. Horses kept in an open shed, even in the colder areas, are healthier and suffer fewer respiratory diseases than horses kept in enclosed barns.

Figure 10.8 A horse shed, open to the south, away from the direction of the prevailing winds and toward the sun.
(Courtesy, American Quarter Horse Association, Amarillo, Texas)

Sheds are usually open to the south or east, preferably opposite to the direction of the prevailing winds and toward the sun. They are enclosed on the ends and sides. Sometimes the front is partially closed, and in severe weather drop-doors may be used. The latter arrangement is especially desirable when the ceiling height is sufficient to accommodate a power manure loader.

So that the bedding be kept reasonably dry, it is important that sheds be located on high, well-drained ground; that eave troughs and downspouts drain into suitable tile lines, or surface drains; and that the structures have sufficient width to prevent rain and snow from blowing to the back end. Sheds should be a minimum of 24 feet in depth, front to back, with depths up to 36 feet preferable. As a height of 8½ feet is necessary to accommodate some power-operated manure loaders, when this type of equipment is to be used in the shed a minimum ceiling height of 9 feet is recommended. The extra 6 inches allow for the accumulation of manure. Lower ceiling heights are satisfactory when it is intended to use a blade or pitchfork in cleaning the building.

The length of the shed can be varied according to needed capacity. Likewise, the shape may be either a single long shed or in the form of an L or T. The long arrangement permits more corral space. When an open shed is contemplated, thought should be given to feed storage and feeding problems, and how water will be provided.

Sometimes hayracks are built along the back wall of sheds, or next to an alley, if the shed is very wide or if there is some hay storage overhead. Most generally, however, hayracks, feed bunks, and watering troughs are placed outside the structure.

SHADE

Shade, either from trees or man-made, should be provided for horses that are in the hot sun.

The most satisfactory man-made horse shades are (1) oriented with a north-south placement, (2) at least 12 to 15 feet in height (in addition to being cooler, high shades allow a mounted rider to pass under), and (3) open all around.

FEED AND WATER EQUIPMENT

The design of feed and water equipment should fill the basic need for simple and effective equipment with which to provide hay, concentrates, minerals, and water without waste or hazard to the horse. Whenever possible, for convenience and safety, feed and water equipment should be located so it can be filled without the caretaker entering the stall or corral.

Figure 10.9 Nature's shade — trees — are excellent for horses. This shows Standardbred mares and foals on pasture. (Courtesy, The U.S. Trotting Association, Columbus, Ohio)

Feed and water equipment may be built-in or detached. Because specialty feed and water equipment is more sanitary, flexible, and suitable, many horsemen favor it over old-style wood mangers and concrete or steel tanks. Bulk-tank feed storage may be used to advantage on large horse establishments to eliminate sacks, lessen rodent and bird problems, and make it possible to obtain feed at lower prices by ordering large amounts.

The kind, size, and location of the most common equipment used to hold concentrates, hay, minerals, and water are described.

CONCENTRATE PAIL, TUB, BOX, OR PORTABLE FEEDER

A pail or tub can be made of metal, plastic, or rubber. Usually it has screw eyes and hooks or snaps so it can be suspended. The capacity should be 16 to 20 quarts for horses and 14 to 16 quarts for ponies.

In a stall, the pail or tub should be at the front. The height should be two-thirds the height of the animal at the withers, or 38 to 42 inches for horses and 28 to 32 inches for ponies.

In a corral put the tub or pail along a fence line and at the same height as in a stall.

For sanitary reasons, removable concentrate containers are preferable so they can be easily and frequently cleaned. This is especially important after feeding a wet mash.

A wooden box for horses should be 12 to 16 inches wide, 24 to 30 inches long, and 8 to 10 inches deep. A box for ponies should be 10 to 12 inches wide, 20 to 24 inches long, and 6 to 8 inches deep.

Figure 10.10 Feed tubs are handy, especially for feeding away from home, such as at horse shows and on trail rides. Rubber or plastic feed and water containers are safer than metal ones. (Courtesy, *Western Horseman,* Colorado Springs, Colorado)

The location and height of a box in a stall are the same as for a pail or tub. Do not use a wooden box in a corral.

If desired, a wedge-shaped metal pan set on a wooden shelf can be mounted in a front corner of the stall and pivoted so it can be pulled out for filling and cleaning and then pushed back into the stall and locked in place.

HAYRACK OR MANGER

A stall rack may be made of metal, fiber, or plastic. A rack for horses should hold 25 to 30 lb. of hay and a rack for ponies, 10 to 15 lb. It should be in a corner of the stall. The bottom of the rack should be the same height as the horse or pony at the withers.

Hayracks lessen hay contamination, parasitic infestation, pawing by horses, and hay waste. Racks should open at the bottom so dirt, chaff, and trash may be removed or allowed to fall out. For stallions and broodmares, use high racks to lessen injury hazards.

A wooden manger may be used. It should be 30 inches wide and 24 to 30 inches long for horses and 20 inches square for ponies. Put the manger in the front or in a corner of the stall. The height should be 30 to 42 inches for horses and 20 to 24 inches for ponies.

Corral racks are usually made of wood. They should be large enough to hold a one-day supply of hay for the intended number of horses. Put the rack in the fence line of the corral if horses feed from one side only. Put it on high ground if horses feed from both sides.

The top of the rack may be 1 to 2 feet higher than the horses at the withers. Corral hayracks that feed from both sides should be portable.

Figure 10.11 Hayrack.

MINERAL BOX OR SELF-FEEDER

A box may be made of wood and a self-feeder may be made of metal or wood. In a stall, the box or self-feeder should be in a corner of the stall and should be the same height as the box or pail used for concentrates.

In a corral, mineral containers should be in a fence corner. The height should be two-thirds the height of the horse at the withers. If a mineral container is in the open, it should be protected from wind and rain. Mineral containers should have two compartments; one for the mineral mix, and the other for the salt.

WATERING FACILITIES

Automatic waterers are made of metal. Waterers should be located in a front corner of a stall or in a fence corner of a corral or pasture.

Watering equipment should be designed to facilitate draining and cleaning. Locate waterers a considerable distance from feed containers if possible. Otherwise, horses will carry feed to the waterer or drip water in the concentrate container. A large, 20- by 30-inch automatic waterer will accommodate about 25 horses; a 2-cup waterer, about 12.

The daily water requirements for horses are: mature horse, 12 gallons; foal to two-year-old, and pony, 6 to 8 gallons. In cold areas, waterers should be heated and equipped with thermostatic controls. A satisfactory water temperature range in winter is 40° to 45° F and in summer 60° to 75° F.

Check automatic waterers daily.

A water pail may be made of plastic, rubber, or metal. It should be located in the front of the stall. The height should be two-thirds the height of the horse at the withers, or 38 to 42 inches for horses and 28 to 32 inches for ponies.

Figure 10.12 Stall waterer for one stall. Stall waterers must be cleaned regularly, so that algae will not build up in them.

A water tank may be concrete or steel. It is used in a corral and should be set in the fence so there are no protruding corners. If it is out in a corral or pasture away from a fence, it should be painted white so the horses can see it at night.

A tank should be 30 to 36 inches high. Allow 1 linear foot of tank space to each 5 horses. A tank should be equipped with a float valve that is protected from the horses.

FENCES FOR HORSES

Good fences (1) maintain boundaries, (2) make horse training and other operations possible, (3) reduce losses to both animals and crops, (4) increase property values, (5) promote better relationships between neighbors, (6) lessen the likelihood of car accidents from animals getting on roads, and (7) add to the attractiveness and distinctiveness of the premises.

Large pastures in which the concentration of horses is not too great may be fenced with woven wire. The mesh of the woven wire fence should be small so horses cannot get their feet through it. Stallion, corral, paddock, and perimeter fences should be higher and sturdier than fences for large pastures. Also, owners should check on, and meet, any fencing requirements of the area.

Figure 10.13 Horse fence.

The deficiencies of board and pole fences are: they must be kept painted; they splinter, break, and rot; and they are chewed by horses. Hardwood post-and-rail fences are attractive but expensive; since they are not painted, they too deteriorate over time. Conventional metal fences of steel, aluminum, wrought iron, chain link, or cable have one or more deficiencies.

Two new types of fencing materials for horses have recently come upon the market. Details follow:

1. *Polymer plastic or PVC (polyvinyl chloride).* Fences made of this plastic or polymer (a) resemble traditional white board fences; (b) are durable, safe, and low-maintenance; and (c) cannot be chewed by horses. This material is available both as round rails and as 2 in. × 6 in. planks, with round or square posts to match, which are set in concrete. The major disadvantage of this type of fence is the initial cost, which is twice that of a board fence.

2. *Rubber-nylon fence.* This fencing material is made from belting, cut in strips 2 in. to 4 in. wide. Because the strips are maintained under tension, it is important that the anchor posts be well braced. When properly constructed, rubber-nylon fence is durable, safe, low-maintenance, and gives the appearance of a black board fence when viewed from a distance. It is relatively inexpensive.

Figure 10.14   Chain-link gate and fence for a horse paddock.
(Courtesy, California Thoroughbred Breeders Association,
Arcadia, California)

Table 10.4 lists the materials and specifications commonly used for
horse fences.

SHOW AND SCHOOLING RINGS

Schooling rings have no standard or required specifications for ring
size, type of construction, or maintenance.

For most purposes, a ring 125 feet × 250 feet will suffice. However,
many good show rings are either smaller or larger than this. For example, the ring of the famous Devon Horse Show, which is often used for
jumpers, is 150 feet × 300 feet. But the ring at the Spanish Riding
School in Vienna is only 59 feet × 180 feet.

The surface of a show ring must be resilient and firm to assure proper
footing, and it also must be free of dust. In outdoor rings, proper drainage and a good tract base are necessary for all-weather use. A ring can
be drained by (1) locating it high enough for water to drain away from
it, and (2) installing drainage tile or perforated steel pipe, with the
perforations on the bottom side of the pipe, in ditches just outside the
perimeter of the arena.

The track usually will be firm if it is covered with a mixture of organic
matter and dirt or sand. For example, the ring at the Spanish Riding
School is covered with a mixture of two-thirds sawdust and one-third
sand. It is sprinkled with water at intervals to keep down the dust.

In many indoor rings in the U.S., 6 to 8 inches of tanbark are used on

Table 10.4 HORSE FENCES

Post and Fencing Material	Post Length and Diameter	Size of Rails, Boards, or Poles and Gauge of Wire	Fence Height (in.)	Number of Rails, Boards, or Poles and Mesh of Wire	Distance Between Posts on Centers (ft.)
Steel or	7½ ft.	10 or 20 ft. long	60	3 rails	10
aluminum post	7½ ft.	10 or 20 ft. long	60	4 rails	10
and rails[1]	8½ ft.	10 or 20 ft. long	72	4 rails	10
Wooden post and boards	7½ ft.; 4–8 in.	2 × 6 or 2 × 8 in. boards	60	4 boards	8
	8½ ft.; 4–8 in.	2 × 6 or 2 × 8 in. boards	72	5 boards	8
Wooden post and poles	7½ ft.; 4–8 in.	4–6 in. diameter	60	4 poles	8
	8½ ft.; 4–8 in.	4–6 in. diameter	72	5 poles	8
Wooden post and rails	7½ ft.	4–6 in. diameter	60–72	3 or 4 rails	10
Wooden post and woven wire[2]	7½ ft.; 4–8 in.	9- or 11-gauge staywire	55–58	12-in. mesh	12

[1] Because of the strength of most metal, fewer rails and posts are necessary than when wood is used.
[2] Use either 1 or 2 strands of barbed wire — with barbs 3 to 4 inches apart — or an electric wire on top of the fence.

a dirt base. Unless tanbark is watered frequently, it will pulverize and give poor footing. Some rings are covered 18 to 24 inches deep with shavings or sawdust mixed with dirt or sand. Other rings are covered with approximately 9 inches of wood shavings, 2 inches of sawdust, and 4 inches of sand, all mixed together and treated. Still other rings are covered with a wood-fiber mix or shredded rubber mixed with sand. Salt may be added because it holds moisture when wetted down and reduces dust.

In outdoor rings, organic matter for resilience is sometimes provided by seeding rye or other small grain on the track during the off-season and disking under the green crop.

No matter how good the construction, a show ring or schooling ring must be maintained. It must be smoothed and leveled, holes must be filled, and when it gets too hard, the ground must be broken. A flexible, chain-type harrow is recommended for show-ring maintenance.

Besides ring size, construction, and maintenance, other factors to be considered are (1) ring layout to facilitate reversing a performance class in a ring that has turf or other decorative material in the center; (2) attractiveness of the ring; (3) spectator seating capacity, comfort, and visibility; (4) nearby parking; and (5) handling the crowd.

DEPRECIATION ON BUILDINGS AND EQUIPMENT

For tax purposes, the following "useful life" guidelines are generally accepted: horse buildings, ten years; automobiles, pick-up trucks, and certain other equipment, five years.

TACK

Figure 11.1 Tack, attire, and Half-Arabian used in a competitive trail ride by Ruth Waltenspiel, Healdsburg, California. Note that she uses an English saddle and rides in boots and breeches. (Courtesy, Ruth Waltenspiel)

Tack includes all articles of gear, or equipment, used on or attached to riding and driving horses. Each horse should have his own saddle, bridle, halter, and lead shank so they can be adjusted to fit.

Superior quality tack usually is cheaper in the long run. With proper care, it will last for many years. Some common items of tack are discussed in the following sections.

BRIDLES AND HACKAMORES

Lightweight bridles and bits usually indicate competent horsemen and well-mannered horses. Bridles may be either single or double. A single bridle is equipped with one bit, whereas a double bridle is ordinarily equipped with both a snaffle bit and a curb bit, two headstalls, and two pairs of reins. Only one rein is used with western bridles.

371

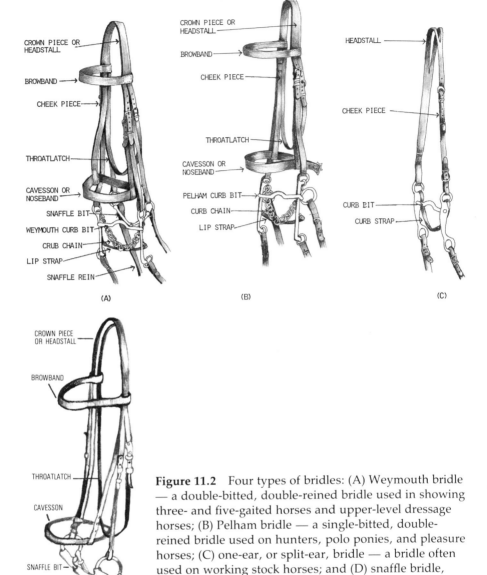

CROWN PIECE OR
HEADSTALL

BROWBAND

CHEEK PIECE

THROATLATCH

CAVESSON OR
NOSEBAND

SNAFFLE BIT

WEYMOUTH CURB BIT

CRUB CHAIN

LIP STRAP

SNAFFLE REIN

(A)

CROWN PIECE OR
HEADSTALL

BROWBAND

CHEEK PIECE

THROATLATCH

CAVESSON OR
NOSEBAND

PELHAM CURB BIT

CURB CHAIN

LIP STRAP

(B)

HEADSTALL

CHEEK PIECE

CURB BIT

CURB STRAP

(C)

CROWN PIECE
OR HEADSTALL

BROWBAND

THROATLATCH

CAVESSON

SNAFFLE BIT

(D)

Figure 11.2   Four types of bridles: (A) Weymouth bridle
— a double-bitted, double-reined bridle used in showing
three- and five-gaited horses and upper-level dressage
horses; (B) Pelham bridle — a single-bitted, double-
reined bridle used on hunters, polo ponies, and pleasure
horses; (C) one-ear, or split-ear, bridle — a bridle often
used on working stock horses; and (D) snaffle bridle,
used when starting horses in training — and in many
horse sports.

All bridles should be properly fitted, and the headstall should be
located so that it neither slides back on the horse's neck nor pulls up
against his ears. The cheek straps should be adjusted in length so the
bit rests easily in the mouth without drawing up the corners. And the

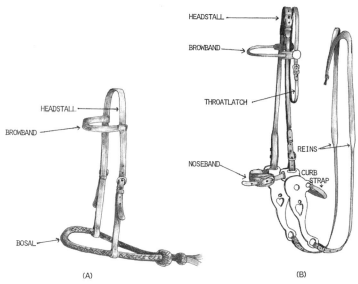

Figure 11.3 Two types of hackamores: (A) bosal hackamore —
a popular hackamore for breaking horses; (B) hackamore bit-
bridle — a hackamore with a removable mouthpiece that is used
on western cow ponies and on young horses when they are
being broken, because it eliminates the possibility of injuring
the mouth.

throatlatch should be buckled loosely enough to permit the hand, when
held edgeways, to pass between it and the horse's throat.

The bosal hackamore and the hackamore bit-bridle are used on horses
with tender mouths and as training devices for western horses.

The bosal hackamore has a pair of reins and an ordinary headstall
that holds in place a braided rawhide or rope noseband knotted under
the horse's jaw. It is an excellent device for controlling a young horse
without injuring his mouth and is used extensively in training polo and
cow ponies.

When properly adjusted, the hackamore should rest on the horse's
nose about 4 inches from the top of the nostrils, or a little below the
base of the cheek bones. It should also permit the passage of two fingers
held edgeways between it and the jaw.

The hackamore bit-bridle is a "fake" bridle; it has the shanks on each
side but no mouthpiece.

The kind of bridle or hackamore used will depend on the horse's
training and intended use. Figures 11.2 and 11.3 show the most common types of bridles and hackamores.

HOW TO BRIDLE A HORSE

Bridling is made easy by the procedure that follows.

Take the crownpiece of the bridle in the left hand and the reins in the right. Approach the horse from the left side opposite the shoulder. With your right hand slip the reins over his head, allowing them to rest on the crest directly behind the ears. Remove the halter — if there is one. Place yourself just behind the horse's head, facing front. Then, step by step, bridle him as follows:

- *Step 1* — Take the crownpiece of the bridle in your right hand and slip the horse's nose between the cheek pieces (and in the cavesson or noseband, if the bridle is so equipped). Raise the bridle with the right hand, until the crownpiece or headstall is just in front of the ears and the bit is dangling against the teeth. With your left hand, cup the horse's chin firmly, holding the bar of the bit across the palm and keeping it against the teeth with your thumb.

- *Step 2* — Slip the ends of your fingers between the horse's lips on the far side and into the animal's mouth. Thereupon, he will open his mouth and curl back his lips.

- *Step 3* — With a quick pull on the crownpiece, bring the bridle into position — that is, the bit in his mouth and the crownpiece slipped over his ears.

- *Step 4* — Buckle the throatlatch.

From these steps and the accompanying figure, the novice should not get the impression that in bridling a horse each step is so distinct and different as to be marked by intermittent pauses. Rather, when properly executed, bridling is a series of rhythmic movements, and the entire operation is done so smoothly and gracefully that it is difficult to discern where one stage ends and the next one begins.

BITS

The bit is the most important part of the bridle. In fact, the chief use of the other parts of the bridle are to hold the bit in place in the horse's mouth. The bit provides communication between the rider or driver and the horse.

Figures 11.5, 11.6, and 11.7 show the most common types of bits. There are many variations of each of these types.

The proper fit and adjustment of the bit is very important. It should rest easily in the mouth and be wide enough so it will not pinch the cheeks or cause wrinkles in the corners of the mouth. As a rule, a curb-type bit rests lower in the mouth than a snaffle. All bits should have large rings or other devices to prevent them from passing through the mouth when either rein is drawn in turning the horse.

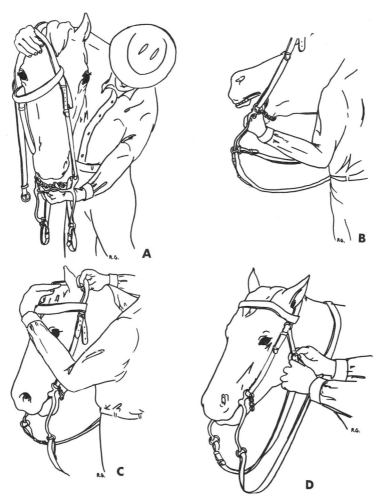

Figure 11.4 Steps in bridling a horse: (A) Step 1 — Bridle in position, with the horse's nose between the cheek pieces, the crownpiece in front of the ears, and the bit dangling against the teeth; (B) Step 2 — Mouth open; (C) Step 3 — Bridle on, with bit in mouth and crownpiece over ears; and (D) Step 4 — Throatlatch buckled.

The following points about bits should be remembered:

- Usually, the snaffle bit is used when a horse is started in training.
- The egg-butt snaffle is used on hunters and jumpers and dressage horses.
- The curb bit is a more severe bit than the snaffle and it may be used either alone or with the snaffle.

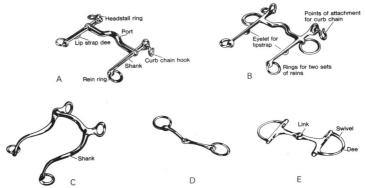

Figure 11.5   Five common types of English riding bits:
(A) Weymouth curb bit — used along with a snaffle bit in a
Weymouth bridle for three- and five-gaited horses and upper-
level dressage horses; (B) Pelham curb bit — used in a Pelham
bridle for hunters, polo ponies, and pleasure horses;
(D) Walking Horse bit — often used on Walking Horses;
(D) snaffle bit — the most widely used of all bits; (E) D-ring
snaffle bit — often used on Thoroughbred racehorses and
occasionally on hunters and jumpers.

- The Pelham bit is one bit that is used with two reins and a curb chain.
  It is a combination of a snaffle and a curb bit and is used in park or
  pleasure riding and hunting.

- The Weymouth bit combined with a snaffle bit is known as a bit and
  bridoon. A double bridle with this combination is used for the most
  advanced levels of dressage, when more collection is required.

- Western bits are similar to the curb bit but they have longer shanks
  and are larger. Usually, they are used with a solid leather curb strap
  but sometimes they have a small amount of chain in the middle of
  the leather curb strap.

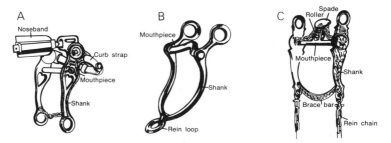

Figure 11.6   Three common types of Western riding bits:
(A) Hackamore bit — used on most cow ponies, (B) Roper
curved-cheek bit — used on many roping horses, (C) Spade-
mouth bit — used on many stock horses.

Figure 11.7 Three common types of driving bits: (A) Liverpool bit — a curb used on heavy harness horses and many pleasure driving horses; (B) bar bit — used on trotting harness horses that carry checkreins and are driven with a strong hand; (C) half-cheek snaffle bit — used on harness racehorses, roadsters, and fine harness horses.

SADDLES

The English and Western saddles are the two most common types, but individual styling within the types may vary considerably.

ENGLISH SADDLE

English saddles include the flat types that are modified specifically for pleasure riding, training, racing, jumping, or polo. English saddles are characterized by their relatively flat seat and generally light weight.

The following points are pertinent to the use of English saddles:

Figure 11.8 English tack used in a competitive trail ride by Moire Donald (left) and Ruth Waltenspiel (right). (Courtesy, Ruth Waltenspiel, Healdsburg, California)

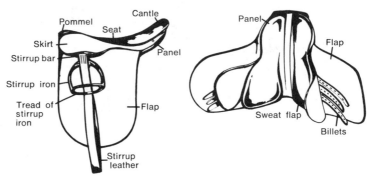

Figure 11.9   An English saddle in upright position (*left*); underside (*right*).

- When an English saddle is used on a show horse, use a leather or nylon girth.
- A saddle pad (square or shaped like the saddle's flaps) is used with an English saddle.
- For English pleasure riding or showing, use an English saddle and a double or Pelham bridle bit.
- For dressage showing and training, use a snaffle bit until the horse has reached the most advanced levels, when a double bridle with a combination of snaffle and curb is used.
- When hacking (going on a trail ride) for pleasure, use a snaffle unless your horse bolts at everything and requires more restraint.
- For hunting and jumping, use a forward seat English saddle and a hunting snaffle or Pelham bit.

WESTERN SADDLE

A Western saddle (Figure 11.10) is the common saddle used by cowboys and western stockmen. The essential features are a steel, light metal, or wooden tree; a pommel, topped by a horn for roping, and a cantle (the height of the pommel and cantle vary according to the uses to which the saddle is to be put and the personal preference of the rider); a comparatively deep seat; heavy square or round skirts; a double cinch, usually, but a single cinch may be used; and heavy stirrups that may be hooded or open.

A Western saddle is designed to give comfort for all-day riding and provide enough strength to stand up under the strain of calf roping. The average Western saddle weighs 35 to 40 lb., but it may range up to 65 or 70 lb.

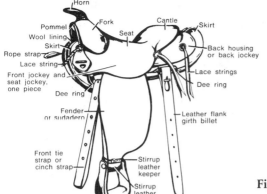

Horn
Fork
Pommel
Cantle
Seat
Skirt
Wool lining
Skirt
Rope strap
Back housing
or back jockey
Lace string
Front jockey and
seat jockey,
one piece
Lace strings
Dee ring
Dee ring
Fender
or sudadero
Leather flank
girth billet
Front tie
strap or
cinch strap
Stirrup
leather
keeper
Stirrup
leather
Stirrup

Figure 11.10 A Western saddle.

HOW TO SADDLE THE MOUNT

Regardless of the type of saddle — English or Western — it should be placed on the horse's back so that the girth (in English saddles, it's a girth; in Western saddles, it's a cinch) will come about 4 inches to the rear of the point of the horse's elbow.

When first adjusted, the girth should be loose enough to admit a finger between it and the horse's belly. After tightening the saddle, it is

Figure 11.11 Western tack, attire, and Quarter Horse mare used in a competitive trail ride by Ashley Stone, San Luis Obispo, California. (Courtesy, Ruth Waltenspiel, Healdsburg, California)

always good practice to "untrack" the horse — that is, to lead him ahead several paces before mounting. This procedure serves two purposes: first, if the horse is the kind that "blows up" so that he cannot be cinched snugly, the "untracking" will usually cause him to relax; and second, if a horse has any bad habits, he will often get them out of his system before the rider mounts.

After the horse has been ridden a few minutes, the girth should always be re-examined and tightened if necessary. The saddle should always be cinched tightly enough so that it will not turn when the horse is being mounted, but not so tight as to cause discomfort to the horse.

The length of stirrups will depend upon the type of riding. It may vary, from very short on running horses to quite long on stock horses. The stirrup leather on English saddles should always be turned so that the flat side of the leather comes against the leg of the rider.

For correct posting, in English riding, the stirrup straps or stirrup leathers must be adjusted to the right length. If stirrups are too short, posting will be high and exaggerated. For English riding, the stirrups can be adjusted to the approximate correct length before mounting by making them about one inch shorter than the length of the rider's arm with fingers extended. When the rider is sitting in the saddle, with the legs relaxed downward and the feet out of the stirrups, the bottom of the stirrup iron should touch just below the ankle bone. For Western riding, the length of stirrups may be considered as about right when there is approximately a 3-inch clearance between the saddle tree and the crotch of the mounted rider standing in the stirrups.

HARNESS

It is not within the scope of this book to cover all types and parts of harness. But some conception of the subject can be obtained by studying the illustrations on the next page and in Chapter 12.

OTHER TACK

It is beyond the scope of this book to list and describe all of the many articles of horse tack. Nevertheless, the most generally used items, in addition to those already described, follow.

BLINKERS (Blinders or Winkers)

Blinkers are an attachment to the bridle or hood, designed to restrict the vision of the horse from the sides and rear and to focus the vision forward. Driving blinkers (or winkers) are made of leather, often with a

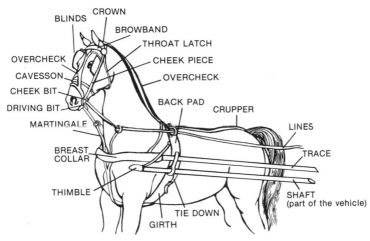

Figure 11.12 Show or jogging harness.

crest or embellishment on the outside. Racing blinkers are in the form of a hood with leather cups that act as shields.

BOOTS (for Horses)

Boots are used to protect the legs or feet against injuries. The most common injuries requiring such protection are those caused (1) by brushing, when the inside of the leg, usually on, or in the region of, the fetlock joint, is knocked by the opposite foot; (2) by overreaching, when the hind toes strike into the rear of the foreleg; or (3) by speedy cutting, when the inside of the leg is struck high above the joint, usually under

Figure 11.13 Racing blinkers — a hood with leather cups.

Figure 11.14   Ankle boot.

the hock. The shins (either front or hind) may also be endangered as a result of striking an obstacle when jumping.

Various types of boots are available to protect the horse from the different kinds of injuries listed above; among them, the quarter boots to prevent bruising of a front heel from a hind toe, worn by five-gaited Saddle Horses, Tennessee Walking Horses, and harness horses; the shin boots worn by the polo pony to guard cannons from injury by the mallet; and many others. Galloping or brushing boots are often worn by event horses, to protect their legs from injuries due to interference or hitting a solid fence.

Quarter Boot; Bell Boot

This is a flexible boot attached above the coronet which extends down over the hoof. It is designed to protect the quarter of the front heel from the hind toe.

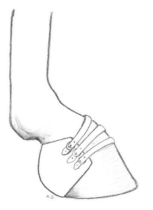

Figure 11.15   Quarter boot on a five-gaited horse. Because of the speed at which five-gaited horses are expected to perform at the trot and the rack, they are permitted to wear quarter boots to protect the heels of the front feet, a practice that is forbidden in three-gaited classes.

Figure 11.16 Bell boots also protect the heels from injury, but they encircle the entire hoof. (Photo by Barbara R. Stratton)

BREASTPLATE; BREAST COLLAR

A hunter breastplate usually consists of a short, wide strap that passes over the neck in front of the withers, two adjustable straps that run from each end of the short strap back to the saddle, two adjustable straps that run down the shoulders to a ring on the breastplate, and another adjustable strap that runs from this ring and attaches to the girth after passing between the forelegs (see Figure 11.17). Sometimes this type is equipped with a strap that runs from the ring on the breastplate to the noseband, and acts as a standing martingale, or with a pair of straps that act as a running martingale.

The breast collar serves the same purpose as a breastplate. Figure 11.18 shows a breast collar.

Either a breastplate or a breast collar is frequently used on slender-bodied horses and on horses which require some special security to prevent the saddle from slipping to the rear (such as racehorses, polo ponies, and event horses). With both articles, it is important that they be adjusted as loosely as possible consistent with holding the saddle in place, with proper allowance made for motion and for movement of the horse's neck.

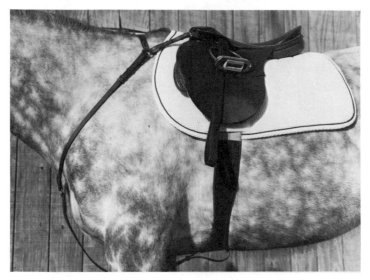

Figure 11.17 A hunter-type breastplate. Breastplates keep the saddle from slipping backward but should not interfere with the horse's freedom of movement. (Photo by Barbara R. Stratton)

HALTER (Head Collar)

A halter is used for leading a horse or tying him. There are many types of halters made from a number of different materials. The rope halter (formerly made of cotton, now made of nylon) is very strong and inexpensive. It will outlast most leather halters, and it is easy to put on and take off. But care must be taken to fit it loosely, otherwise it will rub the cheekbones. A nylon halter also will not break if a horse panics or catches it on something, but some nylon halters have a special "breakaway" buckle designed to release under stress.

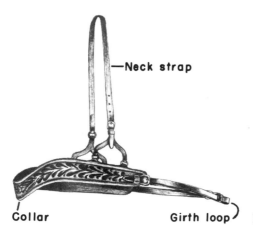

—Neck strap

Collar   Girth loop   **Figure 11.18**   Breast collar.

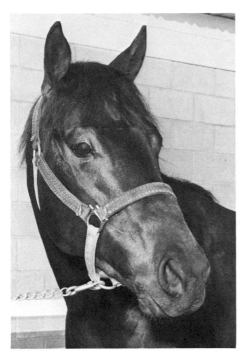

Figure 11.19   A nylon halter.

Leather halters are also widely used. The better ones are mounted with brass. Show halters are of finer, lighter leather than the ordinary stable halter, and they often have brow bands.

Sometimes the novice has difficulty in figuring out how to put a halter on. The following procedure will alleviate this problem: take the buckle in the left hand and the strap in the right hand, making sure that the three short parallel straps are on the bottom; slip the horse's nose through the noseband; swing the strap over from the far side, place it behind the ears, catch it with the left hand, bring the right hand back, and buckle the strap snugly enough to prevent the horse from getting it over his head.

Never leave a halter on a horse in the pasture. Although a haltered horse may be easier to catch, there is risk of the halter getting caught on some object and the animal not being able to free himself.

LONGE (Lunge)

The longe is a strong light strap (usually made of webbing or leather) about 30 feet long, one end of which is attached by a swiveled snap to the noseband of the cavesson. The young horse can begin training at an early age by means of the longe line. He can be circled to the left and to the right; made to walk, trot, canter, and halt; and trained to get used to and obey words of command. The longe is especially useful for

Figure 11.20   A nylon longe line.

urban-raised foals, who are limited in space for exercising on natural footing, but take care not to work a very young horse on a small circle; it puts too much strain on his joints.

Although a young horse can do all kinds of gymnastics without injury when running loose in a corral or pasture, he can be injured by improper use of the longe line. If his head is pulled at the wrong time, or too quickly or too severely, his balance will be destroyed and he may injure a foreleg or foot, throw a curb, be stifled, or even fall down.

MARTINGALES

Martingales are of two types: standing (or sometimes called a tie-down) and running (or ring). The standing martingale consists of a strap which extends from around the girth, between the forelegs, to the noseband and a light neck strap to keep the martingale from getting under the horse's feet when the head is lowered. When properly adjusted, it has the effect of preventing the elevation of the head beyond a certain level without cramping the horse. The standing martingale is most generally employed on saddle horses that rear or throw their heads up and on polo ponies and stock horses that endanger their riders by throwing their heads up in response to a severe curb when pulled up sharply. On the other hand, some competent horsemen prefer to use the run-

Figure 11.21   Correct method of longeing a horse, with a long web tape longe line. (Courtesy, *From Dawn to Destiny*, by Frank Jennings and Allen F. Brewer, Jr., published by The Thoroughbred Press, Lexington, Kentucky)

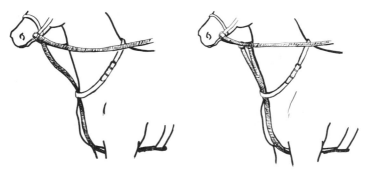

Figure 11.22 The two types of martingales: standing martingale (left), also called a tie-down because it does not give once it is attached; and a running martingale (right), which allows more freedom of movement. (Drawings by Steve Allured)

ning martingale on horses that habitually rear. They feel that the standing martingale sets the head too high.

The running martingale is not attached to the noseband but terminates in two rings through which the reins pass. It is used for the same purpose as the standing martingale but permits more freedom of movement. Thus, it is better adapted to and more frequently used for jumping than the standing martingale.

Proper adjustment of the running martingale is obtained when, with the horse's head in a normal position, the snaffle reins stretched from the pommel form a straight line from bit to pommel.

SADDLE BLANKET OR PAD (Numnah or Corona)

In theory, an English saddle should fit well enough that a blanket or pad is not necessary, *if* the saddle is thoroughly cleaned after each ride, the rider uses a balanced seat, and the mount is properly groomed. When kept clean and when properly used, however, a blanket or pad will usually prevent a sore back. For this reason, even with English saddles, many good horsemen always insist on the use of a saddle blanket or pad.

Figure 11.23 Felt pad.

A saddle blanket or corona is almost always used with a Western saddle.

Felt, mohair, or pad blankets that are adapted to the various types of saddles may be secured. Many good horsemen even prefer a folded Navajo blanket, with a hair pad inside. The corona is a blanket cut to the shape of the saddle and has a large colorful roll around the edge that is quite showy for use with a stock saddle.

The saddle pad or blanket should be placed well forward on the horse's neck and then slid back into position so as to smooth down the hair. It should come to rest smoothly and in such manner that 2½ to 4 inches of it will show in front of the saddle. After being used, the blanket or pad should be hung up to dry. It then should be brushed thoroughly to eliminate hair and dried sweat. Many types of machine-washable fleece pads are now available.

TWITCH

A twitch is a rope run through the end of a stick, used on the horse's upper lip; it is tightened by twisting in order to attract the horse's attention so it will stand still.

CARING FOR TACK

Good tack is expensive and should have good care. If it is properly cared for, it will last for years.

Ideally, each article should be cleaned thoroughly every time it is used on a horse. However, the owner or caretaker of pleasure horses may not have time to do this. A busy person, therefore, should clean

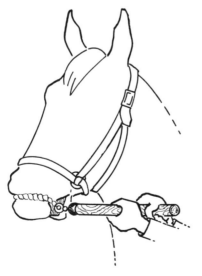

Figure 11.24 Twitch.

the vital parts after each use and then thoroughly clean all tack once a week. After each use, the underside of the saddle and the inside of the bridle should be cleaned; the bit should be washed; and the pad or blanket should be brushed after it has dried out and before it is reused. When necessary, the saddle pad or blanket should be washed, but make sure that the detergent has been rinsed out thoroughly.

All tack used on race and show horses should be thoroughly cleaned after each use. Proper cleaning of tack will

- Extend the life of leather and metal.
- Make leather soft and pliable.
- Help keep the horse comfortable. He will get fewer saddle and harness sores than he will from dirty, crusty, or stiff leather and less irritation and infection than he will from a rusty, moldy, or dirty bit.
- Assure that minor tack defects are noticed and repaired before they become serious. This lessens the likelihood of breaking a rein or line, girth, girth strap, stirrup leather, or other vital part.
- Impart pride and pleasure in the ownership and use of tack; the horse, rider or driver, and tack will all look good.

EQUIPMENT FOR CLEANING TACK

The following items of cleaning equipment are commonly used.

1. A saddle rack on which to clean the saddle. Preferably, the rack should be designed to hold the saddle with either the seat up or the bottom up so both sides can be easily cleaned.
2. A bridle rack, peg, or hook on which to hang the bridle for cleaning.
3. A rack for cleaning harness, if harness is used.
4. A bucket for warm water.
5. Three sponges, preferably, although one sponge is enough if it is rinsed properly — one sponge for washing off sweat and dirt, another for applying leather preservative or glycerine soap, and a third for occasional application of neat's-foot or similar oil.
6. A chamois cloth for drying off leather.
7. About a yard of cheesecloth for applying metal polish.
8. A flannel rag for polishing.
9. Saddle soap or castile soap for cleaning.
10. A leather preservative or glycerine soap for finishing.
11. Neat's-foot or similar oil.
12. Metal polish.
13. Petroleum jelly.

HOW TO CLEAN TACK

To assure that all parts of all articles of tack are properly cleaned, some practical order of cleaning should be followed. Any order that works is satisfactory.

Once a week all leather should be washed with saddle soap or castile soap as described in the section on washing the saddle, and then neat's-foot oil or other leather dressing should be lightly applied. Do not use too much oil; it will darken new leather and stain clothing.

Wooden parts of equipment may be sanded, varnished, and waxed whenever necessary.

The following order of cleaning is suggested for the saddle, bridle, and saddle pad or blanket.

The saddle — clean the saddle as follows:

1. Remove the girth and clean it first, the same way the rest of the saddle is cleaned.
2. Turn the saddle upside down and wash the panel (the part of the saddle that touches the horse's back) and the gullet (the underside center of the saddle). Use a sponge that has been wetted in warm water and wrung out to apply saddle soap to the leather. Rub the leather well to work up a stiff lather that will remove sweat and dirt before it hardens. Wash until clean.
3. Turn the saddle over and wash the rest of it the same way.
4. Dry the saddle with a chamois.
5. Dampen a clean sponge slightly and apply leather preservative or glycerine soap without suds to all parts of the saddle.

The bridle — clean the bridle as follows:

1. Wash the bit in warm water.
2. Clean the leather parts the same way the saddle was cleaned.
3. Use a cheesecloth to apply metal polish to all metal parts of the bridle and then use a flannel cloth to polish them. If the bridle is not to be used for several days, clean and dry the bit and then apply a light coat of petroleum jelly to keep it from pitting or rusting.

The blanket or pad — clean blankets and pads as follows:

1. Hang up or spread out blankets and pads to dry.
2. When dry, brush off hair and dried sweat.
3. Machine wash and dry synthetic fleece pads when necessary.

STORING TACK

After cleaning — handle tack as follows:

1. Store all tack in a cool, dry place.

2. Hang the bridle on its rack so all parts drape naturally without bending.

3. Put the saddle on its rack.

4. Cover the saddle, bridle, and harness (if harness is used).

CAPARISONED HORSE WITH BOOTS IN REVERSE POSITION

In the funeral processions of both President Dwight (Ike) Eisenhower and President John (Jack) Kennedy there was a riderless horse, led by a man in uniform. The horse was properly saddled, but the stirrups held in reverse position a pair of polished cavalry boots with spurs. Also, a glittering saber was hanging to the right side of the saddle. The significance of this follows.

A riderless horse, decked out with the ornamental trappings described above, accompanies the bodies of general officers and former cavalry officers. Also, this consideration may be accorded to a U.S. President, as Commander-in-Chief.

The practice of having the caparisoned (or decked out) charger of the deceased military officer led in the funeral procession stems from an ancient custom surrounding the burial of warriors. The horse bore a saddle with the stirrups reversed and a sword through them to symbolize that the warrior had fallen and would ride no more. Also, the horse was sacrificed at the time, because it was believed that the equine spirit would find his master in the hereafter; otherwise, the departed warrior would have to walk. Horses are no longer sacrificed. But a riderless horse, with the boots and spurs reversed, is still led in the funeral procession to symbolize that the warrior has fallen.

HORSE-DRAWN VEHICLES

Figure 12.1   Out for a Sunday afternoon spin. (Photo by Joan S. Byrne; courtesy, American Saddlebred Breeders Association, Lexington, Kentucky)

Man made much use of saddle horses and packhorses before the carriage came into general use. Also, primitive sliding vehicles preceded the use of wheels. The coming of the wheel made as big an impact on civilization as did the internal combustion engine years later. The Egyptians are believed to have been the original makers of wheels; the first vehicles were probably the wagons and chariots referred to in the Old Testament.

The earliest carriage still in perfect condition to be found today is the State Chariot of Tutankhamen (1361–1352 B.C.) in the Cairo Museum, in Egypt. The first known carriage to be built in Great Britain was made by William Rippon for the second Earl of Rutland in 1555.

Originally, horse-drawn vehicles evolved to meet practical needs, following which they were embellished to meet individual tastes. There was the dignified family carriage with fringe on top; the buckboard with

Figure 12.2 Bronze horse-drawn cart, with umbrella over man, taken from a tomb of the late Eastern Han dynasty (A.D. 25–220) and now on display in Beijing, People's Republic of China. (Photo by A. H. Ensminger)

its jump seat — the pickup truck of grandfather's time; the governess cart, with its door at the rear and two seats facing each other; the high two-wheeled dog cart, for transporting hounds to the hunt; the high-seated rig of the society matron; the old-fashioned top buggy of the country doctor; and the roadster of the young gallant.

The golden age of the carriage arrived in the 18th century. Many different styles of vehicles were built. The high phaeton was a popular vehicle of the period. Later, it was succeeded by the pony phaeton — a long, low vehicle. The names of different types of carriages often came from the name of the builder or the place in which they were made. Although carriages were built throughout the world, it was generally accepted that French and British carriage builders were the masters of their craft.

Even hitches evolved for practical reasons. Tandem driving, for example, was originated by the huntsmen of Old England. Wishing to spare their hunting mount as they traveled to and from the meet, these ingenious huntsmen devised the method of driving the hunter ahead, where he trotted between slack traces, while the horse to the rear did all the work.

Today, most horse-drawn vehicles either are used for recreation and sport, drawn by heavy harness horses, fine harness horses, roadsters, or ponies, or are of historical significance only — they are reminiscent of the horse and buggy era. Both driving for pleasure and competitive driving are becoming more popular again in areas where these activities can be pursued.

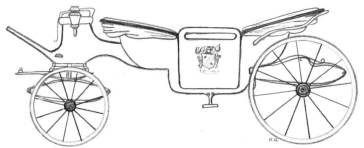

Figure 12.3 Landau, the convertible of great-grandfather's time. It was named after Landau, Germany, where it was first manufactured about 1790. The Landau was a four-wheeled covered carriage with the top divided into two sections. The back section could be left up to shield the passengers from road dust or the elements, or it could be let down or thrown back on a nice day. The front section could be removed or left stationary. Landaus held four people and were usually drawn by two horses. This vehicle was very popular in England from mid-Victorian times onward.

KINDS OF VEHICLES

Drawings and descriptions of both a landau and a phaeton are presented (see Figures 12.3 and 12.4). Note that both of them are embellished with the Ensminger coat of arms — the coat of arms of the author — as was the custom of the day.

Figure 12.4 The park phaeton. The phaeton was a four-wheeled vehicle of which there were many varieties. The early phaetons were built very high, but those of the 19th century were considerably lower and were made in many different shapes and sizes. There was the pony phaeton, made in 1824 for King George IV. Then in 1828 came the massive male phaeton, driven exclusively by men. Elegant ladies' phaetons followed.

Figure 12.5 World champion pleasure driving Morgan, Carlyle Ten, shown to a two-wheeled vehicle. (Courtesy, Bob McLemore and Company, Apple Flat Farm, Monroe, North Carolina, and The American Morgan Horse Association, Shelburne, Vermont)

Through the years, two- and four-wheeled vehicles of many styles and uses have evolved. Pictures of some of these follow.

ORIGIN OF SOME DRIVING CUSTOMS

The history of some driving customs follows.

SHOWING ROADSTERS

The sport of showing roadsters originated in the horse and buggy era, to satisfy the desire to own an attractive horse that possessed the necessary speed to pass any of his rivals. In the show-ring, roadsters may be shown hitched (1) to a sulky, or (2) to buggy or road wagon; the latter may be singly or in pairs. Roadster vehicles must be attractive and light, but strong. Roadster horses are also shown under saddle.

HANDSOME AND HEAVY

Heavy harness horses (Hackneys) in horse shows are harnessed with heavy leather and hitched to heavy vehicles. The heavy leather used on these animals was first decreed by fashion in England, where it stemmed from the idea that to drive handsomely one had to drive

Figure 12.6 Singles, pairs, tandems, or teams of four horses can compete in driving events. Here Charles Cheston is successfully negotiating a tight turn through a hazard on the cross-country or "marathon" phase of the Myopia Driving Event in South Hamilton, Massachusetts. (Photo by Margo Ward; courtesy, Mr. and Mrs. Charles Cheston, Lothian Spring Farm, Topsfield, Massachusetts)

Figure 12.7 Sulky or bike. These racing vehicles, with bicycle-type spoked wheels and pneumatic tires, were first introduced in 1892 and are used in harness races. Sulkies weigh from 29 to 37 pounds. (Courtesy, U.S. Trotting Association, Columbus, Ohio)

Figure 12.8 Handsome and heavy. A Hackney heavy harness horse in action. (Courtesy, Mrs. Dean J. Briggs, Garden Plain, Kansas)

heavily. In this country, heavy harness horses are reminiscent of the Gay Nineties, when bobtailed hackneys hitched to high-seated rigs made a dashing picture as they pranced down the avenue.

Vehicles for hackneys must be of heavy construction, elegant design, and devoid of shiny parts (the latter tends to blind spectators).

WHY DRIVE TO THE RIGHT?

The American custom of driving to the right on the road instead of to the left, as is the practice in some parts of the world, originated among the Conestoga (named after the Conestoga Valley, a German settlement in Pennsylvania) wagon drivers of the 1750s, who transported freight overland to and from river flatboats and barges along the Ohio, Cumberland, Tennessee, and Mississippi Rivers. The drivers of these four- and six-horse teams either sat on the left-wheel horse or on the left side of the seat, the better to wield their whip hand (the right hand) over the other horses in the team. Also, when two Conestoga drivers met, they pulled over to the right so that, sitting on the left-wheel horse or on the left side of the seat, they could see that the left wheels of their wagons cleared each other. Lighter vehicles naturally followed the tracks of the big Conestoga wagons. Even with the development of highways and automobiles, the American custom of driving to the right persisted.

CLOTHES FOR RIDERS

Figure 13.1   English rider in handsome attire. (Courtesy, Kentucky Horse Park, Lexington, Kentucky)

Western riding clothes change more frequently than English attire. However, regardless of style, both Western and English are usually utilitarian. Close-fitting legs eliminate wrinkles that might cause chafing. Chamois leather linings inside the knees and calves keep the muscles of the legs from pinching under the stirrup leathers and increase the firmness of the leg grip. Boots or jodhpurs protect the ankles from the stirrup irons. And high boots also keep the breeches from snagging on objects along the trail, shield the trouser legs from the saddle straps and the horse's sides, and protect the legs from rain and cold.

The time of day, the kind of riding horse, and the class in which the horse is shown at horse shows determine the riding attire. In addition to selecting proper clothes, well-groomed and experienced riders place emphasis on fine tailoring, good materials, and proper fit. Also, when riding a gaited show horse, do not wear gaudy colors, excess jewelry, or sequins, except in parade classes.

For information on clothes for riders for specific show classes, see the official rule book of the American Horse Shows Association.

Appropriate riding clothes for the most common occasions are herewith described.

CLOTHES FOR WESTERN RIDING

Coat — Coats and jackets usually not worn except in bad weather; tailored equitation suits may be worn (matching shirt and pants).

Pants — Western cut, bell-bottom pants of gabardine, cotton twill, cavalry twill, or wool worn with chaps, shotgun chaps, or chinks; a conservative color and well tailored.

Vest — Optional; leather or cloth.

Shirt — Western type; color to match or contrast with western pants; solid or patterned fabric acceptable; long sleeved.

Neckwear — Knotted kerchief, dogger-type tie, choker, or silk scarf tied ascot style and tucked into open neck of shirt.

Hat — Western hat, wide brimmed, felt or straw.

Boots — Western cowboy boots. Western boots are more than a handsome trademark of the range; they're practical, too. The high heel is designed to give the wearer protection against losing his stir-

Figure 13.2 Rider in Western attire competing in a stock horse class. (Courtesy, Appaloosa Horse Club, Moscow, Idaho)

Figure 13.3 Clothes for the rider. Note that there is considerable difference in the riding attire for (1) Western riding, (2) pleasure riding, (3) riding gaited show horses, and (4) riding in a fox hunt or in a hunter class in the show ring.

rups at critical moments; it prevents the foot from slipping through when pressure is applied for quick stops and turns. The top protects the ankles and calves of the legs against inclement weather, brush, insects, and snakes.

Modern western boots possess two added features; namely, (1) comfort, and (2) adaptation for walking, so that the wearer can walk without it being a painful experience.

Gloves — Optional; leather.

Jewelry and other accessories — Hand-carved belt and Western belt buckle; carry a rope or riata; if closed reins are used in trail and pleasure horse classes, carry hobbles; spurs optional.

CLOTHES FOR ENGLISH PLEASURE CLASSES

1. Informal park or school riding, morning or afternoon classes:

Coat — Any conservative color, tweeds or checks, usually light in weight.

Jodhpurs or breeches — Jodhpurs of stretch gabardine, whipcord, corduroy, or stretch twill in colors to match or to contrast with the coat; Kentucky-style breeches with bell bottoms and no flare at the hips.

Vest — Optional; light, solid color or tattersall check.

Shirt — Man's shirt, white or colored, broadcloth or oxford cloth, or a long-sleeved sweater.

Neckwear — Four-in-hand tie or bow tie.

Hat — A soft Panama hat.

Boots — Black or brown strap or elastic jodhpur boots, casual style.

Gloves — Optional; leather gloves to blend with habit.

Jewelry and other accessories — Cuff links, tie pin, belt; spurs of unroweled type and whip or crop optional.

2. Semiformal, afternoon or evening classes:

Coat — Gabardine, wool gabardine, dress worsted, or other men's wear materials; inverted pleats in back; dark colors preferred; in summer, linen or tropical worsted.

Jodhpurs or breeches — Jodhpurs of same material as coat, to make

Figure 13.4 Handsome Western dress boots.

a matching riding habit; Kentucky-style breeches with bell bottoms, no flare at the hips, and no cuff.

Vest — Solid color or tattersall check, to match outfit or to contrast.

Shirt — Man's shirt in white or light color to match suit.

Neckwear — Man's four-in-hand tie to match or contrast with the coat.

Hat — Saddle derby to match suit.

Boots — Black or brown jodhpur boots.

Gloves — Optional; leather in a natural shade or to match suit.

Jewelry and other accessories — Tie clasp, cuff links, belt; spurs and riding whip optional.

CLOTHES FOR GAITED SHOW HORSE CLASSES

1. Five-gaited horse; formal evening riding:

Coat — Black or midnight blue tuxedo-style riding coat with one button in front and inverted pleats; men usually wear a dark suit instead of a tuxedo. Conservative colors are required; in addition to black and midnight blue, may wear gray, green, beige, or brown.

Jodhpurs or breeches — Material and color to match coat.

Figure 13.5 Linda Fahn showing a National Show Horse in a three-gaited class. Note the difference between saddle-seat attire and hunt-seat attire (Figure 13.6). (Courtesy, National Show Horse Registry, Louisville, Kentucky)

Vest — Any solid color to match habit.

Shirt — Man's shirt.

Neckwear — Four-in-hand or bow tie.

Hat — Saddle derby or soft hat.

Boots — Black patent jodhpur boots with tuxedo; brown or black with a suit.

Gloves — Leather gloves to match habit.

Jewelry and other accessories — Cuff links and tie pin; gaited riding whip, crop, and spurs optional.

2. **Three-gaited horse; formal evening riding:**
   Coat — Tuxedo model in black, dark gray, dark brown, or midnight blue; shawl collar with satin lapels; soft pastel-colored coats also can be worn; white coat in summer. Equitation classes must wear a dark tuxedo-style coat with a silk top hat in the evening and a matched suit with a derby in the daytime.

   Jodhpurs or breeches — Material and color to match coat; satin stripe down outside of jodhpurs.

   Vest — Optional; white piqué vest or cummerbund.

   Shirt — Formal-style, white, stiff-front tuxedo; shirt with wing collar and pleated front.

   Neckwear — Black, white, or midnight blue bow tie.

   Hat — Silk top hat.

   Boots — Black leather or patent leather jodhpur boots.

   Gloves — Leather gloves to match habit.

   Jewelry and other accessories — Formal shirt studs; walk-trot stick optional.

CLOTHES FOR HUNTING AND JUMPING

1. **Hunting** *(informal):*
   Coat — Black oxford or English tweed.

   Jodhpurs or breeches — Jodhpurs with peg and cuff or breeches; colors of brick, tan, beige, or canary.

   Vest — Optional; hunting yellow or tattersall.

   Shirt — Stock shirt or ratcatcher in white, light blue, maize, mint, pink, gray, or rust.

   Neckwear — Choker, stock, or ratcatcher tie.

   Hat (hard) — Brown or black hunting derby (hunt cap if 18 years old or younger, with chin harness and foam rubber head cushion).

Figure 13.6   Rider in hunt-seat attire, competing at a local hunter show. Note the protective hard hat with chin harness. (Photo by Phaneuf/Gurdziel Photography; courtesy, Joan Downing, Ipswich, Massachusetts)

Boots — Black or brown boots; high or jodhpur.

Gloves — Brown leather gloves or rain gloves of string.

Jewelry and other accessories — Stock or choker pin, hunting crop, and spurs with straps that match boots.

2. **Hunt seat equitation:**

Coat — Oxford or wool melton hunt coat; black or other conservative color. Conservative wash jacket in season.

Jodhpurs or breeches — Buff, brick, or gray breeches.

Vest — Optional; canary with black coat.

Shirt — Ratcatcher or stock shirt.

Neckwear — Optional; white stock or choker.

Hat — Hunting derby; approved hunt cap with chin harness if 18 years old or under.

Boots — Black hunt boots.

Gloves — Optional.

Jewelry and other accessories — Stock pin worn straight across on a stock tie or choker; spurs of unroweled type; crop or bat optional.

3. Member of a hunt *(formal):*

Coat — Black or navy hunt coat of melton or English cavalry twill; may wear a black or midnight blue coat of shadbelly or other cutaway-type scarlet hunt livery; collar should be same material and color as the coat unless the rider has been invited to wear the hunt club's colors, in which case the collar should conform to hunt livery.

Jodhpurs or breeches — No-flare, in beige, brick, white, or canary with a black coat; men wear white breeches if they wear a scarlet coat.

Vest — Buff or yellow; hunt colors if members of hunt club.

Shirt — White stock shirt.

Neckwear — White stock fastened with a plain gold safety pin worn straight across stock.

Hat (hard) — Silk or velveteen hunting hat; hat guard required with scarlet coat or black shadbelly; staff members and juniors wear hunt caps; adults wear a derby with a hat guard when a black coat is worn.

Boots — Regular hunting boots of black calf with tabs; black patent leather tops permissible for women; brown tops for men on the staff.

Gloves — White or beige string rain gloves or brown leather gloves.

Jewelry and other accessories — Sandwich case, flask, and regulation hunting whip; spurs of heavy pattern with a moderately short neck, preferably without rowels and worn high on the heels.

Boot garters — Plain black or black patent leather with patent leather or black boot tops; brown with brown boot tops; white with white breeches.

4. Jumping:

Coat — Any color of hunt coat in solid or check; jumping coat may be of any informal forward-seat type.

Jodhpurs or breeches — No-flare breeches of a color contrasting with coat.

Vest — Checkered or solid color.

Shirt — Man's shirt; ratcatcher shirt when stock or choker is worn.

Neckwear — Stock or four-in-hand tie.

Hat (hard) — Hunting derby or hunt cap, black velvet.

Boots — Black hunting boots.

Gloves — Optional.

Jewelry and other accessories — Stock pin and belt; jumping bat and spurs optional.

CLOTHES FOR OTHER RIDING OCCASIONS

Clothes for special riding occasions follow.

SIDE-SADDLE FORWARD SEAT FOR HUNTING

Silk hunting hat, hat guard required; dark melton habit with matching skirt; black boots without tops, spurs are optional; white or colored rain gloves. Neckwear, coat collar, vest, sandwich case, and flask are the same as for a member of a formal hunt.

SIDE-SADDLE SHOW SEAT

Habit of dark blue, black, or oxford gray with matching or contrasting skirt; black jodhpur boots; four-in-hand or bow tie; white shirt; hard derby; white or pigskin gloves.

Figure 13.7   Dressage riders in formal attire. In upper-level competition, a top hat and shadbelly coat with tails are customary; attire for the lower levels is less formal, but a dark coat, white breeches, black boots, and a hunt cap are usually worn. (Photo by Barry Kaplan)

Figure 13.8 The rider's attire for the stadium-jumping phase of an event (*left*) is more formal than for the cross-country phase (*right*). (Courtesy of Meadow Ridge Farm, Essex, Massachusetts)

WALKING HORSE

Clothes should be the same as those worn for riding three- or five-gaited horses; men can wear a soft felt hat; women seldom wear a hat.

DRESSAGE

Formal attire; white breeches, white stock shirt with stock, hunt cap or bowler with short black coat (top hat if longer shadbelly coat is worn), black boots, usually with spurs (check A.H.S.A. *Rule Book* for approved types), black or white gloves. A dressage whip is usually carried.

EVENTING

Clothes for the dressage phase are the same as for a dressage rider. On cross-country, riders usually wear white or light-colored breeches and a brightly colored knit shirt or turtleneck. Attire for the stadium phase is more formal, with white breeches, a stock shirt, and a dark coat (usually black or navy). A whip or bat is carried in both jumping phases, but riders are not allowed to carry a whip in the dressage ring. An approved jumping helmet with a safety chin harness must be worn. For details, check the A.H.S.A. rules for combined training.

RIDING THE HORSE

Figure 14.1   Balanced seat on a racehorse. The jockey rides his mount with very short stirrups and a pronounced forward position. (Courtesy, *Appaloosa Journal,* Moscow, Idaho)

Riding has become increasingly popular in recent years. It adds zest, balance, understanding, appreciation, and pleasure to the workaday world for many (the outside of a horse is good for the inside of a man). Children build character through riding — automatically acquiring pride, confidence, self-control, and patience — all through companionship with their good friend and stout companion, the horse.

For greatest enjoyment, one should learn to ride correctly; riders should acquire the art of horsemanship, as opposed merely to "pulling leather" or sticking on. A few of the basics of equitation are herewith presented. These should be supplemented by lessons from a competent instructor and much practice.

MOUNTING AND DISMOUNTING, ENGLISH

Before mounting, two precautions should be taken: always check the saddle girth for tightness and the stirrup straps or leathers for length. A loose girth may let the saddle slip down on the horse's side or belly, especially when one is mounting and dismounting. When the girth is adjusted properly, one should be able to get only the first half of the fingers under it without considerable forcing.

When all precautions have been taken, the steps in mounting and dismounting a horse are as shown in the illustrations on the next two pages.

From the illustrations the novice should not gain the impression that in mounting and dismounting each step is so distinct and different as to be marked by intermittent pauses. Rather, when properly executed, mounting or dismounting is a series of rhythmic movements, and the entire operation is done so smoothly and gracefully that it is difficult to discern where one stage ends and the next one begins.

Dismounting is just the reverse of mounting. In succession, the rider should carefully gather the reins in the left hand, place the left hand on the horse's withers and the right hand on the pommel of the saddle, stand up in the stirrups, kick the right foot free from the stirrup, transfer the weight to the left foot as the right leg is swung backward across the horse's back and croup, shift the right hand to the cantle of the saddle, descend to the ground, and remove the left foot from the stirrup.

Another accepted way of dismounting from the English saddle consists in removing the left foot from the stirrup and sliding down the left side with relaxed knees. The rider will never get hung in the stirrups when dismounting in this manner and small children can get off a horse easily and without assistance.

Figure 14.2 Mounting, English. (Courtesy, Allen I. Ross, Stanford Riding School)

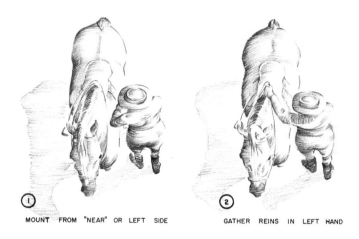

Figure 14.3   Sequence of steps in mounting and dismounting, English riding.

⑤ SWING RIGHT LEG OVER HORSE'S BACK

⑥ EASE DOWN INTO THE SADDLE

⑦ SECURE RIGHT STIRRUP
WITHOUT LOOKING DOWN

⑧ SIT EASILY, ALERT, HEAD
UP AND HEELS DOWN

Figure 14.4   Mounting, Western.

MOUNTING AND DISMOUNTING, WESTERN

The steps in mounting a horse in Western riding are: (1) take the reins in the left hand and place the left hand on the horse's neck in front of the withers; (2) keep the romal or end of the reins on the near side; (3) grasp the stirrup with the right hand and place the left foot in the stirrup with the ball of the foot resting securely on the tread; (4) brace the left knee against the horse, grasp the saddle horn with the right hand, and spring upward and over; and (5) settle into the saddle and slip the right foot into the off stirrup.

Figure 14.5   Western pleasure horse, properly ridden. (Courtesy, Al-Marah Arabians)

HOLDING THE REINS

The rider may hold the reins either in the left hand alone or in both hands. In Western riding, only one hand, usually the left, holds the reins.

When holding the reins with both hands — as is usual in show-ring riding and training — toss the "bight" (ends) of the reins to the right (off) side of the horse's neck; in hunting and jumping, toss the bight to the left.

When holding the reins in one hand, the left for example — as in Western riding — the bight should fall to the left side of the horse's neck and the right hand should be dropped loosely down the side or placed comfortably on the thigh of the right leg. The free hand should never be placed on the pommel of an English saddle or on the pommel or horn of a Western saddle.

The pictures on this page and the next illustrate better than words the correct methods of holding the reins.

In no case should the rein pressure be more vigorous than absolutely necessary, nor should the reins be used as a means of staying on the horse. A horse's mouth is tender, but it can be toughened by unnecessary roughness. Good hands appear to be in proper rhythm with the head of the horse. Beginners are likely to let the hands bob too much, thus jerking the horse's mouth unnecessarily and using the reins as a means of hanging on the horse. The desired light hands exist when a light feeling extends to the horse's mouth via the reins.

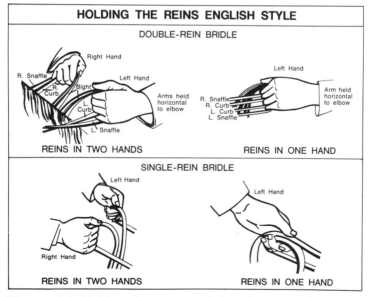

Figure 14.6 Holding the reins, English style: top, double-rein bridle; bottom, single-rein bridle.

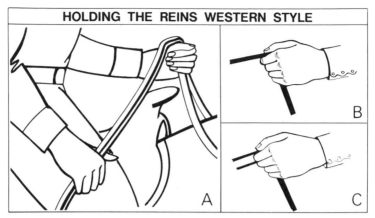

Figure 14.7   Holding the reins, Western style. (A) Only one hand can be used and hands cannot be changed. The hand must be around the reins (B) with no fingers between reins unless split reins are used; when using split reins (C), one finger between reins is permitted.

SEAT

As in any type of sport, correct riding must include rhythm and balance. The rider's movements must be in complete harmony with the horse's movements, for this assures greater security of the rider and freedom of action by the horse.

The illustrations below and on the next page show the correct riding seats for a three-gaited horse, a five-gaited horse, a plantation walking horse, and a Western horse.

BALANCED SEAT

The balanced seat may be defined as that position of the mounted rider that requires the minimum of muscular effort to remain in the saddle and which interferes least with the horse's movements and equilibrium.

Figure 14.8   Correct saddle seat and riding attire for a three-gaited horse.

Figure 14.9 Correct saddle seat and riding attire for a five-gaited horse.

Figure 14.10 Correct saddle seat and riding attire at the running walk.

Figure 14.11 Correct Western seat and riding attire.

In essence, it means that the rider must be "with the horse," rather than ahead of or behind him. When a balanced seat is maintained, the center of gravity of the rider is directly over the center of gravity of the horse. With the proper seat, the minimum use of aids will be necessary to get immediate and correct response from the horse at any gait.

The balanced seat is obtained largely through shifting the point of balance of the upper body from the hips up; the knees, legs, ankles,

Line of body

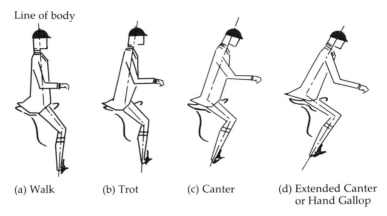

(a) Walk   (b) Trot   (c) Canter   (d) Extended Canter
                                                          or Hand Gallop

Figure 14.12   Balanced seat. Note the position for the walk (A),
the trot (B), the canter (C), and the extended canter or hand
gallop (D). The degree of forward inclination of the upper body
will vary according to the speed and gait of the horse, but the
rider should always remain in balance over his base of support.

and to a great extent the thighs remain in fixed position. Thus, the
degree of forward inclination of the upper body will vary according to
the speed and gait of the horse; but always the rider should remain in
balance over his base of support. The eyes, chin, and chest are lifted,
thus permitting clear vision ahead and normal posture of the back. It
must also be remembered that the greater the speed and the inclination
of the body forward, the shorter the stirrups. The jockey, therefore,
rides his mount with very short stirrups and reins and a pronounced

Figure 14.13   Balanced seat on a
jumper — a pronounced forward
position with security. (Courtesy,
Kentucky Horse Park, Lexington,
Kentucky)

forward position. He rises out of his saddle and supports himself almost entirely with the stirrups, knees, and legs. In steeplechasing or eventing the position of the rider is less extreme than in flat racing, for in this type of riding it is necessary to combine speed with security.

From what has been said, it can be readily understood that there are different seats or positions for different styles of riding. For example, a dressage rider rides with a deeper seat and longer leg than a rider over fences (see photos). Fashion, particularly in the show ring, also decrees that certain form be followed.

Each style of riding differs in appearance, but the end result is the same — balanced riding. An accomplished rider can and does change the seat to meet the style of riding.

RULES OF GOOD HORSEMANSHIP

Horsemen should always practice safety and show consideration for other riders. The following are some of the rules of good horsemanship.

Figure 14.14 Mona Sansoucy Gaudet and her Morgan stallion, Big Bend Doc Davis, competing in the New England Dressage Show, Hamilton, Massachusetts. Note the rider's deep seat and long leg. (Courtesy, American Morgan Horse Association, Shelburne, Vermont)

Figure 14.15   Galloping position for an event rider. Molly Bliss on Hey Charlie, starting out on a cross-country course. The rider's upper body is forward, but her weight is well down in her lower legs and heels, for security. (Photo by Margaret Williams)

- Approach a horse on his left. Never walk or stand behind a horse unannounced; let him know you are there by speaking to him and placing your hand on him. Otherwise, you may get kicked.
- Pet a horse by first placing your hand on his shoulder or neck. Do not dab at the end of his nose.
- When leading a horse, grasp the reins close to the bit on his left side.
- Walk a horse to and from the stable; this prevents him from running to the stable and from refusing to leave the stable.
- To prevent a sore back, make sure the saddle blanket or pad is clean and free of any rough places.
- Check the saddle and bridle, or hackamore, before mounting. The saddle should fit just back of the withers; it should not bear down or rub the withers, but also it should not be placed too far back. The girth should be fastened snugly and should not be too close to the forelegs. Be sure that the bridle, or hackamore, fits comfortably and that the curb chain, or strap, is flat in the chin groove and fastened correctly.
- Mount and dismount from the left side. The horse must be made to stand still until the rider is properly seated in the saddle or has dismounted.

- Sit in the correct position for the style of riding.
- Keep the proper tension on the reins; avoid either tight or dangling reins.
- Keep the hand and voice quiet when handling a horse. Never scream, laugh loudly, or make other noises that will upset the horse. Do not slap a horse with the ends of the reins when he is excited.
- Warm up a horse gradually; walk him first and then jog him slowly.
- Keep to the right side of the road except when passing. Yield the right-of-way courteously.
- Walk a horse across bridges, through underpasses, on pavements and slippery roads, and when going up or down a hill. Do not race a horse; he will form bad habits and may get out of control.
- Slow down when making a sharp turn.
- Keep a horse moving when a car passes. If he stops, he may back into the passing vehicle.
- Anticipate such distractions as cars, stones, paper, trees, bridges, noises, dogs, and children.
- Vary the gaits; do not force a horse to take a rapid gait such as a canter, rack, or trot for more than a half mile without allowing a breathing spell.
- Keep a horse under control at all times if possible. Try to stop a runaway horse by sawing the bit back and forth to break his stride and his hold on the bit; in an open space, pull one rein hard enough to force the horse to circle.
- Be firm with a horse and make him obey. At the same time, love and understand him and he will be a good friend.
- Never become angry and jerk a horse; a bad-tempered person can make a bad-tempered horse.
- Lean forward and loosen the reins if a horse rears. Do not lean back and pull because the horse might fall over backward.
- Pull up the reins of a bucking horse and keep his head up. Loosen the reins and urge a horse forward with your legs if he starts backing. Do not hold the reins too tightly when a horse is standing still.
- Walk a horse at the end of a ride to let him get cool.
- Do not allow a horse to gorge on water when he is hot; allow a warm horse to drink only a few swallows at a time.
- Do not turn a horse loose at the stall entrance. Walk into the stall with him and turn him around so that he is facing the door. In a tie stall, make certain that the horse is tied securely with a proper length of rope.
- Groom a horse thoroughly after each ride.

Figure 14.16   Pair, in which horses should look alike and riders should dress alike. (Courtesy, Al-Marah Arabians)

- Wash the bit thoroughly before it is hung in the tack room. Remove hair and sweat from the saddle and girth before putting them on the rack.
- When riding in a group, keep about 5 feet apart when abreast or a full horse's length behind other mounts when in line, to prevent kicking.
- Never rush past other riders; this may startle the horses and riders and cause an accident. Instead, approach slowly and pass cautiously on the left side.
- Never dash up to another horse or group of horses at a gallop; this can injure riders or horses.
- Wait quietly when a rider must dismount. Do not start moving again until he has remounted and is ready to go.
- Never chase a mounted runaway horse because this will only make him run faster; if possible, another rider should circle and come up in front of him. In case a rider is thrown, stop the other horses and keep quiet; generally the loose horse will return to the group, where he can be caught.
- Do not trespass on private property.
- Leave gates closed; otherwise, livestock may get out.

HORSE ACCIDENTS

A horse accident is a sudden event or change occurring without intent, usually through carelessness, unawareness, lack of information, or a combination of causes, and resulting in a person, horse, or object getting hurt. In most horse accidents, the rider is to blame. Either he has been reckless or uninformed, or he is not a good enough horseman for the mount that he is using.

Most accidents result from a failure of the horseman to communicate with the horse. The aids are mutual language between horse and horseman; hence, they should be understood and used properly. But an accomplished horseman does more — he communicates with the horse so that each understands and anticipates the other. A horseman understands the sight and sound of the horse that he is leading; he has a feel for the horse that he is riding or driving; and he interprets the stance of the horse or the movement of his ears, eyes, and/or muscles. Until such time as communication of this type exists, accidents can best be avoided by the horseman entrusting himself only to a well-trained, mature horse.

F I F T E E N

SHOWING HORSES

Figure 15.1 There is no higher achievement or greater thrill than breeding and showing a champion horse — an animal representing an ideal which has been produced through intelligent breeding, then trained, fitted, and shown to the height of perfection. (Courtesy, Tom McNair Internationale, Pinehurst, Texas)

Horse shows provide spectator entertainment, and recreation, sport, and competition for the exhibitors. Also, the show ring has been, and will continue to be, an important medium for getting horses and people together in one place and at one time to compare, design, and engineer the most desirable models. But the educational value of horse shows has not been exploited. Many people who attend a horse show for the first time are bewildered by the procedure and the many breeds and classes that they see. Others have never gone to a horse show because they feel that their lack of knowledge would prevent them from enjoying it. It is the author's fond hope that this book will result in more people enjoying more horse shows with informed appraisal.

HORSE SHOWS

Horse shows have increased in numbers in recent years, on both local and national levels. Also, they have grown in terms of number of spectators and prize money, as is evidenced in Table 15.1.

In addition to spectator entertainment, horse shows stimulate improved breeding, for winning horses (and their relatives) bring good prices.

The American Horse Shows Association (A.H.S.A.) oversees the rules and schedules of all the big shows. Recognized shows include all regular shows, local shows, combined training events, and dressage competitions in which the A.H.S.A. participates.

CLIPPING AND SHEARING

Custom decrees that some breeds be clipped and sheared according to certain haircuts and hairstyles. These are illustrated on page 425.

SHOWING THE HORSE

The successful showman knows the rules of the classes and follows the correct showing techniques. Broadly speaking, this calls for knowledge

Table 15.1 HORSE SHOWS[1]

Item		Nationally Sanctioned	Locally Sanctioned	Total
Total shows	No.	7,348 (20%)	29,392 (80%)	36,740 (100%)
Spectators	No.	4,577,094	19,898,384	24,475,478
Prizes	$	29,886,067	61,517,456	91,403,523
Total Expenses	$	84,832,882	187,303,694	272,136,576
Admissions	$	5,984,587	39,414,672	45,399,259
Total Revenues	$	96,059,559	221,615,680	317,675,239
Charity (donations)	$	8,618,425	19,104,800	27,723,225

[1] From *Economic Impact of Horse Shows 1979*, a report based on a survey conducted by the American Horse Council, Washington, D.C. Note that 20% of the horse shows were *nationally sanctioned* and 80% were *locally sanctioned*.

Figure 15.2   A beautifully fitted and groomed Half-Arabian mare. (Courtesy, International Arabian Horse Association, Denver, Colorado)

of both performance and breeding (in hand) divisions, as well as of the several classes within each division.

PERFORMANCE CLASSES

Performance classes for horses are so numerous and varied that it is not practical to describe them here. Instead, the showman should refer to the official rule book of the American Horse Shows Association and to the rules printed in the programs of local horse shows.

IN HAND (Halter, or Breeding Classes)

Breeding classes are discussed here. They are shown "in hand," which means the horses are exhibited wearing a halter, preferably, or a bridle. The halter should be clean, properly adjusted, and fitted with a fresh-looking leather or rope lead. If the horse is shown wearing a bridle, the exhibitor should not jerk on the reins hard enough to injure the mouth.

The following practices are recommended for showing in hand, or at halter.

1. Train the horse early.
2. Groom the horse thoroughly.
3. Dress neatly for the show.

Figure 15.3a The natural-appearing mane and tail of the Arabian and Morgan.

Figure 15.3b The tightly braided mane and the docked and set tail of the Hackney.

Figure 15.3c Typical mane and tail treatment of the Tennessee Walking Horse.

Figure 15.3d The clipped or roached mane and the cut, set, and shaved tail of the three-gaited American Saddle Horse.

Figure 15.3e The clipped or roached mane and the tightly braided tail of the polo pony.

Figure 15.3f The full mane with braided foretop and first lock and the full waterspout tail of the five-gaited American Saddle Horse.

Figure 15.3g The usual mane and tail treatment of the Quarter Horse. Both the mane and tail are shortened and shaped by pulling.

Figure 15.3h The braided mane and the thinned tail and braided dock of the hunter.

Figure 15.3 Common mane and tail treatments for different breeds and different styles of riding and competing.

Figure 15.4   A three-gaited saddle horse in a performance class.
(Courtesy, *The National Horseman,* Louisville, Kentucky)

4. Enter the ring promptly and in tandem when the class is called.
   Line up at the location indicated by the ringmaster or judge unless
   directed to continue around the ring in tandem.

5. Stand the horse squarely on all four feet with the forefeet on
   higher ground than the hind feet if possible. The standing position
   of the horse should vary according to the breed. For example,
   Arabians are not stretched, but American Saddlers and park-type
   Morgans are trained to stand with their front legs straight under
   them and their hindlegs stretched out behind them. Other breeds
   generally stand in a slightly stretched position, somewhat
   intermediate between these two examples. When standing and
   facing the horse, hold the lead strap or rope in the left hand 10 to
   12 inches from the halter ring. Try to make the horse keep his
   head up.

6. Unless the judge directs otherwise, the horse should first be
   shown at the walk and then at the trot. Move the horse as follows:
   a. Reduce the length of the lead strap or rope by a series of
      "figure-eight" folds or by coils held in the left hand. Hold the
      upper part of the lead strap or rope in the right hand and
      lead from the left side of the horse. If the horse is well

mannered, give him 2 to 3 feet of lead so he can keep his head, neck, and body in a straight line as he moves forward. But keep the lead taut so the horse is always under control. Do not look back.

b. The exhibitor should keep the horse's head up and briskly move him forward in a straight line for 50 to 100 feet as directed.

c. At the end of the walk, turn to the right. That is, the exhibitor should turn the horse away from himself and walk around the horse. If the horse is turned toward the exhibitor, the horse is more likely to step on the exhibitor. Make the turn in as small a space as practical, and as effortless as possible. When showing at the trot, bring the horse to a walk and move him slightly in the direction of the exhibitor before turning.

d. The exhibitor should lift his knees a little higher than usual when he is showing in the ring.

e. Trail the horse with a whip if it is permitted and desired. Most light horses are given early training by trailing with the whip but usually they are shown without this aid. If a

Figure 15.5 A five-gaited saddle horse in action. (Courtesy, *The National Horseman*, Louisville, Kentucky)

Figure 15.6 World Champion fine harness horse. (Courtesy, Irene Zane, Scott City, Kansas)

"trailer" is used, he should follow at a proper distance. The distance should not be so near he might get kicked but not so far he would be ineffective. The trailer should keep the animal moving in a straight line, avoid getting between the judge and the horse, and always cross in front of the horse at the turn.

Figure 15.7 Grand Champion Morgan stallion. (Courtesy, The Morgan Horse Club, Inc., Shelburne, Vermont)

Figure 15.8 Correct method of leading when showing a horse "in hand."

7. Walk the horse down about 50 feet and walk back; then trot down about 100 feet and trot back. To save time, the judge may direct that horses be walked down and trotted back, which is a proper procedure. After the horse has been walked and trotted, stand him promptly in front of the judge. After the judge has made a quick inspection, move to the location in the line indicated by the ringmaster or judge.

8. Keep the horse posed at all times; keep one eye on the judge and the other on the horse.

9. When the judge signals to change positions, the exhibitor should back the horse out of line, or if there is room, turn him to the rear of the line and approach the new position from behind.

10. Try to keep the horse from kicking when he is close to other horses.

11. Keep calm; a nervous showman creates an unfavorable impression.

12. Work in close partnership with the horse.

13. Be courteous and respect the rights of the other exhibitors.

14. Do not stand between the judge and the horse.

15. Be a good sport; win without bragging and lose without complaining.

GLOSSARY OF HORSE TERMS

Behavior — the movements that horses make. (Photo by Mrs. Buddy Banner, Willow Springs Ranch, Oracle, Arizona)

A mark of distinction of a knowledgeable horseman is that he "speaks the language" — he uses the correct terms and knows what they mean. Even though horse terms are used glibly by old-timers, often they are baffling to the newcomer.

Some terms that are defined or explained elsewhere in this book are not repeated in this chapter. Thus, if a particular term is not listed herein, the reader should look in the index or in the particular chapter and section where it is discussed.

A

Across the Board   A combination pari-mutuel (race) ticket on a horse is known as "across the board," meaning that you collect something if your horse runs first, second, or third.

Actinobacillosis   See **Navel Infection.**

Action   Movement of the feet and legs — it should be straight and true.

Aficionado   Ardent follower, supporter, or enthusiast; a fan.

Age   The age of a horse is computed from the first of January.

Aged Horse   Correctly speaking, a horse 8 years of age or over; but the term is often used to indicate a horse that is smooth mouthed — that is, 12 years of age, or older. Since 1 year of a horse's life corresponds to approximately 3 of man's, it follows that at age 7 a horse "comes of age," or attains maturity.

Aids   The legs, hands, weight, and voice used in controlling a horse.

Alter   To castrate a horse; to geld.

Anatomy   The science of the structure of the animal body and the relation of its parts.

Anthrax (Splenic Fever, Charbon)   An acute, infectious disease caused by *Bacillus anthracis,* a large, rod-shaped organism.

Antihistamines   Drugs used to neutralize and treat allergic conditions in the body.

Appointments   Equipment and clothing used in showing.

Arab   Used interchangeably with Arabian; hence, a breed of horses.

Ascarids   See **Roundworms, Large.**

Aseptic   Refers to something being free from the living germs of disease.

Asterisk   Used in front of a horse's name, an asterisk (*) indicates "imported." Used in front of a jockey's name, it indicates that he is an apprentice rider.

Astringent   A drug, such as tannic acid, alum, and zinc oxide or sulfate, that causes contraction of tissues.

At the End of the Halter   Sold with no guarantee except title.

Azoturia   See **Tying-up.** In the draft-horse era, the disease was known as azoturia. Today, it is known as tying-up.

B

Babesiasis   See **Equine Piroplasmosis.**

Back   The command to move backward.

Balanced Seat   That position of the mounted rider that requires the minimum of muscular effort to remain in the saddle and which interferes least with the horse's movements and equilibrium.

Bald Face   A white face, including the eyes and the nostrils, or a portion thereof.

Balky Horse   Balking refers to any horse that stands still — refuses to go. This vice was not uncommon in the draft horse and horse-and-buggy era. The causes of balking are numerous; among them, too severe

Don't you believe it! The "fire cure" won't work. The singed horse will move forward just far enough to burn up the load of hay.

punishment when overloaded, and sore shoulders. The legendary cures (none recommended by the author) included (1) pounding on one shoe to divert the balky horse's attention, (2) pouring sand in one ear, which was supposed to shake the idea of balking out of his head, and (3) building a fire under him. The author recalls the incident of a neighboring farmer who tried the "fire cure," only to have the singed horse move forward just enough to burn up the load of hay which it was pulling.

In the old days, when selling a balky horse at auction, it was generally announced that he "sells at halter." Belatedly, some uninformed buyer learned that this meant that the horse was prone to balk, and that he wouldn't pull the hat off your head.

Banged   Hair of the tail cut off in a straight line.

Bangtail   Slang term for a racehorse, as in the old days running horses usually had banged tails, often banged close to the dock, or docked and banged. Also, a wild horse.

Barefoot   Unshod.

Barren   A mare that is not in foal.

Bars   May refer either to the bars of the mouth, or of the hoof.

Base Narrow   Standing with front or rear feet close together, yet standing with legs vertical.

Base Wide   Standing with front or rear feet wide apart, yet with legs vertical.

Bean-shooter   A horse that throws its front feet violently forward at the trot, with a little flexion, "landing" about 12 inches above the ground. A very undesirable trait.

Beefy Hocks   Thick, meaty hocks, lacking in quality.

Behavior, Animal   Behavior is the reaction of animals to certain stimuli, or the manner in which they react to their environment. Stated simply, behavior is the movements animals make.

Bell Boots   Rubber protective boots that are bell-shaped, fitting over the coronet bands and down on the hoof.

Bellerophon   The Prince of Corinth in Greek mythology who tamed the winged horse, Pegasus. According to legend, Bellerophon used a golden bridle to coax the curious animal from his favorite meadow, then made him captive and rode him off to destroy the dragonlike monster, the Chimera. Success encouraged him to try to fly to Olympia to live with the gods. However, Zeus, angered by this mortal's ambition, sent a gadfly to sting Pegasus, causing him to unseat his venerable and conceited master, who fell to earth crippled and blinded.

Big Hitch   A hitch of draft horses in fours, sixes, eights, or even more.

Bight of the Reins   The part of the reins passing between thumb and fingers and out the top of the hand.

Bishoping   The practice of artificially altering the teeth of older horses in an attempt to make them sell as young horses.

Blaze   A broad white marking covering almost all of the forehead, but not including the eyes or nostrils.

Blemishes   Those abnormalities that do not affect the serviceability of the horse, including such things as wire cuts, rope burns, nail punctures, shoe boils, and capped hocks.

Blindness   Partial or complete loss of vision.

Blinker   An attachment to the bridle or hood, designed to restrict the vision of the horse from the sides and rear and to focus the vision forward.

Blistering   Blistering consists of applying an irritating substance such as Spanish fly and iodide of mercury (one common preparation consists of 15 parts Spanish fly, 8 parts iodide of mercury, and 120 parts of lard) as treatment for a blemish or unsoundness. Before applying a blister, the hair should be closely clipped from the affected area, the scurf brushed from the skin, and the animal tied so that it cannot rub, lick, or bite the treated area. The blistering agent is then applied by rubbing it into the pores of the skin with the palm of the hand. Three days later the blistered area should be bathed with warm water and soap, dried, and treated with sweet oil or Vaseline to prevent cracking of the skin.

Blood-horse   A pedigreed horse. To most horsemen, the term is synonymous with the Thoroughbred breed.

Blood Spavin   A varicose vein enlargement which appears on the inside of the hock but immediately above the location of bog spavin.

Bloodworms   See **Strongyles, Large and Small.**

Bloom   Hair that is clean and of a healthy texture.

Blow   To exhale forcibly after strenuous exercise.

Blowfly   The blowfly group consists of several species of flies that breed in animal flesh.

Blow Out   To walk or exercise a horse either to loosen its muscles by further exercise, or to prevent chilling and stiffening after a hard work-out.

Blue Eye   An unsound eye with a blue appearance; the sight may or may not be entirely gone.

Bog Spavin   A filling of the natural depression on the inside and front of the hock. A bog spavin is much larger than a blood spavin.

Bolting   1. The name given to the habit that ravenous horses have of eating too fast. This condition may be controlled by adding chopped hay to the grain ration or by placing some large, round stones, as big or bigger than baseballs, in the feed box.
2. An animal breaking out of control or trying to run away is said to be bolting.

Bone   The measurement of the circumference around the cannon bone about halfway between the knee and fetlock joints. Eight inches of bone is average for the Thoroughbred. "Flat bone" indicates that the cannon and the back tendon are parallel, with the tendon well defined and standing well away from the cannon bone. The word "flat" refers to the appearance of the cannon, which is wide and flat when viewed from the side although narrow from the front; it does not mean that the bone itself is flat.

Bone Spavin (or Jack Spavin)   Bone spavin (or jack spavin) is a bony enlargement that appears on the inside and front of the hind leg(s) below the hock at the point where the base of the hock tapers into the cannon bone.

Boots   Protective covering for the legs or feet, generally used when exercising. Some types of boots are used for balance and perfection in the horse's gait.

Bosal   The braided rawhide or rope noseband of a bosal hackamore. The bosal is knotted under the horse's jaw.

Bots (*Gasterophilus* spp.)   Four species of bots have been found in the U.S., but only three are serious pests of horses.

Bowed Tendons   Enlarged tendons behind the cannon bones, in both the front and hind legs. The descriptive terms "high" or "low" bow are used by horsemen to denote the location of the injury: the high bow appears just below the knee and the low bow just above the fetlock. This condition is often brought about by severe strains, such as heavy training or racing, especially in poor footing. When bowed tendons are pronounced, more or less swelling, soreness, and lameness are present. Treatment consists of blistering or firing. The object of blistering and firing is to convert a chronic into an acute inflammation. This hastens nature's processes by bringing more blood to the part, thus inducing a reparative process which renders the animal suitable for work sooner than would otherwise be the case. Careful bandaging, followed by rest (preferably several months to a year at pasture) are also indicated. Surgery has had only limited success because excessive scar tissue usually develops.

Bow-legged Wide at the knees, close at the feet.

Brace Bandages Resilient bandages on the legs of horses worn in some cases in an effort to support weak or lame legs, and worn in other cases to protect a horse from cutting and skinning its legs while racing, jumping, or playing polo.

Brand A mark used as means of identification.

Break To teach a young horse to obey commands, and accept direction and control.

Breaking The act of leaving gait (trot or pace) and "breaking" into a gallop. A trotter or pacer must remain on gait in a race. If it makes a break, the driver must immediately pull it back to its gait. Show horses are also marked down for breaking from the canter back to the trot too early, or vice versa.

Breeder Owner of the dam at the time of service who was responsible for the selection of the sire to which she was mated.

Breeding An attempt to regulate the progeny through intensive selection of the parents.

Breedy Smart and trim about the head and front part of the body.

Breezing A race workout in which a horse is running at a controlled speed.

Bridoon The correct name for the little snaffle bit in the full bridle.

Brittle Hoofs Hoofs that are abnormally dry and fragile.

Broke 1. Tamed and trained to a particular function, as halter-broke. A green-broke horse is not fully trained, unlike a horse that is "dead-broke" on the flat — very responsive and predictable at the walk, trot, and canter.
2. To leave or alter gait; e.g., the trotter broke stride.

Broken Crest A heavy neck which breaks over and falls to one side.

Broken Knees Knees with scars on them, indicating that the horse has fallen. Often scars are an indication that the horse is awkward and inclined to stumble.

Bronchitis A condition of the respiratory system, characterized by the inflammation of the bronchial tubes, with signs similar to heaves.

Broodmare A mare kept for breeding or reproductive purposes.

Broomtail A wild and untrained western range horse of inferior quality.

Brothers (or Sisters)   *Full brothers* — By the same sire and out of the same dam.

Half brothers — Out of the same dam, by different sires. This is one of the most frequently misused terms. Horses by the same sire and out of different dams are referred to as "by the same sire," or else the name of the sire is used, as "by Man O' War." This distinction is for a definite purpose, for only a few horses can be half brothers (or half sisters) to a famous horse, but hundreds can be by the same sire. This restricted definition tends to give a little of the credit to good broodmares instead of leaving the meaning ambiguous.

Brothers in blood — By the same sire out of full sisters; or by full brothers out of the same dam, or any combination of exactly the same blood.

Three-quarter brothers — For example, horses having the same dam and whose sires have identical sires but different dams.

Seven-eighths brothers — The progeny of a horse and his son produced by the same mare, or similar combinations of lineage.

Brush   To force a horse to top speed over a short distance.

Brushing   Striking the fetlock with the other hoof, which results in just roughing the hair of the fetlock, or in an actual injury.

Bucked Shins   A temporary racing unsoundness characterized by a very painful inflammation of the periosteum (bone covering) along the greater part of the front surface of the cannon bone, caused by constant pressure from concussion during fast workouts or races.

Bucking   Springing with a quick leap, arching the back, and descending with the forelegs rigid and the head held as low as possible.

Buck-kneed   See **Knee-sprung.**

Bug Boy   An apprentice jockey.

Bull Pen   Auction ring.

C

Calf-kneed   Standing with knees too far back, directly opposite to buck-kneed or knee-sprung.

Calico-pinto   A multicolored or spotted pony.

Calf Roping   A skill required of cowboys to capture and hold calves when branding, dehorning, and doctoring them on the range.

Calk   Grips on the heels and the outside of the front shoes of horses, designed to give the horse better footing and prevent slipping.

Calking   Injury to the coronary band by the shoe of the horse. Usually incurred by horses whose shoes have calks, or by horses that are "rough-shod," as for ice.

Canter   The canter is a slow, restrained, three-beat gait in which the two diagonal legs are paired, thereby producing a single beat which falls between the successive beats of the other unpaired legs.

Capped Elbow See **Shoe-Boil.**

Capped Hock An enlargement at the point of the hock; it is usually caused by bruising.

Capriole An intricate movement performed by the Lipizzan horses in the Spanish Riding School in Vienna. It is considered the ultimate of all high-school and classical training. The horse leaps into the air, and, while in the air, kicks out with the hind feet. The capriole also, like so many other forms of high-school work, belongs to the medieval methods of combat, in which, by means of such jumps by the horse, the surrounded rider could rid himself of adversaries. By kicking out the hind legs, the horse prevented the enemy from getting within striking distance with sword and lance.

Cast Refers to a horse's falling or lying down close to a wall or fence so that it cannot get up without assistance.

Cat-hammed Having long, relatively thin thighs and legs.

Cavesson Headstall with a noseband (often quite large) used for exercising and training horses.

Centaurs The centaurs were an ancient mythical Greek race dwelling in the mountains of Thessalay. They were imagined as men with the bodies of horses and half-bestial natures.

Champing A term that describes the horse's playing with the bit. Its development is encouraged in bitting a young horse by using a bit with "keys" attached to the mouthpiece, which tends to make the saliva flow and keep the mouth moist — an aid in producing a "soft" mouth.

Charbon See **Anthrax.**

Check Short for checkrein.

Checkrein A strap coupling a bit of a bridle to the harness backband to keep the head up and in position.

Cheek A cheek strap, a part of the bridle.

Chestnut The horny growth on the inside of the horse's legs, above the knees and below the hocks.

Chukker A seven-and-one-half-minute period in a polo game. (From the Hindi language, meaning "a circle.")

Cinch Girth of a Western saddle.

Claiming Race A race in which all the horses are entered at stated prices and may be claimed (purchased) by any other owner of a starter in the race. In effect, all horses in a claiming race are offered for sale.

Clean A term indicating that there are no blemishes or unsoundnesses on the legs.

Clicking Striking the forefoot with the toe of the hind foot on the same side. Also known as forging.

Cluck   To move the tongue in such a way as to produce clucks. The command to go, proceed; the signal to increase speed.

Coarse   Lacking in quality — shown in texture of hair, hairy fetlocks, all-over lack of refinement, common head; flat and shelly feet, and gummy legs.

Cob   A close-knit horse, heavy-boned, short-coupled and muscular, but with quality, and not so heavy or coarse as to be a draft animal. A cob is usually small, standing under 15 hands.

Cobby   Close-coupled, stoutly built. Like a cob.

Cocked Ankles   Bent forward on the fetlocks in a cocked position.

Cock Horse   An extra horse used with English stagecoaches, ridden behind the coach in ordinary going, but hitched before the team for added draft when approaching steep hills or heavy going. The cock horse was usually of a flashy color.

Coffin Bone   A major bone in the foot of a horse, enclosed within the hoof.

Cold-backed   Describes a horse that humps his back and does not settle down until the saddle has been on for a few minutes. Some "cold-backed" horses will merely tuck their tails and arch their backs when first mounted, but others will take a few crow hops until warmed up.

Cold-blood   A horse of draft-horse breeding.

Cold-jawed   Tough-mouthed.

Colic   A severe indigestion, which causes abdominal pain and discomfort.

Collected   The term applied to a horse when ridden well up to its bit, with its neck flexed, jaw relaxed, and hocks well under it. A collected horse has full control over its limbs at all gaits and is ready and able to respond to the signals or aids of its rider.

Colt   A young stallion under three years of age; in Thoroughbreds, the age is extended to include four-year-olds.

Combination Horse   One used for saddle and driving.

Condition   The state of health, as evidenced by the coat, state of flesh, and general appearance.

Conformation   Body shape or form.

Congenital   Acquired during development in the uterus and not through heredity.

Contracted Feet   A condition characterized by a drawing in or contracting at the heels.

Cool Out   To cause a horse to move quietly after heavy exercise.

Coon-footed   Having long, low pasterns and shallow heels.

Corn Injury to the sensitive laminae of the sole, frog, bars, or posterior quarters of the hoof.

Corns A bruise to the soft tissue underlying the horny sole of the foot which manifests itself in a reddish discoloration of the sole immediately below the affected area.

Coupling The section between the point of the hip and the last rib. A short-coupled horse is considered to be an easy keeper, while a long-coupled horse is said to "take a bale of hay a day." The width of four fingers is considered to constitute a short coupling.

Cow Hocks (Cow-hocked) Standing with the joints of the hocks bent inward, with the toes pointing outward.

Crab Bit Bit with prongs extending at the horse's nose. Purpose is to tip the horse's head up and help prevent him from ducking his head, bowing his neck, and pulling hard on the rein.

Cradle A device made of wood or aluminum and worn around the neck of the horse which prevents the horse from chewing at sores, blankets, bandages, etc.

Crest The top part of the neck. This is very well developed in stallions.

Cribber (Wind Sucking, or Stump Sucking) A horse that has the vice of biting or setting the teeth against some object, such as the manger, while sucking air.

Crop A riding whip with a short, straight stock and a loop.

Crop-eared Refers to an animal which has had the tips of its ears either cut off or frozen off.

Crossbred Produced by a sire and a dam of differing breeds.

Cross-firing A defect in the way of going, generally confined to pacers, which consists of a scuffing on the inside of the diagonal forefeet and hind feet.

Crow Hops Mild or playful bucking motions.

Crupper A leather strap with a padded semicircular loop. The loop end goes under the tail and the strap end is affixed at the center of the back band of a harness or the cantle of a saddle to prevent the saddle from slipping forward over the withers.

Cryptorchid A stallion with one or both testicles retained in the abdomen; sometimes called a ridgeling.

Curb 1. An enlargement at the rear of the leg and below the point of the hock.
2. Also, a bit mouthpiece, designed to bring pressure to bear on the horse's bars.

Curry Cleaning (grooming) with a currycomb, dandy brush, body brush, sponge, rub rag, hoof pick, etc.

Cutback Saddle   A long, flat saddle that rests low on the horse's back and is designed to place the rider's weight toward the rear. The name is derived from the U-shaped cutaway slot for the withers. It is used primarily for showing.

Cut-out   The cutting out of certain animals in a herd.

Cutting Horse   A cow horse used in cutting cattle from the herd. To promote the cutting horse and establish uniform rules for his exhibition, cutting horse enthusiasts are banded together in the following association:

National Cutting Horse Association
4704 Highway 377 South
Fort Worth, Texas 76116-8805

D

Daisy-cutter   A horse that seems to skim the surface of the ground at the trot. Such horses are often predisposed to stumbling.

Dam   The female parent of a horse.

Dapple   Small spots, patches, or dots contrasting in color or shade with the background, such as dapple-gray.

Dash   Race decided in a single trial.

Dead Heat   A racing term referring to two or more horses that arrive simultaneously at the finish line.

Deerfly   A biting insect that inflicts a painful bite.

Denerving   The removal of part of the nerve trunk and/or nerves in certain areas.

Dental Star   A marking on the incisor teeth of horses, used in judging their age. It first appears on the lower central and intermediate incisors when the horse is about eight years of age.

Derby   A word that stems from a classic race exclusively for three-year-olds which was initiated at Epsom Downs, in England, in 1780, by the twelfth Earl of Derby. This race became so famous that today, the word "derby" is considered synonymous with any well-known race; hence, there is the Kentucky Derby, the Japan Derby, etc. In England, the word is pronounced "darby," whereas in the U.S. it is pronounced "derby."

Diagonal   Refers to the forefoot moving in unison with its opposite hind foot at the trot. If it is the left forefoot, it is called the left diagonal.

Dish-faced   A term used if the face is concave below the eyes, and, especially in Arabians, if the profile shows a definite depression below the level of the eyes. This term is also applied to some horses and many ponies that have flat or concave foreheads with prominent temples, but this type is the absolute opposite to the "dish" of the Arab, which has a prominent forehead.

Dishing   Carrying the foot forward in a lateral arc in a trot, but advancing the knee in a straight line.

Disqualification   A fault so serious that it disqualifies a horse for registry or show.

Distaff Side   The female side, as in a pedigree.

Distemper   See **Strangles.**

Dock   The solid portion of the tail.

Docked   A tail in which part of the dock has been removed.

Docking and Setting   Removing part of the dock of the tail, cutting the tendons, and "setting" the tail to make the horse carry it high.

Doping   The administering of a drug to a horse to increase or decrease his speed in a race or to improve his performance (perhaps by masking lameness) in some other type of competition. Race course and show officials run saliva tests, urine tests (urinalyses), etc., in order to try to detect any horses that have been doped. Usually such tests are conducted on the winners of every race and on the first three to finish in stakes races. Where doping is proved, the horse may be banned from the track for a period of time, the owner may have his entire stable banned from racing for a period of time, and/or the trainer or jockey may lose his license; with the penalty determined by the circumstances.

The American Horse Shows Association *Rule Book,* in a section on "Drugs and Medications," details their rules that apply to competitions recognized by the Association.

Double-gaited   A term applied to a horse that can both trot and pace with good speed.

Drafty   Having the characteristics of a draft horse. Heavy and lacking in quality.

Drag Hunt   A hunt staged on horseback with hounds following a previously laid trail, made by dragging a bag containing anise seed or litter from a fox's den.

Dressage   The guiding of a horse through natural maneuvers without emphasis on the use of reins, hands, and feet. Dressage means "training," but is also a form of competition in which certain exercises of progressive difficulty are performed.

Drover   A word reminiscent of one of the most thrilling chapters in American history. Prior to the advent of railroads and improved highways, great herds of cattle, sheep, and hogs were driven on horseback over famous trails, often many hundreds of miles long. The crew of "drovers" usually consisted of the boss (often the owner of the herd), a man to ride along each side, and a fourth man to lead.

The "drovers" — those who did the driving — were rugged, and their lives were filled with adventure. The work was accompanied by an almost ceaseless battle with the elements, clashes with thieves, and no small amount of bloodshed.

Dutchman's Team   It is customary to hitch the smaller horse of a team on the left side. When a careless horseman hitches his larger horse on the near side, he is said to be driving a "Dutchman's team."

Dwelling   A noticeable pause in the flight of the foot, as though the stride were completed before the foot reaches the ground. It is most noticeable in trick-trained horses.

E

Ear Down   To restrain an animal by biting or twisting its ear.

Eastern (Oriental)   Applied to horses of Arab, Barb, or similar breeding.

Encephalomyelitis (or Sleeping Sickness)   A virus, epizootic (epidemic) disease that may be carried by birds and mosquitoes. It is caused by four different viruses. The two most common ones are known as the Eastern type and the Western type.

Endurance Rides   Trials of speed and endurance. Eleven 300-mile endurance rides used to be held, seven in New England and four in Colorado, but these were discontinued in 1926. Today, there are several well-known 50- to 100-mile competitive trail rides in the U.S. The time for the different courses varies according to the topography, elevation, and footing, but it is approximately 17 hours for 100 miles and 6 hours for 50 miles. Awards are given for the best-conditioned horse as well as the winners.

Entire   An ungelded male.

Equestrian   A man or woman engaged in horse work or activities.

Equestrienne   A female equestrian.

Equine   A horse. Correctly speaking, the term includes all the members of the family Equidae — horses, zebras, and asses.

Equine Abortion   The premature expulsion of the fetus.

Equine Infectious Anemia (or Swamp Fever)   An infectious virus disease.

Equine Influenza   An infectious disease caused by a myxovirus that has properties of the Type A influenza viruses.

Equine Piroplasmosis (Babesiasis)   Caused by *Babesia caballi* or *B. equi*, protozoan parasites that invade the red blood cells.

Equitation   The act or art of riding horseback.

Ergot   1. The horny growth at the back of the fetlock joint; the spurs of a horse's hoofs.
2. A fungus disease of plants.

Estrus   The estrus period is commonly called "heat."

Ewe Neck   A neck like that of a sheep, with a dip between the poll and the withers. Also termed a "turkey-neck" and "upside-down neck."

Extended Trot   A ground-covering trot in which the horse is asked to lengthen his stride without changing the rhythm of the gait. To achieve this, the rider applies pressure with the calves of legs as he or she comes down into the saddle while posting.

Exudate   Refers to the discharge of fluid and tissue material from an oozing sore or wound. When it dries, it usually forms a dry crust or scab.

F

Face Fly   Face flies gather in large numbers on the faces of horses, especially around the eyes and nose.

Fallen Neck   See **Broken Crest.**

Family   The lineage of an animal as traced through either the males or females, depending upon the breed.

Farcy   See **Glanders.**

Farrier   A horseshoer.

Far Side   The right side of a horse.

Favor   To favor one leg; to limp slightly.

Feather in Eye (or Speck in Eye)   A mark across the eyeball, not touching the pupil; often caused by an injury, it may be a blemish or some other defect.

Feral   Describes a wild horse — one that has escaped from domestication and become wild, as contrasted to one originating in the wild.

Fetlock Joint   The connection between the cannon and the pastern bones.

Fetus   The unborn animal as it develops in the uterus.

Figure-eight Bandage   A style of bandaging, applied in a figure-eight fashion, which allows for expansion at the flexing of hocks and knees.

Filly   A young female horse under three years of age; in Thoroughbreds, it includes four-year-olds.

Film Patrol   The practice of recording a race on film.

Firing   Applying a hot iron or needle to a blemish or unsoundness as a treatment.

First Lock   The first lock of the mane on or in back of the poll (when the poll is clipped). The first lock is sometimes braided with a ribbon, as is the foretop or forelock.

Fistulous Withers   An inflamed condition in the region of the withers, commonly thought to be caused by bruising.

Flat Bone   See **Bone.**

Flat Foot   A foot the angle of which is less than 45°, or one in which the sole is not concave, or one with a low, weak heel.

Flat Race   A race without jumps.

Flat-sided   Lacking spring in ribs.

Flaxen   A light-colored mane or tail.

Flea-bitten   1. A white horse covered with small, brown marks. 2. Any "mangy-looking" animal.

Floating   Filing off the sharp edges of a horse's teeth.

Foal   A young, unweaned horse of either sex.

Foaling   Giving birth to a foal.

Follicle   A bubblelike structure on the ovary which contains an egg.

Foot-lock or Feather   Long hair which grows back of the fetlock.

Forage   Vegetable material in a fresh, dried, or ensiled state which is fed to livestock (pasture, hay, silage).

Forehand   The "front" of the horse, including head, neck, shoulders, and forelegs — in other words, that portion of the horse in front of the center of gravity.

Foretop (Forelock)   The lock of hair falling foward over the face.

Forging   See **Clicking.**

Form   The past performance of a racehorse; often a table giving details relating to a horse's past performance.

Founder   See **Laminitis.**

Four-in-hand   A hitch of four horses, consisting of two pairs, with one pair in front of the other.

Fox Hunt   A hunt with hounds, staged on horseback, after a live fox. The fox may have been released from captivity or tracked and flushed out of hiding by the hounds. See also **Drag Hunt.**

Fox Trot   A slow, short, broken type of trot in which the head usually nods. In executing the fox trot, the horse brings each hind foot to the ground an instant before the diagonal forefoot.

Frog   A triangular-shaped, elasticlike formation in the sole of the horse's foot.

Full Bridle   Just another term for either a Weymouth or double bridle.

Full Brothers (or Sisters)   Horses having the same sire and the same dam.

Furlong   A racing distance of one-eighth mile.

Futurity   A race in which the animals entered were nominated before birth.

G

Gait   A particular way of going, either natural or acquired, which is characterized by a distinctive rhythmic movement of the feet and legs.

Gallop   See **Run.**

Galton's Law   The theory of inheritance expounded by Sir Francis Galton (1822–1911). According to this genetic theory, the individual's inheritance is determined as follows: ¼ by its sire and ¼ by its dam; ¹⁄₁₆ by each of the four grandparents; ¹⁄₆₄ by each of the 8 great grandparents; and on and on, with each ancestor contributing just ¼ as much to the total inheritance as did the one a generation nearer to the individual. "Galton's law" is correct in the sense that the relationship between ancestor and descendant is halved with each additional generation which intervenes between them. It is not correct in the sense that the individual's heredity is completely determined by the heredity of its ancestors. Rather, in a random-bred population, the individual is ¼ determined by each parent and ½ determined by chance in Mendelian segregation. Determination by more remote ancestors is included in the determination by the parent. Galton's law is often used as a stamina index by Thoroughbred breeders.

Gamete   A mature sex cell (sperm or egg).

Gaucho   The South American cowboy. In particular, the term is used in the pampas area of Argentina. The gaucho is considered by many to be the world's finest roughrider.

Gear   The equipment and accessories used in harness driving (except the vehicle) and in polo playing (except the bridles and saddles). (See **Tack.**)

Gee   The teamster's term signaling a turn to the right.

Geld   To cut or castrate a male horse.

Gelding   A male horse that was castrated before reaching maturity.

Genotype Selection   Selection of breeding stock not necessarily from the best-appearing animals but from the best-breeding animals, according to genetic makeup.

Germ Plasm   Germ cells and their precursors, bearers of hereditary characters.

Get   Progeny or offspring.

Get-up   The command to go; proceed; move forward. When repeated, it means to increase speed. "Giddap," slang.

Girth   The strap or webbing that holds the saddle or backband in place.

Girth-place   The place for the girth, as the name implies, is marked by a depression in the underline just in back of the front legs.

Glanders (or Farcy)   An acute or chronic infectious disease caused by *Malleomyces mallei,* a bacterium.

Glass-eyed   The term applied to an eye that is devoid of pigment.

Good Mouth   Said of an animal 6 to 10 years of age.

Goose-rumped   An animal having a short, steep croup that narrows at the point of the buttocks.

Grade   An animal of unknown ancestry. If it shows some specific breed characteristics, it may be suffixed with the name of that breed; e.g., grade Shetland.

Grain   Harvested cereals or other edible seeds, including oats, corn, milo, barley, etc.

Granulation   The formation of excess or scar tissue in early wound healing and repair. Also known as "proud flesh."

Gravel   A condition which is usually caused by penetration of the protective covering of the hoof by small bits of gravel or dirt. Access to the sensitive tissue is usually gained by the "white line" or junction of the sole and wall, where the horn is somewhat softer. Once in the soft tissue inside the wall or sole, bacterial infection carried by the foreign material develops rapidly, producing pus and gas which create pressure and intense pain in the foot. In the untreated cases, the abscess breaks out at the top of the coronary band and the pus and gas are forced out through this opening.

Grease Heel (or Scratches)   A low-grade infection affecting the hair follicles and skin at the base of the fetlock joint, most frequently the hind legs. It is similar to scratches, but in a more advanced stage.

Green-broke   A term applied to a horse that has been hitched or ridden only one or two times.

Gummy-legged   Having legs in which the tendons lack definition, or do not stand out clearly.

Gymkhana   A program of games on horseback.

H

Hack   A horse used for riding at an ordinary gait over roads, trails, etc.

Hair   A slender outgrowth of the epidermis which performs a thermoregulatory function, to protect the animal from cold or heat. It becomes long and shaggy during the winter months in cold areas, especially if the horse is left outside. Then, during the warm season, or when the animal is blanketed, the horse sheds and the coat becomes short.

Hair Colors   The five basic horse coat colors are bay, black, brown, chestnut, and white. Additionally, there are five major variations of these colors: dun (buckskin), gray, palomino, pinto (calico or paint), and roan.

Half-bred When capitalized, this denotes a horse sired by a Thoroughbred and registered in the Half-bred Stud Book.

Half-stocking White extends from the coronet to the middle of the cannon.

Halter Puller A horse that pulls back on the halter rope.

Halter Pulling Pulling back on the halter rope when tied in the stable.

Hammer-head A coarse-headed animal.

Hamstrung Disabled by an injury to the tendon above the hock.

Hand A 4-inch unit of measurement. See **Height.**

Hand-canter A semiextended canter, midway between a promenade canter and a gallop.

Hand gallop An extended canter, but the horse remains collected, unlike the flat-out run when the horse's gait almost returns to a four-beat status.

Handicap A race in which chances of winning are equalized by assigned weights; heaviest weights are given to the best horses, and lightest weights to the poorest.

Hard-mouthed Term used when the membrane of the bars of the mouth where the bit rests have become toughened and the nerves deadened because of the continued pressure of the bit.

Hat-rack An emaciated animal.

Haute école See **High School.**

Haw The teamster's term signaling a turn to the left.

Hay Belly Having a distended barrel due to the excessive feeding of bulky rations, such as hay, straw, or grass. Also called "grass belly."

Heat 1. One trip in a race that will be decided by winning two or more trials.
2. A common term for the estrus period.

Heaves Difficulty in forcing air out of the lungs. It is characterized by a jerking of the flanks (double-flank action) and coughing after drinking cold water.

Height Tallness of a horse as measured from the withers to the ground. It is expressed in hands (each hand being 4 inches).

Heredity Characteristics transmitted to offspring from parents and other ancestors.

Hernia (or Rupture) The protrusion of any internal organ through the wall of its containing cavity, but it usually means the passage of a portion of the intestine through an opening in the abdominal muscle.

Herring-gutted (or Shadbelly) Lacking depth of flank, which is also termed "single-gutted."

Heterozygous   Having unlike genes, which can be present for any of the characteristics, such as coat color, size, etc.

Hidebound   Having a hide that is tight over the body.

High School (or Haute école)   The highest form of specialized training of riding horses.

Hippology   The study of the horse.

Hitch   1. To fasten a horse; e.g., when hitched to a rail.
2. Connection between a vehicle and a horse.
3. A defect in gait noted in the hind legs, which seem to skip at the trot.

Hitching   1. Having a shorter stride in one hind leg than in the other.
2. Fastening a horse to an object or vehicle.

Hives   Small swellings under or within the skin, similar to human hives. They appear suddenly over large portions of the body and can be caused by a change in feed.

Hobbles   Straps which encircle the pasterns or fetlock joints on the front legs of the horse and are connected with a short strap or chain to prevent the horse from roaming too far when turned out to graze. Another type of hobble is used on the hind legs (often around the hocks) of a mare in breeding, to prevent her kicking the stallion.

Hogged Mane   A hogged mane is one that has been clipped short.

Homozygous   Having like genes, which can be present for any of the characteristics of the animal, such as coat color, size, etc.

Homozygous Dominant   A dominant character that produces only one kind of gamete.

Homozygous Recessive   A recessive character that produces two kinds of gametes; one carries the dominant gene and the other carries the recessive gene.

Honda   A ring of rope, rawhide, or metal on a lasso through which the loop slides.

Hopples   The term applied to hobbles (leather or plastic straps with semicircular loops) used in harness racing, which are placed on the gaskin and forearm, connecting the fore and hind legs of the same side in pacers, and running diagonally in trotters, connecting the diagonal fore and hind legs. Such hopples, which were invented by a railroad conductor named John Browning in 1885, are used to keep a horse on gait; i.e., to prevent trotters from pacing and pacers from trotting.

Hormone   A body-regulating chemical secreted by a gland into the bloodstream.

Horn Fly   Primarily pests of cattle, but they sometimes seriously annoy horses.

Horse   In the restricted sense this applies to an entire (an ungelded male), not a gelding or mare.

Horsefly   A biting insect that inflicts a painful bite.

Horsemanship   The art of riding horseback.

Horse Meat   In France and Belgium, and other parts of the world, horse meat is considered a delicacy for human consumption. In this country, many horses that have outlived their usefulness or that are less valuable for other purposes are processed in modern sanitary slaughtering plants for pet food.

Horsepower   The historical importance of horses is attested to by the continued use of the term "horsepower." Originally, it was a measure of the power that a horse exerts in pulling. Technically speaking, a horsepower is the rate at which work is accomplished when a resistance (weight) of 33,000 lb. is moved 1 foot in 1 minute, or 550 lb. is moved 1 foot in 1 second. Despite their sophistication, modern motors are rated in horsepower, based on tests made on a machine known as the dynamometer.

Hot-blooded   Of Eastern or Oriental blood.

Hot-walker   One employed to cool out horses.

House Fly   Nonbiting, nuisance insect.

Hunt   Pursuit of game. As used by horsemen, the term usually implies a hunt on horseback with hounds.

Hunt Seat Saddle   Much like the jump saddle, but with less incline to the cantle. A close-contact jumping saddle, also called a "flat" saddle, is often used for hunter and jumper classes and hunt-seat equitation.

Hybrids   Crosses of species, not breeds. The mule is a hybrid — a cross between the horse family and the ass family. Most mules are infertile.

Riding sulky plow, about 1881.

I

Import   To bring horses from another country.

Importing   In registering horses from another country in the registry's stud book of their breeds, the certificates of registration issued bear the abbreviation Imp. and the country of export: e.g., Imp. Hydroplane (Eng.). When a name, such as Hydroplane has been previously granted to a horse foaled (born) in this country, a symbol is added; e.g., Imp. Hydroplane — II (Eng.). Imported is also denoted by an asterisk in front of the name; e.g., *Hydroplane II (Eng.).

Indian-broke   Horses trained to allow mounting from the off side.

Indian Pony   A pinto.

Influenza   A contagious virus disease, characterized by respiratory inflammation, fever, muscle soreness, and often a loss of appetite.

In-hand   Refers to horses shown in halter classes.

Interfering   The striking of the fetlock or cannon by the opposite foot that is in motion is known as interfering. This condition is predisposed in horses with base-narrow, toe-wide, or splay-footed standing positions.

Itch   See **Mange.**

J

Jack   1. A bone spavin.
2. The male of the ass family.

Jack Spavin   See **Bone Spavin.**

Jennet   Female of the ass family.

Jerk Line   A single rein, originally used in western U.S. It was fastened to the brake handle and ran through the driver's hand to the bit of the lead animal.

Jockey Club   Probably the most exclusive club in America, limited to fewer than 100 members. The Jockey Club is custodian of the American Stud Book, registry of Thoroughbred horses.

Jockeys   Professional riders of horses in races. Jockeys are both born and made. They were born to be small people; and they are made as jockeys if they possess courage and intelligence. Jockeys weigh anywhere from 94 to 116 lb., with an average of about 105 lb. A famous observation, which the author once overheard in a jockey's room before a race, was, "What would we all be if it weren't for racing? We'd all be bellhops." But, the jockey might well have added that they would be bellhops anyway if they didn't have the courage to ride down a track at 40 miles an hour, delicately balanced in a pair of short stirrups, amid 48 flying steel plates (shoes) and six thundering tons of horseflesh — calmly, but in a split second, planning every move as they ride.

They're off! At the starting gate, the bell rings, the little doors fly open, the jockey yells, hunches foward, and urges with all his might as the horse plunges forward — all in a split second. (Courtesy, *From Dawn to Destiny*, by Frank Jennings and Allen F. Brewer, Jr., published by The Thoroughbred Press, Lexington, Kentucky)

Jockey Stick   A stick fastened to the hame of the near horse and the bit of the off horse for use in driving with a single rein to prevent crowding.

Jog Cart   A cart longer and heavier than a racing sulky, used in warm-up miles because it's more comfortable for the driver than a sulky.

Jogging   A slow warm-up exercise of several miles with the horse going the wrong way of the track.

Joint Ill   See **Navel Infection.**

Jughead   A stupid horse. Also one with a large, ugly head.

Jump Seat Saddle   A saddle with a high cantle (back) which inclines the rider's weight forward to keep in balance with the horse when going over jumps. It usually has forward flaps with knee rolls to help maintain balance.

K

Kick   Movement by a horse of the back legs, with intent to hit a person, horse, or other object.

Knee-sprung (or Buck-kneed)   A condition of over in the knees, or with the knees protruding too far forward.

L

Lameness   A defect that can be detected when the affected foot is favored when standing. In action, the load on the ailing foot is eased, and there is a characteristic bobbing of the head of the horse as the affected foot strikes the ground.

Laminae   The flat tissue in the sole or base of the hoof.

Laminitis (or Founder)   An inflammation of the sensitive laminae of the hoof. All feet may be affected, but the front feet are most susceptible.

Lead   The leading foot (leg) of a horse under saddle. When cantering circularly, the foot to the inner arc of the circle — clockwise, a right-foot lead; and counterclockwise, a left-foot lead. In counter-canter, the horse is on the outside lead instead of the inside lead.

Lead Line   A chain, rope, or strap, or combination thereof, used for leading a horse.

Leaders   The head team in a four-, six-, or eight-horse hitch.

Leathers   The straps running from the saddle to the irons on an English saddle.

Left Lead   Left front foot and left rear foot lead on the canter.

Leg Bracer   A solution, lotion, or liniment containing a large amount of alcohol used as a stimulant for the legs, causing increased blood circulation to the applied area.

Legs Out of the Same Hole   Very narrow-fronted. Such horses usually stand base wide; i.e., the feet stand wider apart than the distance across the legs at the chest.

Levade   An exercise of the haute école, especially as performed in the Spanish Riding School at Vienna. In the levade the horse is in a half rearing position, with the forelegs well bent and the hind legs in a crouching position.

Lice   Small, flattened, wingless insect parasites.

Lineback   An animal having a stripe of distinctive color along the spine.

Lines (or Reins)   A leather strap, webbing, or rope attached to the bit or bits for control and direction. In driving, lines are sometimes called reins. In riding, reins are never called lines.

Lip Strap   The small strap running through the curb chain from one side of the bit shank to the other. Its primary function is to keep the horse from taking the shank or the bit in its teeth.

Lockjaw   See **Tetanus.**

Long-coupled   Too much space between the last rib and the point of the hip.

Longe   The act of exercising a horse on the end of a long rope or line, usually in a circle.

Lope   The Western adaptation of a very slow canter. It is a smooth, slow gait in which the head is carried low.

Lop-neck   See **Broken Crest.**

Lugger   A horse that pulls at the bit.

Lugging and Pulling   Some horses pull on the reins, "lug" on one rein, or bear out or in with the driver, making it hard to drive them and to rate the mile at an even clip.

Lunge   See **Longe.**

Lungworms (*Dictyocaulus arnfieldi*)   Lungworms may be found in the air passages of the horse and other equines. The male worm reaches a length of about 1 inch and the female may be about 2 inches long. The equine lungworm is very rare in the U.S.

M

Maiden   1. A mare that has never been bred.
2. On the racetrack, it refers to a horse (stallion, mare, or gelding) that has not won a race on a recognized track; and in the show ring, it refers to a horse or rider that has not won a first-place ribbon in a recognized show in the division in which he or she is showing.

Mane   Long hair on the top of the neck.

Mange (or Scabies, Scab, or Itch)   A specific contagious disease caused by mites.

Manners   A way of behaving.

Mare   A mature female four years or older; in Thoroughbreds, five years or older.

Mascot   A companion for a horse. The most common mascots are ponies, goats, dogs, cats, and chickens.

Matron   A mare that has produced a foal.

Mites   Very small parasites that cause mange (scabies, scab, and itch).

Mixed-gaited   Said of a horse that will not adhere to any one true gait at a time.

Mohammed's Ten Horses   In the days of Mohammed, intelligence and obedience were the main requisites of the Arab's horse. For war purposes, only the most obedient horses were used, and they were trained to follow the bugle.

Legend has it that the Prophet himself had need for some very obedient horses, so he inspected a certain herd to make personal selections.

The horses from which he wished to make selections were pastured in a large area bordering on a river. The Prophet gave orders that the animals should be fenced off from the river until their thirst became very great. Then, he ordered the fence removed, and the horses rushed for the water. When they were just about to dash into the river to quench their thirst, a bugle was sounded.

All but 10 of the horses ignored the call of the bugle. The obedient 10 turned and answered the call of duty, despite their great thirst. The whimsical story goes on to say that these 10 head constituted the foundation of the "Prophet Strain."

Moon Blindness (or Periodic Ophthalmia)   A cloudy or inflamed condition of the eye which disappears and returns in cycles that are often completed in about a month.

Morning Glory   A horse that works out in record time in the morning but does not live up to its promise in an actual race.

Mosquito   A biting insect.

Mottled   Marked with spots of different colors; dappled, spotted.

Mounting   The act of getting on a horse.

Mouthing   Determining the approximate age of a horse by examining the teeth.

Mudder   A horse that runs well on a track that is wet, sloppy, or heavy.

Mustang   Native horse of the Western Plains.

Mutation   A sudden variation which is later passed on through inheritance and which results from changes in a gene or genes.

Mutton-withered   Low in the withers, with heavy shoulder muscling.

Muzzle   The lower end of the nose, which includes the nostrils, lips, and chin.

N

Narragansett Pacer   A fast type of pacer, descended from the indigenous horse of Narragansett Bay area of Rhode Island and evolved during the time of the Revolutionary War (1775–1781). During this period, racing was illegal except in Rhode Island.

Navel Ill   See **Navel Infection.**

Navel Infection (or Joint Ill, Navel Ill, Actinobacillosis)   An infectious disease of newborn animals caused by several kinds of bacteria.

Navicular Disease   An inflammation of the small navicular bone and bursa of the front foot. It is often impossible to determine the exact cause of the disease. Affected animals go lame; have a short stubby stride; and usually point the affected foot when standing. Few animals completely recover from the disease. Treatment consists of special shoeing. In cases of persistent and severe lameness, unnerving may be performed by a veterinarian to destroy the sensation in the foot.

Near Side   The left side of a horse.

The custom of working from the left side of the horse evolved quite logically in two ways:

1. In the days when horsemen wore swords, they hung to the left. Hence, the sword would have interfered with the rider by hanging between his legs had he tried mounting from the right.

2. In England, traffic keeps to the left. Therefore, when working around horses the coachman stood on the left side if possible in order to be on the side of the road and out of the line of traffic.

In both the above situations horsemen were most often on the left side of horses; hence, logically it became known as the "near side," and the right side became the "off" side. With a team of horses, the one on the left is the "near" horse, the one on the right is the "off" horse.

Neck Rein   To guide or direct a horse by pressure of the rein on the neck.

Neigh   The loud, prolonged call of a horse.

O

Off Side   The right side of a horse.

Open Bridle   Bridle without blinds or blinkers covering the eyes. Some bridles are rigged with blinds that shut off vision to the rear and side and a few horses are raced with goggles or "peekaboo" blinds.

Open-hocked   Wide apart at the hocks with the feet close together.

Oriental   See **Eastern.**

Orloff Trotter   A breed of horses originating in Russia (now the U.S.S.R.) in the 18th century, principally through the interest of Count Alexis Gregory Orloff Chesminski. Used in the Soviet Union for light work, pleasure driving and riding, exhibition at fairs in various forms of competition including dressage, and extensively in harness racing.

Osselets   A rather inclusive term used to refer to a number of inflammatory conditions around the ankle joints. Generally it denotes a swelling that is fairly well defined and located slightly above or below the actual center of the joint, and, ordinarily, a little to the inside or outside of the exact front of the leg. When touched, it imparts the feeling of putty or mush, and it may be warm to hot. The pain will be in keeping with the degree of inflammation as evidenced by swelling and fever. Afflicted horses travel with a short choppy stride and show evidence of pain when the ankle is flexed.

Outlaw   A horse that cannot be broken.

Ovary   The female organ that produces eggs. There are two ovaries.

Overreach   The hitting of the forefoot with the hind foot.

Overshot Jaw (or Parrot Mouth)   The upper jaw protruding beyond the lower jaw.

Ovulation   The time when the follicle bursts and the egg is released.

Ovum   Scientific name for egg.

P

Pace   A fast, two-beat gait in which the front and hind feet on the same side start and stop simultaneously.

Paddling   Throwing the front feet outward as they are picked up. This condition is predisposed in horses with toe-narrow or pigeon-toed standing positions.

Pair   1. Two horses hitched abreast.
2. Used in reference to two horses ridden side by side, as in pair classes.

Palisade Worms   See **Strongyles, Large and Small.**

Pari-mutuels   Machine-controlled pool betting, invented in France in 1865, by a perfume-shop proprietor named Pierre Oller, who, embittered by a losing streak with the bookies, worked out the idea of the betting pool and began selling tickets over his store counter. His take was five percent; the rest was divided equally among the winners.

Parrot Mouth   See **Overshot Jaw.**

Passage   1. A movement of the haute école. This is a slow, cadenced, rather high trot with a fairly long period of suspension, giving the impression that the horse is on springs, or "trotting on air."
2. A term for diagonal movement of the horse while facing straight forward, at the walk or trot.

Pastern   That part of the leg between the fetlock joint and the coronary band of the hoof.

Pedigree   A record of the ancestry of an animal.

Pedigree Breeding   Selection on the combined bases of the merits of the individual and the average merits of its ancestry.

Pegasus   A word of Greek origin, meaning strong. Legend has it that the winged horse, Pegasus, was fashioned from the body of Medusa, daughter of a sea-god who, in her youth, was as mortal as she was beautiful. At his birth, the frisky colt flew to Mount Helicon, where he created a fountain (Horsewell) with one swift blow of his hoof. Using a golden bridle, Bellerophon coaxed the curious animal from his favorite meadow, made him captive, and rode him off. Later, Pegasus unceremoniously dumped his venerable and conceited master and flew into outer space where he became the constellation that bears his name.

Pelham Bit   A one-piece bit equipped to handle four reins. Two are snaffle reins, used for guiding the horse and lifting the head; and two are curb reins, used for control and for setting the head. Snaffle reins are always heavier than curb reins.

Periodic Ophthalmia   See **Moon Blindness.**

Piaffe   A dressage movement in which the horse does a cadenced trot in place, without moving from the spot. It is the foundation of all high-school movements.

Piebald   Refers to black-and-white coat color.

Pigeon-toed   Pointing toes inward and heels outward.

Pig-eyed   Having small, narrow, squinty eyes, set back in the head; also, having thick eyelids.

Pin-firing   A method of inserting an electric needle into an injured area. This induces healing at the site.

Pinto   A multicolored, spotted horse.

Pinworms (*Oxyuris equi, Probstmyria vivipara*)   Two species of pinworms, or rectal worms, frequently are found in horses. *Oxyuris equi* are whitish worms with long, slender tails. *Probstmyria vivipara* are so small they are scarcely visible to the eye.

Pirouette   A dressage exercise in which the horse holds its forelegs more or less in place while it moves its hindquarters around them.

Pivot   A movement in dressage in which the horse pivots around its hindquarters, holding one hind leg more or less in place and sidestepping with the other hind foot.

Place   To finish second in a race.

Placenta   The membrane by which the fetus is attached to the uterus. Nutrients from the mother pass into the placenta and then through the navel cord to the fetus. When the animal is born, the placenta is expelled. It is commonly called the "afterbirth."

Plug   A horse of common breeding and poor conformation.

Point   The team in back of the leaders in an eight-horse hitch.

Pointing   1. Perceptible extension of the stride with little flexion is called pointing. This condition is likely to occur in the Thoroughbred and Standardbred breeds — animals bred and trained for great speed with a long stride.
2. Referring to a standing position when one of the front legs is extended ahead of the other. This occurs when a horse with a sore foot places the ailing foot ahead in order to take the weight off it.

Points   Black coloration from the knees and hocks down, as in most bays and browns, and in some buckskins, roans, and grays.

Poll Evil   An inflamed condition in the region of the poll (the area on top of the neck and immediately behind the ears), usually caused by bruising the top of the head.

Polo Pony   A "pony" used for playing polo. Polo ponies of today are mostly of Thoroughbred breeding. They must be fast, and tough and courageous enough to stand the bumping, riding-off, and the many quick stops and turns.

Pop-eyed   Refers to a horse whose eyes are generally more prominent or bulge out a little more than normal; also to a horse that is "spooky" or attempts to see everything that goes on.

Popped Knee   A general term describing inflammatory conditions affecting the knees, so named because of the sudden swelling that accompanies it.

Post   The starting point of a race.

Posting   The rising and descending of the rider with the rhythm of the trot.

Post Position   Refers to race starting position. Beginning with position number 1 nearest the rail, horses line up at the starting gate according to number.

Poultice   A moist, mealy mass, applied hot to a sore or inflamed part of the body.

Pounding   A "heavy foot" contact with the ground, common in high-going horses.

Prepotency   Refers to breeding power, as measured by the degree in which parent likeness is transmitted to offspring.

Produce   Offspring.

Progenitor   One that originates or precedes.

Progeny   Refers to offspring or descendants of one or both parents.

Puffs   Wind galls, bog spavins, or thoroughpins.

Pulled Tail   A tail thinned by hairs being pulled.

Pulling Record, World   The world's record in pulling contest was established in the 1965 Hillsdale County Fair, in Michigan. It is held jointly by Frank Vurckio, Sun Down, New York; Fowler Bros., Montgomery, Michigan. It was made on a dynamometer with a tractive pull of 4,350 lb. (equal to 56,493 lb., over 28 tons, on a wagon).

Purebred   An animal descended from a list of ancestors of the same breed but not necessarily registered. This should not be confused with "Thoroughbred," a breed of horse.

Purse   Race prize money to which the owners of horses in the race do not contribute.

Q

Quality   Refinement, as shown in a neat and well-chiseled head, fine texture of hair with little or no fetlock, clean bone, good texture of hoof, etc.

Quarter Crack (or Sand Crack)   A vertical split in the horny wall of the inside of the hoof (in the region of the quarter), which extends from the coronet or hoof head downward.

Quittor   A deep-seated running sore which occurs on the coronet band or hoof head. It is caused initially by an injury or puncture wound in the area of the sole of the foot.

R

Rack (or Single-foot)   A fast, flashy, unnatural, four-beat gait in which each foot meets the ground separately at equal intervals; hence, it was originally known as the "single-foot," a designation now largely discarded.

Random   Three horses hitched in single file, usually to a dogcart.

Rangy   Elongated, lean, muscular, of slight build.

Rat Tail   A tail with a short hair coat.

Rattlers   Rattlers (wooden, rubber, or plastic balls) or links of light chain fastened about the pasterns of high-going harness and saddle horses and ponies. Weighted boots are also used to enhance action.

Reata   Spanish for lariat.

Recessive Character   A characteristic which appears only when both members of a pair of genes are alike. Opposite of dominant.

Red Worms   See STRONGYLES, LARGE AND SMALL.

Reins   See **Lines**.

Remuda   A collection of riding horses at a roundup from which are chosen those used for the day. A relay of mounts.

Ribbed-up   Said of a horse on which the back ribs are well arched and incline well backwards, bringing the ends closer to the point of the hip and making the horse shorter in coupling.

Ridgeling   A horse with at least one testicle in the abdomen. A ridgeling is difficult to geld, and often retains the characteristics of a stallion. Also called a cryptorchid.

Right Lead   Right front foot and right rear lead on the canter.

Ringbone   A bony growth on the pastern bone in the area of the coronet. It is generally on the forefoot, although occasionally the hind foot is affected.

Ringer   A horse passed off under false identity, with the idea of entering it in a race below its class where it is almost certain to win.

With today's lip tattoo system of identification, ringers are a thing of the past.

Ringworm   This is a contagious infection of the outer layers of skin caused by an infestation of microscopic fungi.

Roach-backed   Arched-backed, razor-backed.

Roached Mane   A mane that has been cut short and tapered so that it stands upright. It is not so short as a clipped mane.

Roarer   A wind-broken animal that makes a loud noise in drawing air into the lungs, especially when respiration is speeded up with exercise.

Rollers (Rattlers)   Wooden balls on a cord, encircling a horse's pastern to give more action.

Rolling   Excessive lateral shoulder motion, characteristic of horses with protruding shoulders, is known as rolling.

Roman-nosed   Refers to a horse having a profile that is convex from poll to muzzle.

Rope-walking   See **Winding.**

Roundworms, Large (or Ascarids) (*Parascaris equorum*)   The female varies from 6 to 22 inches long and the male from 5 to 13 inches. When full grown, both are about the diameter of a lead pencil.

Rubdown   A rubbing of the body with a rough towel, usually given after exercise, to promote circulation and remove fatigue.

Run (Gallop)   The run, or gallop, is a fast, four-beat gait where the feet strike the ground separately; first one hind foot, then the other hind foot, then the front foot on the same side as the first hind foot, then the other front foot, which decides the lead.

Running Walk   A slow, four-beat gait, intermediate in speed between the walk and rack. The hind foot oversteps the front foot from a few to as many as 18 inches, giving the motion a smooth gliding effect. It is characterized by a bobbing or nodding of the head, a flopping of the ears, and a snapping of the teeth in rhythm with the movement of the legs.

Rupture   See **Hernia.**

S

Saline   Consisting of or containing salt.

Saliva Test   The testing of saliva for the presence of drugs or narcotics.

Sand Crack   See **Quarter Crack.**

Scab   See **Mange.**

Scabies   See **Mange.**

Scalping   That condition in which the hairline at the top of the hind foot hits the toe of the forefoot as it breaks over.

Schooling   Training and developing natural characteristics in a pony.

Sclerostomes   See **Strongyles, Large and Small.**

Scoring   Preliminary warming up of horses before the start. The horses are turned near the starting point and hustled away as they will be in the race.

Scotch Collar   Housing over the collar of draft show harness.

Scraper   A metal or wooden tool, slightly concave, shaped like a hook at the upper end and used with one hand for scraping sweat and liquid from the body. Also, a thin metal strip with handles affixed at either end, used with both hands for scraping sweat and liquid from the body.

Scratches   See **Grease Heel.**

Screwworm   Maggots of the screwworm fly, which require living flesh of animals on which to feed.

Scrotum   The sac-like pouch of the male animal that suspends the testicles outside the body.

Scrub   A low-grade animal.

Self-colored   A term applied to the mane and tail when they are the same color as the body coat.

Sell at Halter   To sell with no guarantee except the title.

Semen   Sperm mixed with fluids from the accessory glands.

Serviceably Sound   Said of a horse that has nothing wrong that will materially impair its value for the intended use.

Sesamoid Fractures   The fracture of one or both of the two pyramid-like bones that form a part of the fetlock or ankle joints (on both front and rear legs) and articulate with the posterior part of the lower end of the cannon bone.

Set-tail   A tail in which the cords have been cut or "nicked" and the tail put in a set.

Sex Cells   The egg and the sperm, which unite to create life. They transmit genetic characteristics from the parents to the offspring.

Shadbelly   See **Herring-gutted.**

Shoe-boil (or Capped Elbow)   A soft, flabby swelling at the point of the elbow; hence, the common name "capped elbow." It is usually caused by contact with the shoe when the horse is lying down.

Short-coupled   Describes a horse having a short distance (usually not more than four fingers' width) between the last rib and the point of the hip.

Show   Finishing third in a race.

Show Bridle   Same as Weymouth bridle, but the leather usually is cut finer and the bits often are more severe.

Sickle-hocked   The hind legs set too far forward, giving the impression of a sickle when viewed from the side.

Sidebones   Ossified lateral cartilages immediately above and toward the rear quarter of the hoof head. They occur most commonly in the forefeet.

Side Step   See **Traverse.**

Sign   The word used when speaking of animal symptoms. Animals show "signs" of abnormality, whereas people can relate their symptoms of ill health. In horses, one must observe these signs.

Single-foot   Now called a "rack." See RACK.

Sire   The male parent.

Sisters   See **Brothers.**

Skewbald   Refers to coat color other than black — such as bay, brown, or chestnut — combined with white.

Skirt   That part of the saddle against which the knees and calves of the rider are placed.

Slab-sided   Flat-ribbed.

Sleeping Sickness   See **Encephalomyelitis.**

Sloping Shoulders   Shoulders properly angulated and laid back.

Slow Pace   See **Stepping Pace.**

Smoky Eye   A whitish-clouded eye. See **Walleye.**

Smooth   Unshod, "barefoot."

Smooth Coat   Short, hard, close-fitting coat of hair.

Smooth-mouthed   No cups in the teeth. Indicates a horse is 12 years of age or older.

Snaffle Bit   A mouthpiece with a joint in the center. The ring may be either circular or D-shaped. The most widely used of all bits.

Snip   A white mark between the nostrils or on the lip.

Snorter   An excitable horse.

Soft   Easily fatigued.

Solid Color   Having no white markings.

Sound   Said of a horse free from injury, flaw, mutilation, or decay; also one that is guaranteed free from blemishes and unsoundnesses.

Spavin   See **Blood Spavin, Bog Spavin,** and **Bone Spavin.**

Spay   To remove a mare's ovaries.

Speck in Eye   A spot in the eye, but not covering the pupil. It may or may not impair the vision. See **Feather in Eye.**

Speedy Cutting   A condition of a horse at speed in which a hind leg above the scalping mark hits against the shoe of a breaking-over fore-foot. In trotters, legs on the same side are involved. In pacers, diagonal legs are involved.

Sperm (Sperm Cell)   Male sex cell produced in the testicles.

Splenic Fever   See **Anthrax.**

Splints   Abnormal body growths found on the cannon bone, usually on the inside surface, but occasionally on the outside. They are most common on the front legs.

Spooky   Nervous.

Sprinter   A horse that performs best at distances of a mile or under.

Spurs   The artificial aid worn over a boot, used to achieve a desired result when riding.

Stable Fly   A biting insect that bites principally on the legs.

Stag   A male horse that was castrated after reaching maturity.

Stake Races   A stake, short for sweepstake, is just what the name implies. Each owner puts up an equal amount of money (nominating fees, fees for keeping them eligible, and starting fees) and the winner takes all. Also, the track usually puts up added money. Actually, few stake races are run on a winner-take-all basis; rather, the money is divided between the first four horses.

Stall   Space or compartment in which an animal is placed or con-fined. It may be a straight stall with the animal tied at the front end (a tie-stall) or a compartment with the animal loose inside (box-stall).

Stallion   A male horse four years old or older; in Thoroughbreds, five years old or over.

Standing Halter   Similar to a martingale, it is a strap that runs from the girth to a tight halter on the horse's head. It helps keep the horse from throwing its head up and going into a break.

Star   Any white mark on the forehead located above a line running from eye to eye.

Stargazer   A horse that holds its head high in an awkward position.

Steeplechaser   A horse used in cross-country racing with jumps.

Stepping Pace (or Slow Pace)   A modified pace in which the objec-tionable side or rolling motion of the true pace is eliminated because the 2 feet on each side do not move exactly together. Instead, it is a 4-beat gait with each of the 4 feet striking the ground separately.

Sterile   A term used to designate a stallion that is infertile.

Stifle   The counterpart of the knee joint in man. The junction of the horse's tibia and patella in the hind leg.

Stifled   A horse is said to be stifled when the patella (or kneecap) slips out of place and temporarily locks in a location above and to the inside of its normal location.

Stirrup Iron   The metal D-shaped device on the saddle through which the leather runs and on which the foot rests.

Stock Horse   In the West this term designates a cow horse. In other localities it can also mean a stallion used at stud.

Stocking   White extends from the coronet to the knee. When the white includes the knee, it is known as a full stocking.

Stomach Worms (*Habronema* spp., *Trichostrongylus axei*)   A group of parasitic worms that produces inflammation of the stomach.

Straight Shoulder   Said of shoulder lacking sufficient angulation.

Strangles   A widespread contagious disease of horses, especially among young animals, caused by *Streptococcus equi*, a bacterium.

Stride   The distance covered by one foot when in motion. Greyhound, with a trotting record at 1:55¼, had a stride of more than 27 feet.

Stringhalt   A condition characterized by excessive flexing of the hind legs. It is most easily detected when backing a horse.

Stripe   A narrow white marking that extends from about the line of the eyes to the nostrils.

Strongyles, Large and Small (*Strongylus* spp. and others)   There are about 60 species of strongyles. Three are large worms that grow up to 2 inches long. The rest are small and some are barely visible to the eye. Large strongyles are variously called bloodworms (*Strongylus vulgaris*), palisade worms, sclerostomes, and red worms.

Stud   1. A male horse (stallion) kept for breeding.
2. Also, an establishment or farm where animals are kept for breeding.

Stud Book   The permanent book of breeding records.

Stump Sucking   See **Cribber.**

Substance   A combination of good bone, muscularity, and width and depth of body.

Suckling   A foal that is not weaned.

Sulky or Bike   Light racing rig with bicycle-type wheels used in harness races. The sulkies weigh from 29 to 37 lb., and usually have hardwood shafts, although aluminum and steel sulkies have been introduced recently.

Summer Sores   These are irritated spreading sores which develop from a wound. The sore may be as small as a dime but will enlarge rapidly within a week's time.

Surcingle   A belt, band, or girth passing over a saddle or over anything on a horse's back to bind the saddle fast.

Suspensory Ligament Sprain   The suspensory ligament is situated over the back of the leg and passes over the fetlock or ankle joint, both in the forelegs and hind legs. Its principal function is to support the fetlock. This ligament is frequently the object of severe strain; the swelling begins just above the fetlock and extends obliquely downward and forward over the sides of the fetlock. Should the injury be further up on the leg, the exact location at first may appear obscure, as the ligament is covered by the flexor tendons.

When the suspensory ligament is affected, the swelling will be found right up against the bone. If it is the flexor tendons that are involved, the swelling will be farther back, near the surface on the back of the leg.

Swamp Fever   See **Equine Infectious Anemia.**

Swan Neck   A long, slim, swanlike neck.

"Swap Horses in Midstream"   The origin of the saying, "Don't swap horses in midstream," appears to be clouded in obscurity.

Upon being congratulated when renominated for the presidency, Lincoln said, "I do not allow myself to suppose that either the convention or the league have concluded to decide that I am either the greatest or the best man in America, but rather they have concluded it is not best to swap horses while crossing the river, and have further concluded that I am not so poor a horse that they might not make a botch of it in trying to swap." One historian of that period credited the utterance to a Dutch farmer; and H. L. Mencken reports that the phrase was used some 24 years earlier than when Lincoln used it.

Swaybacked   Having a decided dip in the back. Also termed "easy-backed" and "saddle-backed."

Sweat Scraper   An instrument for removing excess sweat from a hard-worked horse.

Sweeney   A depression in the shoulder due to atrophied muscles.

Sweet Feed   Refers to horse feed which is characterized by its sweetness due to the addition of molasses; usually a commercial horse feed mixture.

Swing Team   The middle team in a six-horse hitch, or the team in front of the wheelers in an eight-horse hitch.

Swipe   Racetrack slang for a groom, stable hand, or exercise boy.

Synovial Fluid   The fluid that lubricates the joint.

T

Tack   Equipment used in riding and driving horses, such as saddles, bridles, harness, etc.

Tack Room   Place for storage of tack and accessories used in riding or driving. Also a display room for pictures, prizes, ribbons, trophies, and the like.

Tail, Styles   A tail is banged if the hair is cut off in a straight line below the dock; it is thinned if it is shortened; and it is thinned and tapered if the hairs are pulled and broken.

Tail Female   The female line, or bottom line of a pedigree.

Tail Male   The sire line, or top line in a pedigree.

Tail Rubbing   Persistent rubbing of the tail against the side of the stall or other objects.

Tail-set   A crupperlike contrivance, with a shaped section for the tail, which brings the tail high so that it can be doubled and tied down, to give it an arch and extremely high carriage; but a tail so set must first be "nicked" to give such results. The set is worn most of the time while the horse is in the stable, and until a short time before the horse is to be shown. Horses with set tails are sometimes "gingered" before entering the ring, in order to assure high tail carriage while being shown.

Tally Ho   The cry of the hunt once the fox is sighted.

Tandem   Said of two horses, one hitched in front of the other.

Tapadera   A long, decorative covering over the stirrup used in parade classes.

Tapeworms (*Anoplocephala magna, A. perfoliata, Paranoplocephala mamillana*)   Internal parasites of horses, of which there are three species. *Anoplocephala perfoliata* is the most common and most damaging.

Teaser   A horse, usually a stallion or a ridgeling, used to test the response of a mare prior to breeding, or used to determine if a mare is in heat and ready to breed.

Temperament   Refers to the horse's suitability for the job it is to perform.

Temperature   Normal rectal temperature for the horse is 100.5° F. Normal range is 99.0–100.8° F.

Testicle   A male gland which produces sperm. There are two testicles.

Tetanus (or Lockjaw)   Chiefly a wound-infection disease caused by a powerful toxin, more than 100 times as toxic as strychnine, that is liberated by the bacterium *Clostridium tetani*, an anaerobe.

Thick Wind   Difficulty in breathing.

Thong   The lash of the whip.

Thoroughpin   A puffy condition in the web of the hock. It can be determined by movement of the puff, when pressed, to the opposite side of the leg. The swelling is more or less rounded or oval in shape and can be observed from both sides.

Threadworms (*Strongyloides westeri*)   Parasites; they are known as strongyloides.

Thrifty Condition   Healthy, active, vigorous.

Throatlatch   The narrow strap of the bridle, which goes under the horse's throat and is used to secure the bridle to the head.

Thrush   A disease of the foot, caused by a necrotic fungus characterized by a pungent odor. It is most commonly found in the hind feet and is caused by unsanitary conditions in the animal's stall. Thrush causes a deterioration of tissues in the cleft of the frog or in the junction between the frog and bars. This disease produces lameness and, if not treated, can be serious.

Ticks   External insects, several kinds of which may be found on the horses. The most common ones are the winter tick, *Dermacentor albipictus;* the lone star tick, *Amblyomma americanum;* and the spinose ear tick, *Otobius megnini.*

Tie   To attach or fasten by use of halter and a shank.

Toe Weight   A metal weight (knob) fitted to a spur previously placed on the front hoof to induce a change of balance in motion. Used extensively in the training and racing of harness horses.

Tongue-loller   A horse whose tongue hangs out.

Tooth Rasp   A file with a long handle, used for floating or removing sharp edges from the teeth.

Totalizator   The mechanical "brains" of the pari-mutuel system.

Tote Board   The indicator board of the totalizator on which is flashed all pari-mutuel information before or after a race.

Tout   A low-order con man who peddles tips, betting systems, etc., to the unwary racegoer.

Traces   The parts of a harness which run from the collar to the singletree.

Tracheotomy   An operation on the throat to cure roaring, or to keep a horse from suffocating in an emergency.

Trail Ride   A cross-country ride over paths or unimproved roads. On competitive rides the horse must work over or through obstacles and (usually) hilly terrain and its fitness to continue is verified at certain checkpoints.

Trappy   A short, quick, choppy stride. This condition is predisposed in horses with short, straight pasterns and straight shoulders.

Traverse (or Side Step)   The traverse or side step is simply a lateral movement of the animal to the right or left as desired, without moving forward or backward.

Troika   The word "troika" is a Russian word meaning trio or three. A troika hitch is a three-horse combination team hitched to a vehicle; e.g., a carriage, wagon, sleigh, or sled. The carriage is the vehicle of common use and it is known as a caleche. It is a light four-wheeled two-passenger vehicle with an elevated seat for the driver.

Trot   A natural, rapid, two-beat, diagonal gait in which the front foot and the opposite hind foot take off at the same split second and strike the ground simultaneously.

Tucked-up   Having the belly under the loin. Refers also to a small-waisted horse. Differs from "herring-gutted" and similar conditions in that a horse may be "tucked-up" temporarily due to hard work, lack of water, lack of bulk in the diet, etc. Also, called "gaunted-up" or "ganted-up."

Twitch   A rope run through the end of a stick, used on the horse's upper lip; it is tightened by twisting in order to attract the horse's attention so it will stand still.

Two-track   The horse moves forward and diagonally at the same time.

"Tying-up" (*Azoturia*, black-water, Monday-morning disease)   The "tying-up" syndrome is characterized by muscle rigidity and lameness affecting the muscles of the croup and loin, accompanied by pain, disinclination to move, a variable temperature, and brownish-colored urine. The cause is unknown, although it does seem to be associated with nervousness and an imbalance between diet, conditioning, and exercise.

Type   Type may be defined as an ideal or standard of perfection combining all the characteristics that contribute to the animal's usefulness for a specific purpose.

U

Underpinning   The legs and feet of the horse.

Undershot Jaw   The lower jaw is longer than the upper jaw.

Unicorn   An unusual three-horse hitch with two horses hitched as a pair and a third hitched in front of the pair.

Unsoundnesses   Those more serious abnormalities that affect the serviceability of the horse.

Utility Saddle   A saddle that is between the jump seat and the show seat and is designed for general purpose use, except jumping.

V

Vesicular Stomatitis   A contagious disease of the mouth caused by a virus.

Veterinarian   One who treats diseases or afflictions of animals medically and surgically; a practitioner of veterinary medicine or surgery.

Vice   Any of the multitude of bad habits that a horse may acquire.

Viceroy   A lightweight, cut-under, wire-wheeled show vehicle with curved dash, used for some heavy harness classes, and especially for Hackney Ponies, Shetlands, and Harness Show Ponies.

W

Walk   A natural, slow, flatfooted, four-beat gait; the latter meaning that each foot takes off from and strikes the ground at a separate interval.

Walleye (or Smoky Eye)   Also termed glass, blue, china, or crockery eye; refers to lack of color in a horse's eye.

Warm-up, Warming Up   The process or routine of graduated exercise until the horse is properly conditioned for a more strenuous effort.

Weanling   A weaned foal.

Weaving   A rhythmical swaying back and forth while standing in the stall. The prevention and cure are exercise, with ample room and freedom from stress.

Weymouth Bridle   A double bridle in which the snaffle bit and the curb bit are separate.

Wheelers   The team on the pole or tongue, hitched directly in front of a rig or wagon in a four-or-more-horse hitch.

Whinny   The horse's sound that denotes happiness, or anticipation of more pleasure.

Whip   1. An instrument or device of wood, bone, plastic, leather, fiber glass, metal, or combination thereof with a loop or cracker of leather or cord at the upper end; used for disciplining or goading an animal. Sometimes a required accessory when exhibiting (driving), as in a horse show.
2. One who handles a whip expertly, one who drives a horse in harness other than racing, or one who "whips in" or manages the hounds of a hunt club.

Whip (in the Senate)   The term "whip" is derived from the British fox-hunting term "whipper-in," the Huntsman's principal assistant whose job is to keep the hounds from leaving the pack. The principal job of the whip in the U.S. Senate is to round up the party's senators for important votes and to try to make sure that they vote in keeping with the wishes of the party leaders.

White Line   The union between the sole and the wall of the foot.

Whoa   The command to stop; stand. When repeated softly, means to slow down, but may also mean attention.

Windgall   See **Windpuffs.**

Winding (or Rope-walking)   A twisting of the striding leg around in front of the supporting leg so as to make contact in the manner of a "rope-walking" artist is known as winding or rope-walking. This condition most often occurs in horses with very wide fronts.

Windpuffs (or Windgall)   An enlargement of the fluid sac (bursa) located immediately above the pastern joints on the fore and rear legs. They are usually the result of too fast or too hard road work, especially on hard surfaces.

Wind Sucking   See **Cribber.**

Windy (or Wind-broken)   Said of an animal that whistles or roars when exerted.

Winging   Winging is an exaggerated paddling, particularly noticeable in high-going horses.

Wrangling   Rounding up range horses.

Y

Yearling   A horse between one and two years of age.

APPENDIXES

HORSE BOOKS

Without claiming that either all or the best horse books are listed, the books that follow are recommended as the kind that will provide valuable reference material for the horseman's bookshelf and enhance the home library.

America's Quarter Horses, P. Laune, Doubleday & Co., Inc., Garden City, NY, 1973.

Anatomy and Conformation of the Horse, G. B. Edwards, Dreenan Press Ltd., Croton-on-Hudson, NY, 1973.

Anatomy and Physiology of Farm Animals, R. D. Frandsen, Lea & Febiger, Philadelphia, PA, 1965.

Anatomy of the Domestic Animals, S. Sisson, W. B. Saunders Co., Philadelphia, PA, 1953.

Anatomy of the Horse, The, R. F. Way and D. G. Lee, J. B. Lippincott Co., Philadelphia, PA, 1965.

Animal Behavior, 2nd ed., J. P. Scott, The University of Chicago Press, Chicago, IL, 1972.

Animal Breeding Plans, J. L. Lush, Collegiate Press, Inc., Ames, IA, 1963.

Animal Disease and Human Health, J. H. Steele, Food and Agriculture Organization of the United Nations, Rome, Italy, 1962.

Animal Parasitism, C. P. Read, Prentice-Hall, Inc., Englewood Cliffs, NJ, 1972.

Animal Science, 9th ed., M. E. Ensminger, Interstate Publishers, Inc., Danville, IL, 1991.

Animal Wastes, E. P. Taiganides, Applied Science Publishers, Ltd., Fosel, England, 1977.

Appaloosa, F. Haines, Amon Carter Museum of Western Art, Fort Worth, TX, 1963.

Appaloosa Horse, The, F. Haines, et al., R. C. Bailey Printing Co., Lewiston, ID, 1957.

Appaloosa, The Spotted Horse in Art and History, F. Haines, University of Texas Press, Austin, TX, 1963.

Arab Breeding in Poland, E. Skorkowski, Your Pony, Columbus, WI, 1969.

Arabian Horse Breeding, H. H. Reese, Borden Publishing Co., Los Angeles, CA, 1953.

Art of Horsemanship, The, Xenophon, trans. by M. H. Morgan, J. A. Allen & Co., Ltd., London, England, 1962.

471

Art & Science of Horseshoeing, The, R. G. Greeley, J. B. Lippincott Co., Philadelphia, PA, 1970.

Asiatic Wild Horse, The, E. Mohr, trans. by D. M. Goodall, J. A. Allen & Co., Ltd., London, England, 1971.

At the Horse Show with Margaret Cabell Self, M. C. Self, Arco Publishing Co., Inc., New York, NY, 1966.

Beginner's Guide to Horses, The, C. R. Melcher, A. S. Barnes & Co., Inc., Cranbury, NJ, 1974.

Behavior of Domestic Animals, The, 3rd ed., ed. by E. S. E. Hafez, Williams and Wilkens Co., Baltimore, MD, 1975.

Biography of the Tennessee Walking Horse, B. A. Green, The Parthenon Press, Nashville, TN, 1960.

Bit by Bit, D. Tuke, J. A. Allen & Co., Ltd., London, England, 1965.

Black Beauty, A. Sewell, Collins, London, England, 1970.

Book of the Horse, The, P. Hamlyn, The Hamlyn Publishing Group, Ltd., New York, NY, 1970.

Book of Horses, The, D. Williams, J. B. Lippincott Co., Philadelphia, PA, 1971.

Breeding and Improvement of Farm Animals, V. A. Rice, et al., McGraw-Hill Book Co., New York, NY, 1967.

Breeding and Raising Horses, Agr. Hdbk. No. 394, M. E. Ensminger, U.S. Department of Agriculture, Washington, D.C., 1972.

Breeding the Racehorse, F. Tesio, J. A. Allen & Co., London, England, 1964.

Breeding Thoroughbreds, J. F. Wall, Charles Scribner's Sons, New York, NY, 1946.

Business of Horses, The, K. A. Wood, Wood Publications, P. O. Box 963, Rancho Santa Fe, CA, 1973.

Care and Training of the Trotter and Pacer, J. C. Harrison, et al., The U.S. Trotting Assn., Columbus, OH, 1970.

Carts and Wagons, J. Vince, Spurbooks Ltd., Buckinghamshire, England, 1975.

Cavalletti, R. Klimke, trans. by D. M. Goodall, J. A. Allen & Co., Ltd., London, England, 1973.

Cavalry Manual of Horsemanship and Horsemastership, The, ed. by G. Wright, Doubleday & Co., Inc., Garden City, NY, 1962.

Color of Horses, The, B. K. Green, Northland Press, Flagstaff, AZ, 1974.

Complete Book of the Horse, The, ed. by E. H. Edwards and C. Geddes, Ward Lock Ltd., London, England, 1973.

Complete Encyclopedia of Horses, The, M. E. Ensminger, A. S. Barnes & Co., Inc., Cranbury, NJ, 1977. (Now reprinted by Oak Tree Publications, San Diego, CA).

Complete Horseshoeing Guide, The, R. F. Wiseman, University of Oklahoma Press, Norman, OK, 1968.

Conditioning to Win, ed. by D. M. Wagoner, Equine Research Publications, Grapevine, TX, 1974.

Dealing with Horses, J. F. Kelly, Arco Publishing Co., Inc., New York, NY, 1969.

Descriptive Bibliography of 1001 Horse Books, A, ed. by W. E. Jones, Caballus Publishers, Fort Collins, CO, 1972.

Determining the Age of Farm Animals by Their Teeth, Farmers' Bull. No. 1721, U.S. Department of Agriculture, Washington, D.C.

Diseases of the Horse, U.S. Department of Agriculture, U.S. Government Printing Press Office, Washington, D.C., 1942.

Disorders of the Horse, E. Hanauer, A. S. Barnes and Co., Inc., Cranbury, NJ, 1973.

Diseases Transmitted from Animals to Man, 5th ed., ed. by T. G. Hull; Charles C. Thomas, Publisher, Springfield, IL, 1963.

Domestic Animal Behavior, J. V. Craig, Prentice-Hall, Inc., Englewood Cliffs, NJ, 1981.

Draft Horse Handbook, EB 1135, L. C. Luce and J. B. Johnson, Washington State University, Pullman, WA, 1982.

Dukes' Physiology of Domestic Animals, 9th ed., ed. by M. Swenson, Cornell University Press, Ithaca, NY, 1977.

Economic Impact of the U.S. Horse Industry, The, The American Horse Council, Washington, D.C., 1987.

Effect of Environment on Nutrient Requirements of Animals, D. R. Ames, Chairman, NRC, National Academy Press, Washington, D.C., 1981.

Elegant Carriage, The, M. Watney, J. A. Allen & Co., Ltd., London, England, 1969.

Elements of Environmental Health, D. F. Newton, Charles E. Narrill Publishing Co., Columbus, OH, 1974.

Elements of Farrier Science, D. M. Canfield, Enderes Tool Co., Inc., Albert Lea, MN, 1966.

Emerging Diseases of Animals, Veterinary Research Laboratory, Onderstepoort, South Africa, Food and Agriculture Organization of the United Nations, Rome, Italy, 1968.

Encyclopedia of the Horse, The, ed. by C. E. G. Hope and G. N. Jackson, The Viking Press, Inc., New York, NY, 1973.

English Pleasure Carriages, W. B. Adams, Adams & Dart, Bath, Somerset, England, 1971.

Environmental and Functional Engineering of Agricultural Buildings, H. J. Barre, L. L. Sammet, G. L. Nelson, Van Nostrand Reinhold Co., New York, NY, 1988.

Environmental Quality, R. W. Peterson, Chairman, U. S. Government Printing Office, Washington, D.C., 1976.

Equestrian Sport in Five Continents, ed. by E. A. Sarasin, Federation Equestrian International, FEI, Germany, 1963.

Equine Medicine & Surgery, 2nd edition, ed. by E. J. Catcott and J. F. Smithcors, American Veterinary Publications, Inc., Wheaton, IL, 1972.

Ethology: The Biology of Behavior, 2nd ed., I. Eibl-Eibesfeldt, Holt, Rinehart, and Winston, New York, NY, 1975.

Every Horse Owner's Cyclopedia, J. H. Walsh, Porter & Coates, Philadelphia, PA, 1871.

Evolution of the Horse, W. D. Matthew and S. H. Chubb, American Museum of Natural History, New York, NY, 1921.

Fair Exchange, H. S. Finney, Charles Scribner's Sons, New York, NY, 1974.

Famous Horses of America, Porter & Coates, Philadelphia, PA, 1877.

FAO Yearbook, Food and Agriculture Organization of the United Nations, Rome, Italy, annual.

Farm Animal Manures: an overview of their role in the agricultural environment, J. Azevedo, P. R. Stout, Agricultural Publications, University of California, Berkeley, CA, 1974.

Feeding and Care of the Horse, L. D. Lewis, Lea & Febiger, Philadelphia, PA, 1982.

Feeding Ponies, W. C. Miller, J. A. Allen & Co., Ltd., London, England, 1968.

Feeding to Win, ed. by D. M. Wagoner, Equine Research, Grapevine, TX, 1973.

Feeds & Nutrition, 2nd ed., M. E. Ensminger, J. E. Oldfield, W. W. Heinemann, Ensminger Publishing Co., Clovis, CA, 1990.

Feeds & Nutrition Digest, 2nd ed., M. E. Ensminger, J. E. Oldfield, W. W. Heinemann, Ensminger Publishing Co., Clovis, CA, 1990.

First Aid Hints for the Horse Owner, W. E. Lyon, Collins, St. James's Place, London, England, 1971.

First Horse, R. Hapgood, Chronicle Books, San Francisco, CA, 1972.

First Horsemen, The, F. Trippet, Editors of Time-Life Books, Time-Life Books, New York, NY, 1974.

Foundation Sires of the American Quarter Horse, R. M. Denhart, University of Oklahoma Press, Norman, OK, 1976.

From Dawn to Destiny, F. Jennings and Allen F. Brewer, Jr., The Thoroughbred Press, Inc., Lexington, KY, 1962.

Genetic Principles in Horse Breeding, J. F. Lasley, Columbia, MO, 1970.

Genetics of the Horse, W. E. Jones, R. Bogart, Edwards Brothers, Inc., Ann Arbor, MI, 1971.

Genetics of Livestock Improvement, 3rd ed., J. F. Lasley, Prentice-Hall, Inc., Englewood Cliffs, NJ, 1978.

Gentle Giants, R. Whitlock, Lutterworth Press, Guildford and London, England, 1976.

Great Ones, The, ed. by K. Hollingsworth, The Blood-Horse, Lexington, KY, 1970.

Grooming Horses, R. W. Collins, The Blood-Horse, Lexington, KY, 1959; reprinted under special arrangement, by The Thoroughbred Record Co., Inc., 1971.

Grooming Your Horse, N. Haley, A. S. Barnes & Co., Inc., Cranbury, NJ, 1974.

Guide for Veterinary Service and Judging of Equestrian Events, American Association of Equine Practitioners, Golden, CO, 1974.

Guide to American Horse Shows, A, D. A. Spector, Arco Publishing Co., Inc., New York, NY, 1973.

Hagan's Infectious Diseases of Domestic Animals, 6th ed., D. W. Bruner, J. H. Gillespie, Cornell University Press, Ithaca, NY, 1973.

Hammond's Farm Animals, J. Hammond, Jr., I. L. Mason, T. J. Robinson, Butler & Tanner, Ltd., Frome and London, England, 1971.

Handbook of Veterinary Procedures and Emergency Treatment, R. W. Kirk, S. I. Bistner, W. B. Saunders Co., Philadelphia, PA, 1975.

Harper's Encyclopedia for Horsemen: The Complete Book of the Horse, L. Taylor, Harper & Row, New York, NY, 1973.

Health Issues Related to Chemicals in the Environment: A Scientific Perspective, A. L. Craigmill, Chairman, Council of Agricultural Sciences and Technology, Ames, IA, 1987.

History of American Jacks and Mules, F. C. Mills, ed. by H. L. Hall, Hutch-Line, Inc., Hutchinson, KS, 1971.

History of Domesticated Animals, A, F. E. Zuener, Harper & Row, Publishers, Inc., Great Britain, 1963.

History of Horse Racing, The, R. Longrigg, Stein and Day, New York, NY, 1972.

History of The Arabian Horse Club Registry of America, Inc., The, A. W. Harris, The Arabian Horse Club Registry of America, Inc., Chicago, IL, 1950.

History of the Percheron Horse, A, A. H. Sanders, W. Dinsmore, Breeder's Gazette Print, Chicago, IL, 1917.

History of Thoroughbred Racing in America, The, W. H. Robertson, Prentice-Hall, Inc., Englewood Cliffs, NJ, 1965.

Horse, The, J. W. Evans, et al., W. H. Freeman and Co., San Francisco, CA, 1977.

Horse, The, J. M. Kays, A. S. Barnes and Co., Inc., Cranbury, NJ, 1969.

Horse, The, I. P. Roberts, The Macmillan Co., London, England, 1913.

Horse, The, P. D. Rossdale, The California Thoroughbred Breeders Assn., Arcadia, CA, 1972.

Horse, The, through fifty centuries of civilization, A. Dent, Phaidon Press Ltd., London, England, 1974.

Horse America Made, The, L. Taylor, American Saddle Horse Breeders Association, Louisville, KY, 1961.

Horse-Breeding Farm, The, L. C. Willis, A. S. Barnes and Co., Inc., Cranbury, NJ, 1973.

Horse from Conception to Maturity, The, P. Rossdale, California Thoroughbred Breeders Assn., Arcadia, CA, 1972.

Horse Owner's Vet Book, The, E. C. Straiton, J. B. Lippincott Co., New York, NY, 1973.

Horse Behavior and Training, R. W. Miller, Montana State University Bookstore, Bozeman, MT, 1974.

Horse Breeding and Stud Management, H. Wynmalen, J. A. Allen & Co., Ltd., London, England, 1950.

Horse Breeds of the West, F. S. Harris, Cordovan Corp., Houston, TX, 1973.

Horse Buyer's Guide, The, J. K. Posey, A. S. Barnes and Co., Inc., Cranbury, NJ, 1973.

Horse Feeding and Nutrition, T. J. Cunha, Academic Press, New York, NY, 1980.

Horse Psychology, M. Williams, A. S. Barnes and Co., Inc., Cranbury, NJ, 1969.

Horseman's Encyclopedia, The, M. C. Self, A. S. Barnes and Co., Inc., Cranbury, NJ, 1963.

Horseman's Handbook on Practical Breeding, A, J. F. Wall, Thoroughbred Bloodlines, Camden, SC, 1950.

Horseman's Scrapbook in Verse and Prose, A, D. J. Kays, Long's College Book Co., Columbus, OH, 1954.

Horseman's Short Course, Proceedings, Staff, Washington Horse Breeders Assn., Seattle, WA, 1968.

Horseman's Tax Guide, J. O. Humphreys, The Blood-Horse, Lexington, KY, 1963.

Horsemanship, Mrs. A. W. Jasper, Boy Scouts of America, New Brunswick, NJ, 1963.

Horsemanship and Horse Care, Agr. Inf. Bull. No. 353, M. E. Ensminger, U.S. Department of Agriculture, Washington, D.C., 1972.

Horsemanship and Horsemastership, vol. 2, The Cavalry School, Fort Riley, KS, 1946.

Horsemanship and Horsemastership, ed. by G. Wright, Doubleday & Co., Inc., Garden City, NY, 1962.

Horsemen's Veterinary Adviser, J. B. Davidson, Horse Publications, Columbus, OH, 1966.

Horses, G. G. Simpson, Oxford University Press, New York, NY, 1951.

Horses, M. C. Self, A. S. Barnes & Co., Inc., Cranbury, NJ, 1953.

Horses and Americans, P. D. Strong, Frederick A. Stokes Co., New York, NY, 1939.

Horses and Tack, M. E. Ensminger, Houghton Mifflin Co., Boston, MA, 1991.

Horses in America, F. Haines, Thomas Y. Crowell Co., New York, NY, 1971.

Horse's Astrologer, A, Chadwell and Sellers, Cordovan Corp., Houston, TX, 1973.

Horses' Injuries, C. L. Strong, Arco Publishing Co., Inc., New York, NY, 1973.

Horse Show, At the, M. C. Self, Arco Publishing Co., Inc., New York, NY, 1973.

Horse Science Handbook, vols. 1–3, ed. by M. E. Ensminger, Agriservices Foundation, Clovis, CA, 1963, 1964, 1966.

Horseshoeing, A. Lungwitz, J. W. Adams, Oregon State University Press, Corvallis, OR, 1966.

Horseshoeing Theory and Hoof Care, L. Emery, J. Miller, N. Van Hoosen, Lea & Febiger, Philadelphia, PA, 1977.

Horses, Their Selection, Care and Handling, M. C. Self, A. S. Barnes & Co., Inc., Cranbury, NJ, 1943.

Horses of Today, H. H. Reese, Wood & Jones, Pasadena, CA, 1956.

Horses and Horsemanship, 6th ed., M. E. Ensminger, Interstate Publishers, Inc., Danville, IL, 1991.

Horses and Horsemanship, L. E. Walraven, A. S. Barnes and Co., Inc., Cranbury, NJ, 1970.

Horses and Horsemanship Through the Ages, L. Gianoli, Crown Publishers, Inc., New York, NY, 1969.

Horses! Horses! Horses! M. E. Ensminger, Pegus Co. Clovis, CA.

Horses, Horses, Horses, S. Wilding, Van Nostrand Reinhold Co., New York, NY, 1970.

Horse Shows, A. N. Phillips, The Interstate Printers & Publishers, Inc., Danville, IL, 1956.

Horses & Men, R. Albaugh, The Printer, Davis, CA, 1974.

Horse: Structure and Movement, The, R. H. Smythe and Rev. P. C. Goody, J. A. Allen & Co., London, England, 1972.

Horse Today — and Tomorrow?, The, H. Lange, K. Jeschko, Arco Publishing Co., Inc., New York, NY, 1972.

"Hosses," C. W. Gray, Garden City Publishing Co., Inc., Garden City, NY, 1927.

How to Buy a Race Horse, A. Bower, Cromwell Bookstock Agency, Lexington, KY, 1968.

Illustrated Veterinary Encyclopedia for Horsemen, The, ed. by Staff, Equine Research Publications, Grapevine, TX, 1975.

Infectious Diseases of Domestic Animals, 3rd ed., W. A. Hagan, D. W. Bruner, Comstock Publishing Associates, Ithaca, NY, 1957.

Introduction to Light Horse Management, An, R. C. Barbalace, Caballus Publishers, Fort Collins, CO, 1974.

Introduction to the Wonderful World of Horses, An, Roundup, Inc., McHenry, IL, 1968.

Judging Manual for American Saddlebred Horses, J. Foss, American Saddle Horse Breeders Association, Louisville, KY, 1973.

Kellogg Arabians, The, H. H. Reese and G. B. Edwards, Borden Publishing Co., Los Angeles, CA, 1958.

Kingdom of the Horse, The, H. H. Isenbart and E. M. Buhrer, Time-Life Books, New York, NY, 1969.

King Ranch Quarter Horses, The, R. M. Denhardt, University of Oklahoma Press, Norman, OK, 1978.

Know About Horses, H. Disston, The Devin-Adair Co., New York, NY, 1961.

Know Your Pony, D. M. Goodall, A. S. Barnes and Co., Inc., Cranbury, NJ, 1973.

Lame Horse, The, J. R. Rooney, A. S. Barnes and Co., Inc., Cranbury, NJ, 1974.

Lameness in Horses, 2nd edition, O. R. Adams, Lea & Febiger, Philadelphia, PA, 1966.

Latest Developments in Livestock Housing, Seminar, University of Illinois, Urbana-Champaign, IL, 1987.

Law and Your Horse, The, E. H. Greene, A. S. Barnes & Co., Inc., Cranbury, NJ, 1971.

Lectures, Stud Managers Course, Stud Managers Course, Lexington, KY, intermittent since 1951.

Leg at Each Corner, A, N. Thelwell, E. P. Dutton & Co., Inc., New York, NY, 1963.

Light Horse Breeds, The, J. W. Patten, A. S. Barnes & Co., Inc., Cranbury, NJ, 1960.

Light Horse Management, R. C. Barbalace, Caballus Publishers, Fort Collins, CO, 1974.

Light Horses, Farmers' Bull. No. 2127, M. E. Ensminger, U.S. Department of Agriculture, Washington, D.C., 1965.

Livestock behaviour, a practical guide, R. Kilgour, C. Dalton, Westview Press, Boulder, CO, 1984.

Livestock Environment, Proceedings, Second International Livestock Environment Symposium, D. S. Bundy, Planning Chairman, American Society of Agricultural Engineers, St. Joseph, MI, 1982.

Livestock Waste Management and Pollution Abatement, Symposium, American Society of Agricultural Engineers, St. Joseph, MI, 1971.

Managing Livestock Wastes, Proceedings, American Society of Agricultural Engineers, St. Joseph, MI, 1975.

Manual of Horsemanship of the British Horse Society and The Pony Club, The, The British Horse Society and the Pony Club, The British Horse Society, Warwickshire, England, 1968.

Manure Gases in the Animal Environment, G. A. Nordstrom, J. B. McPuitty, University of Alberta, Edmonton, Alberta, 1976.

Mare Owner's Handbook, ed. by T. Rogers, Cordovan Corp., Houston, TX, 1971.

Mares, Foals and Foaling, F. Andrist, J. A. Allen & Co., London, England, 1959.

Marvels & Mysteries of Our Animal World, Reader's Digest Association, Pleasantville, NY, 1964.

Master Farrier, The, B. Beaston, Oklahoma Farrier's College, Sperry, OK, 1975.

Mechanisms of Animal Behavior, P. Parler, W. J. Hamilton, III, John Wiley & Sons, New York, NY, 1966.

Mechanics of the Horse, The, J. R. Rooney, Robert E. Krieger Publishing Co., New York, NY, 1980.

Merck Veterinary Manual, The, 6th ed., ed. by O. H. Siegmund, Merck & Co., Inc., Rahway, NJ, 1986.

Modern Breeds of Livestock, 4th ed., H. M. Briggs, The Macmillan Co., New York, NY, 1980.

Morgan Horse Handbook, The, J. Mellin, Stephen Greene Press, Brattleboro, VT, 1973.

Natural History of the Horse, The, J. Clabby, Weidenfeld and Nicolson, London, England, 1976.

Nationwide System for Animal Health Surveillance, A, National Research Council, National Academy of Sciences, Washington, D.C., 1974.

Nutrient Requirements of Horses, no. 6, 5th ed., rev., National Research Council, National Academy of Sciences, Washington, D.C., 1989.

Old Horseman's 1974 Almanack, The, ed. by S. W. Brotchie, TRT Publications, Inc., Beverly, MA, 1973.

Organic Farming: current technology and its role in a sustainable agriculture, ed. by D. M. Kral, American Society of Agronomy, Madison, WI, 1984.

Our Friendly Animals and Whence They Came, K. P. Schmidt, M. A. Donohue & Co., Chicago, IL, 1938.

People with Long Ears, R. Borwick, Cassell & Co., Ltd., London, England, 1970.

Percheron Horse, The, M. C. Weld, O. Judd Co., New York, NY, 1886.

Personality of the Horse, The, ed. by B. Aymar and E. Sagarin, Bonanza Books, New York, NY, 1963.

Pinto, The, Yearbook and Studbook of the Pinto Horse Assn. of America, 1958–59.

Practical Horse Breeding and Training, J. Widmer, Charles Scribner's Sons, New York, NY, 1942.

Practical Light Horse Breeding, J. F. Wall, The Monumental Printing Co., Baltimore, MD, 1936.

Practical Parasitology: General Laboratory Techniques and Parasitic Protozoa, C. J. Price, J. E. Reed, United Nations Development Programme, and Food and Agriculture Organization of the United Nations, Rome, Italy, 1970.

Principles of Genetics, I. H. Herskowitz, The Macmillan Co., New York, NY, 1973.

Principles of Horseshoeing, The, D. Butler, Doug Butler, Maryville, MO, 1985.

Proceedings of the First International Conference on Equine Infectious Diseases, ed. by J. T. Bryans, et al., The Grayson Foundation, Lexington, KY, 1966.

Progress in Equine Practice, vol. 1, ed. by E. J. Catcott, J. F. Smithcors, American Veterinary Publications, Inc., Santa Barbara, CA, 1966.

Progress in Equine Practice, vol. 2, ed. by E. J. Catcott, J. F. Smithcors, American Veterinary Publications, Inc., Santa Barbara, CA, 1966.

Racehorse in Training, The, W. Day and A. J. Day, Cassell and Co., Ltd., New York, NY, 1925.

Reproduction in Farm Animals, 4th ed., E. S. Hafez, Lea & Febiger, Philadelphia, PA, 1980.

Reproductive Physiology, A. V. Nalbandov, W. H. Freeman and Co., Publishers, San Francisco, CA, 1958.

Rule Book, The American Horse Shows Assn., Inc., New York, NY, annual.

Saddlery, E. H. Edwards, A. S. Barnes & Co., Inc., Cranbury, NJ, 1963.

Saddle Up!, C. E. Ball, J. B. Lippincott Co., Philadelphia, PA, 1970.

Safe and Effective Use of Pesticides, The, P. J. Marer, University of California Press, Oakland, CA, 1988.

Science of Genetics, The, G. W. Burns, The Macmillan Co., New York, NY, 1972.

Scientific Aspects of the Welfare of Food Animals, F. H. Baker, Chairman, Council for Agricultural Science and Technology, Ames, IA, 1981.

Shetland Pony, The, L. F. Bedell, Iowa State University Press, Ames, IA, 1959.

Shetland Pony, The, M. C. Cox, Adam and Charles Black, Ltd., London, England, 1965.

Some Diseases of Animals Communicable to Man in Britain, ed. by O. Graham-Jones, Pergamon Press, Ltd., London, England, 1968.

Some Important Animal Diseases in Europe: Papers Presented at the Animal Disease Meeting, Warsaw, 1948, K. V. Kesteven, Food and Agriculture Organization of the United Nations, Rome, Italy, 1952.

Spanish Riding School, The, H. Handler, McGraw-Hill Book Co., Ltd., Maidenhead, England, 1972.

Stable Management & Exercise, 6th ed., M. H. Hayes, Stanley Paul & Co., Ltd., London, England, 1968.

Stagecoaches & Carriages, I. Sparkes, Spurbooks Ltd., Buckinghamshire, England, 1975.

Statistical Abstracts of the United States, U.S. Department of Commerce, Bureau of the Census, Washington, D.C., annual.

Steeplechasing, J. Hislop, J. A. Allen & Co., Ltd., London, England, 1970.

Stockman's Handbook, The, 7th ed., M. E. Ensminger, Interstate Publishers, Inc., Danville, IL, 1991.

Structures and Environment Handbook, Midwest Plan Service, Iowa State University Press, Ames, IA, 1972.

Stress Physiology in Livestock, vol. 1, *Basic Principles,* vol. 2, *Ungulates,* vol. 3, *Poultry,* M. K. Yousef, CRC Press, Inc., Boca Raton, FL, 1985.

Stud Farm Diary, A, H. S. Finney, J. A. Allen & Co., Ltd., London, England, 1973.

Stud Managers Course, Lectures, Stud Managers Course, University of Kentucky, Lexington, KY. Intermittent years since 1951.

Stud Managers' Handbook, The, ed. by M. E. Ensminger, Agriservices Foundation, Clovis, CA. Published annually since 1965.

Studies on Reproduction in Horses, Y. Nishikawa, Japan Racing Assn., Tokyo, Japan, 1959.

Summerhays' Encyclopedia for Horsemen, compiled by R. S. Summerhays, Frederick Warne and Co., Inc., New York, NY, 1966.

Tales of the King's Horses, L. Rosenvold and D. Rosenvold, Rosenvold Publications, Montrose, Canada, 1958.

Thelwell's Riding Academy, N. Thelwell, E. P. Dutton & Co., Inc., New York, NY, 1967.

Thoroughbred Bloodlines, J. F. Wall, Monumental Printing Co., Baltimore, MD, 1935.

Thoroughbred Racing Stock, Lady Wentworth, Charles Scribner's Sons, New York, NY, 1938.

Top Form Book of Horse Care, F. Harper, Popular Library, New York, NY, 1966.

Touch of Greatness, A, C. W. Anderson, The Macmillan Co., New York, NY, 1945.

Training the Arabian Horse, H. H. Reese, The Cruse Publishing Co., Inc., Fort Collins, CO, 1961.

Training Horses for Races, G. W. L. Meredith, Constable and Co., Ltd., London, England, 1926.

Training the Quarter Horse Jumper, H. P. Levings, A. S. Barnes and Co., Inc., Cranbury, NJ, 1968.

Training Thoroughbreds, P. M. Burch, The Blood-Horse, Lexington, KY, 1961.

Training Tips for Western Riders, L. N. Sikes, The Texas Horseman, Houston, TX, 1960.

Trotting Horse of America, The, H. Woodruff, University Press; Welch, Bigelow, & Co., Cambridge, MA, 1871.

TV Vet Horse Book, TV Vet, Farming Press Ltd., Ipswich, Suffolk, England, 1971.

Understanding and Training Horses, A. J. Ricci, J. B. Lippincott Co., Philadelphia, PA, 1964.

Using the American Quarter Horse, L. N. Sikes, The Saddlerock Corp., Houston, TX, 1958.

Utilization, Treatment, and Disposal of Waste on Land, Proceedings, Soil Science Society of America, Inc., E. C. A. Runge, President, Madison, WI, 1986.

Veterinary Medicine, D. C. Blood, J. A. Henderson, The Williams & Wilkins Co., Baltimore, MD, 1960.

Veterinary Notebook, W. R. McGee, *The Blood-Horse,* Lexington, KY, 1958.

Veterinary Notes for Horse Owners, M. H. Hays, Arco Publishing Co., Inc., New York, NY, 1972.

Veterinary Notes for the Standardbred Breeder, W. R. McGee, U.S. Trotting Assn., Columbus, OH., 1950.

Veterinary Parasitology, 2nd ed., G. Lapage, Charles C. Thomas, Publisher, Springfield, IL, 1968.

Veterinary Treatments & Medications for Horses, ed. by Staff, Equine Research Publications, Grapevine, TX, 1977.

Western Equitation, Horsemanship and Showmanship, D. Stewart, Vantage Press, Inc., New York, NY, 1973.

Western Horse Behavior & Training, R. W. Miller, Doubleday & Co., Inc., Garden City, NY, 1975.

Western Horse, The, J. A. Gorman, The Interstate Printers & Publishers, Inc., Danville, IL, 1967.

Wild Animals in Captivity, H. Hediger, Dover Publications, Inc., New York, NY, 1964.

Wild Horse of the West, The, W. D. Wyman, University of Nebraska Press, Lincoln, NE, 1945.

Wonderful World of Horses, The, ed. by B. Weikel, Roundup Incorporated, McHenry, IL, 1968.

World Dictionary of Breeds, Types, and Varieties of Livestock, A, I. L. Mason, Commonwealth Agricultural Bureaux, Farnham House, Farnham Royal, Slough, Bucks, England, 1951.

World of Horses, The, J. Campbell, The Hamlyn Publishing Group Ltd., New York, NY, 1969.

World of Pinto Horses, The, ed. by R. D. Greene, The Pinto Horse Assn. of America, Inc., San Diego, CA, 1970.

Young Horseman's Handbook, Vols. 1–9, H. Disston, The Jarman Press, Charlottesville, VA, 1961.

Your Horse, A Sporting Life Publication, The Sporting Life, Long Acre, London, England, 1967.

HORSE MAGAZINES

The horse magazines publish news items and informative articles of special interest to horsemen. Also, many of them employ field representatives whose chief duty is to assist in the buying and selling of horses.

In compiling the magazine list that follows, no attempt was made to list the general livestock magazines, of which there are numerous outstanding ones. Only those magazines that are chiefly devoted to horses are included. Cognizance is taken of the fact that some magazines may not be listed, simply because the author is not acquainted with them.

BREEDS

AMERICAN BASHKIR CURLY	*Curly Cues,* Box 453, Ely, NV 89301
AMERICAN MUSTANG	*American Mustang World,* P. O. Box, 338, Yucaipa, CA 92399
AMERICAN SADDLEBRED	*American Saddlebred Newsletter,* 49093 Iron Works Pike, Lexington, KY 40511
	Bluegrass Horseman, The, P. O. Box 389, Lexington, KY 40501
	Saddle and Bridle, 375 N. Jackson Ave., St. Louis, MO 63130
	Saddle Horse Report, P. O. Box 1007, Shelbyville, TN 37160
ANDALUSIAN	*The Spanish Bit,* 1941 Old Mill Road, Springfield, OH 45502
APPALOOSA	*Appaloosa Journal,* Box 8403, Moscow, ID 83843
	Cal-Western Appaloosa, 3097 Willow #15, Clovis, CA 93612
ARABIAN	*Arabian Horse Country,* P. O. Box 4607-A, Portland, OR 97208
	Arabian Horse Express, P. O. Box 845, Coffeyville, KS 67337
	Arabian Horse Times, The, R. R. 3, Waseca, MN 56093
	Arabian Horse World, 409 Sherman Ave., P. O. Box 60910, Palo Alto, CA 94306
	Crabbet Influence in Arabians Today, The, 12723 Road 34¾, Madera, CA 93638
DONKEY AND MULE	*Brayer, The,* 2901 N. Elm, Denton, TX 76201
DRAFT HORSES (all breeds, and mules)	*Draft Horse Journal,* Box 670, Waverly, IA 50677
BELGIAN	*Belgian Review* (annual), P. O. Box 335, Wabash, IN 46992

BUCKSKIN	*Buckskin Country*, 4627 W. Frier Drive, Glendale, AZ 85301
HACKNEY	*Hackney Journal, The*, P. O. Box 200, Crawfordsville, IA 52621
HAFLINGER	*Haflinger Highlite*, 2061 Kenyon Ave., S.W., Massillon, OH 44646
LIPIZZAN	*Lipizzan Journal, The*, c/o United States Lipizzan Registry, 12479 Duncan Plains Rd., N.W., Johnstown, OH 93031
MINIATURE HORSE	*Miniature Horse World, The*, American Miniature Horse Assn., The, P. O. Box 129, Burleson, TX 76028
MISSOURI FOX TROTTING HORSE	*Missouri Fox Trotter*, Box 191, West Plains, MO 65775
MORGAN	*Morgan Horse, The*, The American Morgan Horse Assn., Inc., P. O. Box 960, 3 Bostwick Road, Shelburne, VT 05482
MORAB	*Morab World, The*, W3174 Faro Springs Rd., Hilbert, WI 54129
NATIONAL SHOW HORSE	*National Show Horse*, 10401 Linn Station Rd., Louisville, KY 40223
NATIONAL SPOTTED SADDLE HORSE	*National Spotted Saddle Horse Journal*, P. O. Box 898, Murfreesboro, TN 37133-0898
NORWEGIAN FJORD HORSE	*Fjord Times, The*, Norwegian Fjord Assn. of North America, 24570 W. Chardon Rd., Draplake, IL 60030
PAINT HORSE	*Paint Horse Journal, The*, P. O. Box 18519, Fort Worth, TX 76118
PALOMINO	*Palomino Horses*, P. O. Box 71, Meridian, MS 39302-9984
	Palomino Parade, P. O. Box 324, Jefferson City, MO 65101
PASO FINO	*Paso Fino Horse World*, P. O. Box 600, Bowling Green, FL 33834
PERCHERON	*Percheron Notes*, P. O. Box 141, Fredericktown, OH 43019
PERUVIAN PASO	*Caballo Magazine*, P. O. Box 1959, Corona, CA 91718-1959
	International Peruvian Paso, 7228 Kentwood Ave., Westchester, CA 90045
PINTO HORSE	*Pinto Horse, The*, 1900 Samuels Ave., Fort Worth, TX 76102
PONY OF THE AMERICAS	*Pony of the Americas*, 5240 Elmwood Ave., Indianapolis, IN 46203
QUARTER HORSE	*Canadian Quarter Horse Journal*, P. O. Box 7065, Ancaster, Ontario, Canada L9G 3L1
	Intermountain Quarter Horse, The, 2225 E. 4800 So., Suite 110, Salt Lake City, UT 84117
	Quarter Horse Journal, The, P. O. Box 32470, Amarillo, TX 79120

Quarter Racing Journal, The, P. O. Box 32470, Amarillo, TX 79120

Quarter Week, 10554 Progress Way, Suite G, Cypress, CA 90630

Western Rider, The, P. O. Box 7065, Ancaster, Ontario, Canada L9G 3L1

SPANISH MUSTANG *Spanish Mustang Registry* (annual), 8328 Stevenson Ave., Sacramento, CA 95828

Newsletter, The (quarterly), 8328 Stevenson Ave., Sacramento, CA 95828

SPOTTED SADDLE HORSE *Spotted Saddle Horse News,* P. O. Box 1046, Shelbyville, TN 37160

STANDARDBRED *Harness Horse, The,* P. O. Box 10779, Harrisburg, PA 17105

Hoof Beats, 750 Michigan Ave., Columbus, OH 43215

Horseman and Fair World, The, 904 N. Broadway, Lexington, KY 40505

TENNESSEE WALKING HORSE *Voice of the Tennessee Walking Horse,* P. O. Box 286, Lewisburg, TN 37091

Walking Horse Report, P. O. Box 1007, Shelbyville, TN 37160

THOROUGHBRED *Arizona Thoroughbred,* P. O. Box 41774, Phoenix, AZ 85080-1774

Backstretch, The, 19363 James Couzens Hwy., Detroit, MI 48235

Blood-Horse, The, Box 4038, Lexington, KY 40544-4038

British Columbia Thoroughbred, 17687 56A Ave., Surrey, British Columbia, Canada B3F 1G4

Florida Horse, The, P. O. Box 2106, Ocala, FL 32678

Maryland Horse, The, P. O. Box 427, Timonium, MD 21093

Texas Thoroughbred, The, P. O. Box 14967, Austin, TX 78761

Thoroughbred of California, The, 201 Colorado Place, Arcadia, CA 91006

Thoroughbred Record, The, 367 W. Short St., Lexington, KY 40507

Thoroughbred Times, P. O. Box 8237, Lexington, KY 40533

Washington Thoroughbred, The, P. O. Box 88258, Seattle, WA 98178

TRAKEHNER *American Trakehner, The,* 5008 Pine Creek Dr., Ste. B, Westerville, OH 43081

TROTTINGBRED *Trottingbred, The,* 575 Broadway, Hanover, PA 17331

WELARA PONY *Welara Journal,* P. O. Box 401, Yucca Valley, CA 92284

WELSH

GENERAL

Welsh Roundabout, 5051 Townline Rd., East Troy, WI 53120

American Farriers Journal, 63 Great Rd., Maynard, MA 01754-2025

California Horseman's News, P. O. Box 474, San Marcos, CA 92069

California Horse Review, P. O. Box 2437, Fair Oaks, CA 95628

Carriage Journal, The, R.D. #1, Box 115, Salem, NJ 08079

Chronicle of the Horse, The, P. O. Box 46, Middleburg, VA 22117

Cuttin' Hoss Chatter, The, 4704 Highway 377, South, Fort Worth, TX 76116

Dressage & CT, 211 W. Main St., New London, OH 44851

Equestrian Trails, 13741 Foothill Blvd., Suite 220, Sylmar, CA 91342-3105

Equus, 656 Quince Orchard Rd., Gaithersburg, MD 20878

Horses All, P. O. Box 9, Hill Spring, Alberta, Canada T0K 1E0

Horse and Horseman, P. O. Box HH, Capistrano Beach, CA 92624

Horse Illustrated, P. O. Box 57549, Boulder, CO 80322-7549

Horse & Pony, P. O. Box 2050, Seffner, IL 33584

Horse & Rider, 941 Calle Negocio, San Clemente, CA 92672-6202

Horseplay, P. O. Box 130, Gaithersburg, MD 20884

Horse, Of Course, RFD, Temple, NH 03084

Horse Show, 220 E. 42nd St., New York, NY 10017-5806

Horse World, P. O. Box 1007, Shelbyville, TN 37160

Horseman, 25025 I-45 North, Suite 390, Spring, TX 77380

Horsemen's Corral, P. O. Box 110, New London, OH 44851

Horsemen's Yankee Pedlar, 785 Southbridge St., Auburn, MA 01501

Lariat, The, 12675 S.W. First St., Beaverton, OR 97005

Modern Horse Breeding, P. O. Box 50197, Boulder, CO 80321-0197

National Horseman, The, P. O. Box 43397, Middleton, KY 40243

Northeast Equine Journal, P. O. Box 623, Keene, NH 03431

Practical Horseman, Gum Tree Corner, Unionville, PA 19375

Record Horseman, P. O. Box 1209, Wheat Ridge,
CO 80034

Southern Horseman, The, P. O. Box 71, Meridian,
MS 39302

Spur, P. O. Box 85, Middleburg, VA 22117

Tack n' Togs, 12400 White Water Dr., #160,
Minnetonka, MN 55343

Trail Rider, The, Rt. 1, Box 1004, Chatsworth,
GA 30705

Turf and Sport Digest, 26 West Pennsylvania
Ave., Towson, MD 21204

USCTA News, 292 Bridge St., South Hamilton,
MA 01982

Washington Horse, The, 13470 Empire Way
South, Seattle, WA 98178

Western Horseman, The, P. O. Box 7980, Colorado Springs, CO 80933

INDEX